INTERNATIONALIZATION OF BUSINESS: An Introduction

INTERNATIONALIZATION
OF BUSINESS: An Introduction

Richard D. Robinson

Alfred P. Sloan School of Management
Massachusetts Institute of Technology

THE DRYDEN PRESS

Chicago   New York   Philadelphia
San Francisco   Montreal   Toronto
London   Sydney   Tokyo   Mexico City
Rio de Janeiro   Madrid

Acquisitions Editor: Anne Elizabeth Smith
Project Editor: Ruta S. Graff
Managing Editor: Jane Perkins
Design Director: Alan Wendt
Production Manager: Mary Jarvis

Text and cover designer: Gordon Stromberg
Copyeditor: Anne Knowles
Indexer: Jennifer Gordon
Compositor: Modern Typographers, Inc.
Text type: 10/12 Palatino

Library of Congress Cataloging in Publication Data

Robinson, Richard D., 1921–
  Internationalization of business.

  Includes bibliographical references and index.
  1. International business enterprises—Management.
I. Title.
HD62.4.R615   1983   658'.049   83-11710
ISBN 0-03-060301-3

Printed in the United States of America
456-038-98765432

Address orders to:
383 Madison Avenue
New York, New York 10017

Address editorial correspondence to:
One Salt Creek Lane
Hinsdale, IL 60521

CBS College Publishing
The Dryden Press
Holt, Rinehart and Winston
Saunders College Publishing

To Carol
Whose boundless enthusiasm, personal devotion, and
profound insight into human interactions
provided continuing inspiration
for this undertaking.

The Dryden Press Series in Management

Arthur G. Bedeian, *Consulting Editor*

CONTENTS

Chapter 7   **Financial Strategy** 180

Chapter 8   **Legal Strategy** 218

Chapter 9   **Control Strategy** 262

Chapter 10   Public Affairs Strategy 306

PREFACE

International business management, as a field of theory, research, education, and practice, has to do with generating, maintaining, and controlling international flows of people, information, funds, goods, and services for a commercial purpose. It differs from the purely domestic in that it involves operating effectively:

- within and among different national sovereignties;
- under widely disparate economic and cultural conditions;
- with people living within very different value systems;
- as part of an industrial revolution set in the *contemporary* world;
- over great geographical distances;
- in national markets varying greatly in structure, population, and area.

In fact, the domestic managerial system may be seen merely as a special case within the much larger international system.

The phrase **commercial purpose** relates to the effort to fulfill some human need or want through the transfer of goods and services from one condition or place to another, or from one person or group to another, for a mutual profit stated in explicit terms on a quid pro quo basis. For example, the production and sale of goods by a governmental entity for an internal financial profit is a business activity, but payment of social security benefits or foreign aid is not.

There are essentially two ways to organize a textbook on international business management. One is to focus on major issues, such as minimizing political risk, protecting proprietary rights, managing joint ventures, developing intercultural communication skills, and the like. This approach tends to lead to a certain disjointedness as one jumps from one issue to another. The second is the functional or strategic decision-making focus, in which material is organized around the major choices of **strategy** facing a firm, with emphasis on those aspects not present in a purely domestic business, or at least not present to the same degree. If one opts for this second organizational principle, one finds that discussion of major issues falls into place within the appropriate decision-making areas. For example, political risk has a number of facets; the issue arises in virtually every strategic decision-making area, but in different ways. Protecting proprietary rights, we find, has both legal and control strategy implications. Managing joint ventures relates to the financial, organizational, legal, and control strategy areas. Intercultural communication is an issue most appropriately dealt with in relation to labor and management strategies.

I find that this second approach coincides more closely with the way in which decision-making responsibility within firms is actually allocated. Hence, as in my previous texts, I follow that outline here.

As an organizational vehicle, I use "the decision circle" (Figure P.1), which is simply an interrelated set of strategic choices forced upon any firm faced with the internationalization of its markets. These choices have to do with marketing, sourcing, labor, management, ownership, finance, law, control, and public affairs. It will be noted that the first two—marketing and sourcing—constitute the basic strategies that encompass a firm's initial considerations. Essentially, management is answering two questions: to whom are we going to sell what, and from where and how will we supply that market? We then have a series of input strategies—labor, management, ownership, and financial. They are addressed essentially to the query, with what resources are we going to implement the basic strategies? That is, where will we find the right people, willingness to carry the risk, and the necessary money? A third set of strategies—legal and control—respond to the problem of how the firm is to structure itself to implement the basic strategies, given the resources it can muster. A final strategic area, public affairs, is shown as a basic strategy simply because it places a restraint on all other strategy choices.

Although these strategy areas are shown separately in the decision circle and treated separately in the body of the text, they obviously do not stand alone. There must be constant reiteration as one moves around the decision circle. The sourcing strategy obviously influences marketing strategy, as well as the reverse. The target market may enjoy certain preferential relationships with other markets. That is, everything influences everything else. Inasmuch as the number of options a firm faces is multiplied as it moves into international markets, decision making becomes increasingly complex the deeper the firm becomes involved internationally. One is dealing with multiple currency, legal, marketing, economic, political, and cultural systems. Geographic and demographic factors differ widely. In fact, as one moves geographically, virtually everything becomes a variable: there are few fixed factors. Figure P.2 maps some of these complexities.

For our purposes here, a strategy is defined as an element in a consciously devised overall plan of corporate development that, once made and implemented, is difficult (i.e., costly) to change in the short run. By way of contrast, an **operational** or **tactical decision** is one that sets up little or no institutionalized resistance to making a different decision in the near future. Some theorists have differentiated among strategic, tactical, and operational, with the first being defined as those decisions that imply multi-year commitments; a tactical decision, one that can be shifted in roughly a year's time; an operational decision, one subject to change in less than a year. In the international context, I suggest that the tactical decision, as the phrase is used here, is elevated to the strategic level because of the rigidities in the international environment not present in the purely domestic—for example,

Figure P.1
The Decision Circle

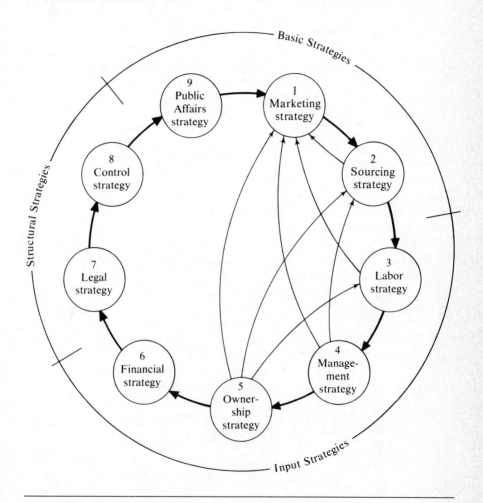

Each strategy area contains a number of subsidiary strategy options. The decision process, which normally starts in the marketing strategy area, is an iterative one. As the decision maker proceeds around the decision circle, previously selected strategies must be readjusted. Only a portion of the possible feedback adjustment loops are shown here. The numbers refer to the chapter sequence of this book.

work force planning and overall distribution decisions. Changes may be implemented domestically in a few months, but if one is operating internationally, law, contract, and custom may intervene to render change difficult unless implemented over several years.

Figure P.2
Variables in the International System

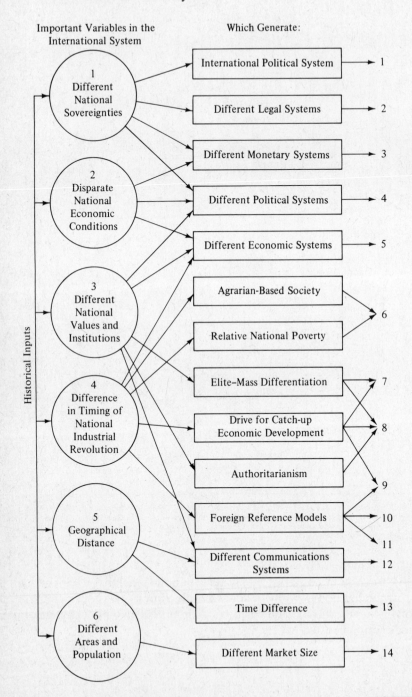

Important Variables in the International System

Which Generate:

1. Different National Sovereignties
2. Disparate National Economic Conditions
3. Different National Values and Institutions
4. Difference in Timing of National Industrial Revolution
5. Geographical Distance
6. Different Areas and Population

Historical Inputs

- International Political System → 1
- Different Legal Systems → 2
- Different Monetary Systems → 3
- Different Political Systems → 4
- Different Economic Systems → 5
- Agrarian-Based Society → 6
- Relative National Poverty
- Elite–Mass Differentiation → 7
- Drive for Catch-up Economic Development → 8
- Authoritarianism → 9
- Foreign Reference Models → 10
- → 11
- Different Communications Systems → 12
- Time Difference → 13
- Different Market Size → 14

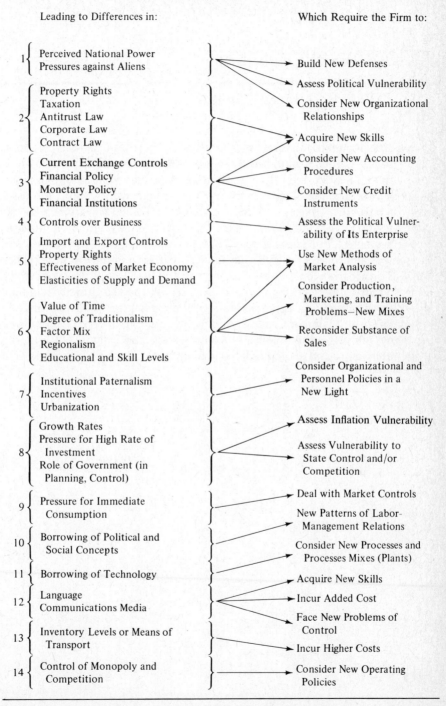

Leading to Differences in:

Which Require the Firm to:

1 {
Perceived National Power
Pressures against Aliens

2 {
Property Rights
Taxation
Antitrust Law
Corporate Law
Contract Law

3 {
Current Exchange Controls
Financial Policy
Monetary Policy
Financial Institutions

4 {
Controls over Business

5 {
Import and Export Controls
Property Rights
Effectiveness of Market Economy
Elasticities of Supply and Demand

6 {
Value of Time
Degree of Traditionalism
Factor Mix
Regionalism
Educational and Skill Levels

7 {
Institutional Paternalism
Incentives
Urbanization

8 {
Growth Rates
Pressure for High Rate of
    Investment
Role of Government (in
    Planning, Control)

9 {
Pressure for Immediate
    Consumption

10 {
Borrowing of Political and
    Social Concepts

11 {
Borrowing of Technology

12 {
Language
Communications Media

13 {
Inventory Levels or Means of
    Transport

14 {
Control of Monopoly and
    Competition

Build New Defenses

Assess Political Vulnerability

Consider New Organizational
    Relationships

Acquire New Skills

Consider New Accounting
    Procedures

Consider New Credit
    Instruments

Assess the Political Vulner-
    ability of Its Enterprise

Use New Methods of
    Market Analysis

Consider Production,
    Marketing, and Training
    Problems—New Mixes

Reconsider Substance of
    Sales

Consider Organizational and
    Personnel Policies in a
    New Light

Assess Inflation Vulnerability

Assess Vulnerability to
    State Control and/or
    Competition

Deal with Market Controls

New Patterns of Labor-
    Management Relations

Consider New Processes and
    Processes Mixes (Plants)

Acquire New Skills

Incur Added Cost

Face New Problems of
    Control

Incur Higher Costs

Consider New Operating
    Policies

Note: Many important relationships are not charted here. This scheme is presented only as an illustration.

ACKNOWLEDGMENT

The writing of a textbook is never an individual thing. Many people contribute in diverse ways, directly or indirectly. It is possible, however, to mention only a few by name. First on the list are colleagues associated with the International Business Group at the Sloan School of Management with whom I discussed many of the issues: Professors Donald R. Lessard, J. Daniel Nyhart, and Eleanor Westney, and Dr. Raj Rao. Then there are the invaluable contributions made by the two reviewers, Professors James C. Baker of Kent State University and G. Eric Hansen of Saint Mary's College. Substantive assistance in manuscript preparation was provided by both Carol A. Robinson and Joan Wyatt. The copyeditor, Anne Knowles, deserves special praise for her careful and constructive editing. I also wish to express my appreciation for proofreading and indexing done by Robert Beran and Jennifer Gordon. And finally, but too numerous to list, were the many students who added useful information and insight. To all go my profound thanks—and apologies if the final product falls short of their expectations.
R. D. R.
Cambridge, Mass.
January 1983

CHAPTER 1

UNDERLYING THEORY

comparative advantage the concept that nations undertake international trade to gain from exporting those goods and services they can produce at lowest cost (compared to other goods and services) and to import those which other nations produce at relatively lowest cost.

company resources capital, personnel, technical knowledge, goodwill, intangibles (patents, copyrights, trademarks, trade secrets), distribution system, political leverage, and so forth.

direct investment an investment of capital made with the intent of exercising some control and assuming some degree of participation in management.

hard goods merchandise.

intermediates manufactured or processed goods which are inputs into a good produced for delivery to the final consumer.

learning curve the graphic representation of a company's increasing efficiency (i.e., decreasing per-unit cost of product) as it becomes more skilled. Also called the experience curve. It is a function of aggregate volume, time, and the capacity of a firm to capture its own experience.

multinational corporation an internationally integrated production system over which equity-based control is exercised by a parent corporation that is owned and managed essentially by the nationals of the country in which it is domiciled.

product the embodiment of a package of services, or value-added chain, in which all the producing company's efforts are involved, and which it delivers to a customer.

social costs costs a firm incurs in damage suits, legal expenses, work stoppages, insurance premiums, building and maintaining security systems, taxes, compliance with government regulation, and general training of employees not covered by public education.

software human skills, technical know-how, and information.

structure organizational rigidities difficult to alter significantly in the short run.

technical efficiency the relationship between the labor, materials, and capital required per unit of production. Normally, the greater the technical efficiency, the lower the relative per-unit cost of production.

time horizon the time over which the inputs and outputs (cost and benefits) relevant to a decision or plan are considered.

The internationalization of business challenges managers in new and exciting ways, even those on the entry level. Virtually no executives in a profit-seeking enterprise can remain insensitive to the opportunities and threats inherent in the process without jeopardizing future earnings.

The internationalization process is the business response to the internationalization of markets as products and factors of production become increasingly mobile, less country specific. Why should that be? There are many answers. With but slight exception, the entire world has opted for industrialization (that is, mechanization) so as to provide more goods and services with which to gratify a nearly universal craving for an easier, more secure, longer life. Even where the appeal of less materialistic religions and ideologies is supposed to dominate, in fact the pressure for increased consumption has become psychologically and politically compelling. The way of one's forebearers is no longer adequate, which was not true only a few short years ago in many regions of the world. Whether capitalist or socialist, almost all national leaders now speak of efficiency of production and equity of distribution.

This rising tide of expectations is, of course, coupled with transportation and communication technologies which have reduced the cost of moving goods and people, of transferring funds, and of transmitting information. The worldwide information explosion has made even the most backward, isolated, impoverished villagers aware of the array of goods and services being consumed by the more affluent. The spread of education enhances that awareness. Demand is multiplied and intensified by both the media and by education. A politically-imposed "iron curtain" may be effective against the movement of people and goods, but not against electronically driven information. Eventually, even the most authoritarian of regimes are forced to permit international transactions in goods, and hence in technology and capital as well, even though the technology be limited to that embodied in the goods and the capital, used to finance their purchase.

1.1 Processes of International Trade

A nation dedicated to improving the lot of its own people must import those goods and services that are either not available locally or cost more than the foreign-produced counterparts—and sell its own products in order to buy those imports. For a time, a country may borrow foreign savings with which to buy foreign goods and services, but not indefinitely. Eventually, it must repay. And to do so, it must sell or lease something. That something can be a manufactured good; a nonrenewable raw material (e.g., oil); a renewable resource (e.g., agricultural produce); labor (via the temporary export of people); technology (the result of investment in research and development); services (e.g., education, medical care, insurance, transportation, marketing, engineering, design, construction, banking, military); savings (e.g., capital in either equity or debt form, for which dividends or interest is received); political-military support (for which grants or subsidized loans may be received—that is, "foreign assistance"); or land in the form of either lease or outright sale).

Some countries, the United States included, at times try to prevent the competition of foreign goods and services by erecting various trade barriers, such as special taxes on imports (tariffs) or one or more nontariff barriers, such as quotas or discriminatory standards. Over the years, the combined pressures from domestic consumers and foreign trading partners have liberalized international trade. Still, governments intervene in international markets in a variety of ways. They may subsidize exports to generate more foreign earnings with which to purchase imports. In such case, of course, the foreign consumer gains; the local consumer pays. Or a government may screen incoming investment capital to make certain that it is being used in ways perceived to be socially and economically desirable. Or it may monitor contracts for the import of technology or technical services to ascertain that exhorbitant payments are not being extracted by foreign contractors. Whenever a government finds itself without adequate foreign currency reserves, it may well inhibit the outward flow of capital and offer special incentives to attract foreign capital. And, almost universally, governments restrain the entry of foreign labor.

There are many measures of the internationalization of markets, and hence, of business. International trade in goods and services reported by governments seems to be outpacing growth in the world's total production. This means that the percentage of world production moving in international trade is increasing. If one then adds three more elements, (1) the value of production for domestic consumption by firms owned by foreigners, (2) international capital movements, and (3) the earnings of expatriate labor (e.g., the guest workers in Europe; the Egyptians, Turks, and Koreans in Arab countries; the Mexicans and other Hispanics in the United States), the total for the international sector adds up to something like one quarter to one third of world production. And that percentage seems to have been moving up over the past several decades. On top of this, one should add the *unreported* international movements, that is, the illegal traffic among nations, which must amount to several billions of dollars annually. The more governments regulate and tax, the larger the illegal flows become. In some countries the illegal or "off the books" economy runs well over 25 percent of the national product.[1]

The point of this argument is to underline the growing importance of international markets in goods, money, technology, labor, and skills. Just think of all the ways that even the relatively small business, far removed from a coastal city, may feel the impact.

Perhaps most obviously, the small firm may be adversely affected by the local sale of an imported product at a lower price. Why the lower price? Obviously, the foreign producer either faces lower cost for one or more inputs (labor, capital, technology, raw materials, intermediates, government—i.e., taxes) or is willing to shave margins more than the domestic producer. Margin shaving may be possible if the larger volume generated by increased sales abroad reduces per-unit cost. Such a reduction could take place for several reasons. Perhaps investment is "lumpy" (i.e., a certain investment is required no matter what the output, up to a certain level), or overhead cost per unit of output is high; that is, the fixed cost for management, research and development, and marketing must be maintained at a certain level to be effective almost regardless of output. If one can spread that fixed cost over larger volume, the per-unit cost goes down. Or reduced cost may be associated with volume simply because the firm is pushed further down its **learning** or **experience curve**. And why should that happen?

It is generally agreed that an enterprise becomes better—more efficient—in producing anything as it becomes more skilled. It becomes more skilled as it learns or accumulates experience, which is associated very closely with cumulative volume. Thus, a foreign producer may enter your market at what seems to you an unfair price, one pegged at below cost. But what the foreign competitor may in fact be doing is simply trying to pick up volume to be able to move down his learning curve. International competition can boil down largely to a question of who can reduce per-unit cost most quickly via the learning process.

One suspects that a number of factors may be important in impeding or accelerating that process. The motivation and stability of a firm's labor force may be a key, likewise the degree of communication among managers, technicians, and producers (labor). The firm that faces the least resistance to innovation has an important advantage. It can introduce changes without delay. Resistance to change may be lowered because employees do not feel

---

[1]Geoffrey Carroll, "The Underground Economy," *Europe*, November–December 1981, p. 41.

threatened or exploited. The point is that firms that can retain their experience via employment stability, generalize that experience through open internal communication, and activate change with little delay, have a distinct advantage in the international market.

The reason all of this takes on special importance as markets become international is that the attitudes, values, and institutions—in short, the culture—of one country may be peculiarly favorable to, or supportive of the behavior required to compete successfully in international markets. Another culture may be less so. It is also true that firms producing in and exporting from countries in which various **social costs** are relatively low have distinct advantages over those operating in countries with relatively high social costs. By social cost I mean those costs the firm incurs in damage suits, legal expenses, work stoppages, insurance premiums, building and maintaining security systems, taxes, compliance with government regulations, and general training of employees, which may be part of public education elsewhere. Social or national efficiency is one thing; technical efficiency is another. Without the former, the benefits of the latter may be lost.

1.2   Theory of Comparative Advantage

The usual explanation for international trade is stated in terms of **comparative advantage**. A country may be more efficient than any other in producing virtually everything, from guns to butter. But it can be demonstrated that if a country is relatively more efficient in producing guns, it gains if it expends its resources in producing as many guns as possible and buying the butter it needs from others. (A country is always *relatively* more efficient in producing certain goods rather than others.) Furthermore, the country at the other end of the transaction gains as well, for now it can get guns at a relatively lower price in exchange for its butter. If it attempted to produce guns itself, the trade-off between guns and butter would not be so attractive. (Of course, whether guns will really do the purchasing country any good is another matter, but it must perceive that they will or it would not trade.)

Relevance to Management Decisions

The trouble with this concept is that it is almost wholly irrelevant to managerial decision making. The firm may produce butter only; it is very unlikely to produce butter *and* guns. Hence, management's interest is in building markets for butter, not guns. It is not interested in the trade-offs from the national point of view. Furthermore, its efficiency in butter production may be well above or below the national average. The point is that the theory of national comparative advantage is based on *average* efficiency. It also assumes that resources can be moved from butter production to gun production without serious cost, which is a fallacy. The capital equipment, technology, and skills—even the geographical location within a country—that are appropriate for the butter industry may be completely inappropriate for the munitions industry. Resources can be shifted only over the very long run and possibly only with government subsidy to those suffering loss in the process. A society that encourages close government-business collaboration and in which large business combines are tolerated may be very much better at shifting resources to take advantage of national comparative advantages in international trade. But in doing so, it must acquiesce to a degree of international interdependence that may seriously erode the nation's sense of independence and national security. To produce only guns and no butter, or all butter and no guns, may not be appealing choices, unless a society is committed to the notion of international interdependence and maximum economic growth and perceives little external threat—perhaps an unrealistically enlightened approach!

In a society that does not tolerate such close government-business collaboration or the formation of large business combines, there may be some advantage in organizing large conglomerates. Such conglomerates can internalize some of these trade-offs and so take advantage of national comparative advantage in international trade. A conglomerate may embrace both butter and gun production, and it can shift resources from one to the other with relative ease. Even the large general trading company can exert pressure in this direction by making advantageous trade-offs and thereby push the nation's allocation of resources in the direction of comparative advantage. It may be able to buy and sell guns as well as butter internationally. Such a firm can be more responsive to comparative advantages. Thus, even though we said initially that the theory of comparative advantage was irrelevant to the individual firm, this is not quite true if we are talking of the large conglomerate or international trading company, both of which seem to be of growing significance internationally.

Our relatively small, mid-country firm, however, will sell butter in international trade only if it can compete successfully in overseas butter markets in terms of price, quality, consumer credit, and/or service (e.g., frequency of delivery). Conversely, it may suffer foreign competition in its own local market via imported butter if the foreign producer can do one or more of these things better. We assume that neither government subsidizes the export of butter in any way, nor makes its import more costly by imposing import duties or special nontariff barriers of some sort.

But let us assume that our relatively small, mid-country firm can avoid competition. Perhaps it joined with competitors to lobby effectively for tariff protection or some sort of import quota system. Or perhaps its product is bulky and of low per-unit value—or perishable, as butter—thereby rendering long-distance transport uneconomic, thereby giving it a degree of natural protection. It could still be in trouble from foreign competitors.

If a foreign firm believes that its cost advantage is transferable, it might make a direct foreign investment and start up a local manufacturing facility. It might make such a move if management felt that it had superior technology, more highly skilled technicians, a product more appealing to the consumer for some reason (such as a recognized brand name or demonstrably better performance), superior management, access to lower-priced intermediates by reason of its foreign affiliation, or access to lower-priced capital by reason of its ability to tap international capital markets. In other words, the foreign management may perceive some advantage over the local firm.

Economic theorists speak of market imperfections in this context. If all markets were perfect (open to all comers on equal terms, regardless of nationality and size), then there would be little reason for direct international investment. Direct investment occurs because of market imperfections, because a foreign firm has some advantage over the local.

Other theorists speak of the relatively greater **efficiency** (i.e., lower cost) of internal or administered transactions as opposed to market transactions. The first category refers to those movements of goods, funds, technology, skills, and information *within* a firm; the second, to purchases and sales between the firm and external markets. For example, researchers have demonstrated that the transfer of technology within a firm, from one affiliate to another, is less costly than a transfer between two unrelated entities. Indeed, firms would not exist at all unless the internal transaction costs within some area of activity were not less than open market transactions. Otherwise, we would all act as individuals, and buy and sell from each other on an arms-length basis.

Let us assume now that our firm has avoided foreign competition in its own market and no foreign firms have perceived any advantage in entering its domestic market via their own manufacturing facilities. Can management then ignore the international marketplace? Not at all. It may well find itself unable to compete effectively with another *domestic* firm that has availed itself of certain foreign inputs. For example, a domestic competitor may have entered into a license for a superior foreign technology, say a way of increasing the shelf-life of butter. It may be producing for a foreign firm under a manufacturing contract, thereby gaining experience and reducing its per-unit cost. It may have acquired lower-priced capital abroad by finding foreign debt capital or by taking in a foreign partner. It may have discovered that certain intermediates can be manufactured more cheaply overseas, say a part requiring a lot of hand tooling or handling, and has entered into a subcontract with a foreign manufacturer. An example might be packaging materials. It may even have shifted a major part of its manufacturing abroad where certain economies can be realized, and now imports the nearly finished product back into the local market. Or it may have located a domestic plant to better utilize lower-cost foreign labor coming into the country.

Capital Intensive versus Labor Intensive Goods

Although I argued earlier that the theory of comparative advantage was largely irrelevant to managerial decision making because few firms—except possibly the largest conglomerates or general international trading companies—were in the business of selling *both* guns and butter, in another sense that theory can be very relevant. All manufacturing firms, our small domestic firm included, do have the choice of selling either **hard goods** or the **software** (human skills and knowledge) which make the production and distribution of those hard goods possible. The reason the theory of comparative advantage may be relevant here is that management may well have the choice between selling in international markets the hard goods the firm manufactures and/or the software it develops; and, generally speaking, software is very much more capital intensive than hardware. Hence, if one country is particularly well endowed with capital, such that its ratio of capital cost to labor cost is low relative to the comparable ratio for another country, the two countries should trade. The first should export that which requires a lot of capital to produce (capital intensive goods) and buy that which requires a lot of labor to produce (labor intensive goods). Both countries would gain in the trade.

It can be demonstrated that, from the point of view of a national society (not necessarily that of the firm), the most capital intensive goods are the products of highly skilled people and the technology they have developed over time. If so, the greatest comparative advantage for a country in which capital is relatively cheap lies in the area of high-level human skills and technology. Theoretically, then, a firm located in such a country should make more money in international trade by exporting software than hardware, *unless* it can extract a monopoly profit via the exploitation of certain market advantages, such as an exclusive right to use a valuable technology or know-how or a brand name for which strong consumer preference has developed. However, if it is true, as I have hypothesized below, that there is a general slowdown of commercially valuable technological innovation, and an internationalization of markets via increased competition, then the basis for maintaining any sort of monopoly in international markets is being eroded. We would then expect a dramatic increase in the international flows of software from those countries relatively well endowed with capital embodied in human skills and technology, and an increase in the export of hard goods from those countries not so well endowed—both of which appear to be happening.

One of the difficulties in demonstrating empirically that this shift is indeed occurring is that some important software flows are not reported in international trade statistics because the consumer moves in order to purchase the software—as in the case of educational, legal, engineering, and medical services. Every institution of higher learning, every medical center, every large law firm, every major engineering and design firm has foreign clients. Their purchase of services often does not enter into trade statistics. Those foreign students sitting in class using this book, for instance, are creating an international flow—an export—of educational services, which is very capital intensive from the point of view of society. To produce a frontier researcher, practitioner, or educator requires the investment by society of hundreds of thousands of dollars over twenty or more years. It takes that long before the individual begins to contribute.

1.3 Business in the International Marketplace

When all is said and done, few managers can afford to ignore the internationalization of markets. Everywhere there is mounting competition from foreign goods, foreign technicians, foreign managers, foreign technology, foreign labor, foreign owners, foreign finance. This is the stuff of world development, of world unity. To stop the process now and divide up permanently into trading blocs would be costly in terms of heightened prices, slowed economic development, and mounting political conflict.

Hence, to compete effectively in the decades ahead, many, if not most, firms will need to internalize new skills—skills in language, political-economic analysis, negotiation, trading, product modification, process engineering that assumes different factor costs and scale, culturally-sensitive management, international communication, and training. To capture such skills at reasonable cost probably means removing all national barriers to corporate recruitment and promotion as a matter of corporate policy. It also may mean, in some instances, the international dispersion of certain research and development activities, as well as sourcing of products.

Multinational Corporations

It should be made clear at the outset that the study of international business is not confined to the study of the **multinational corporation**. The MNC is only one type of business organization involved in international transactions, and it may already be fading. The multinational, as it developed following World War II, can be described as an internationally integrated production system over which equity-based control is exercised by a parent corporation that is owned and managed essentially by the nationals of the country in which it is domiciled. That is, control is based on ownership of assets, not on their use under contract. The emphasis is on the international integration of *manufacturing* facilities, not simply of markets, which would be the case of an international trading company. The central management is dominated by parent-country nationals, as is its ownership. And the parent—or center of control—is located within the country with which most of the top managers and owners identify. Hence, neither management nor ownership is truly international. Legally, the parent corporation is a creature of one country. All of these parameters may be changed; a subject discussed at greater length in Chapter Nine. The important point here is that the multinational corporation cannot be equated with international business. One must also talk of the management of exporting firms, importing organizations, trading companies, and the international service companies—for example, engineering and construction firms, banks and insurance companies, consultants, transportation and communication organizations.

Foreign Direct Investment

Note that one of the hallmarks of the multinational corporation is foreign
direct investment. Although one may entertain considerable misgivings
about the accuracy of international trade and investment statistics, there is a
good deal of evidence that the flow of foreign direct investment, as a
percentage of the total international flow of commercial resources, is declining. What appear to be growing most rapidly are the flows of services, skills,
technology, information, and proprietary rights (patents, trademarks,
copyrights, trade secrets) under contract.

Statistically, the definition of foreign direct investment is an arbitrary
one, and the reporting of flows of services and information under contract is
done very inadequately by many countries. For purposes of statistical definition, an investment generally is termed "direct" if it constitutes more than
10 percent (sometimes 25 percent) of the equity of the enterprise in which
the investment is made. Technically, though, direct investment is an investment of capital made with the intent of exercising some control and assuming some degree of participation in management. In this sense, an investment may be direct even though the equity held by the investor is less than a
given percent; it depends upon how the rest of the equity is distributed.
Further, an investment of over a given percent may not lead to control or
management participation. Then there is the problem of control flowing
from debt, not equity. If the debt/equity ratio is very high, effective control
may be in the hands of the creditors (other than the owners). There is the
further problem of control arising out of a purely contractual relationship,
whether that relationship be represented by management contract, manufacturing contract, or a restrictive license or technical assistance agreement
of some sort.

An interesting question arises when one assumes that the international flows of commercially valuable goods and services under contract are
coming to dominate; namely, what is causing the relative demise of direct
foreign investment? Are the conditions and requirements being imposed on
direct foreign investors by many governments eroding equity-based control
to such a degree as to discourage the direct foreign investor? How does
management justify the assumption of risk implicit in direct investment
when "adequate" control is threatened at every turn? Increasingly, host
governments are limiting foreign managerial options in respect to plant
location, choice of technology, level of employment, definition of target
markets, changes in production, definition of product mix, financial structure, ownership, appointment of key executives, legal form of organization,
purchase or buy decisions, and sourcing decisions. As the form and time of
government intervention becomes less predictable, the equity investor perceives heightened risk and uncertainty. The result is that the investor has to
be able to anticipate a very much higher level of earnings, so as to overcome
the higher rates by which those earnings must be discounted to the present
to factor in the heightened risk and uncertainty. That swollen stream of

earnings introduces even more political risk; host political authorities may object. Remittance of earnings above a certain level may be blocked.

On the other hand, the underlying dynamics that explain the declining relative importance of direct foreign investment may lie with the massive balance-of-payments surpluses piled up by the oil-exporting countries and the recycling of these funds via Western financial intermediaries to the less developed countries in the form of bank loans—that is, in portfolio debt rather than direct investment. Financial resources thereby become available to many countries from sources other than the direct foreign investors of North America, Japan, and Western Europe. It may be relevant to note that of the larger corporations in the world, those growing most rapidly are the large general trading companies and large international service corporations, not those primarily involved in manufacturing. For these trading and service enterprises, foreign direct investment is only of marginal or transient interest, primarily as a strategy to develop a source of supply or a customer to be spun off to local ownership as soon as practicable. Long-run profit is derived largely from commissions and fees arising out of the international flows of goods and services, much less from dividends.

We cannot yet answer definitely the two questions begged in this discussion: (1) Is direct foreign investment, in fact, declining in the long run relative to other international commercial flows, specifically those of skills, technology, information, proprietary rights? and (2) Is the underlying cause the intervention of governments or a shift in the source of financial resources, or both? One suspects that the answer may be both and, indeed, a third possible explanation may be contributing to the apparent shift away from multinational corporate control. That explanation has to do with the loss of technological advantage of the large, globally integrated industrial firms—the multinationals.

Shifting Advantages

If, as many claim, the rate at which significantly new technology is being commercialized has slowed down worldwide, an increasing share of the world's technology is becoming relatively mature. Mature technology tends, on average, to be more labor intensive than new technology. Less research and development takes place. Relevant skills become more widely disseminated, and the firm needs to invest less in internal training. Markets become more predictable and inventory requirements, lower. Producers of capital goods (i.e., machinery) become more competitive, which reduces the cost of equipment and thereby lowers per-unit investment cost. Obsolescence rates decrease. Risk and uncertainty are generally reduced. All of these developments tend to reduce the amount of capital utilized per unit of output, thereby rendering the industry more labor intensive.

If all of this be so, manufacturing could be expected to shift slowly to those countries in which labor is relatively cheap compared to capital. In fact, we seem to be entering a period of rather rapid shift in the production of manufactured goods to the more advanced of the less developed countries, the so-called newly industrializing countries (NICs). If the MNCs are indeed losing both relative financial and technological advantage, their continued control via ownership (equity)—which is the control characteristic of the MNCs—becomes intolerable. For this reason, neither host government intervention nor the rise of the international trading and service companies is surprising.

Note that from 1970 to 1980, U.S. imports from non-oil-producing (non-OPEC) developing countries grew at an average annual rate of over 22 percent, compared to the growth of only 17 percent of U.S. imports from industrialized countries—and these percentages are diverging.[2] Also, the industrialized countries as a group are sourcing an increasing share of their manufactured imports from LDCs (7 percent in 1970, 13 percent in 1980.)[3] The big exporters are Singapore, South Korea, Taiwan, Hong Kong, Brazil, and Mexico, a group of NICs with a real economic growth rate of 9.4 percent per annum during the 1970s (versus 6 percent in Japan and 3 percent in the United States).[4] If the rate at which new technology is being commercialized is in fact slowing, manufacturing will continue to shift. Accelerating this shift is the increasingly rapid dissemination of relevant technical and managerial skills, also symptomatic of maturing technology.

There seems to be substantial evidence that the rate of increase in world per capita production and consumption of goods is slowing, one symptom of which is global inflation. As this happens, pressure for distributing that consumption more equally mounts. Mass communication has enhanced awareness of widely disparate levels of per capita consumption within and among national societies. Catch-up consumption targets become psychologically compelling. And the world's supply and distribution systems are further strained, and inflation accelerates.

The importance of this process to the corporate strategist is that he or she is driven to the assumption that governments of the poorer countries will, in the long run if not the short, intervene increasingly in international markets, in the desperate effort to capture more of the wherewithal of consumption for their own frustrated peoples. One can anticipate increasingly sophisticated, honest, and effective efforts by governments to force foreign-owned enterprises to employ more and more local resources, whether they be raw materials, the capacities of local subcontractors, local technical and managerial skills, or, as product and technology mature and risk and uncertainty fall, local equity, possibly to the point of extinguishing foreign ownership.

Associated with this pressure for local value-added and local control is growing pressure from employees almost everywhere for greater influence in decision making. As populations become more literate, educated, and

[2]John A. Mathieson, "U.S. Trade with the Third World: The American Stake" (Stanley Foundation, Occasional Paper 28, January 1982), pp. 8–10.

[3]International Bank for Reconstruction and Development, *World Development Report 1982* (Washington, D.C., 1982), p. 12.

[4]Luis Kraar, "Make Way for the New Japans," *Fortune*, August 10, 1981, p. 176.

industrially mature, the conventional prerogatives of people called managers are destined to change. Note that the owners of a mature enterprise often, in fact, take less risk than employees do. Markets and costs are more predictable. And the owners have a better opportunity to diversify risk than does the run-of-the-mill employee, whose sole source of livelihood may be his or her job. Hence, the highest priority objective of enterprises may, more and more, be the maintenance and increase of employee income and benefits, on the Japanese or Yugoslav model. (See pp. 82–83 for further discussion of these systems.) In such event, management is very likely to maximize return to labor, not return to owners, which comes to be viewed as more or less a fixed cost.

One other pressure pushing in the direction of local control should be noted. The scale factor in much of international production may be in the process of being reduced significantly. Small-batch production and the mini-plant may prove increasingly competitive to the products of world-scale plants, which require vast inputs of capital and ready access to world markets. If this be true, the large multinational loses another bit of rationale for maintaining centralized control.

All of these forces add up to increased difficulty for a corporation that maintains equity-based, centralized control over an internationally integrated production system—that is, for the modern multinational corporation.

1.4   Long-Term Strategy

The argument goes that corporate strategists will increasingly feel compelled to take a long hard look at the bundle of services their respective firms market, called a "product." A product is, of course, nothing more than the embodiment of a *package* of services, or "value-added chain," from information gathering and sorting, to purchasing, hiring, research and development, engineering, training, the application of labor and technical and managerial skills to a series of production processes, marketing, distribution, and the financing of the entire process.

For a U.S. firm (or European, or Japanese) facing an increasingly internationalized market, and with decreasing competitive edge derived from financial advantage and technological superiority, the problem is reduced to ascertaining what it can do better by reason of its experience and organization and the fact of being based in a relatively large, wealthy, technologically sophisticated market. One would normally zero in on those services that appear to be peculiarly sensitive to economies of scale (such as relatively easy access to international information and distribution systems), services that are relatively capital intensive (such as R&D and entrepreneurial activities), and those that require the highest levels of technical sophistication.

One firm's comparative advantage might lie in a combination of information gathering, purchasing, research and development, marketing, and distribution. If so, its long-term strategy might well be to meet international competition via international subcontracting or, if an Eastern European source is seen as desirable, coproduction. If information gathering, purchasing, and marketing are seen as the firm's areas of greatest comparative advantage, the corporation might move toward a trading company mode. Or, if it sees its real strength as lying in R&D, it might opt for a strategy of licensing and technical assistance/training contracting.

But, some might say—and do say—how is the corporation to maintain control with such strategies? Control of what? Is control something justified at any cost, including loss of market position? What of quality of product? one might ask. If quality will deteriorate without parent control—which control, I assume, means having people responsible only to the parent firm at the product reject button—then there must be demand for a product of lesser or different quality. Quality, one needs to remind oneself, is not an absolute; it relates to the satisfaction of a set of needs. A cheaper, less durable, less finely tooled, less automated product may well be better in some sense where the cost of capital is very high and labor is relatively cheap.

I suggest that if one talks about control without specifying the return on corporate assets committed, one is talking about power, not about profit maximizing. Consider the alternatives. Which is personally more satisfying—conducting a global business with 50,000 employees which earns a 20 percent return for the corporate stockholders, or conducting a business of 500 people which concentrates on domestic production and transfer of technology to others under contract, but which earns a return of 40 percent on resources committed? Which would you find more satisfying?

The Decision-Making Process

One might argue that a reasonable business approach to the selection of appropriate strategies for the exploitation of overseas opportunities is posed by this query: Given

- the domestic environment,
- the socioeconomic environment of the host nation,
- the structure of the international economic and political system—all three of which generate legal restraints, among others—and,
- company resources,

what is the most effective strategy for achieving corporate goals? (See Figure 1.1.)

Considerable noise and rigidity—that is, inability to communicate accurately and to respond in an appropriate manner—are generated in this ideal decision-making system by at least four other variables:

- past company experience (the historical input),
- existing company structure (structural rigidities),
- the quality of the communications system (the linkages), and,

Figure 1.1
The Decision-Making Process

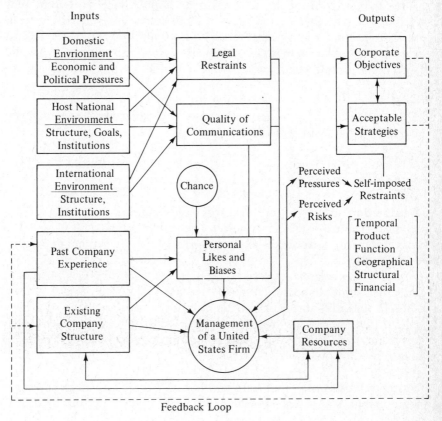

- personal likes and biases (partly chance occurrence; for example, the degree of sensitivity of key people to the demands of the surrounding society).

These variables are, of course, closely interrelated. Company structure and personal likes and biases in part determine the quality of the communications system. The quality of communications and personal likes and biases have the impact of altering the management's perception of external and internal environments.

These four variables, *in interaction with the other variables as seen by management* (the international environment, the host national environment, the domestic environment, company resources), produce a set of perceived pressures and perceived risks. This system very commonly generates a set of self-imposed restraints, most common of which are:

1. A time dimension in thinking—that is, those strategies are deemed best that most nearly achieve corporate objectives within a *given period of time*— one year, two years, five years. Profit, however and wherever determined, is maximized over that period. This dimension varies remarkably from company to company. It is probably safe to say that a longer time dimension is required for success in international business than in the purely domestic because of the growth factor and associated restrictions on monetary movement.

2. A limitation on the products to be sold or produced overseas (e.g., oil production, cement, intermediates).

3. A functional limitation (on selling, assembly, manufacture, construction, engineering, consulting, licensing).

4. A limitation on the geographical scope of operations (e.g., within Latin America or the European Community). Such a limitation is often related to the development of export sales by the firm. That is, investment in productive facilities abroad tends to follow the development of export sales, but export sales may be greater precisely for those products in which the parent country has some distinct advantage, and are therefore not necessarily a measure of the advantages of local manufacture. The advantage may be in cost or in the identity of the goods with a given natural source. In fact, imports may be a more convincing indication of advantages accruing to overseas production.

5. Structural restraints—that is, refusal to consider other than certain types of relationship, such as an agency, 100 percent ownership, or license.

6. Financial restraints (such as refusal to seek external debt or equity capital). For a company to face a growth situation requiring expansion precisely at the rate that can be financed out of earnings would be a rare coincidence. The point is, of course, that a firm operating under a policy of expanding only at the rate permitted by retained earnings is disinclined to examine investment opportunities once that growth rate is approached, hence, the apparent coincidence of rates. The further afield the opportunity is in distance or substance, the less likely management is to see it.

It is within the parameters of these six self-imposed restraints, many of which may be entirely reasonable, that management defines corporate objectives, recognizes alternative strategies, and perceives the relevant variables.

Restraints of Time

Perhaps the greatest impact is management's **time horizon**, whether determined implicitly or explicitly. It is of particular relevance in the international area because of the greater time lag between decision and implementation than in the typical domestic case and the greater range of long-run strategies. Some relevant variables in setting an appropriate time horizon include the firm's available resources, its present geographical spread, the nature of the product, and growth conditions within markets where the firm is presently operating (particularly in the domestic market). If one or more of these factors do not rule out a time horizon longer than the current fiscal period, then management should probably not impose such a time restraint on its foreign market strategists. Figure 1.2 suggests some of the relationships that may exist between management's time horizon and acceptable strategies. The point is that it is wasteful of time and effort, and therefore costly, to permit analysts to consider strategies that management will not accept, particularly in the international field, because of the greater time and cost involved in investigating and implementing many projects. Bear in mind that there is a significant difference between what management *can* and *is willing* to accept. This difference should be made explicit by management after careful study of company's resources and its commitment to present markets.

Restraints of Structure and Resources

A word about company structure as related to the selection of corporate objectives and acceptable strategies to accomplish them is appropriate here. **Structure** means those organizational rigidities difficult to alter significantly in the short run, such elements as ownership, independence of management, board status (internal or external), divisional independence, divisional basis (product, region, function, composite), size of company, contractual relationship or interdependence in respect to other firms (e.g., as supplier or buyer). Indeed, if this last relationship is very important, management may be prone to enter overseas markets only in concert with the associated domestic firm, say in joint ventures, thereby limiting its ownership strategy to minority participation with other domestic firms, which is called a "piggy-back operation." Great size may limit consideration of overseas opportunities to international, regional, or multinational markets, thereby ruling out production for a single national market. Great size may also render product and process modification difficult, thereby eliminating market-oriented modifications of either. On the other hand, small size may limit overseas commitments to one or two national markets, thereby ruling out geographical dispersion and resulting in increased risk.

A Ford executive once commented that, after all, Ford could not build cars in mud huts, nor could it turn out a specially designed truck for use on the Arabian Peninsula. A small firm specializing in trucks could and did design a special truck for Arabia, though admittedly it was not produced in mud huts. More recently, General Motors has been feuding with the government of South Korea over how vehicles should be produced in Korea. GM wanted to make parts for its world car in Korea, thereby incorporating

Figure 1.2
Time Horizon of Management and Its Implications

	Now	1 yr.	2 yr.	3 yr.	4 yr.	5 yr.	10 yr.	20 yr.
	Sell Present Product		Consider By-products (Services, Rights, Finance)			Full Consideration of By-products		
		Market Research = Statistical Study		Market Research = Detailed Study of Selected Target Markets		On-the-spot Market Analysis	Continuing Market Analysis	
		Limited Penetration (Skimming)		Moderate Penetration		Full Penetration		
		Limited Promotion (Largely Spillover)		Some Specially Designed Promotion		Full Promotion		
		No Servicing		Provision for Servicing		Full Servicing		
		No Investment Related to Foreign Sales		U.S. Investment Related to Foreign Sales		Foreign Investment		
		No Product Modification		Minor Product Modification		Product Redesign	Special Products	
		Use Present Supply Sources		Overseas Assembly in Leased Facilities or Contract Manufacturing		Overseas Manufacturing	Global Integration Among Manufacturing Facilities	
Acceptable Strategies		Direct Mail Order and/or Independent Exporters		Either		Overseas Agents or Representatives	Foreign Sales Branch or Subsidiary	Internationally Oriented Operation
		No Specialized Personnel		Specialized Expert Personnel		Specialized Staff Personnel	Internationally Oriented Staff	Multinational or Transnational Organization
		No Organizational Changes		Slight Organizational Changes		Major Organizational Changes	Internationally Oriented Organization	
		Tight Control from U.S.		Tight Control		Looser Control	Decentralized Control	Near Autonomy for Foreign Operations (but see Chapter 9;
		Correspondent Relationships Only		Contractual Relations or Branch		100 Percent-owned Foreign Subsidiary	Joint Ventures	Multinational or Transnational Ventures

its Korean plant into its global assembly line. Its Korean associate, and the Korean government, wanted to build a totally Korean vehicle.

By **company resources**, one refers to such variables as financial resources, personnel, technical knowledge, goodwill, intangibles (patents, copyrights, trademarks, trade secrets), distribution system, and political leverage. A management may or may not utilize its resources to secure external financing or contractual relationships. Past experience or company structure or personal likes and biases may rule out the use of a resource such as goodwill for such purposes, thereby possibly requiring wholly owned ventures as the vehicle for overseas expansion, if indeed the firm feels able to do more than select some form of exporting. In any event, the rate of expansion overseas is curtailed. Meanwhile, the more geographically limited involvement overseas can heighten risk.

Optimum Strategy

A few words about corporate objectives are necessary or our concern about optimum strategy is without purpose. Optimum for what? Some object to the use of the word "optimum" because, with nine strategy sets and all their feedback loops and complexities, a management can never truly select, or know that it has selected, *the optimum* of anything. Granted. Optimum is used here to refer to an objective a management moves toward but never really achieves. Let us agree that the primary objective of the firm is to maximize profit. But to maximize profit where, for whom, over what length or period of time? Profit maximization is meaningless unless management first defines these parameters. If it does not, the system may be irrational because management is not doing what it set out to do, namely, to maximize profit. There are, of course, a number of perfectly valid reasons for limiting the international scope of the firm. One reason would be financial and personnel inadequacies—although management should ascertain that these inadequacies are not caused by some unnecessary self-imposed restraint (stemming, for example, from limitations on ownership and salaries, from an incompetent and insecure management, or from imperfections of communications) but are genuine, externally imposed inadequacies. Self-imposed restraints may sometimes flow from management's fear of losing control by moving into unfamiliar areas, such as the international market or a new functional area, and the employment of new people with unfamiliar expertise.

To operate effectively in the increasingly internationalized markets ahead, one must, I contend, be conscious of the *nonmarket biases* possibly operating in the corporate strategic decision-making system and explicitly factor them out to the extent possible. Those biases are essentially four in number:

- The power or control bias.
- The engineering bias, which acts so that preference is given to the most complex, newest technology regardless of its appropriateness for where it is to be used.

- The distance bias, the tendency to assign higher risk and uncertainty to places, functions, or products the further removed they are from one's own personal experience and expertise.
- The bias of past success, the most deadly of them all, given the rapidly changing environment surrounding us.

CHAPTER 2

MARKETING STRATEGY

agent one who buys nothing from a firm, its principal, but who acts on the firm's behalf as defined by agreement, for which the agent receives a fee and/or commission.

bilateral trade agreement an agreement between two countries that commits the two to exchange specified amounts of listed goods and services over a given amount of time.

branch an unincorporated entity, legally and financially indistinguishable from the parent firm.

clearing dollars the value of the imbalance of exchange between two countries committed to a bilateral trade agreement.

distributor one who contracts to buy a firm's goods or services for sale to third parties.

dumping the sale of foreign-produced goods at less than fair market value.

general trading companies organizations handling a broad spectrum of goods and sales without geographical restriction, either on a commission basis or on their own account, or both.

income elasticity of demand the relationship between the changes in the amount consumed as level of income changes.

inferior good a good for which consumption decreases proportionately as income rises.

parallel trading two or more firms acting in concert either to take a country's goods or services as partial or full payment for products or services sold there, or to supply goods or services in exchange for those received, or both.

risk outcomes whose probability can be inferred from previous experience.

subnational market a market smaller than a national market, defined geographically, by income level, by ethnic identity or some other distinguishing characteristic.

subsidiary an incorporated legal entity, in which the parent owns a controlling interest, and which possesses legal liability distinct from the parent and, hence, possesses a separate financial structure.

superior good a good for which consumption increases proportionately as income rises.

switch trading a complex system of barter trade involving a number of firms and intermediaries.

The purpose of a commercial enterprise is to sell something to someone at a profit. For the corporate strategist, the point of departure is a series of questions: what is the firm going to sell, to whom, how much, over what period of time, via which channels, to be serviced by whom, promoted by whom, supplied from where (i.e., what is the source preference of the buyer), and at what price?

The difference between the marketing mix in a purely domestic situation as opposed to the international is that the latter is very much more complex. Many givens in the domestic case become variables when you move across international borders. In one's home country, one may face a highly skilled, affluent, literate population with given age, ethnic, and geographical distributions. These factors can reasonably be assumed to change only over the very long run, well beyond the planning horizon of the corporation. But in another geographic market, these factors may be very different. Abrupt changes as one moves geographically across national borders obviously relate to the choice of marketing strategy—or should. What works in the domestic market cannot be assumed to work in another. In fact, the chance is very good that it will not.

Consider the difference between selling in the United States and selling in, say, India. The unit in which the product is sold may have to be altered. Aspirin tablets may best be sold in packages of 5 rather than bottles of 50 or 100, to bring the price to a level the Indian consumer can tolerate. Distribution may be through thousands of small outlets, largely located in rural hamlets. There may be no central distribution system. In fact, most may be dispensed by physicians. Brand name may not be important. So it goes.

To return to our set of sales-related questions set forth in the first paragraph, obviously, the answer to each is closely related to all others. The pricing decision may rule out trying to tap the mass market in India, which is characterized by low levels of income and literacy. That decision will impact on the choice of channels, and so on. Decisions cannot be made in splendid isolation, a fact that has obvious organizational implications for the firm. Those making the pricing decision must communicate with those selecting channels. The targeted Indian consumer may have a strong preference for locally produced aspirin. In that case, those in marketing must talk with those responsible for making sourcing decisions, that is, those responsible for the investment of corporate resources in production. Ideally, all concerned should know something about the Indian environment. Hence, in the first instance, all decisions are first approximations until their implications are worked through the other strategy sets and thus close the decision circle.

2.1 Substance of Marketing

Goods and Services

Unless a firm has been service-oriented in its previous activities (e.g., in research, engineering, architecture, construction, finance, insurance, transport, communications, management consulting, or advertising), management is likely to look at foreign markets only in terms of merchandise (hard goods). Yet every manufacturing firm has valuable services which it could sell, specifically, engineering, manufacturing, managerial, and marketing know-how. In addition, many manufacturers have valuable rights which are marketable: process and product patents, copyrights, trademarks, brand names, commercially valuable secrets. From time to time, a firm may also find obsolete but very usable machinery on its hands, or surplus cash for which an investment opportunity is needed.

There is reason to believe that in many foreign markets, the return to be realized from the sale of services, valuable rights, used machinery, and investable funds (for debt or equity in a portfolio sense) may be substantially greater than the profit to be earned on the export of goods or the return generated by direct investment in a foreign-based productive enterprise. The point is, the manager does not know unless he or she makes careful calculation of expected earnings in each case.

Also, unless the firm has operated in a sufficiently differentiated domestic market which has induced a feedback into product design, the chances are that a management will see a foreign market (whether for marketing or sourcing) only in terms of the goods the firm has been producing at home. The greater the regional variation, or market sensitivity, in product design in the domestic market, the better prepared a management is likely to be to analyze *overseas* market opportunities in terms of the most appropriate product within the capability range of the firm.

In fact, very few international divisions possess their own research and development sections. Frequently, R&D activity is concentrated within the firm's domestic market. The result is that many firms seem to export products designed for the domestic market with little thought to whether the design should be altered in some way to make it more appropriate overseas or, indeed, to invent a new or significantly different product. Consider this list of environmental factors and their possible design implications. You probably can add others.

Level of technical skills ⟶	Product simplification
Level of literacy ⟶	Remarking of product
Differences in language ⟶	Changes in product marking and instructional materials
Level of labor cost ⟶	Automation or manualization of product
Level of income ⟶	Quality and price change; change in unit size
Level of interest rates ⟶	Quality and price change
Level of maintenance capability ⟶	Change in product tolerances and ease of repair
Climatic differences ⟶	Product modification
Isolation ⟶	Product simplification and reliability improvement
Differences in standards of number system →	Recalibration of product and resizing
Availability of complementary products →	Greater or lesser product integration
Availability of materials ⟶	Change in product structure and fuel
Power availability ⟶	Resizing and redesign (e.g., from power-driven to animal-driven or man-driven)
Cultural taboos ⟶	Use of particular colors, words, and materials

This list is by no means all-inclusive. For example, there is the possibility of national political pressures generated by environmental or health concerns to restrict or make more costly the manufacture of disposable (short-lived) products, nonbiodegradable products, or dangerous products. One should expect differences in national sensitivities.

Export of Skills

But perhaps no *product* is really appropriate, if we distinguish product from services. Perhaps the firm can make more money by training someone else to do what it has learned to do. Two thoughts may be useful here. One has to do with political vulnerability and the other, with comparative cost advantage. Consider the first.

For a variety of reasons which will be explored later, alien ownership[1] of overseas production facilities almost always heightens risk. This is particularly true where (1) the enterprise represents an obvious and relatively

---

[1]Ownership is equated with management control arising through equity investment. See also the definition of "direct investment" on next page.

large feature on the national economic landscape (or an important sector thereof), and (2) the owners are identified with a national state very much more affluent or powerful than the host state. On the other hand, the movement of merchandise—exports—into a national state is often more easily subject to host government control than are services. Sale and purchase agreements relating to merchandise are relatively short-term, often thirty to ninety days. On the other hand, the skills and valuable rights discussed above typically move into a national market under the umbrella of relatively long-term contracts, often five to ten years. Very few instances of deliberate breaching of such contracts by either individuals or governments have been reported. Rather than risk international harassment, a host government is more likely to wait out the term of the contract and then refuse to approve its renewal, in which case the firm may be forewarned several years in advance and thus have time to shift its strategy with a minimum of loss. The point is that a contract does not bestow a vested interest unlimited in time, as does the ownership of tangible property. Yet a contract does more or less assure a market for a given period of time, which a simple sale (the export of a product or outright sale of a right) does not.

The second reason for giving careful consideration to the export of skills, which are embodied in people, and valuable rights lies in their possible competitive advantage. Here we run into the theory of comparative advantage in international trade again, the relevance of which has been discussed in Chapter One. High-level skills and technology are, of course, very capital intensive. Firms based in countries in which capital is relatively cheap should have a comparative advantage in this area.

For these two reasons then—political vulnerability and comparative cost—many firms operating internationally and based in the more developed countries would do well to consider carefully the export of skills, valuable rights (which are produced by high-level skills), and capital in the form of debt or portfolio equity, rather than thinking only in terms of the export of merchandise or direct investment. In this context, direct investment means investment made for the purpose of acquiring or maintaining management control, control being defined as final decision-making authority over dividend and investment policies, choice of product, volume of production, discretionary costs, and employment of key personnel.

As nations become more sensitive to the requirements of economic development, to their own economic interests, and to comparative costs, pressure will mount to limit imports from the more developed nations to goods and services rich in high-level skills and technology. The poorer nations will then be in a position to employ more of their own resources, predominately labor. This pressure, in turn, may well heighten the political vulnerability of firms relying upon the export to these markets of consumer goods, which tend to be labor intensive, and of capital in the form of direct investment. Domestic experience and a history of successful export of merchandise and of direct investment overseas may not be adequate guidelines for the future.

2.2   Marketing Target (Geographical)

It should be recognized that the use of historical export sales to predict future trends of exports is hazardous. Although possibly valid in the short run, export sales are subject to sudden changes. Such a change may arise because of the collapse of a competitive position (with the appearance of local production), imposition of import controls at the other end of the pipeline for revenue or consumption control purposes, imposition or release of export controls by the exporting nation, or an official decision to compel local production in the long run. Imports into the domestic market of comparable products may be a better guideline to overseas markets, though possibly not to be supplied from a domestic plant. But even imports have a serious flaw as a guide; a product may enjoy substantial demand in a given foreign market but none domestically due to disparate income and wealth levels, values and institutions, climate, geography, and style of living. In addition, there may be many services produced domestically that have not yet appeared in the export stream, but which theoretically should enjoy substantial overseas markets. Because of their generally capital intensive nature they would not show up as imports into the domestic market. Therefore, the present flow of international trade in many cases provides only a first, short-run approximation of foreign market opportunities, which is not to deny its importance.[2] There are other problems with published trade statutes in that many flows are either not reported or reported inadequately: smuggling, flows of services when the clients move, countertrade.

Analysis of Potential Markets

Logically, a firm should look periodically at every potential national market in order to allocate its resources in an optimum fashion. Given the limited managerial, production, marketing, and financial resources at the disposal of a firm, a policy of exerting equal energy in developing each national market is obviously not possible. Stripped to its essence, the decision then is to determine which market the firm should concentrate on, *forgetting for the moment the source of supply for that market*. Does a sufficient demand exist for a product, valuable right, or service (within the capability of the firm to supply) that would make the market more attractive than others? Securing a convincing answer to that question is costly, and this represents a major obstacle to international business.

---

[2]The United Nations, U.S. Department of Commerce, the Organization for Economic Cooperation and Development (OECD), and the various common market and trade bloc organizations publish historical series of trade by commodities, using several classification systems: the International Standard Industrial Classification (ISIC) is used by the United Nations and 85 countries for listing all products and economic activities; the Standard International Trade Classification (SITC, revised in 1960) by the United Nations for classifying commodities in international trade; the Standard Industrial Classification (SIC) by the U.S. Department of Commerce for purposes of classifying domestic industries and Schedule B for classifying United States exports (shifted as of January 1, 1965, to SITC); and the Brussels Tariff Nomenclature (BTN) by roughly 100 nations plus several of the regional trade groups.

A flow of detailed studies of virtually every national market is available to the businessman.[3] But one needs to have a precise notion of where the market lies before this mass of information becomes valuable.

Eliminated immediately from the list of potential markets for firms controlled by U.S. nationals or legal entities are those closed by U.S. Government action through export control, which operates for capital equipment, technical information, and skills, as well as merchandise. The Export Administration Act of 1979 regulates exports to all countries other than Canada in order to provide support for American foreign policy, national security interests, and the domestic economy (for short supply reasons). Most goods can move to non-Communist bloc countries via a general license, which requires no formal application. Validated licenses are required for certain types of strategic goods regardless of destination, and in almost all cases for strategic goods destined to certain Communist countries. In addition, there is an almost complete embargo on trade with North Korea, Albania, and Cuba. The so-called Battle Act, the Mutual Defense Control Act of 1951, authorizes the president to deny aid to any nation that knowingly permits the export of specific strategic goods or data. Such goods and data are generally those agreed upon by the members of the Coordinating Committee (COCOM), including Japan and most North Atlantic Treaty Organization (NATO) countries. This list is subject to annual review and has been pared periodically. It is limited currently to those things likely to be used even in peacetime for military-industrial production and similar purposes. Currently, the United States tends to deny license for any export if it is believed that it would make a significant contribution to the military or economic potential of the recipient nation that would be detrimental to U.S. security and welfare, even though available elsewhere and not embargoed by the COCOM. Transactions of U.S.-controlled foreign enterprise are similarly restrained in respect to the transfer of unpublished American-origin technical data, or in selling commodities included on the COCOM list. Published technical data, or that freely disclosed to the general public upon request, may be exported under a general license to any destination other than those subjected to a complete embargo.

Some firms set out the range of goods, rights, and services within their capability and attempt to relate the market of each to certain aggregate national statistical measures.[4] Some of these are:

---

[3]See *Business America* published by the U.S. Department of Commerce; also the bibliography in the quarterly *The International Executive*. For trade statistics see *U.S. Bureau of Census Report FT 410* (monthly and quarterly, value and quantity of United States imports and exports by commodity and country); *OECD Statistical Bulletins A, B,* and C (quarterly and annually, trade statistics for OECD members and North America); *World Trade Annual* (Walker and Company, New York; trade statistics for 1312 commodities for 22 principal trading nations); and the United Nation's *Commodity Trade Statistics*. Both the OECD and UN publish monthly lists of publications. See also *A Basic Guide to Exporting* and *How to Build an Export Business* (U.S. Department of Commerce, 1981).

[4]Some standard sources: *The Gallatin Annual of International Business* and *The Gallatin Newsletter, Business International, London Economist Intelligence Unit Reports, International Reports, Inc., The International Executive* (bibliography), *Overseas Business Reports* and *Global Market Surveys* (U.S. Department of Commerce), the OECD *Country Studies* and *Main Economic Indicators,* the UN annual regional economic summaries, the UN *Demographic Yearbook* and the UN *Statistical Yearbook.* Also see *Social Indicators III* (U.S. Department of Commerce, 1980).

1. Per capita gross national product (bear in mind that comparisons across currency frontiers are very tricky; to secure comparable purchasing powers in terms of local goods and services, dollar figures derived from official exchange rates for the poorer countries must be multiplied by a factor of two or three; also the size of the underground economies vary).
2. Distribution of personal income (tends to be highly unreliable except for the more developed countries).
3. Degree of socialization (the percentage of gross national income represented by government revenues and expenditures).
4. Class structure (may be estimated from educational and occupational breakdowns, also by rural-urban split).
5. Degree of industrialization (may be estimated from sectoral breakdown of gross national product).
6. Degree of urbanization (population statistics, rural and urban, are generally available).
7. Degree of integration of the national market as opposed to a regionalized market (may be estimated from cargo and passenger miles by land transport as a ratio of the total estimated tonnage of marketable goods and total population, respectively, or by cost of internal transport and domestic freight insurance).
8. Existence of specific industries, services, or agricultural activity (input-output tables are rarely available, although crude approximations may be derived).
9. Literacy (local definitions may be misleading; what constitutes literacy?).
10. Age distribution.
11. Availability of certain natural resources (including water and power).
12. Skill levels (may be deduced from education and occupation statistics).

Unresolved questions: (1) projected trends for each of these measures and (2) the presence of an attractive regional (subnational) or segmented market. In respect to the first, given the inertia of traditional or nearly traditional society, changes may appear as rather abrupt discontinuities. That is, they could not be predicted on the basis of a historical series. For over 3000 years, those living in Anatolia (now Turkey) used a solid-wheeled ox cart. Between 1955 and 1965 these carts disappeared from whole regions. Rural society may be under great economic pressure for many years and yet resist urbanization. Then, almost without warning, the dam bursts. It requires a social anthropologist to predict such shifts with any degree of accuracy.

An attractive **subnational market** may be well hidden by aggregate statistics. The poverty of India, considered in the aggregate, does not alert one to the existence of a large, relatively affluent subnational market for many sophisticated products. The set of cultural variables constituting a market for a given product should not be equated necessarily with a *national* market. And even though a given national market may not appear large enough to warrant more than a reading of the statistics, one may combine segments of different national markets lying within a convenient geographical or cultural area,[5] thereby justifying the commitment of company resources to further exploration, or at least to a study of the more detailed literature.

If some of the aggregate indicators suggest that one or more of a firm's products might be sold in a centrally planned economy, it is essential that management learn something about the national economic plan. It is not only in the socialist countries that such a plan may provide market guidance, but also in a number of other countries that plan to a somewhat lesser degree, such as France, the United Kingdom, India, Turkey, Korea, and many others. Not infrequently, a careful reading of the plan, which is generally made public in some form, will reveal where special development emphasis is to be put and, hence, may identify marketing opportunities. Particularly in the less developed countries, the plan will reveal priorities for the allocation of foreign exchange to purchase foreign goods and services. In general, the more centrally controlled an economy, and the more restricted its foreign exchange earning capacity and reserves vis-à-vis the demand for foreign goods and services, the more critical the national economic plan is in assessing market opportunity.

It is important to note that the socialist countries vary significantly along a number of dimensions, such as the ability of foreign sellers and buyers to contact industrial enterprises directly; to set up permanent representational offices; to advertise and promote locally; to establish equity joint ventures; to contract for external arbitration of trade-related disputes; and to obtain protection for patents, copyrights, trademarks, and trade secrets. Their relations with individual nonsocialist countries likewise vary. For example, in the case of the United States, differences may be noted in respect to diplomatic recognition, most-favored-nation treatment, availability of export-import bank facilities, availability of assistance from the Overseas Private Investment Corporation (OPIC), the existence of a tax treaty, the presence of a relevant science and technology agreement, the existence of a trade agreement or long-term economic cooperation agreement, freedom to borrow in the U.S. money market, and in the rigor with which export controls are enforced. Countries also differ in respect to membership in various international economic and commercial institutions, such as the General Agreement on Trade and Tariffs (GATT), the International Monetary Fund (IMF), the International Bank for Reconstruction and Development (IBRD, or World Bank), the Berne Convention on Copyright Protection, the Paris Union on the Protection of Industrial Property Rights (patents, trademarks), and the Liaison Committee of the International Chamber of Commerce.

---

[5]Of particular importance in this regard are the many trade blocs, customs unions, free trade areas, common markets and arrangements in relation to specific industries or commodities. One should be alert to the fact that "natural" pressures for or against such market integration may well outlive or redirect politically inspired integration.

Obstacles to Standardized Analysis

There have been a number of efforts to rank or classify national markets in general terms, the idea being that if several countries are similar along relevant dimensions, standardization of the corporate planning process may be justified. The problem is that the market dimensions relevant to one firm may not be relevant to the next. The products a firm sells are often related to a very specific, and often unique, set of variables. Thus, it is of doubtful value to start with the general classification of markets by such variables as literacy, education, occupational breakdown, per capita wealth, income distribution, power consumption per capita, levels and direction of foreign trade, and degree of urbanization. The relevant market variables for Coca Cola are likely to be very different from those for General Motors. Rather, one would best start with those specific environmental factors known to be associated with the sale of the firm's products in markets where it has had experience.

What may be misleading, of course, is the fact that the variables may shift significantly in value from one market to another. It is known, for example, that the United States farmer on average buys fewer cameras than the nonfarm population. Therefore, the farming-nonfarming occupational breakdown becomes important in constructing a consumption function for camera sales in the United States. But can one make the same assumption, say, in the case of the Japanese farmer? One cannot be certain. In the United States and Western Europe, the consumption of margarine may be related significantly to the level of urbanization. Can one therefore assume that the market for margarine is limited to the urban centers of Turkey? (In fact, it turned out that it was not.) Hence, one takes those variables known from experience and/or analysis to be linked to demand in familiar markets, then reexamines them critically in the context of an unfamiliar market. Variables given a zero rating (those seen as constant) in the former, may be found to swamp estimates in the latter. An example might be the imposition of government restrictions on the import of goods seen as nonessential in order to conserve foreign exchange reserves in the face of persistent balance-of-payments crises.

Income Elasticities

If you are dealing with historical market data, beware of the underlying dynamics. The importance of coming to grips with the dynamics of a market is reflected in the notion of **income elasticity of demand**, which describes the relationship between the amount consumed and level of income (i.e., level of economic development). It answers the question, what difference in consumption is triggered by a change in income, both being represented in percentages? Thus:

$$\frac{\Delta C_A}{C_A} \bigg/ \frac{\Delta Y}{Y}, \tag{2.1}$$

where C_A and Y represent initial values (quantity of Good A consumed and personal income), and ΔC_A and Δ_Y represent the change in values over some period of time, say a year.

If this ratio is greater than one (i.e., has an elasticity greater than unity), it means that proportionately more of Good A is consumed as income moves up. It is a **superior good**. If the ratio is less than one, then proportionately less of Good A is consumed as income moves up. It is an **inferior good**. The concept of income elasticity aids the researcher concerned with predicting growth in demand for particular goods in international markets, provided he or she can approximate the goods' income elasticities. Bear in mind that an income elasticity can be calculated either by looking at consumption preferences for people with different incomes at one point in time (cross-sectional analysis), or by charting changes in consumption over time as incomes increase (time series). The two approaches may produce different results. Note that market projections based on income elasticities assume that (1) one can plot income change and (2) past relationships will hold in the future.

2.3   Study and Penetration of Selected Market

One useful way of looking at a foreign market is to think in terms of six levels of research and analysis:

1. Potential need (which is a constant over the relevant time horizon and is physically determined);
2. Felt need (which is culturally determined and may be stimulated, albeit slowly, if the potential need is there);
3. Potential demand (which is economically determined);
4. Effective demand (which may be equated with potential demand modified by political considerations);
5. Market demand (which is commercially determined, such as by cost of selling); and
6. Sales (which are determined by competitive conditions).

One may think of these levels as a six-tiered filtering process, as illustrated in Figure 2.1. Consider the sorts of information required at each level to justify the added investment in the commitment of company resources (executive time and cash expenses) to research the more important questions at the next level (see Table 2.1).

Market Research

From table 2.1 it is apparent that an expensive overseas junket is unnecessary until one establishes a reasonable presumption that there exists a specific demand for a particular product or service of sufficient size to be attractive within the target market. If management has gone this far in

Figure 2.1
The Market Research Filter

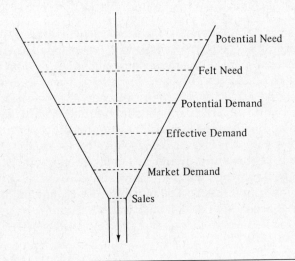

studying a given geographical sales target and has satisfied itself concerning the existence of a relatively attractive demand, competitive conditions with which it can live, and apparently feasible costs, the next step is an on-site survey. Inasmuch as this is a costly procedure, a management is well advised to be relatively certain of its ground before dispatching a survey group.

Various methods for on-site market surveys are:

1.   Measuring response to exhibition at local trade fairs, professional meetings, world trade centers.
2.   Sampling customer response by questioning, through the mail or face-to-face.
3.   Pretesting the market via free samples or a concerted sales effort for a given period of time without regard for profit.
4.   Consulting market analysts and/or social anthropologists familiar with the area.

The choice of methods depends upon several variables: the nature of the market (industrial, professional, or consumer), size and homogeneity of the market, geographical concentration of expected consumers, literacy, number of markets being surveyed, customer reaction to the questionnaire approach, availability of dependable surveyors, resources of the firm, and availability of competent market analysts or social anthropologists in the area. One should be forewarned against unconsciously making culturally conditioned assumptions about the (1) use of the product being tested and the general identity of the potential customers (for example, one firm did not

Table 2.1
Data Required before Entering or Expanding in a Foreign Market

Level	Major Categories of Data Needed (dependent upon nature of product or service)
1. *Potential need (physically determined)*	Climate, natural resources, land use, population (demography), occupational breakdown, life expectancy, topography, overall level of wealth. *Key question*: Is there a potential need?
2. *Felt need (culturally determined)*	Existence of linking products and services,* values and institutions (class structure, influence on elite, life style), market exposure (means of communication and transport, literacy, mobility, urbanization). *Key question*: What effort (cost) is required to transform a potential need into a felt need of significant intensity and aggregate size to be attractive (profitable)?
3. *Potential demand (economically determined)*	Disposable income level, income distribution, consumption as a function of income, family budget studies, traditional trading patterns (external and internal). *Key question*: Are there economic and organizational factors beyond the firm's influence that will block the development of a felt need into a potential demand?
4. *Effective demand (politically determined)*	"Buy national" restrictions, foreign exchange restrictions, import duties, import quotas, imposition of national law regarding standards (public health, sanitation, safety, security, pollution), conflict with locally owned rights (patents, copyrights, trademarks), taxation, rationing, subsidy programs, price and wage controls, special external trade relations (such as bilateral trade treaties), effectiveness of commercial law, extent of law and order, relative importance of the government sector in total consumption, government control over communications, state planning. *Key questions*: To what extent are market factors permitted to operate? And to what extent can the firm circumvent or change politically imposed restraints?
5. *Market demand (commercially determined)*	Cost or availability of internal distribution (degree of market dispersion, market organization, credit facilities, insurance, transport costs, special storage and handling facilities), advertising and promotion facilities and effectiveness. *Key question*: Can the firm get its product or service to the customer at reasonable cost relative to other products and services for which there is also effective demand?
6. *Specific demand (sales potential: competitively determined)*	Appropriateness of the firm's and competitors' product or service in terms of quality, design, sizing, packaging, and pricing; credit terms; currency accepted (source of product); delivery time; service and warranties offered. *Key questions*: Can the firm meet the terms offered by competitors in the supply of the same or similar products and services? What is its likely market share?

*For example, a felt need for gasoline requires vehicles; a felt need for transmission lines, electric power; and so on. A very real danger is the use of what some have dubbed "self-reference criteria," which refers to a tendency to ascribe to others our own preferences and reactions. An example is the promotion of filtered cigarettes on the basis that they reduce tar and nicotine content and so promote longer life expectancy, in a country where the average life expectancy is 40 years.

expect its margarine to be eaten like cheese and therefore overlooked the part of the population not using butter on its bread); (2) propensity of people to buy a given type of product (for instance, pills in the absence of medical advice); (3) probability that people will respond to a market survey honestly or at all; (4) the location of the buy-or-not-buy decision-making authority; (5) relation between enthusiasm for a free sample and the willingness to buy; (6) generalization from a sample (overlooking significant bias in a sample because of the presence, in undue numbers, of a religious, racial, class, caste, educational, or occupational group not recognized as relevant by the marketeer).

In any event, let us assume that your firm has, one way or another, established an attractive probability that a specific demand for its products exists in Country X.

Market Penetration

To what depth should your firm try to penetrate the market of Country X? That is, what percentage of the market should it try to capture? The answer is probably related to the time horizon of management, the quality of your product, its design, the degree to which your product is specialized in use, its price, access to distribution channels, and availability of funds for investment or promotion. Some of the more significant questions you might ask yourself are:

1. Are the assumptions I am making about the necessary durability and performance standards of my product really justified, given customer taste, skill, and income in Country X? (Bear in mind that quality is relative to use; it is not an absolute dimension.)
2. Will the design of my product generate maximum demand? (Consider packaging, marking, color, size, measures, skill required to use)
3. Is the degree to which my product is specialized in use or function really necessary?
4. Does my product rely unnecessarily on the presence of other products or materials in Country X?
5. Can the price of my product be shifted significantly if changes suggested in one, two, three, and four above are made, or by developing an alternative source to that now existing?
6. Would access to channels of distribution in Country X be less costly if my firm were to go into some sort of partnership with local interests?
7. At what point, in terms of market share, is my firm likely to run into politically imposed restraints arising out of pressure developed by local competitors who are losing business to us?
8. Is our promotion budget really adequate to eliminate unjustified consumer bias against the national identity of our product when the local customer begins perceiving that a locally manufactured good is just as good?

2.4   Time Horizon

Prior to an on-site market survey, management should normally have made explicit the **time horizon** it will use in determining the return from company resources committed to the exploitation of that market (see Figure 1.2). If the time horizon is very short, only a minimum commitment is justified, possibly no more than reading the aggregate statistics and talking with one or two persons familiar with the area. In such a case, management will be concerned only with existing conditions in the market, not its dynamics. A short time horizon also normally implies no consideration of supply sources other than those already existing, certainly not new direct investment in productive facilities, in either your home country or abroad, from which to supply the target market. Although risk is thereby reduced, because market conditions of the near future can be predicted with greater probability of accuracy than those of the more distant future, market opportunities inherent in aggregate growth and structural changes in the target market may be hidden from view.

2.5   Choice of Channels to Reach a Foreign Market

The first decision to be made in this category is whether your firm itself should undertake responsibility and the risk of moving its product to Country X or employ an external agency. In making this decision, you should consider the availability of specialized export skills presently within your organization, the desirability of direct relation with its foreign markets (the feedback effect), the likelihood of eventual assembly or manufacture within Country X, the possibility of supplying Country X from a third source, and the cost of developing internal exporting expertise. All of these considerations are related to management's time horizon and to the potential importance of Country X in relation to your firm's total sales.

Export

It should be clearly understood that export requires a set of highly specialized skills having to do with packaging, marking, documentation, selection of carriers, insurance, export controls, foreign import regulations, foreign exchange regulations, export finance, the selection of overseas commission houses, representatives, and agencies, and the sensitivity to know when direct entry into the market via a foreign sales branch or subsidiary is advantageous. Figure 2.2 illustrates the choices. As one moves down Figure 2.2, the **risk** incurred by the firm increases and payments to external intermediaries decline. The risk—and hence financial liability—is generally least for the firm when it sells outright domestically to resident export houses, foreign buyers, and commission houses. The risk is moderate in the case of independent export managers who operate on a commission basis, and somewhat greater for export brokers, who simply negotiate sales contracts

Figure 2.2
Alternate Export Routes

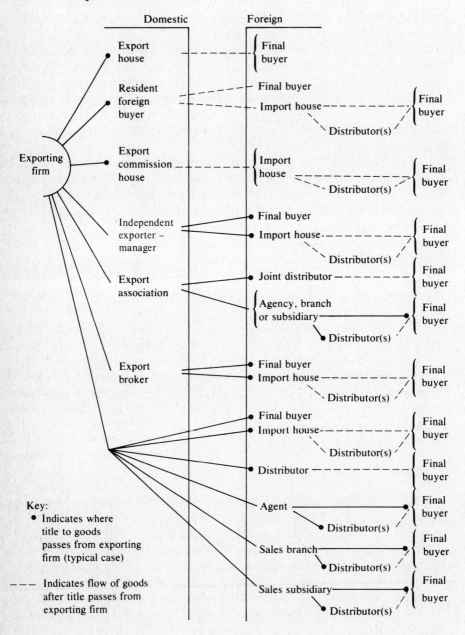

Export (or import) house—an integrated distributor that buys, stocks, and distributes on its own account. Includes trading companies and foreign trade organizations where the purchasing is done in the country of the supplier.

Resident foreign buyer (governmental or private)—the subsidiary, branch, or agent of an overseas buyer charged with the responsibility of buying on behalf of its overseas principal or owner.

Export commission house—a merchant who acts as the representative of specific foreign buyers and who negotiates purchases on behalf of foreign clients.

but assume none of the risk, for the independent export manager operating on a flat fee basis, and for the cooperative export association.

Management should note that it is frequently contrary to the interest of external exporting agencies to recommend the development of another source of supply vis-à-vis a target market—for example, some variety of overseas assembly or manufacturing—despite strong arguments in its favor. Therefore, even though employing such external agencies, management should periodically undertake an internal or independent check on its foreign markets. Furthermore, promotion, servicing, and product design feedback may be substantially less than optimum. Management should be forewarned not to finance the development of market expertise external to the firm.

A firm may, in a sense, also export its distribution services by buying goods and services of overseas origin—imports—for distribution in the domestic or third markets. Inasmuch as importing requires a set of highly specialized skills, not the least of which is moving goods through U.S. customs, the firm is faced with a similar set of alternatives as in the exporting situation, and a similar set of variables is relevant (see Section 3.3).

One of the dangers in comparing the costs to the firm of these various channels is that at least a portion of the activities performed by the firm itself may be charged to general overhead and not be allocated to the export or import function. Therefore, the real costs of the various alternatives are not strictly comparable.

This comment leads into a discussion of the firm that opts for performing these functions itself. What this really means is that the firm is shouldering the risk for the movement of the goods or services to or from the foreign market. It may merely go to the frontier if only a mail order or purchase business is involved. Other alternative strategies involve penetration into the foreign market to a greater or lesser degree. The establishment of a foreign sales subsidiary possibly represents the greatest degree of penetration, for in that case the firm comes face to face with the internal distribution system or supply channels of the foreign market. The size of the market, the nature of the product, the importance of the market feedback, legal restric-

Figure 2.2 Definitions (*continued*)

Independent exporter-manager (may be combined with a consulting service)—one who acts as the firm's export manager on a fee basis, generally does not buy and sell on its own account.

Export association—a cooperative activity undertaken by several firms, sometimes under a separate incorported entity. (In the United States, it could be a Webb-Pomerene Association [so named for its congressional sponsors] a Joint Export Association, or an Export Trading Company licensed under the 1982 law on the subject.)

Export broker—one who negotiates export sales contracts for a fee.

Distributor—one who contracts to buy a firm's goods or services for sale to third parties.

Agent—one who buys nothing from a firm, its principal, but acts on the firm's behalf as defined by agreement (in a sense, acts as a branch of the firm), for which the agent receives a fee and/or commission. (A manufacturer's agent sells in the name of the principal; an ordinary commission agent sells in its own name.)

Branch—an unincorporated entity, legally and financially indistinguishable from the parent firm. An act of a branch is an act of the parent, for which the parent is fully liable.

Subsidiary—an incorporated legal entity, in which the parent owns a controlling interest, that possesses legal liability distinct from the parent and, hence, a separate financial structure.

tions, and the resources available to the firm (including the necessary associated skills) are controlling. Again, management should be cautioned not to make domestically conditioned assumptions about any one of these factors.

General Trading Companies

In this context, special comment about the **general trading companies** of Japan, the *sogo shosha*, is warranted. The largest trading companies in the world are Mitsubishi Shoji Kaisha and Mitsui & Co. All told, there are some 6500 trading companies in Japan, but only 300 or so are engaged in foreign trade, and of these only a few are large *general* trading companies that handle highly diversified lines and are organized on a worldwide basis. These have offices in all of the major trading centers, providing the structure for a vast information system, all linked electronically.

The general trading company defies our previous classification of international trading routes because it can assume the role of virtually any type of intermediary. The only functions that the general trading companies normally do not perform are production and retailing, but they may become involved in even these activities through joint ventures. Their export-import services are complete and expert. The trading company conducts thorough detailed market studies and advises the seller. It will then supervise the overseas shipment in all stages from packaging, scheduling, insurance coverage, inland shipment, stowage, overseas shipment, warehousing, and distribution, to the choice of wholesale outlets. For potential buyers, the trading company provides the reverse set of services and, on occasion, will actually trade on its own account. It also provides financing, from short- and medium-term commercial credit to long-term production financing. The latter has led the trading company to be active in establishing overseas joint ventures on behalf of third parties, frequently involving the trading company as well. In recent years, trading companies have become increasingly active in the international transfer of technology. Many now research available technology for sale or license in one country for possible buyers in another. Indeed, the larger trading companies have in-house engineering and technical capacity to advise on the construction of factories and public works. Contractual relationships are maintained with external R&D organizations, as Mitsubishi does with Battelle Memorial Institute of Columbus, Ohio.

Who owns and manages a Japanese trading company? Although formally associated with industrial-banking cartels (the Zaibatsu), since World War II these groups have tended to fall apart and to be replaced by a number of less formal associations. The larger trading companies are still linked with groups of Japanese banks and manufacturing firms, but more through debt financing than through equity. However, several of the trading companies have plowed their profits into equity holdings of Japanese growth industries so that the trading company itself may approach the status of a holding company. In short, the trading company is a corporate entity whose stock and debt are held in large part by related banking, commercial, and manufacturing enterprises.

In dealing with the trading company, one should realize that the top management level is involved with coordination of policy and financial agreements with affiliated producing and service companies. Operational control is usually at the managing director level, where there may be 20 or more people but only a few involved with import-export. Thus, the foreign seller's real point of contact is the department head or section chief. Initial contact is often through one of the branches located in the exporter's home country.

A relatively new form of collaboration between Japanese trading companies and non-Japanese commercial groups is appearing. An example is a small U.S. corporation that enters into a joint venture with one of the Japanese trading companies for the purpose of stimulating U.S. firms to export through the trading company's worldwide network. For a relatively small fee, the U.S. company's products are plugged into the network for distribution. If and when products are sold, a commission is paid to the joint venture. The Japanese trading companies are motivated to sell U.S. products in Japan or in third markets because of the pressure on them from both the Japanese and U.S. Governments to help improve the U.S. balance of payments, the imbalance of which is due in large measure to the imbalance in United States-Japanese trade. All of the major *sogo shosha* are attempting to divorce themselves to a greater extent from purely Japanese trade.

There are other trading companies elsewhere, but none offer similar geographical, functional, or product scope. In some countries, as in the United States, there are substantial legal obstacles to the establishment of a true general trading company. Some of these may have been reduced with the passage of the Export Trading Company Act of 1982.

2.6   Choice of Channels within a Foreign Market

Distribution Variables

A firm may go still further, of course, by pushing on toward the ultimate consumer. Various alternative paths of distribution and the possible functions and characteristics of each layer, which are imposed traditionally, are diagrammed in Figure 2.3. In each case, management should analyze the cost of changing the system to conform to its policies elsewhere. For example, for a given product in Country X, wholesalers may traditionally carry large inventories, finance the retailers, and assume responsibility for promotion vis-à-vis the consumer. Can the firm and the retailers perform these functions with equal effectiveness at comparable cost? That they do so in their domestic market may not be important. Relevant variables are: ability of one layer (including the manufacturer or foreign sales branch or subsidiary) to perform functions of the next; degree of control of each layer by competitors (tie-in backward or forward); adequacy of coverage by each

Figure 2.3
Analysis of a Distribution System

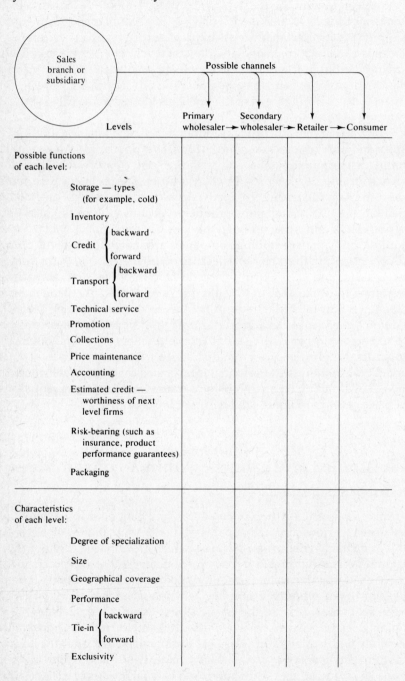

layer; degree to which flow is confined to fixed channels (the extent to which retailers purchase direct from manufacturers or from primary wholesalers); nature of the customer (mass market, industrial market, limited number of consumers); nature of product (durability, need for special handling facilities, ease of adulteration, amount of customer service needed, unit cost); and the existence of a turnover or transactions tax (which may have a pyramiding effect). Inadequate analysis of these variables has led many firms into costly errors and, sometimes, failure.

Marketing in Socialist Countries

The socialist countries pose special problems for the international marketeer. In these countries, the ministry of foreign trade probably administers the national import-export business, generally through a series of state-owned enterprises—the Foreign Trade Organizations (FTOs)—each of which specializes in the procurement and/or sale of specified goods and services. Thus, the first task for the foreign seller is to determine the appropriate FTO. On occasion, an overseas mission or office of an FTO, or a government trade mission on which several FTOs may be represented, takes the initiative in contacting specific Western firms producing goods in which they are interested.[6]

In the recent past, direct contact with the end user in socialist countries has been difficult for a foreign seller, if not prohibited. However, there has been a gradual liberalization in this respect in recent years. Characteristically, each FTO has had full authority to purchase and/or sell goods and services covered by its charter. But now, as one moves away from the Soviet Union and Albania, the most highly centralized of the socialist states, one finds the system much less rigid. In a number of countries—the People's Republic of China and Yugoslavia, for example—some industrial enterprises have almost complete freedom to buy abroad within the limits of the foreign exchange available to them. In such cases, the foreign supplier deals directly with the end user. Trade in high technology goods and services virtually demands such contact.

2.7 Customer Service

For many consumer goods no customer service may be required, although the matter of guarantees of quality and performance may remain. Are such guarantees really necessary and, if not, what is the effect on cost? Where foreign exchange controls operate and time-consuming transport is involved, guarantees of this variety may be inoperable unless local inventories or repair services are maintained. In the event that the complexity, unreliability, and use of a product is such as to require servicing, the firm has the

---

[6]A useful reference is *Sales Promotion Techniques for Marketing in Communist Countries* (U.S. Department of Commerce, 1981).

choice of putting its own servicing agents into the field or leasing or contracting for these services. Prior to the development of a significant market, both courses may be unduly costly and thereby generate pressure in the direction of some sort of regional arrangement. The latter is feasible if freedom and cost of movement within the area are within reason. In some instances a joint arrangement with competitors may be possible, thereby making service costs lower for all concerned.

2.8   Choice of Vehicle for Promotion of Product

Whether the firm itself undertakes promotion in the target market or farms out this task to an external advertising or promotional agency depends in large measure upon the availability of the necessary expertise within the firm and the potential size of the target market, plus management's time horizon. Also, if the firm is likely to move into production within the overseas market in the foreseeable future, the rationale for employing an external agency may be somewhat weakened. One may find it less costly to internalize this expertise in preparation for the more complex problems that local production entails.

There is a further strategy alternative in the selection of an agency: should it be the agency used by the firm in its domestic market or a different one? If the latter, should it be foreign? And if foreign, should it be indigenous to the target market or identified with a third market? In making this choice, of course, the entire international program of the firm should be considered. Directly relevant are the firm's ownership and control strategies and the likelihood of developing foreign profit centers. Major pitfalls are:

1.   Centralizing *control* of foreign promotional campaigns in corporate headquarters, whether firm- or agency-conducted.
2.   Utilizing a domestically based agency for overseas promotion that lacks adequate experience or staff to be effective in the target market.
3.   Having *no* department, subsidiary, or agency directly responsible for promotion in the target market.
4.   Permitting the overseas promotion effort to be overshadowed by and become subsidiary to the domestic effort.

Increasingly important in the promotion of certain goods and services in overseas markets are trade fairs, trade centers, and trade missions. The first tend to be annual affairs in all of the major trading centers of the world, including the Communist. Trade centers often house permanent exhibits and market information channels. Trade missions, organized and sponsored by various government agencies or trade associations, are organized on an ad hoc basis. The varying degree of continuity each institutional device offers, plus the different exposure of each (the public in the case of trade fairs, commercial buyers for trade centers, and specific interested parties for trade missions) determine their relative value to the firm.

2.9   Source of Product

Management should be aware of the fact that price alone may not determine the best strategy in respect to national source of supply for several reasons:

1. Given balance-of-payments pressure, foreign exchange controls, relatively high interest rates, and distance, the customer may be most concerned about the currency in which payment is to be made, and, in descending order of concern, credit terms, delivery time, durability, and price.[7]

2. Production within the foreign market may be justified even though the resulting product price is higher than for a comparable import. This is true because official exchange rates in less developed countries often undervalue (as measured in comparative purchasing powers) the local currency when used to buy certain foreign currencies. Such inequality is in effect a subsidy for imports and a tax on exports. That is, the importer is permitted to buy more units of foreign currency, say dollars, per local currency unit than is economically justified; the exporter is permitted to receive fewer local currency units per dollar value sold. Therefore, an import-substituting industry should be measured not only by the recorded values of the imports thereby rendered unnecessary, but by something more, typically 20 to 30 percent more for many underdeveloped countries. Up to that inflated unit price, the local economy gains even though it could import the same item more cheaply. The point is that, using the official exchange rate, the foreign exchange saved may be worth more than the local resources used, in the calculus of national economic growth. As government economists become more sophisticated, these things are recognized, and official pressures favoring the local product can be expected.

3. In some instances, regulations enforced by customers limit the nationality of source—for example, the Agency for International Development, (AID), NATO, and other national and regional buyers of goods and services. Management should be aware that the definition of source used by such buyers may vary (ownership, registration, place of production, source of materials and personnel).[8]

4. In a given target market, certain countries tend to be associated with desirable attributes of the product in question—for example, German optics, Turkish tobacco, English woolen goods, French wine. In some instances,

---

[7]Useful sources of information relative to financial pressures in a given country are *International Financial Statistics* (published monthly by the International Monetary Fund) and *International Financial News Survey* (published weekly by the Fund).

[8]Of relevance is the U.S. "Buy American" Act, which permits the Department of Defense to award a contract to a United States producer whose price is 50 percent higher than that of a foreign bidder, and other governmental agencies (for example, the General Services Administration) 6 percent higher, or 12 percent if the supplier is located in a distressed area of the United States.

any foreign-made product is assumed to be "better" than a local manufacture.

5. There is a possibility that a foreign subsidiary of a domestic firm, particularly if the latter owns less than a controlling interest, may be able to produce and ship certain goods to Communist countries that would be forbidden if produced within the domestic market. This consideration is particularly relevant for U.S. firms manufacturing goods deemed to be sensitive by the U.S. Government.

Sales in socialist countries are frequently linked with a compensating purchase. And where a firm is trading under bilaterial trade agreement (for example, Soviet-Indian or Canadian-Chinese), the product source is defined for a Western firm (India and Canada in these examples). It is possible, however, for a firm to initiate sales and purchase through either switch trading or parallel trade. All three types of transactions—barter, switch, and parallel trading—are known generally as "countertrade."[9] Increasingly, LDCs are resorting to countertrade.

Countertrade Transactions

Several definitions are needed to understand these concepts, which are really much simpler than the terms suggest. First, I made reference to a **bilateral trade agreement**. This refers to an agreement between two countries that commits the two to exchange specified amounts of listed goods and services over a given time, often five years. In that the value of the exchange is not likely to balance exactly in any one year, the agreement frequently permits an imbalance to develop in either direction up to a specified value. Often the unit value of the goods and services, and of the permitted imbalance, are stated in U.S. dollars—or, more recently, in terms of a special unit of account (see Section 7.4). These imbalances are often referred to as **clearing dollars**.

Say that India is supposed to sell the Soviet Union a certain dollar value of goods and services, but for some reason India does not. The basic agreement may permit the Soviet Union to sell these clearing dollars—which constitute claims on Indian goods and services—to, say, a trading house in Europe. The latter may buy these clearing dollars at a substantial discount and eventually sell them to someone who wishes to buy something from India. In this case, the clearing dollars can only be used to buy Indian goods. If the imbalance were reversed, they could only be used to buy Soviet goods. The reason for bilateral trading is that by so restraining trade, the two countries can maintain a balance of trade within a given plus or minus margin (represented by the limit to the imbalance, a form of credit), and thus

---

[9]A useful reference is *Countertrade Practices in East Europe, the Soviet Union and China: An Introductory Guide to Business* (Washington, D.C., U.S. Department of Commerce, International Trade Administration, 1980).

to a degree they can insulate domestic pricing, employment, and monetary and fiscal policies against balance-of-payments pressures. Particularly for socialist countries, bilateral trading is an important mechanism because domestic prices may have little relevance to international market prices. When a ceiling on the imbalance between the two countries is set in the agreement, there is pressure on both countries to reduce the balance of clearing dollars in favor of one or the other, thereby enabling trade between them to continue. This is the essence of **switch trading**.

Parallel trading involves taking a country's goods or services as partial or full payment for products or services sold there. Usually, the goods are unrelated and one disposes of them through a special barter house, which eventually sells them to a third party.

Both switch and parallel trading can become enormously complicated; many intermediaries may become involved, and as many currencies. As a consequence, such trading is often handled through special trading companies, very frequently headquartered in either Vienna or Zurich. Also, the large general trading companies are organized to handle this kind of trade at relatively low cost, which fact gives them a substantial advantage.

The relationships described here are diagrammed in Figure 2.4. You should bear in mind that many more intermediaries and currencies may be involved than those shown here. Countries X and Y in this example are bilateral traders with a clearing account arrangement.

2.10   Pricing

There are essentially three alternative pricing strategies: a standard world-wide price, dual pricing (domestic/export), or market-differentiated price (see Figure 2.5). Either policy may, of course, include a discount system. Because of the different priorities given by some foreign buyers, discounts for waiving performance warranties, claims for services, payment in certain foreign currencies (e.g., dollars), or delivery within a specified time may be more important than the typical domestic discounts based on quantity, terms of payment, or purchase of associated goods or services.

Standard Worldwide Price

The standard worldwide base price is most likely to be looked upon by management as full-cost pricing, including an allowance for manufacturing overhead, general overhead, and selling expenses. Often ignored are (1) the necessarily arbitrary nature of these cost allocations; (2) differences in costs from market to market (in labor, capital, materials, and management in the case of overseas manufacture; in shipping, crating, insurance, tariffs, taxes, internal transport, distribution, and promotion in the case of exporting); (3) the possibly lower incremental cost of goods moving into foreign markets (particularly in reference to domestically oriented research and de-velopment); (4) differences in competitive position within the foreign

Figure 2.4
Diagram of Switch and Parallel Trading

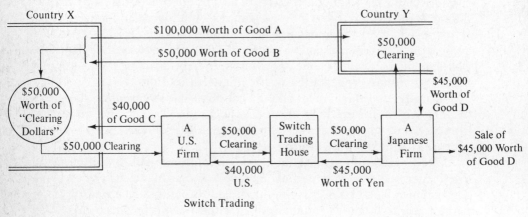

Switch Trading

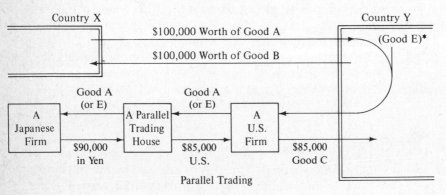

Parallel Trading

*Or good E may be delivered in payment, good E being in excess supply in country Y.

Note: In each case, the trading house has made a profit of $5,000 in yen, which it can use in reverse transactions or sell to someone else. The U.S. firm must price good C so that the discount on the clearing dollars or on the goods delivered to the trading house will be covered. It will be seen that parallel trading does not necessarily affect the balance between countries X and Y unless Y uses the goods received from X as part of the deal with the U.S. firm.

markets; (5) differing degrees of penetration for different foreign markets; and (6) price controls enforced by a government or by a dominant supplier.

Dual Pricing

Dual pricing refers to the practice of quoting one price for the domestic market, a second for exports. The latter is often the lowest of the two, which is justified to the extent that the marketing cost is external to the firm. Also, if the firm is exporting out of a country whose basic tax is the value-added tax (VAT), into a country in which the VAT is not employed, the tax burden on the exported product may be lower than for a product sold domestically to the extent that the VAT is rebated by the exporting country. Of course, a

Figure 2.5
Matrix of International Pricing Strategies

	Cost-Oriented	Market-Oriented
Standard worldwide price: *with net price control*		
with final price control		
Dual pricing (domestic/export): *with net price control*		
with final price control		
Market differentiated prices: *with net price control*		
with final price control		

firm may use a foreign market in which to dump products. Insofar as something over and above the variable cost of production is captured by the firm, a special export price might be justified in the short run so long as such sales do not effect full-cost price sales, either domestically or in other markets. Such a strategy is sometimes called marginal cost pricing.

Market-Differentiated Pricing

A market-differentiated pricing policy, on the other hand, assumes that the head office knows enough about the target market to set the correct price for that market. The best policy in some circumstances is for headquarters to set a price floor and permit local management full pricing discretion beyond that point. A variation is a headquarter-determined price guideline, with local discretion to price below and above within certain percentage limits. The commonality of ownership between the corporate headquarters and the associated foreign firm is obviously an important consideration. If ownership is the same—that is, if the foreign firm is a branch or 100 percent owned by the domestic firm—the degree of price discretion given may be substantial. Profit is 100 percent owned wherever generated. Also, decisions in all of the other marketing strategy areas (particularly in regard to degree of penetration, time horizon, choice of channels, and source of product) are directly relevant to setting pricing policy. It should be noted that the price used by a firm may or may not be the price recognized by local customs officials for the purpose of determining ad valorem duties. (In international tariff negotiations, a recurrent criticism of the United States is its use of American selling price regardless of the foreign price.)

Transfer Pricing and Dumping Restraints

Two further restraints of a legal nature should be considered: transfer pricing for tax purposes and antidumping legislation. Inasmuch as transfer prices determine in part the jurisdiction within which profits are generated, local tax officials are concerned. (See Section 8.2 for further discussion of this point.) As used here, **dumping** refers to the sale of foreign-produced goods at less than "fair value." In the United States, the Secretary of Commerce has the responsibility of determining, upon receipt of a complaint, whether foreign merchandise "is being or is likely to be" sold in the United States at less than its fair value. If the finding is affirmative, the International Trade Commission must determine whether a domestic industry "is being or is likely to be injured, or is prevented from being established" as the result of the dumping. A determination of injury requires the imposition of a special compensatory dumping duty to make up the difference between purchase price (or exporter's sales price) and the foreign market value (actual or imputed). A number of countries have roughly similar provisions.

In any event, your firm should be prepared to quote c.i.f. (cost, insurance, and freight) for the nearest port *abroad* to the foreign buyer (not f.o.b., free on board, for some port in its *domestic* market—see Figure 2.6), give competitive credit terms, provide data in a language and in measures useful to the potential customer, reply promptly and fully to overseas inquiries, provide adequate instructions in a useful language for a product's use, and assure overseas customers of supply as regular as to domestic customers. To do these things requires specialists.

Negotiating International Contracts

The pricing of services, know-how, and rights transferred abroad under contract merits special mention. Many international executives have looked at such transactions as marginal to their principal business and so have not been fully aware of either the full cost or market value of what they were transferring. Those skilled in negotiating international contracts of this sort speak of the "negotiating window." The ledge of that window consists of the actual cost of the transfer, a cost one can very easily underestimate. Included should be all direct costs incurred in the negotiation and transfer, a very large item being management time. Additional costs include legal assistance; training foreign personnel at your plant; and sending your own personnel (engineers, technicians, managers) to the foreign contractor's plant to explain, train, and perhaps even supervise for a time. Included, of course, should be reasonable estimates for supplying documentation in the language, measuring units, and standards required. The upper edge of the

Figure 2.6
The Application of Export Terms

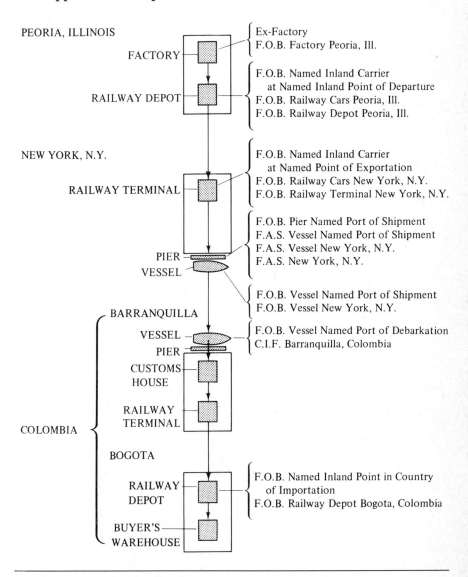

PEORIA, ILLINOIS

FACTORY — Ex-Factory
F.O.B. Factory Peoria, Ill.

RAILWAY DEPOT — F.O.B. Named Inland Carrier
at Named Inland Point of Departure
F.O.B. Railway Cars Peoria, Ill.
F.O.B. Railway Depot Peoria, Ill.

NEW YORK, N.Y.

RAILWAY TERMINAL — F.O.B. Named Inland Carrier
at Named Point of Exportation
F.O.B. Railway Cars New York, N.Y.
F.O.B. Railway Terminal New York, N.Y.

PIER — F.O.B. Pier Named Port of Shipment
F.A.S. Vessel Named Port of Shipment
F.A.S. Vessel New York, N.Y.
F.A.S. New York, N.Y.
VESSEL

F.O.B. Vessel Named Port of Shipment
F.O.B. Vessel New York, N.Y.

BARRANQUILLA

VESSEL — F.O.B. Vessel Named Port of Debarkation
C.I.F. Barranquilla, Colombia
PIER
CUSTOMS HOUSE

RAILWAY TERMINAL

COLOMBIA

BOGOTA

RAILWAY DEPOT — F.O.B. Named Inland Point in Country
of Importation
F.O.B. Railway Depot Bogota, Colombia

BUYER'S WAREHOUSE

Source: Gerald R. Richter, "Basic Principles of Foreign Trade," in *International Trade Handbook*, ed. Leslie L. Lewis (Chicago: Dartnell Corp. prepared in cooperation with the American Institute for Foreign Trade, 1965), p. 32.

negotiating window is the full value of the skills, technology, and rights to the firm receiving them. Perceptions between transferor and transferee may well differ by a wide margin in this respect. Therefore, even if you are confining your export to the transfer of such intangibles, an analysis of the market for the goods to be produced may still be of considerable value. Part of the price extracted may be in terms of obligations, such as the obligation to buy certain goods or materials from the transferring firm, to make available any improvements in product or process developed by the foreign firm, and an agreement to refrain from selling in certain specified countries. To what extent such obligations are legally enforceable under the laws of either country is another matter. There are significant national differences on this score.

In the final analysis, marketing strategy must be adjusted and readjusted in light of the feedback from strategy selections in other areas. No final choices should be made before possible problems in other areas of decision have been thought through. In a sense, everything could be subsumed under marketing strategy as some marketing specialists like to do.

CHAPTER 3

SOURCING STRATEGY

acquisition the take-over of one firm by another. In a sense, one firm buys another.

common market a regional group with no internal tariffs, a common external tariff, and harmonized domestic or common regional law to facilitate unrestricted factor movement.

currency area a group of countries whose currencies are relatively freely convertible, which enforce similar foreign exchange control systems, if any, and hold reserves of scarce or "hard" currencies in a common pool.

degree of integration the percentage of a product manufactured by one plant; or, more broadly, the extent to which a company produces its own goods rather than purchase inputs from external suppliers.

free trade area a regional group with no internal tariffs.

joint venture the participation of two companies jointly in a third enterprise. Both contribute assets, both own the joint venture to some degree, and they share risk.

long-term arrangements bilateral or multilateral agreements calling for the restriction of exports of a specific commodity by one or more producing countries to one or more importing countries whose markets are being disrupted.

manufacturing interchange a setup where each of several plants manufactures a specified set of parts, all exchange with one another, and all assemble the same or similar products.

merger the joining of two or more firms in the formation of a new legal entity. The original firms disappear as separate legal entities. The owners of the merging companies then own the new entity.

rationalize production to concentrate given processes, or the production of certain products, in a limited number of plants within a region, for distribution throughout the region, thereby gaining maximum technical efficiency.

risk refers to outcomes, the probability of which can be inferred from previous experience.

tax treaties two-nation agreements defining source of income for tax purposes and providing for consultation in the event of double taxation, among other things.

uncertainty the probability of an unpredictable outcome, which may be approximated by use of a normal distribution curve based on minimum and maximum estimates.

If management has made tentative strategy choices in respect to sales, it is next faced with a set of production and procurement decisions.

1. From where should the firm supply the target market?
2. To what extent should the firm *itself* undertake production (degree of integration)?
3. To the extent that it does not, what and where should it buy from others?
4. To the extent that a firm opts to do at least some manufacturing, how should it acquire facilities?
5. Should the firm produce in one plant or many, related or autonomous?
6. What sort of production equipment (technology) should it use?
7. What site is best?
8. Where should research and development be located?

Answers to these questions set up a feedback into the marketing strategy area, particularly in respect to product specifications, assessment of competitive position, and national source of supply. For purposes of reducing cost, a firm may use a manufacturing technology different from that used domestically. This difference may impact product design in some way. Or perhaps the firm realizes that it cannot supply the target market at a competitive price using the technology effective at home. Regional trading relationships—such as a common market or free trade area—may effect the sourcing decision.

Let us look briefly at each of the eight questions raised above.

3.1   Source of Supply

An assumption that many managers new to international business make is that there are two possible sources—one's domestic market (via exporting) or the target market (local production). The more experienced manager realizes that production within a *third* market may be a desirable alternative due to lower cost. That is, the supply strategy of producing within a third market and exporting into the target market may result in the lowest cost under certain circumstances.

Let us imagine that the product is very labor intensive (i.e., labor as a percent of total cost of production is relatively high) in a kind of labor—say semi-skilled—that is priced very low in Country X. That is, the wage paid to semi-skilled labor is significantly lower than that paid in either your domestic market or target market. Let us assume further that the good has relatively high value per cubic foot and/or pound so that the shipping cost is relatively unimportant. In addition, Country X may be offering some sort of export incentive, which has the effect of reducing import tariffs. One can also imagine the availability of some material (an input into the manufacture of our product) in which Country X specializes and can therefore supply at a price relatively cheap compared to other sources. Nor should you necessarily think only in terms of the complete product. Perhaps there is some component of which semi-skilled labor and materials of this sort constitute a large percentage. If so, you may decide to manufacture certain parts in Country X, some at home, and some in the target market, where the final product will then be assembled. It all depends upon a careful study of relative costs.

It may be well to think for a moment about some of these costs and common mistakes made in evaluating them.

Take labor, for instance. In many countries the cost of legally imposed fringe benefits (social welfare taxes, the annual bonus, payments into a publicly administered pension plan, and termination pay) may be significantly higher than those to which you are accustomed. Also, the true cost of labor to the firm includes training, the cost of which is increased by a high turnover rate and an inadequate, publicly supported training system. In addition, domestically based assumptions about the number of employees required may not be justified if productivity is substantially different. Finally, labor law in many countries makes labor more of a fixed cost in that termination may be both difficult and costly. Sometimes, one can take advantage of escape clauses relating to "temporary labor," but this is a short-run device at best. Such practices may, in fact, accelerate the turnover rate, thereby adding to training costs.

Energy may be a problem. An inadequate supply may force a firm to provide its own source by installing a generating plant, which can be relatively high cost. Local materials, even though cheap, may be of different quality from those to which you are accustomed, which may in turn require you to install a more rigorous quality control or use a different production technology. Also, both energy and materials may be subject to interruption in their flow for a variety of reasons, including ability of local suppliers to secure foreign exchange with which to import needed supplies.

If one is sourcing a product a long way from the market in which it is to be sold, and air freight is not economic, a relatively large inventory may be necessary—including the goods in the supply pipeline—because of the time required to deliver via ship. Added financial cost may be the result. And management may be more costly than realized if home country nationals (rather than local nationals) are deemed necessary for reasons of control or because of the inadequacy of local managerial talent; the same for technical skills. Setting up an expatriate family abroad can be very costly to the company, possibly adding up to four or five times the employee's domestic salary. Further, sheer distance means added cost in communications, travel, misunderstandings, and tardy handling of problems. If management is local and does not use your native language fluently, a further cost in translation and delay is incurred.

Given a relatively small and untested target market, your foreign factory may develop unused capacity, or the use of more general-purpose machines may be inevitable in order to provide for flexibility in product. Contracting out unused capacity to produce another product is then possible. In the first case, fixed charges per unit of production are probably higher than would otherwise be the case; in the second, more intensive training and supervision may be needed. Costs mount.

Trade Relationships

We mentioned earlier that you should be aware of any special trading relationships between the target market and other countries from which that market might reasonably be supplied. Such a relationship could facilitate commerce in that direction by reducing cost. One can classify these trading relationships as follows in terms of degree of integration, the negotiating group being the least, the federation the most highly integrated.

1. **Negotiating groups**, organized for the purpose of joint commercial negotiation with other countries. An example is the Special Coordinating Committee for Latin America (ECLA) for coordination in negotiating trade preferences (i.e., lower duties) with the European Community (EC) and the United States. The EC (see item 16 below) often acts as a negotiating group. So likewise does the Organization for Economic Cooperation and Development (OECD) and the "Group of 77," representing the more affluent and poorer countries, respectively. It may be important for a firm to try to influence such negotiations so as to get its products included.

2. **Exporters' clubs**, organized for the purpose of consolidating the commercial debt of specified countries, and to extend further credit. The Hague Club (for Brazil) and the Turkish Consortium are examples. The creditworthiness of local buyers is thus affected.

3. Trade control groups, countries with common perceptions of external threat that cooperate to deny strategic goods to potentially hostile nations. The major example is the Coordinating Committee (COCOM) in which all NATO countries plus Japan participate.

4. Defense groups, countries which have joined together to mount a common defense effort, such as the North Atlantic Defense Organization (NATO) and its East European counterpart, the Warsaw Pact.

5. Commodity associations, groups of countries concerned with specific commodities (essentially unbranded raw materials sold in bulk), either as producers or consumers. Their function is largely limited to collecting statistics, research, and providing forums for international consultations between producers and consumers. Such associations are obviously important for firms dealing in the commodity involved. Some of the present associations have to do with cotton, peanuts, lead and zinc, and wool.

6. Producers' cartels, organized by commodity-producing countries to stabilize and/or increase prices, with the hope of maximizing revenues in the long run. A cartel of this sort can work only if most major producing countries are willing to restrict output and to desist from cheating. Examples of producers' cartels: Organization of Petroleum Exporting Countries (OPEC), Council of Copper Exporting Countries (CIPEC), Association of Iron Ore Exporting Countries (AIEC), International Bauxite Association (IBA), Association of Natural Rubber Producing Countries (ANRPC), Union of Banana Exporting Countries (UBEC). OPEC has been the most successful.

7. Commodity agreements, international agreements among commodity suppliers, buyers, or both, relating to buffer stocks, price ranges, export quotas, import quotas, quality controls, and joint promotion. Present agreements relate to wheat, tin, sugar, coffee, and olive oil. They have been notoriously ineffective.

8. Long-term arrangements (LTA), bilateral or multilateral agreements calling for the restriction of exports of a specific commodity by one or more producing countries to one or more importing countries whose markets are being disrupted. The object is to lessen the export-induced disruption of the market of the importing countries without the imposition of quotas or tariffs, since these devices tend to be difficult to remove. Properly used, an LTA provides the importing country or countries with time to shift resources so that the import restrictions may ultimately be lifted with minimum injury. The United States has been a party to such agreements regarding textiles and steel. Long-term arrangements are sometimes called voluntary marketing arrangements (VMA) or orderly marketing arrangements (OMA).

9. Friendship, commerce, and navigation (FCN) treaties generally include a most-favored-nation clause (MFN), which assures the two signatories of the benefit of any more liberal FCN treaty negotiated with other parties, including tariffs and quotas and right of establishment.

10. Bilateral trade agreements, two-nation agreements calling for the exchange of specified commodities at specified trade-off prices up to a stipulated amount. Provision for a clearing account is generally included, which account is a device for permitting temporary imbalances up to agreed-upon limits.

11. Tax treaties, two-nation agreements defining source of income for tax purposes and providing for consultation in the event of double taxation, among other things.

12. General agreement on trade and tariffs (GATT), a multilateral agreement among virtually all major trading countries providing a mechanism for facilitating reciprocal reduction of tariffs and other trade barriers, the standardization of trade formalities, and the resolution of trade disputes. MFN treatment is guaranteed all members except for common markets, free trade areas, and other international agreements specifically excepted by GATT members (for example, the Canadian-United States vehicle accord).

13. Regional cooperation for development, a group of nations with special relationship in regard to economic planning and investment in joint products. Examples are the Central Treaty Organization and the Association of Southeast Asian Nations, plus a number in Africa.

14. Currency area (franc, sterling, dollar), a group of countries whose currencies are relatively freely convertible, which enforce similar foreign exchange control systems, if any, and hold reserves of scarce or "hard" currencies in a common pool. Two variations: monetary area, a group of countries having a special relationship with a currency not their own (e.g., until recently the Persian Gulf principalities' use of the Indian rupee); and a currency union or area, two or more countries that share the same currency (as the Communaute Financiere Africain use of the CFA franc (West and Equatorial Africa), and use of the East African shilling in East Africa).

15. Customs preference area, a group of nations that reciprocally maintain lower tariffs toward each other than with other countries (e.g., historically the British Commonwealth, United States-Philippines).

16. Free trade area (FTA), a regional group with no internal tariffs. Since national external tariffs may vary, rules of origin must be enforced (generally 50 percent of final value for the European FTA). Permitted by the GATT if 85 percent of the trade is free. Major operating FTA's are the European (EFTA) and the Latin American (LAFTA), although the latter has not been very successful, and since 1981 has been renamed the Latin American Integration

Area (LAIA), which is envisioned as leading to a series of preferential bilateral trade treaties and agreements.

17. Customs union, a regional group with a common external tariff and no internal tariffs (the Benelux countries).

18. Common market, a regional group with no internal tariffs, a common external tariff, and harmonization of domestic law in order to facilitate unrestricted factor movement. The major attempts in this direction have been the European Economic Community (EEC), the Central American Common Market (CACM), and the Andean Common Market (ANCOM). A common market may be of a general character (as the EEC), based on the integration of certain sectors of the members' economies (the approach used by the CACM), or limited to specific products (the United States-Canadian accord on vehicles).

19. Economic union, a combination of a common market and a currency union. None now in existence, although the EEC has been moving in this direction.

20. Federation, a political grouping of nations, which implies a special trade relationship, the most likely being an economic union (the West Indies Federation, which broke down in 1962; the United Arab Republic, which has been largely inoperative; Malaysia, which has lost Singapore; and the United Arab Emirates).

Let us now assume that you have considered all of these factors, both costs and trade relationships, and have decided that the target market should be supplied from a particular national source, whether from your home market via export, locally in the target market, or from a third country. We still have not determined whether we should manufacture the product ourselves or pay someone else to do so for us. This brings us to the question of integration.

3.2   Degree of Integration

The **degree of integration** in respect to the production of a particular product may be viewed as a continuum from 100 percent external purchase on one end to 100 percent manufacture at the other, with all degrees of external supply and assembly in between. The more of a product a plant manufactures, the greater degree of integration, a measure of which is the value added as a percentage of the total value of the product. It is difficult to imagine a 100 percent integrated plant, even if the external inputs were limited to raw materials. Any degree of external input implies make-or-buy decisions in respect to both the individual plant and the company at large.

That is, if we decide to buy, should we do so from an associated enterprise (associated via common ownership) or from strangers? We thus introduce a two-dimensional concept, which is illustrated in Figure 3.1.

Various political factors may militate against plant or company integration within a given national market, particularly if the contemplated enterprise would constitute a large part of an important sector of the host economy, either nationally or regionally. An extreme case of the latter is the stimulation of large communities dependent upon the enterprise, for example, the company town. Avoiding such a situation may well be worth the higher cost of external sources of supply. Some firms have attempted to build themselves into the local economy by a process of *local integration*— that is, by subcontracting all processes and services for which local skills are adequate, even to the extent of providing training, financing, and technical assistance to indigenous entrepreneurs. Included is *contract manufacturing* and assembly by otherwise independent local firms. The best strategy may call for changing one's supply or production profile in planned steps. If so, care should be taken not to lose something valuable in the process—such as secret processes, personnel in whose training the firm has invested heavily, or market position. Not infrequently this shift is compelled, as in *compulsory manufacturing*, an example of which is a Mexican government decree that a certain percent of the value of all autos assembled there must be produced locally. In other instances, a firm may be compelled to commit itself to the development of 100 percent local manufacture in a series of steps spread over time. The problem of control, of course, is greatly compounded by shifting supply sources.

3.3   Purchasing

Whether a firm limits purchases to the local market in which it is producing, or scans the international horizon for the best deals, depends on a lot of factors. These include local shortages (persistent, seasonal, cyclical), internationalization of the firm in terms of sales or production, the availability to the company at reasonable cost of the skills needed for successful importing, effectiveness of antiforeign bias on the part of the ultimate customer (for instance, how apparent is the foreign component or the foreignness of the product?), the sensitivity of organized labor (which possibly mounts with the labor intensity of the imported product concerned), the appeal of foreign goods (particularly to market segments, such as the appeal of Israeli goods to the Jewish community in the United States), and the availability of low-cost export financing in the source country.

Overseas purchase involves foreign export controls (see Section 2.2), export financing (Section 7.4), and local import restriction. The latter is frequently linked to a foreign exchange control system, under which a local firm, even though foreign owned, must get an official permit to import the good and to buy the foreign currency needed to pay for it. Thus, both an import license and a foreign exchange permit may be required, in which case

Figure 3.1
The Supply Profile (for a single plant)

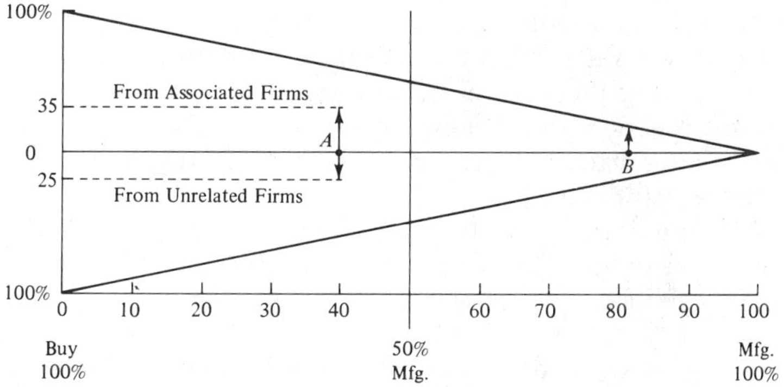

Example: Point A indicates about 60 percent bought, approximately 25 percent being procured externally to the company, 35 percent internally. At point B, the plant manufactures about 80 percent, buying all of the balance from associated firms.

a smooth flow of imported components may be impossible to maintain. Huge inventories of some components, shortages of others, and interrupted production may be the result. Much longer lead time is often required than in the case of local purchase, and therefore the importance of planning is magnified.

You should note that many countries—the United States included—impose a variety of import quotas and prohibitions, specifically:

- absolute quotas (excess imports are either returned or placed in bonded warehouses until the quota period is ended);
- tariff rate quotas (tariff rate increases with quantity imported);
- quotas by source (such as a complete ban on imports from "enemy" countries or those against which trade sanctions have been decreed);
- absolute prohibitions (in the United States, for example, prohibitions against the extension of long-term credit to any nation that has defaulted on obligations to the United States, the import of any product manufactured by forced labor, or the import of agricultural commodities deemed by the president to interfere with the domestic price-support program);
- special tariffs (often following a finding of dumping or an "unfair" business practice such as an export subsidy, in which case a duty designed to equalize the price with a fair market price may be imposed, a so-called countervailing duty);
- voluntary import quotas (in which a government may use public pressure to prevent imports by private business).

What sometimes go unappreciated are the highly specialized skills required for efficient importing. Briefly, they may be summarized as follows:

1.   finding a reliable supplier;
2.   predicting shortages or stoppages (at the source or in transit, e.g., a dock strike) and providing alternative sources;
3.   avoiding unnecessarily high inventories;
4.   passing the tariff barrier, which requires determining the value of goods, placing them in the appropriate lowest duty category, anticipating the final assessment of duties—which may occur many months after actual import—and challenging various official rulings before relevant bodies;
5.   maintaining an import equilibrium in respect to locally manufactured competitive products in order to avoid retaliation by domestic producers via price wars or politically pressured dumping charges or increase in duties;
6.   assuring the availability of associated services to the customer who, of course, may be oneself if the importing firm is the user (e.g., effective guarantees of quality, measure, and so forth);
7.   advising sellers about appropriate markings, documentation, packaging, means of transport; and
8.   following changes in legally imposed import restrictions and foreign exchange controls.[1]

The degree of skill required is related to the degree the firm penetrates the foreign source in its buying. Relatively low-level skill is perhaps adequate if the importing is done external to the firm, via independent importers, resident foreign sellers, cooperative import associations, import brokers, or locally situated distributors. A much higher level of skill is needed if the firm buys abroad direct from overseas export commission houses or merchants, or via its own buyers, agencies, branches, or subsidiaries located overseas. As with exporting, the choice of channel rests largely on volume, legal restraints, the degree to which competitors control existing channels, the international structure of the firm, and existence within the firm of the relevant skills.

3.4   Acquisition of Facilities

If the firm decides to manufacture rather than to buy from others, it is faced with the further choice between acquiring existing facilities or constructing a new plant. Under what circumstances is it the best policy to acquire an established company with operating plants? As in virtually all decisions, the answer is, it depends. In this case it clearly depends upon the relative importance given to acquiring a management, acquiring a labor force, ac-

---

[1]A useful reference is *Importing Into the United States* (Washington, D.C.: Department of the Treasury, U.S. Customs Service, 1981).

quiring channels of distribution, saving time in market entry, eliminating a competitor, preempting acquisition by another firm, technological innovation (that is, new plant versus old plant), and political reprisal. In reference to the last, unless a demonstrable gain can be shown for their respective economies, many host governments are likely to block take-overs of important local firms unless there is a clear need, such as impending bankruptcy. Outcries about the extent of foreign involvement in certain industries in many countries has led frequently to the erection of roadblocks to further major **acquisitions**. Acquisition of only a part interest in overseas facilities via either the **joint venture** or **merger** route may circumvent this difficulty and actually lead to higher rates of return for all parties. Although few international mergers have occurred in contemporary Europe, or elsewhere, the number of international joint ventures among European firms is quite large. Repeated joint venturing can, in time, lead to effective merger.

Under certain circumstances, the acquisition of, or merger with, a foreign enterprise may run afoul of U.S. antitrust laws. For example, if the acquired company is a member of a cartel that restrains the foreign commerce of the United States in some way, the U.S. firm may be vulnerable to prosecution. Other situations risky under U.S. law:

1.   A merger with, or acquisition of, a foreign firm if that firm has U.S. subsidiaries that compete with the acquiring U.S. firm and its subsidiaries in the U.S.
2.   A merger or acquisition that links a U.S. firm with a foreign enterprise and eliminates potential competition within the United States.
3.   Joint-venturing with a firm's domestic competitor—or even a foreign competitor—if judged to have an anticompetitive effect on U.S. trade.

A variety of questions remain without clear answers, such as which products compete (for example, do razors compete with electric shavers; coal with oil; copper with aluminum?), and at what point in terms of market concentration is competition significantly restrained. Geographically, what constitutes a market?

There is the reverse situation in which a foreign firm acquires a U.S. enterprise. Apparently, the same rule applies; witness the U.S. Justice Department's attack of British Petroleum when it acquired Sohio in 1969. If the acquisition is deemed to have an adverse effect on competition in any section of the United States, the courts may force a dissolution or prevent the acquisition, merger, or joint venture. How U.S. courts will treat the Toyota–General Motors joint venture in California remains to be seen. By way of contrast, the European Community regulations on competitition prevent a merger, acquisition, or joint venture only if it is deemed to have an adverse effect on international trade within the Community and if the benefits accruing to the larger or joint enterprise are not passed on in significant degree to the public through lower prices, better service, accelerated research and development, and the like. But a number of governments in effect screen mergers or acquisitions by foreign firms (joint ventures are generally encouraged), and in many cases such foreign involvements are blocked. This has been true of such countries as France, the United Kingdom, Germany, Japan, and Canada, as well as many less developed countries.

Whether your firm decides to acquire (that is, buy) a going plant someplace abroad to supply the target market, or build its own from scratch, we are talking about foreign direct investment. You will recall that we defined FDI as an investment of capital with the intent of participating in management, that is, in exercising some degree of control. The capital can be in various forms—funds, machinery, technology, proprietary rights (such as patents, copyrights, and know-how), or the services of skilled people. Such a move engages a whole new series of special skills, from the analysis of technical and financial feasibility in a different environment, and creation of design and engineering compatible with that environment, to recruitment and training of foreign personnel, integration of foreign managers, and long-distance and continuing communication—possibly in a language other than your own.

Although treated in greater detail in the chapters on financial and ownership strategies, suffice to say here that skill in estimating political and economic risk and **uncertainty** in the new environment assume great importance. After all, you would not want your firm to commit its resources to building a factory in Country X if the probability of significant political or economic changes which would erode profits were high. And the further away we get from our own immediate experience, or that of others whose judgment we have learned to trust, the higher risk and uncertainty appear.

Virtually everyone assumes a certain knowledge and insight about their home environment, and, hence, risk and uncertainty there are generally perceived to be relatively low (though not necessarily). This is not the case when one deals with a relatively unfamiliar setting. Recall that the classical investment rule is that one invests up to the point where the expected stream of future earnings, *discounted to the present*, is higher than, or at least equal to, the cost of the investment. One normally discounts by a rate that is the sum of the cost of capital, the relevant rate of inflation, and the perceived risk. But we shall talk more of this later on. The point is made. To engage in foreign direct investment, the firm needs special analytical skills in respect to the foreign environment—its relevant laws and regulations, the dynamics of the economy, the availability and cost of various inputs, tax law, regulations concerning both imports and exports, possible costs associated with remitting profits home, the easy of entry and exit for your personnel, labor attitudes and organization—to mention only a few of the more important elements. The possibility of change in any or all of these factors must be built into the analysis, hence, the assessment of risk and uncertainty. What is likely to change over our planning period that may impact on our stream of earnings? And by how much? That is the question. In that a foreign direct investment tends to lock corporate resources into fixed assets which cannot be moved readily, such investment should not be undertaken lightly, a fact which many corporations have learned at considerable cost.

3.5 Interplant Relationships

When management determines the degree of manufacturing that the firm should undertake itself in its own facilities and where they should be located to supply the target market, it is left with several additional questions. First: Is a single plant or a multi-plant setup the best? This problem comes up quite frequently in an emerging common market or free trade area. There may be immediate advantages to unity in manufacturing. But on the other hand, a concentration of productive facilities in one national market creates a certain uneasiness about the possibilities that the trade area or common market may eventually pull apart. Hence, one may decide that it is best to have more than a single plant. For example, if the technology is such that once the capacity of a plant is reached it takes a big chunk of additional investment to produce one more unit, it might be well to invest that added capital in a new plant elsewhere.

If one decides on more than one plant, there is a second question. Should each plant specialize, say by product or process? Should the firm **rationalize** production over the region? For long-established plants in Western Europe, for instance, the process of rationalization may be costly—both financially and psychologically—as plants are split apart and new bundles of processes or products brought together. But delay may be even more costly. A third alternative is **manufacturing interchange**, whereby each plant manufactures a specified set of parts, all exchange with one another, and all assemble the same products. For a highly complex product, the problem of flow control is exceedingly difficult. Also, a work stoppage at any one plant shuts down all. Therefore, there is a pressure for large inventories to build up in the system. Finally, different governments may impose varying standards as to size, content, durability, load, and quality.[2]

Whether a management opts for a single or multi-plant solution—and, if the latter, whether specialized or autonomous—depends upon a set of considerations. Chief among these are the economies of scale to be achieved through plant specialization, the relative ease of introducing new products, the cost of reshuffling existing productive facilities (transfer of machines, workers, managers), customer reaction, response by organized labor, political reprisal, legal barriers, effect on inventory levels (and on working capital), adequacy of new local suppliers, the risk (and cost) inherent in specialized plants, probability of controls on product and service flow among the plants becoming unduly costly, nature of the product, nationality of management, and ownership of the various facilities.

In respect to ownership, if it seems necessary to have diverse ownership patterns for the various plants located in different countries or,

---

[2]The United States, represented by the American Standard Association, is one of many nations participating in the preparation of standards issued by the International Organization for Standardization (ISO), a nongovernmental agency with consultative status to the UN Economic and Social Council. Also active in this field are the International Electrotechnical Commission, now functioning as a department of ISO, and the International Bureau of Weights and Measures, which is affiliated with the UN Educational, Scientific, and Cultural Organization (UNESCO). The European Community has made substantial progress in developing common standards.

indeed, anything departing from equity-based control (i.e., over 50 percent) by a single parent, then the intercompany buying and selling inherent in the manufacturing interchange relationship may be deemed illegal under both U.S. and foreign antimonopoly law (see Section 8.3). Potential competitors may be held to be cooperating to an illegal degree. The problem of mutually acceptable prices likewise comes up. Also, if the policy is for the management of each plant to be in the hands of local nationals, the difficulty of instituting effective control over who makes what may be compounded if different products or components have varying prestige values in the minds of key executives (for instance, degree of modernness, size, and complexity), for then elements of national pride may become involved. And if the strategic significance of the alternative products varies (military applications, basic pharmaceuticals, and so forth), official intervention in the allocation among plants located in different countries may be expected.

3.6   Choice of Technology (Plant Design)

The Plant as a Variable

You may find that a management is so domestically oriented that it assumes a plant is a given bundle of processes undertaken with a unique set of machines, whatever the surrounding factor mix (as reflected in a lower natural resource price, higher interest rate, lower ratio of unskilled labor to skilled labor, higher profit expectations, lower tax rates). That is, only one part, or at best, a small part, of the production function is within the range of management vision.

But if management sees a plant as a variable, then the local environment becomes relevant, and a number of decisions are required, which in a general way determine the desired balance between machine and labor skill, given relative capital and labor costs. How much skill should be built into the machine? How much into labor? If skilled labor is scarce and costly, if publicly supported institutions are not producing the skilled persons, then it may be less costly to invest in skilled machines. But skilled machines are often special-purpose machines, which require long production runs to bring down per-unit depreciation cost to a feasible level. On the other hand, more general-purpose machines often require a higher level of labor skill and closer quality control, which in many markets is difficult to come by at a feasible cost. An acceptable solution in this case might be highly flexible, multipurpose skilled machines. Given the range of present technical feasibility, it may be more practical to fragment jobs, thereby simplifying the training function, and superimpose a few highly trained troubleshooters. Capital costs may, of course, be brought down by the installation of second-hand machines, if permission of the host government can be secured for their import and agreement reached as to their capital value.

The actual purchase of the machines deemed most appropriate may well be influenced by considerations other than initial price. Such considerations include the currency in which purchase may be made, durability (in a high-capital-cost country, investment locked in long-lived machines may be unduly costly), ease of repair, and safety features (requirements may vary nationally, as for electrical wiring).

Appropriate Technology

This brings us to the whole subject of appropriate technology, a subject about which there has been much debate within various United Nations agencies and the less developed countries. The LDCs are those with relatively low per capita national products. By definition, those same countries have low savings and hence relatively little capital for investment. This situation implies high cost of capital relative to labor. Therefore, one might conclude that the most appropriate technology for LDCs is that which utilizes the most labor per unit of output, that is, the most labor intensive. The charge has been made that many foreign firms starting up factories in LDCs bring in rather capital intensive technology because that is what they are used to in their home countries. Most capital exporting countries are relatively well endowed in capital, or they would not be investing abroad. Naturally, there is a tendency for the technology developed in such countries to be relatively capital intensive to reduce to a minimum the amount of labor used, since labor is relatively expensive. In fact, much of the pressure for technological innovation has come from the rising cost of labor in the more industrialized countries of North America, Western Europe, and now Japan. The result has been the substitution of capital for labor in the form of capital intensive technology. But this is not the whole story.

One should go back to the original notion of appropriate technology. Appropriate for whom and for what? The only generalizable answer is, that technology which most nearly satisfies national objectives with least cost in terms of use of local resources. The key phrase is national objectives. How are they determined, and by whom? Suppose the priority of objectives leads to conflicting implications, which is not all that rare. Maximum employment might well be a national objective, along with maximum economic growth. To promote the former, one might select the most labor intensive technology. The technology one would select to maximize economic growth is not clear. If one is not concerned with the *distribution* of income and wealth, only with aggregate *growth*, then a fairly capital intensive technology may be appropriate, particularly if the capital can be imported in the form of *foreign* savings at relatively low cost. Also, if the host country is trying to build up an export industry to earn foreign currencies with which to buy high-priority imports, again a relatively capital intensive technology may be appropriate. A standard product of a given quality, often demanded by export markets, is frequently hard to deliver with very labor intensive technology. If tolerances have to be very fine and volume assured because the product is an intermediate for incorporation into manufacturing elsewhere, labor intensive technology may not be appropriate.

On the other hand, if the host society is very concerned about the distribution of income and wealth, a more labor intensive technology may be deemed appropriate. With capital intensive technology, more of the income normally goes to the providers of the capital, the financiers or capitalists. Particularly if the providers of capital are located abroad and all earnings are remitted abroad, local labor benefits only to a limited extent because capital intensive-technology employs relatively few workers, and those few are probably relatively highly paid technicians, an elite within the local labor market. In addition, the earnings are not captured by local capitalists, although the local government will receive some via taxes. Of course, the fact that foreign capitalists carry the risk of failure of the enterprise, at least initially, may make the relationship tolerable. Later, as an enterprise becomes more mature and its success assured, the risk factor may be minimal. Pressure against continued foreign ownership may mount.

The point is that the phrase "appropriate technology" standing outside of a politically determined priority of national objectives is meaningless. Management should be sensitive to this truth, and to the fact that objectives articulated by a government may not actually reflect the long-run priorities perceived by the majority of the populace. If so, political change can be anticipated.

Selection Guidelines

A number of guidelines have been articulated by researchers and practitioners in respect to a firm's choice of technology. The first is that you should control any engineering bias present in your firm by *requiring* consideration of technological alternatives from the point of view of anticipated earnings. By engineering bias is meant the built-in predisposition of engineers in the more developed countries to prefer the newest, most complex, most capital intensive technology, regardless of the circumstances within which it is to be used. Somehow, it is perceived to be "better" in some absolute sense.

Use *local* wage rates in profitability studies, look at *local* technologies and the rationale for their use, consider the use of older generation machines (possibly secondhand) or those built in the LDCs. They may be less automated, easier to operate and repair, and less costly. Require justification for all investment in materials handling equipment and earth moving machinery. Eliminate bias in reporting systems arising from such efficiency measures as numbers of workers or hours of labor per unit of output. Check whether the company's standard plant designs are really appropriate for low-wage countries. And finally, break the manufacturing process down into divisible subprocesses and apply the same analysis to each.

An internationally sophisticated manager is aware of the fact that technology is a variable, and that what is appropriate under one set of circumstances is not under another.

Up to this point we have determined from which country the firm should supply the target market, the extent to which it should itself manufacture, where it should buy that which it does not produce, the degree of plant specialization if we decide on more than one manufacturing facility, and our choice of technology. What we have not decided is the site of the plant—or plants—within the country or countries selected, and the location of research and development activities.

3.7   Site Selection

The only generalization significantly different from those applying to a purely domestic enterprise is that the relative cost of factor and product *mobility* may vary widely from market to market. It may or may not be less costly to locate close to the center of market gravity (the geographical center of the purchasing power of the market), or near an existing power source, an important raw material input, a stable labor supply, in a locale in which management will reside contentedly (because of available intellectual companionship, familiar entertainment, schooling facilities for children), or in a well-policed area. The weights applied to each factor, and the degree to which geographic areas thus defined overlap, will determine the solution. A point to bear in mind is that many less developed countries and regional blocs (such as the EEC) are developing at a quickening pace and their internal markets are expanding and perhaps shifting quite rapidly. Power, resource, and community development may be expected at a very fast rate in some instances. Static analysis may be dangerous; one company located a plant near the largest market only to find that the market center shifted several hundred miles away in a matter of five years. Similar shifts in the domestic U.S. market often move much more slowly because of the market's size and more leisurely expansion rate.

It may be well to note that if one begins with a labor intensive operation but looks forward to the day of an absolute decline in the labor input, location of a plant within a relatively small community—one in which the firm is an important employer—may be asking for trouble. One American firm felt compelled to abandon its Philippine operation precisely for this reason. It was the largest employer in a small Philippine town. With mechanization of its plant, management anticipated that serious political pressures would be generated by the resulting cutback in employment. The United States firm did not wish to be caught in such a situation, and therefore withdrew.

3.8   Research and Development

All that has been said in the preceding paragraphs emphasizes the need for an environmentally oriented research and development effort, whether one speaks of product, process, machines, or site. An R&D division embedded in a domestic operation, where foreign markets are only in the peripheral vision of management, is unlikely to develop the interest and skills necessary for devising solutions to the set of problems posed above. In some instances, as in the pesticide and fertilizer industries, research may be so environmentally oriented as to require a number of foreign sites representative of important climate, soil, and elevation mixes. Proximity to certain types of institutions, academic or otherwise, may likewise be important. It may also be a valid generalization that the more labor intensive a process, the closer the development function should be linked to production. This may demand geographical proximity to the foreign manufacturing plant.

The reason is that development efforts for labor intensive processes may be more restricted than capital intensive processes by cultural factors, such as the ease or cost of introducing new skills, redefining jobs, getting rid of or adding personnel. The cost of R&D may be significantly lower abroad than within the parent country. Finally, on occasion, host governments even insist—as part of the price of entry—that a foreign firm undertake some R&D locally.

A partial solution devised by some companies is the employment of technical liaison personnel to provide better communication between the foreign market environment and domestically based R&D sections. This may prove to be the transmission belt for a useful two-way technical flow as a firm's competitors abroad or foreign researchers come up with new ideas and products. This externally induced stimulation may be important in developing the most effective entry into a given market and maintaining one's position in it. There is, of course, an important feedback into the marketing strategy area; constant adjustment is needed. Organizational structure should facilitate this need.

Having made tentative decisions relating to marketing and sourcing strategies, we are ready to cosider the resources to use in their implementation—the labor, management, and finances (both equity finance, or ownership, and debt).

CHAPTER 4

LABOR STRATEGY

codetermination 50–50 management-labor representation on the board of directors.

flexitime flexible scheduling that permits employees to choose their own work hours within a given time frame.

labor management authority of labor is theoretically preeminent to that of management. Also called self-management.

minority board participation minority representation for labor on the board of directors.

open-door policy a policy of granting employees access to higher management in order to register complaints about the behavior of their immediate supervisors.

paternalism a system where the patron (an individual, group, or corporate entity) assumes responsibility for employees' personal as well as employment needs.

piece rate a rate of pay based on the number of pieces (units of product) a worker produces per unit of time.

profit sharing compensation in addition to workers' basic pay package that is keyed to the company's profitability and intended to create a greater area of common interest between management and labor.

quality circles groups of workers who meet periodically during work hours to discuss ways of improving product quality, efficiency, and morale.

speak-up policy a policy of encouraging employees of all types to register complaints with their supervisors.

works council a body of workers' representatives, or of both workers and management, institutionalizing management-labor relations at the enterprise level.

The most important inputs to production are the human effort and skills required, whether directly employed in the production processes internal to a firm or embodied in the machines and technology it buys from others. We have dealt previously with the choice of technology and plant design, that is, the choice between greater or lesser labor intensity of production. Here, we consider the strategic decisions relating to a firm's employees other than managers, although the labor-management dichotomy is becoming increasingly blurred as production becomes more technologically complex. In some systems, as in the Japanese, it is rare that an individual moves into a managerial function without having served many years in the same firm in nonmanagerial positions and having, in fact, participated in managerial-like functions well before holding managerial rank.

The principal strategic decisions in the labor area are six in number:

1. What range of responsibility toward its employees should management feel, in depth and over time?
2. What degree of labor participation in management should be encouraged?
3. What should the policy toward local unions be?
4. What factors should influence recruitment and job assignment in an overseas enterprise?
5. On what basis should training, development, and promotion be undertaken?
6. Should pay scales and other benefits be the same or greater than those in the surrounding business community?

The casual assumption that the pattern of industrial relations successful at home should be extended automatically to overseas operations may be very costly. Attitudes, expectations, skill levels, law, and institutions differ enormously from society to society.

Also, some of these decisions may be seen domestically as operational or tactical decisions subject to change in the relatively short run. They may become strategic decisions, however, in the international case, where culturally induced and legally enforced rigidities can lead to high cost if the attempt is made to shift policy in the short run.

4.1   Responsibility toward Employees

The possible relationships between management and nonmanagerial employees range from a highly paternalistic to a highly formalized, impersonal one closely regulated by law and collective contract. The relationship runs from a short-term commitment (for example, the life of a contract) to a lifetime commitment, as in many of the larger Japanese corporations. Some observers have concluded that in an increasing number of countries labor is a semifixed cost, reducible only via natural attrition or bankruptcy.

Paternalistic Management

In many less developed countries, where the values of traditional society still persist, the foreign employer may be forced into a paternalistic relationship whether desired or not. An employee expects the relevant elite, official or civilian, to assume certain personal obligations. This **paternalism** is functional, given a traditional society in which status is determined ascriptively, that is, by means other than demonstrated ability, typically by birth into a certain group or class and, to a lesser extent, by age. An elite in such a society retains its status only so long as a system of reciprocal obligations operates between elite and nonelite. Otherwise, the elite class would no longer be viewed as necessary. Responsibility on the part of members of the elite cannot be delegated, for that would challenge the validity of claims to elitism. Eliteness would no longer be seen as restricted to a specific group or class. Upward mobility based on achievement likewise constitutes a challenge to claims to elite status based on ascriptive qualities. Therefore, achievement per se carries little weight in determining status between elite and nonelite; only the fulfillment of traditional obligations does so.

This traditional system becomes even more functional in a country with (1) subsistence level of living for the mass and (2) an ineffective central government that fails to assure minimum services to all individuals, including ability to protect life and property. Then the employer, patron, landowner, officer, governor, chief, or sheikh becomes a protector as well as a master. Subsistence living requires periodic support by others of greater wealth, hence personal loyalties tend to be strong, far stronger than loyalty to abstract values. The system also implies social immobility and a low level of innovation, and, hence, of technical skill.

As one experienced observer commented, the introduction of technical managers "with neither the inclination nor the economic resources to play the paternal role" may create a "malaise" among the workers who have previously known "no other source of vertical job relationship." Unfortunately, the pressure from workers to cast such managers in the "paternal context" may only spur on "their maneuvers to resist the stereotypes."[1]

To retain new employees, in whom a substantial training investment may have been made by the firm because of their low initial level of skill relevant to a modern economic enterprise, the employer may be forced to assume the paternalistic obligations expected of a patron in traditional society. Paternalism may be equated with decision-making authority on the part of one's boss that encompasses much that would be considered reserved for personal decision and institutionalized implementation in a less traditional society, such as granting loans, giving personal assistance in time of disaster, providing housing and medical care, counseling marital relations, and seeing to children's education. Furthermore, nothing less than the *personal* assistance of the patron himself is demanded, for these responsibilities cannot be readily delegated; delegation might well undermine the patron's authority and his ability to command loyalty.

The psychological difficulties thrust upon an alien management in this situation are readily apparent and may constitute a compelling reason for employing local nationals to manage the enterprise. In any event, the transition from a new, relatively small undertaking to a large industrial establishment requires a change in management-labor relations. The door of the boss's office cannot remain open to anyone with a personal problem. Possible steps in this transition are:

1. Delegating responsibility for handling personal problems to someone other than the boss but closely identified with the boss socially, for example, a member of his or her family.
2. Institutionalizing certain functions, such as a housing corporation, a cooperative loan office, a company health clinic.
3. Externalizing all nonbusiness functions as rapidly as possible, by interesting the local government, employing subcontractors, and so forth.
4. Encouraging the employees themselves to assume added responsibility through various clubs, associations, a company union.
5. Restraining from discouraging the organization of an independent labor union and, if it is representative, insisting on bargaining with it collectively.

A trap a number of foreign managements have fallen into is to make irreversible decisions in this area. A perfect case in point is the construction of a company town. Initially, the employer's responsibility to supply decent

---

[1]Charles H. Savage, *Social Reorganization in a Factory in the Andes* (Ithaca, N.Y.: The Society for Applied Anthropology, monograph No. 7, 1964), pp. 3–4.

housing and related services may be entirely acceptable, indeed, expected, by the employee. The government may well be unable to provide what is needed. A differential between company town and traditional community in terms of living standards is thereby created. If, as is so frequently the case in traditional society, the extended family system prevails, the company town grows far more rapidly than expected. Cash income may be sent home, but income in the form of houses and services can only be shared by moving into the town those to whom the employee feels obligated. Services become strained. As the town grows and the population becomes less traditional in the sense of possessing a world view and values increasingly supportive of technological and scientific development, friction within the company frequently develops. There is a tendency to blame the company for anything that goes wrong in the community. Once the situation has progressed to this point, how does the firm backtrack to limit relations with its employees to matters relating directly to the job? Unless outside interests, possibly the local government, are willing to take over responsibility, the firm may eventually be forced to withdraw entirely.

Modern Labor Relations

The alternative route is to externalize as rapidly as possible all functions not directly related to the principal business of the firm. The firm may subsidize housing, education, health facilities, transportation services, and so forth, but actual responsibility remains in the hands of local government or entrepreneurs. For example, providing daily transportation from traditional communities to the place of work may, in the long run, be far less costly than becoming involved in a company town. Ideally, either the government or local entrepreneurs would be paid to provide such services. Subsidies of this sort may be justified in that the firm is creating external costs that should be borne by the enterprise. The subsidies may take the form of grants, training, or technical assistance. The rapid externalization of such social services is particularly important for a foreign-owned firm that might otherwise generate the hostility of local political leaders by appearing to weaken the nationalistic loyalty of its employees. The social services provided by the firm may be seen as a challenge to the host government, an exposure of its weaknesses, and hence, as a force against the creation of a politically cohesive state.

A further step in the creation of a modern labor force—modern in the sense of being more paticularistic by limiting its relations with mangement to matters directly related on the job, more achievement-oriented, and more individualistic in solving problems—is the appearance of employees' associations within the plant and eventual affiliation with an independent labor union.

A parallel step in the modernization of manager-subordinate relations may be the **speak-up** and **open-door** policies introduced by some firms. "Speak-up" refers to encouraging anyone to register complaints with supervisors; "open-door," to granting access to higher management in order to complain about the behavior of one's supervisor. This system can operate effectively only if the investigating process which follows is done objectively as well. Sometimes complementing these processes is an employee opinion survey run periodically, in which individuals are asked to express opinions about working conditions, compensation, impact of job requirements on family, and the like.

Some have said that the paternalistic nature of management-labor relations in Japan, plus the astonishing rate of Japanese economic growth, challenge the notion that there is a unique relationship between "modern" labor relations, as defined above, and high levels of productivity and creativity. Possibly the notion is faulty, but the Japanese case does not prove the point, for it is not paternalistic in the usual sense. True, the range of company-bestowed benefits is wide, and the company seems at times to be all-pervasive in the lives of its employees. But, unlike the true paternalistic model, employees appear to have a great deal to say about company policy. They participate in many important decisions by means of the company union and other devices. What appears to be paternalism (i.e., decision making *external* to the individual concerning personal, non-job related matters as well as those related to the job), plus some degree of participative management, is not paternalism; it is expression of a collective responsibility to the individual as determined by the *collectivity*, including the individual. Furthermore, it is institutionalized.

A more obvious case might be the Yugoslavian enterprise, obvious because its structure is prescribed by law. To the uninitiated, such an enterprise would appear highly paternalistic vis-à-vis the individual worker in terms of the range of benefits received and the pervasiveness of the enterprise in his or her life. Yet, one does not think of the Yugoslavian enterprise in these terms because of the system of self-management by which the workers, through their elected workers' council, select the managing board and general director and consider important policy alternatives, including the allocation of funds to be expended on various employee benefit plans.

Perhaps the sort of identity between manager and worker that the Japanese and Yugoslavian systems in some cases generate within the context of modern industry is the next evolutionary step, something beyond the system North Americans are inclined to call modern, in which management and labor are seen as independent adversaries negotiating contracts. It is well to maintain an open mind on the subject, particularly given the rapidly evolving notions of job-enrichment and industrial democracy.

There is a further dimension in management's responsibility to employees: the time dimension. The laws of many countries inhibit management's freedom to discharge employees; in others, collective agreements have a similar effect but generally over a shorter run. In any case, a discharge may be a very costly business if there is a terminal pay requirement and the individual has been with the company for many years. Although not embedded in law, many of the larger Japanese firms pursue a lifetime employment system, *shushin koyo seido*, which means a lifetime job commitment (i.e., up to retirement) on the part of the firm. Indeed, there is relatively little interfirm movement of labor or managers within Japan, particularly among the larger firms. Such a system has definite advantages: (1) employees work in stable work groups over long periods of time, which probably contributes to better communication and a higher level of company loyalty; (2) the employees (and their unions) need not fear technical innovation; (3) these stable work groups may generate unusually high levels of both effort and innovation; (4) the time horizon of the worker is likely to be longer, and hence his or her objectives more likely to coincide with those of the firm—*if* the firm also sets long-term objectives, which tends to be the case in Japan for a variety of reasons. The disadvantages include, of course, the difficulty of shaking loose less productive or redundant employees, thus incurring a high fixed labor cost, and the elimination of the incentive implicit in the employee's latent fear of his inability to meet physical and culturally induced needs—that is, the fear of being fired. There is also the problem of increasing cost as the average age of employees increases. But, given the total Japanese context, the lifetime employment system obviously has not interferred seriously with Japan's economic growth. Indeed, it may have promoted it.

To what extent could, or should, a *non*-Japanese firm operating in Japan adopt the lifetime employment system? Some firms may be well advised *not* to adopt it, but rather to offer themselves as alternatives to the Japanese system. Clearly, a typical Japanese worker must look upon a job with a foreign firm as more risky. The foreign firm is unlikely to have a long record in Japan. It is likely to be seen as only a relatively small subsidiary operation. Nor is the Japanese government, through the banking system, likely to support the firm if it runs into difficulties. The results are that (1) the foreign firm will have to pay the worker more to compensate for the perceived higher risk and (2) a natural screening process is likely to operate, whereby the firm attracts individuals to its employ who are less motivated by security and more individualistically oriented than are their average compatriots. In a sense, the foreign firm provides an escape device from the more common system.

The idea of a lifetime employment commitment may be edging into the United States. Among the demands of the U.S. Steelworkers Union in 1977 was lifetime income security, thereby adding to the suspicion that indeed labor was becoming a fixed cost. In 1982, the Ford Motor Company initiated guaranteed employment for some of its employees in order to build a more efficient, motivated labor force.

4.2   Degree of Labor Participation in Management

Obviously, one cannot speak of responsibility toward employees without reaching the subject of employees' right to participate in important decisions affecting their welfare, present and future. The real question is, to what extent should workers influence the decision-making process in the firm? Increasingly, the answer is legally determined.

Speaking on Belgian TV in 1971 about European moves toward greater labor participation in management, pundit John Kenneth Galbraith raised a few European hackles by proclaiming,

[Participation] is a pipe dream. I advise you to give up the idea of this kind of reform . . . The very nature of organized and bureaucratic management of a large concern concentrates the power in the hands of men who share the information of specialists in technology and management. Neither the capitalist nor the worker has a part in it.[2]

Notwithstanding such views, a change in the traditional relationship between employee and employer is obviously worldwide as dissatisfaction with the traditional forms of hierarchical corporate control mounts. Labor is demanding a larger role in decision making, at both the job and the enterprise level. Perhaps this pressure arises out of an evolutionary process that, despite apparent short-term evidence to the contrary, is reflected in the increasing awareness of individuals everywhere of their humanity. The need for autonomy and self-fulfillment is now part of the world industrial culture. Whether it leads to maximum economic efficiency may be irrelevant.

Responses take many forms, from flexible work hours (**flexitime**), group-assigned tasks, group assembly operations, workers' councils, co-determination (labor participation at the board level), self-management (labor selection and control of management), and role change (managers working periodically as ordinary labor), to employee ownership and profit sharing. The response may be ideologically justified, introduced for purely pragmatic reasons, or appear as the result of labor dissatisfaction and pressure. In any event, in the process the prerogatives and roles of both managers and workers are redefined, and the socioeconomic disparity between managers and workers is narrowed. In the ultimate model, they become one or are so heavily overlapped as to be virtually indistinguishable. (In some places, such as the United States, the notion that consumers as well should have a voice in the direction of enterprises is gaining support.)

In that the traditional function of organized labor is challenged by many of these reforms or at least seriously altered, organized labor may perceive them as a threat, as- in the United States. Its power could be dampened by workers' management and ownership, for then distinctions between employee and employer tend to melt. Internal accommodation in decision making replaces direct confrontation supported by resources and pressures external to the firm. Theoretically, labor unions could still serve critically important functions in the articulation of grievances, protecting the minority from the tyranny of the majority, reporting irregularities to competent authorities, and in bringing attention to important income disparities

[2]Reported in *Worldwide P & I Planning* (November–December 1972), p. 18.

among similar enterprises. Or the unions may become an integral part of the decision-making system, in part as a compromise solution.

There are many systems and degrees of labor participation in decision making. The following categories would seem to include most of these, although this section should perhaps be read in association with that on participative management in the following chapter, Section 5.5.

Labor Management (Self-management)

Under labor or self-management, the authority of labor is theoretically preeminent to that of management. Examples are the Yugoslavian case, already mentioned, and, theoretically, the Israeli model, where a significant percentage of manufacturing and construction is provided by companies owned and managed by the Histadrut.[3] In addition, there are producers' manufacturing cooperatives in most of Israel's *kibbutzim* and in many separate industrial enterprises.

The Israeli concept differs in theory from the Yugoslavian, for in Yugoslavia virtually all industry is owned by society (not the government) and held in social trust by the workers' community, consisting of all employees of an enterprise, the terms of which are defined in charter or statute. The community (the rough equivalent of stockholders) periodically elects a workers' council (somewhat similar to a board of directors), which in turn names the managing director (president) and the management board (supervisory board). The latter, consisting of both council members and non-council community representatives, selects all other members of management, performs an auditing function, and initiates action at the council level.

Regardless of many criticisms, it is obvious that self-management in Yugoslavia cannot be written off as a failure. It is equally obvious that Western firms will face unusual problems in joining forces with such enterprises.

To what extent the Yugoslavian model will be seized upon by other societies is not yet clear, although innovations introduced in 1971 in Zambia and in 1974 in Peru seem to have been influenced. More recently, the People's Republic of China has exhibited a great deal of interest and is experimenting with the concept.

Codetermination

Until 1972, the principal examples of codetermination, a 50–50 management-labor representation on the board of directors, were the iron, coal, and steel industries of the Federal Republic of Germany. A law introduced in 1951 provided for equal representation on the supervisory boards, or *Aufsichstrat*. After many years of urging by the German Trade Union Federation

[3]General Federation of Jewish Labor in Israel.

(DGB), codetermination *(Mitbestimmung)* was extended in 1976 to all German enterprises employing 2,000 or more (roughly 650 firms employing some 4 million)[4] but with several important differences.

1. Under the new law, high-level white collar personnel (employees with managerial responsibility below that of the senior management group) select one of the employee representatives. (If this representative votes with the shareholders, there is no longer real parity.)
2. The chairman of the supervisory board may be chosen either from the shareholders or employee representatives. But a two-thirds vote of the entire board is required. If a candidate is unable to generate the required votes, then the shareholders may appoint one of their own representatives. (This would seem to assure the shareholders of the chairmanship in most cases.)
3. The board chairman has a double vote in that first he may vote as any other member, and if the board is deadlocked, he may vote again as chairman.

Possibly the most revealing remark reported about the law was made by a German industrialist who did not wish to be named: "The new law doesn't bother me. It doesn't matter if the majority is one or five votes; the important thing is that the new law leaves power with the stockholders."[5] Others, however, fear the union influence. Henry Ford II was moved to declare that the scheme "could lead to a denial of basic property rights."[6]

Although supported by the British Trade Union Congress (TUC), a codetermination proposal put forward by a royal commission in England in early 1977 was not enacted into legislation. Basically what was proposed was equal management and labor representation on corporate boards, with one third of the seats being reserved for a neutral group selected by both parties.

Minority Board Participation

Minority board participation is exemplified by the one-third representation given to employees in German firms (other than in the coal, iron, and steel industries) by the Shop Constitution Law of 1952. This provision still applies for firms with over 500 employees and not more than 2,000. The European Corporation Law drafted by the EC Commission would require one-third labor representation on the supervisory board of all corporations within the EC that satisfy certain criteria, but such a move has not, in fact, been made. At least seven European countries have introduced minority board participation: Sweden, the Netherlands, Norway, Luxembourg, Denmark, Ireland and France. How has it worked? *Business International* reported in mid-1976:

---

[4]Multiple companies are aggregated.

[5]Quoted in Richard Balzer, "What Determines Co-Determination?" (New York: Institute of Current World Affairs, newsletter RJB-44, April 27, 1976), p. 5.

[6]*New York Times*, October 17, 1975, p. 10.

Most companies in Europe have found industrial democracy less alarming than they feared. In fact, in those countries where it is most advanced, e.g., Sweden, Germany, the Netherlands, labor strife is virtually unknown, in stark contrast to the situation in the U.K. and Italy.[7]

Some recent research in Germany confirms that codetermination is working reasonably well and that fears expressed initially by both labor and management were unfounded. Both sides now seem to be reasonably pleased with the results, one of which is much improved industrial relations as mutual confidence and trust has built. Some German subsidiaries of foreign-based corporations, however, appear to have continuing difficulty in dealing with the new system.[8]

This verdict would appear to remain valid. Although there have been no legislative proposals in the United States on the subject as of this book's publication, there are a few straws in the wind. The United Auto Workers Union (UAW) asked Chrysler in 1976 to consider granting seats on the company's board of directors to labor representatives. Chrysler had been singled out possibly because its subsidiary in the United Kingdom had proposed to admit two union representatives to its board in a bid for industrial peace. The demand in the United States eventually led to one union representative on the Chrysler board as part of a last-ditch effort to salvage the company, but whether such will continue to be the case remains to be seen.

Works Councils

Works councils are bodies through which management-labor relations are institutionalized at the enterprise level. A council may consist only of workers' representatives or of both workers and management, as in a joint works council in the United Kingdom. These bodies may or may not have legal status, may or may not be mandatory under the law, and may or may not be established by agreement between trade unions and employers' organizations at the national level.

An example is the German law that requires that the works council (*Betriebsrat*) in any private firm employing five or more people to be a party to company decisions having to do with working conditions, training, methods of payment, hiring and firing, promotion, transfers and regrouping, and work allocation. A council is composed entirely of work force members. Curiously, although there is no requirement that a council member belong to a union and although union membership nationwide is only about 40 percent of the work force in Germany (see Figure 4.4), something like 80 percent of the works council members are reported to be union members. In that nominations are made by list, which must be supported by a minimum number of workers, the union has a substantial edge. Also,

[7]May 28, 1976, p. 172.

[8]Christian Diedrich, "Co-Determination in the Federal Republic of Germany, "unpublished MS thesis, Alfred P. Sloan School of Management, Massachusetts Institute of Technology, 1982, particularly pp. 88–95.

union members seem to wield greater influence on the councils than nonunion members; the union, even though in a minority position, is organized.

A further example is the Dutch Works' Council Act of 1971, which provided for councils in firms with over 100 employees and gave them a voice equal to that of management in such matters as pensions. The councils must also be consulted about personnel policies, annual reports, mergers, expansion plans, and closures.

Particularly worrisome to firms operating internationally is the fact that local input into decision making of the sort we have been describing could well undermine the centralized control necessary to maintain an internationally integrated production system. Even some U.S. unions have tried to secure a veto power over managerial decisions in respect to foreign sourcing if there were an adverse domestic impact on jobs.

Job Enrichment

Any scheme that provides greater autonomy, that is, decision-making capacity, to workers or groups of workers on the shop floor is a form of job enrichment. Flexitime is one of these. The idea apparently originated in certain German enterprises about 1970. Ideally, the individual worker determines his or her own daily and weekly work schedule. In some cases, employees may borrow time to be made up later, or bank time by working more than the contracted number of hours, and then draw upon it as vacation time. Obviously, it is not easy to apply such a system where the public is served or on production lines. A number of pressures seem to push in the direction of such a scheme, specifically, (1) rising levels of education (which engender a demand for individual self-determination), (2) expansion of adult education, (3) the growth of special programs to keep older workers at work, (4) growth in the number of women with a demand for intermittent or part-time work, (5) expansion of the service sector, (6) continuing urbanization (which creates a need to stagger working hours to avoid congestion of services), (7) growing importance of shift work designed to utilize the capacity of increasingly capital intensive industries, (8) rising levels of real income and relative job security (which permits workers to react against rigidity), and (9) a weakening of the work ethic.

Another approach to job enrichment is group assembly as opposed to assembly line organization. The record seems very mixed. In 1973, the Swedish car company, Saab, completely scrapped the assembly line in a new plant. In its stead, work was organized in teams of from three to ten people, who set their own rhythm and divided the work among themselves. Their only obligation was to finish a batch in the same measured time as the assembly line production. After a year, Saab tallied the costs and savings. The biggest saving came from a drop in absenteeism and turnover, which more than offset the increasing training costs. Shortly thereafter Sweden's other car company, Volvo, designed an entire automobile manufacturing plant built to accommodate team (15 to 20 people) assembly work. Olivetti, another success story, had by 1976 switched about half of its 5,000 assembly workers in Italy from conventional assembly lines to "production islands." The result? Higher productivity and lower indirect labor costs. Early in 1974, General Motors Truck and Coach Division experimented with the team approach to assembly, but it was dropped after a few months. The complexity of assembly proved too difficult for a team approach and was deemed too slow to meet GM's production standards.

Job rotation is yet another vehicle for reducing boredom and alienation. United Biscuits of the United Kingdom launched such a program in 1972. Subsequently, employees asked if they could learn more about supervisors' jobs in order to understand the work process better. Management allowed them to take over their supervisors' jobs a day at a time, handling production scheduling, paperwork, and liaison with other departments. So successful was the experiment that the number of supervisors was cut in half over the next two or three years. The result has been lower supervisory costs, as well as less absenteeism and turnover.

Quality Circles and the Scanlon Plan

The notion of job enrichment frequently gives rise to shop floor groups, small groups of production workers who meet periodically to discuss ways of improving product quality, efficiency, and morale. By 1980, considerable discussion had arisen in the world press about the "quality circles," which by then had appeared in large numbers in Japanese industry and were credited with a major contribution to Japan's extraordinary record of economic growth, productivity, and quality of product. Many thousands of these small groups were meeting frequently during work hours in Japanese companies to discuss ways of improving their tasks, and engineers and managers were listening. Monetary rewards and social recognition were given to individuals or groups making useful suggestions. Meanwhile, of course, the individuals involved were given a new sense of their own importance, and morale and company loyalty grew stronger, thereby helping to stabilize employment. The firm was then in a position to reduce costs not only by capturing its own internal experience, but also by disseminating it rapidly throughout the work force. Some observers have suggested that this system was peculiarly compatible to the Japanese social-psychological milieu because of the tradition of consensus decision making and the relatively small differences in remuneration and social distinction between managers and workers. Added is the fact, already mentioned, that Japanese managers—almost without exception—serve long apprenticeships as ordinary workers in factories or offices within the same firm in which they perform managerial functions. North American and Western European firms have been attempting to introduce "quality circles," but often with only limited success.

Interestingly enough, the Japanese notion of the quality circle had its origin in certain ideas developed in the United States, starting with the concept of "Theory Y" management (see below) developed by a professor at the Sloan School of Management, M.I.T., namely Douglas McGregor. The

The ideas embedded in the concepts of Theory X and Theory Y can be summarized thus:

Theory X, one of two theories in a dichotomous management classification system developed by Douglas McGregor, is equated with the "classical" management theory. It assumes that efficiency is measured solely in terms of productivity; that human beings act rationally; that coordination is not achieved unless directed from above; that people prefer the security of a definite task and do not value the freedom to determine their own approach to problems (i.e., they prefer to be directed and will not cooperate voluntarily); that the activities of a group should be viewed on an objective and impersonal basis; that workers are motivated by economic needs and therefore incentives should be in terms of monetary rewards; that people do not like to work, and close supervision and accountability should be emphasized; that authority has its source at the top of a hierarchy and is delegated downward; that managerial functions in varied types of activities have universal characteristics and can be performed in a given manner regardless of environment and the qualities of the person involved.

Theory Y, an alternative set of assumptions (often associated with more "modern" or "participative" management) underlying a normative theory of management derived from Maslow's need hierarchy.* Underlying assumptions are that the expenditure of physical and mental work is natural (that it may be either a source of satisfaction or of punishment, depending upon the circumstances); that individuals will exercise self-direction and self-control in the service of an objective to which they are committed; that commitment to an objective is a function of the reward associated with its achievement (the most important being ego satisfaction and self-actualization needs); that the average human being learns under proper conditions to accept *and* to seek responsibility; that the capacity to exercise a relatively high degree of imagination and creativity in the solution of organizational problems is widely distributed in the population; that under conditions of modern industrial life the intellectual potential of the average human being is only partially utilized.

*A widely-used classification, developed by Abraham Maslow, that divides human needs into three levels: *first level*, intrinsic or physiological (safety, food, shelter); *second level*, extrinsic or social (affiliation, belonging, prestige, status); *third level*, self-actualization (self-esteem, competence, power, achievement). It is assumed that some degree of satisfaction of a lower need is necessary before a higher need becomes motivating.

central idea is that people are capable of *self-directed* effort toward corporate goals. The worker is assumed to be the expert in respect to his or her job. Hence, an important function of management is to seek workers' ideas as to how to improve quality, production, and morale. This notion was incorporated many years ago by Joseph Scanlon, a steel worker, in a plan to tap the ideas of workers. After an initial success, and with the support of McGregor, Scanlon subsequently helped a number of companies in the United States install the plan that bears his name. The basic idea, the implementation of which differs from firm to firm, is the introduction of a committee system and financial incentives. The latter are typically cash bonuses paid to all employees in a plant whenever a saving is achieved as measured against the historical ratio of labor cost to the value of production. The committee seeks out workers' ideas through elected worker representatives, who solicit suggestions from other workers and confer with management. The Scanlon plan has enjoyed modest success in the United States. One authority has observed:

> **Experience under the Scanlon plan suggests an expanded consideration of plans for changing union-management relationships towards cooperation on production decisions . . . [it] can improve labor-management relationships at the local level but it cannot turn collective bargaining into total cooperation.**[9]

Whatever views you may have on the subject, there is clear evidence of a worldwide movement toward more participative management, whether on the work floor or in the board room. It may be useful to think of the various alternatives that have been discussed as a series of concentric rings of authority or self-determination around the individual employee (Figure 4.1).

Negotiating Committees

Negotiating committees assemble periodically to bargain collectively with management. They may be organized on a national level, involving one or more national unions and an employer's association (in which case a question arises as to labor's capacity to enforce an agreement at the local level), or on the local level between management and local or national unions. Agreements reached by negotiating committees may or may not have a legal basis (i.e., they may have the legal status of binding contracts and be enforceable as such, as in the United States, or they may not). Such negotiations may or may not be legally required. In any case, there seems to be a worldwide tendency for negotiators to broaden discussions to cover matters formerly considered to be purely managerial, such as hiring and firing, job security, training, production scheduling, bonuses, promotion, trade and investment policy, and environmental considerations.

[9]James W. Driscoll, "A Change Strategy for Union-Management Cooperation: The Scanlon Plan," unpublished working paper (Sloan School of Management, Massachusetts Institute of Technology, May 1978), pp. 16–18.

Figure 4.1
The Concentric Circles of Worker Participation

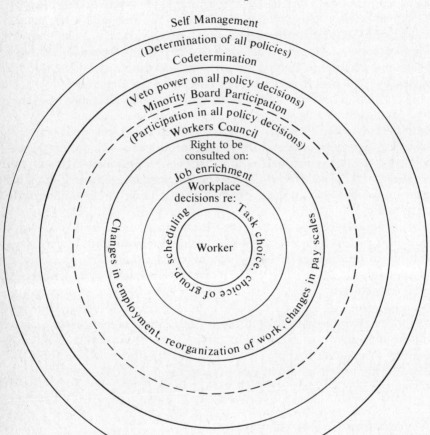

Compulsory Negotiation

Compulsory negotiation is enforced by a national or state network of conciliation and arbitration commissions and courts, as in Australia. Bargaining
may take place at both industry and plant level, but it is largely informal and
supplementary to the arbitration process. Even more than a collective bargaining system, the compulsory settlement of agreements seems to place
labor and management in adversary positions.

Role Change

Role change is only known to have existed on a compulsory basis in the
People's Republic of China, although note the previously cited United
Kingdom case (United Biscuit). At one time, Chinese factory administrators

were apparently required to spend two days a week working on the factory floor as ordinary labor. It is theorized that such a practice, though incurring a social cost (because individuals are not fully exploiting their comparative advantage, that is, their differential skills), may in fact lead to a net gain by lessening social costs generated by increasing job specialization, inability to communicate, social fragmentation, and interpersonal conflict. The Chinese system attempted to achieve closer identification among all people by role change. Results seem to have been mixed.

Informal Communication

Informal communication is a particularly strong method of labor participation when management deliberately removes obstacles to direct communication, as did Imperial Chemical Industry (ICI) in Britain. It took ICI and nine unions several years to formalize the scheme. Without going into detail, two key sections of the agreement are revealing:

Relations in the workplace. **Management should accept the fact that employees have knowledge and skills that can contribute to the solution of workplace problems. Employees should understand the management point of view, the needs of the business, and also have regard for the interest of other groups of employees. Where alterations to working or manning practices seem necessary to improve plant efficiency, there should be joint discussion and agreement among those directly concerned.**

Organization of work. **Work should be organized so that each employee's time, skills, and capacity to accept responsibility can be fully and effectively employed. The joint cooperation of employees and management will be needed to achieve this. The outcome should be more interesting, more responsible, and therefore more highly rewarding jobs. All rearrangement of work will be consistent with the company's policy of safe working.**

The pattern of labor management for which a firm opts is very much a function of law and local custom, over which the firm may have little control. The real question is whether management wishes to move toward a higher level of worker participation than that compelled by law and/or custom, or to invent devices to circumscribe participation. Management's choice rests very heavily on (1) its perception of human nature generally (Theory X or Theory Y?) and (2) its perception of the capabilities and motivations characteristic of a particular labor force at a particular time and place. In regard to the latter, management should be situationally oriented; that is, it should adapt its policy to a given place and time and be sufficiently sensitive and flexible to be able to shift that policy as relevant variables change.

Direct labor participation in management may make the employment of nonnational managers very difficult. This difficulty is circumvented in Yugoslavia by permitting the worker's council to delegate certain managerial authority for a joint business enterprise (Yugoslav-foreign) to a joint managing board or business committee. Apparently, such a board may designate the managers of the joint enterprise for limited periods of time.

Presumably, by prior agreement, non-Yugoslav nationals could be placed in this position, although none seem to have been appointed.

It should be noted that legally imposed conditions vary substantially from country to country in regard to the *procedures* for determining wage and nonwage conditions of employment, the *substance* of such conditions (including employer contribution to employee welfare through the state or other external agency), and *structural relationship* (codetermination of labor representation on the board of directors or at other levels of management, disclosure of company financial records to labor representatives, employee participation in profit). What may be the subject of negotiation in one country may be dictated by law in another. On the other hand, some aspects of labor-management relations may have no legal basis at all, such as the collective agreement or union-management contract in the United Kingdom up to 1971. Until then, such contracts had been held to be mere gentlemen's agreements, not legally enforceable contracts. (Since 1971, however, collective labor contracts have been legally enforceable.)

4.3 Policy toward Labor Unions

The Role of Unions

The role of the union varies from country to country for some of the reasons suggested in Figure 4.2. For example, if the level of union income is low due to high labor mobility (difficulty of holding members), low employment, low per capita labor income and/or the lack of labor homogeneity, then a labor union has need for other sources of income and support. Also, limited income means that the union has but little capacity to suspend work, support research, or undertake welfare on behalf of its members. It is driven into alliance with other organizations—political party, church, or government. Under these circumstances, it is very easy for political or religious issues and ideological commitments to become involved. One result is the wide variance among countries in respect to labor's propensity to walk off the job.

In the United States, the union selected by the majority of workers in a plant has a legal monopoly over all bargaining with the employer, which means that there is no bargaining through other institutions. Collective bargaining in the United States is usually at the local or company level, and any agreement is limited in its application to the union and firm involved in the negotiation. The collective agreement negotiated between the employer and a labor union supercedes any individual employment contracts. In Europe, the right of a union to represent all employees is unknown. European collective bargaining is typically between representatives of an employers' association and representatives of a confederation of unions, sometimes on a national but usually on a regional basis. Agreements so negotiated often set the minimum conditions for an entire industry, although they do not necessarily supercede individual employment con-

Figure 4.2
Environmental Influences on Structure and Posture of Organized Labor

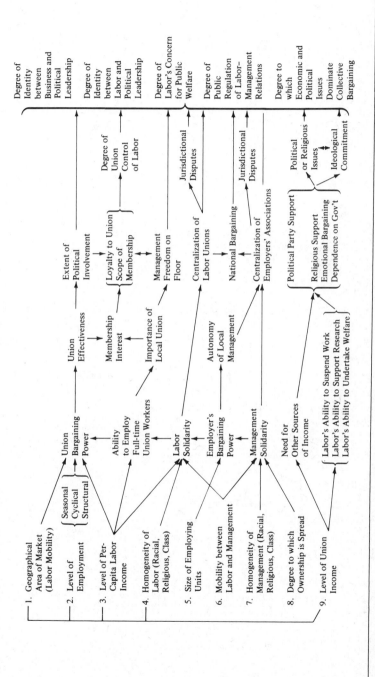

(feedback loops not shown for sake of simplicity)

tracts. Another characteristic European institution, quite apart from the unions, is the works council consisting of elected employee representatives. The works council may act as a consultative agency vis-à-vis management and function as part of the grievance procedure and, as already described, participates in a variety of other decisions. In Japan, the national and regional confederations are relatively weak, and most negotiation is done by what are essentially company or plant unions.

It is generally concluded that the most important method of establishing conditions of work in the major industrial countries remains free collective bargaining in a framework of law and custom. But national differences are great, not only in respect to the level at which bargaining takes place (enterprise or industry level), but also the centralization of union

Figure 4.3
Centralization of Union-Management Structure
Related to Level of Bargaining

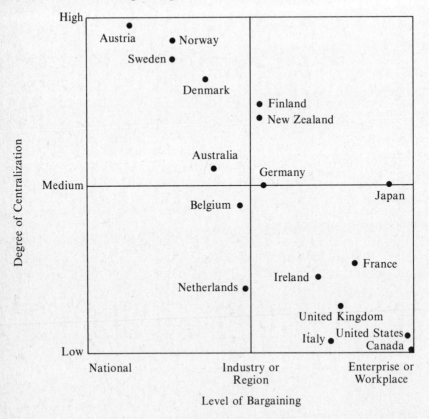

Figure 4.4
Unionization Related to Level of Bargaining

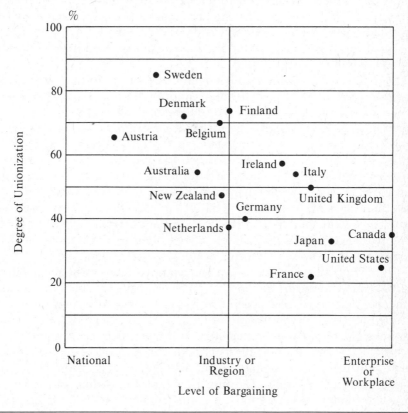

Source: *The OECD Observor*, no. 94, September 1978, p. 4.

management, the scope of bargaining, the degree to which government intervenes, and, of course, the degree of unionization. Figures 4.3 and 4.4 graphically differentiate among countries by relating level of bargaining to degree of union management centralization (Figure 4.3) and level of bargaining to degree of unionization (Figure 4.4).

There is a further difference in respect to organized labor's response to the new, computer-based automated technology allegedly responsible for displacing large numbers of workers. It would appear that as a direct result of union activity, workers in Britain, Germany, Norway, and Sweden have greater influence than U.S. union members on decisions about the introduction of new technology. This influence, although based principally in stronger labor relations laws and contract clauses, is also a product of superior labor education programs dealing with the new technology, greater access to relevant technical expertise, and growing labor involvement in R&D activities by both the public and private sectors. In some places, you may even encounter active, union-trained "technology commit-tees" or "data shop stewards."[10]

Unions also differ markedly from one country to the next in respect to their degree of political involvement. One generalization that can be made is that, characteristically, the poorer the union, the more likely it is to turn to external sources of support, typically to a religious or political organization. There is also the historical input.

The more intimate relationship between unions and political movements or governments in newly independent countries is particularly the result of earlier identification of unions with movements for independence from Colonial powers, and partly the result of other pressures (economic development plans, Communist threats, etc.), which cause governments to control labor movements more than we have in the West. Unions have some freedom and influence even within the "one-party" democracies, such as Egypt, India, and perhaps even Ghana. In many developing countries, there is, as Maurice Neufeld has put it, "the inevitability of political unionism." Thus, our view of the trade union as virtually free of government influence or control will be a long time in developing in these countries at their present stage of political and economic growth.[11]

If the firm has been able to limit its responsibilities essentially to those related directly to the job at hand, it will be in a better position to negotiate with trade unions on strictly economic issues. The broader range of subjects included in negotiations, the more likely is the negotiation to take on a political coloration. Note that negotiation with a union in a company town situation is by definition political. That the union may become politically active on behalf of the company when its "golden egg" is under political attack is beside the point. The firm then becomes vulnerable at best to charges of undermining national union solidarity, at worst to charges of subverting union loyalty to the nation.

It is a safe assumption that sooner or later, regardless of its environment, a firm will be faced with the problem of dealing with a local labor organization. The degree to which union organization is centralized, politically committed, able to capture members, and responsible for its commitments depends on a number of factors, the most important of which are plotted on Figure 4.2. Under most circumstances, it would appear in management's best interest to deal with unions that are strong locally, essentially nonpolitical, representative of the workers, and responsive to their members' best interests. The problem lies in how to encourage whatever unions there are to develop in those directions.

Some experienced international business practitioners suggest the following policies:

[10]"Unions and Management in Europe Seek to Ease Transition to New Technology," *Transatlantic Perspectives*, No. 6 (February 1982), pp. 20 ff.

[11]Charles A. Myers, "The American System of Industrial Relations: Is It Exportable?" Reprinted from the *Proceedings of the Fifteenth Annual Meeting* (Industrial Relations Research Association, 1962), p. 8.

1. Resist, vigorously, bargaining with unions dominated by or committed to a political party or religious establishment, or to particular political or religious ideologies.
2. Resist, but give ground to, labor leadership that seems primarily concerned with bettering working conditions (rather than enlarging support for a political or religious cause). Moderate resistance tends to strengthen such leadership. Outright company encouragement may torpedo its appeal.
3. Bargain with local unions rather than with a national organization if at all feasible. (Possible restraints: legal requirements, a demand for national negotiations through an employers' association because of the industry-wide repercussions, unwillingness on the part of the national labor union to permit local negotiation because of the weakness of local labor leadership, and financial resources.)
4. Encourage the development of responsible labor leadership by contributing to seminars and training courses sponsored by the host government, the International Labor Organization, the World Federation of Free Labor Organizations, the American Federation of Labor and Congress of Industrial Organizations (AFL-CIO), and other organizations.
5. Avoid conditions permitting the creation of an independent third force between local and national unions, such as the interunion, plantwide shop stewards' communities in the United Kingdom.

Two points need expansion. The first is that bargaining with local unions rather than on a national level may so strengthen local labor as to make it virtually independent of national union control. If labor is organized on a craft basis and is represented locally by means of a shop steward system (which may mean one shop steward per shop regardless of the mix of unions represented in that shop), then management faces a power center not controlled by any union. In fact, a plantwide shop stewards' committee may deliberately neutralize union authority on the local level. Given this situation, if the firm opts to negotiate only on the national level, it is in trouble, for the union negotiators are in no position to implement agreements at the plant level. The only leverage they can develop vis-à-vis the local shop stewards would be public appeal or control of funds or valuable services. But it is likely that the shop stewards have developed a virtual communications monopoly through a regular plant newspaper, as well as independent sources of funds through football pools and similar activities. Because they perceive their authority as being challenged by management's refusal to negotiate with them, they are constantly in need of proving their authority. Hence, the probability of wildcat strikes over relatively trivial incidents is high. In an overly simplified form, this describes the pattern of Ford's management-labor relations in its Daggenham plant in Britain during the 1950s and into the late 1960s.

The second point meriting emphasis is that international channels of communication of organized labor are improving, albeit slowly. An agreement reached with labor in Country X may become relevant to negotiations in Country Y. In some internationally oriented firms, a representative of the parent firm either sits in on all important negotiations or approves all important labor-mangement agreements. The critical factor here is the degree of management responsibility held in the local enterprise by the associated international firm. This feedback through international labor channels may be a valid reason for not assigning overall management responsibility to a foreign affiliate, but rather centralizing control over labor-management relations regionally or worldwide.

International Labor Organizations

It is important to realize that nationally based unions face many disadvantages when it comes to dealing with the larger firms operating internationally. Union officials must deal with management personnel subject to pressures or control from abroad. Employment is linked to some degree to the global performance of the firm, and different countries may compete with each other to attract employment. While some corporations effectively coordinate their resources and productive facilities, trade unions have not developed an effective internationally integrated structure. Some of the more aggressive Western unions have focused attention on this problem and have, over the past decade, started to play a more active role in those organizations designed to provide labor with an international forum; namely, the multinational union organizations, the International Trade Secretariats (ITS), and the International Labor Organization (ILO). The most active of the multinational union organizations has been the International Confederation of Free Trade Unions (the ICFTU, headquartered in Brussels), even though the U.S.-based AFL-CIO withdrew some years ago. Possibly of greater significance to corporate managers are the 20 or so ITSs, which are really international federations of national trade unions operating in the same or related industries. They cooperate with the ICFTU and each has its own liaison offices. The significance of the ITS from the point of view of management lies in the fact that behind local unions may lie the expertise and resources of an ITS.

The International Labor Organization, another international channel of labor communication and support, is a specialized agency of the United Nations. Essentially, it is involved in the collection and analysis of statistics concerning labor around the world and in the creation of international labor standards. It deals with such subjects as employment, international labor mobility, skill development, wages and hours, child welfare, social security, and safety standards. There are now about 150 ILO conventions embodying internationally endorsed standards for various working conditions. These conventions are not legally binding unless formally ratified by a government, but they may become relevant to local labor-management negotiations. Additionally, the ILO has issued a hundred or so recommendations. The conventions and recommendations are collectively known as the International Labor Code. At various times and places it may be quoted to managment.

Those who advocate more active international labor collaboration face a set of problems militating against the establishment of effective multinational union bargaining positions, such as union rivalries, the political orientation of some unions, structural variations, ideological differences, personality clashes among leaders, desire to maintain independence, lack of funds and staff support at the international level, lack of union discipline, lack of common contract termination dates, and the simple inertia against changing one's tactics. In addition, proponents confront problems that emanate from the much broader context of society as a whole; differences in the social, economic, and political environment within which the national unions must operate; the ideology and foreign policy orientation of host governments; national customs and laws; the need for full employment; and rising exports everywhere. And finally, the degree of unionization varies greatly from country to country. In the United States, union membership dropped from 28 percent of those employed outside of agriculture in 1970 to 23.6 percent in 1980. In many European countries, the percentage is 40 percent or higher, except for France, where it is 20 percent. (See Fig. 4.4.)

4.4   Basis for Recruitment and Job Assignment

Labor may be recruited on the basis of ability or social status. In many societies, quite apart from demonstrated ability, social status is very largely a complex function of family background and ties, wealth (however defined), sex, number of children, education, race, nationality, regional origin, politics, religion, and former military rank—to mention a few factors. Because of the vast complexity of this subject in view of the variety of social structures in which the firm may be operating, all one can do is to suggest some guidelines that emerge from accumulated experience.

Conforming with Local Traditions

In cultures where patterns of dominance-subordination are socially determined, and are not a function of demonstrated personal ability, management should be cautioned against promoting those of inferior social status to supervisory positions over those of higher social status (for instance, an ex-corporal over an ex-sergeant in societies where former military status is important). A breakdown in communication and morale may be the result.

Similarly, nepotism—in the sense of permitting supervisors and foremen to hire kinfolk, fellow tribesmen, or people from their own village—may result in maximum overall efficiency even though the individual worker may not measure up to other candidates for the job in terms of individual ability. In one's group, the insider may be more effective than the outsider with superior ability.

Discrimination in employment by sex may also have to conform to traditional practice to gain maximum efficiency. Innovation on this score by a foreign management in a highly traditional society may lead to a variety of difficulties. On the other hand, management should be aware of the fact that women make up a higher percentage of the labor force in some countries than in others. For example, in Sweden over 50 percent of the work force is female, and about 71 percent of the women belong to unions—far higher than the United States' female membership of 12 percent, Germany's 20 percent, or Austria's 44 percent. In Sweden, in part because of government policy, it is reported that 60 percent of all married women work. Sweden has been particularly effective in eliminating the dual pay system characteristic of many countries (the United States included), whereby women are paid less than men for the same jobs.[12] Theoretically, such practice is now illegal in the United States, but aggregate statistics indicate that nonconformance with the law is apparently widespread.

Racial, Ethnic, and Religious Minorities

In a multiracial or multiethnic society where social status is related to race or ethnic group by both law and prevailing national values, the firm must conform, withdraw from management responsibility, or somehow satisfy both the law and its own sense of equity. In setting policy, the firm should be sensitive to the effect of its behavior in such a society on attitudes toward the firm in other societies in which it operates. A relevant query is whether or not by restructuring itself legally and administratively, the firm can avoid hostility in these other societies. That is, can it insulate itself from being identified with the enterprise in the country that assigns status on the basis of race? Mining companies operating both in the Republic of South Africa and in areas north of "the line"—say in Zambia—have had to face up to this problem. Another relevant query is how long the status quo is likely to last. The conforming firm may find itself trapped by a racial or ethnic revolution. Total loss of assets may be expected unless the firm is supplying skills or external sales channels not available from other, more acceptable, sources. It should be noted that a firm's *home* government policy may be applied subtly to the firm's overseas operations, encouraging it to be less enthusiastic about observing local customs that are officially repugnant in the home country— as have many European and North American companies in South Africa.

In some situations where parent country law quite clearly prohibits discrimination on the basis of ethnic origin (as in the United States), a corporation may be caught in the middle. It may be prohibited from employing people of a specific ethnic origin abroad—as Jews in Saudi Arabia— yet still be subject to home-government law. The resolution is not clear.

The problem of the multiracial or multiethnic country manifests itself particularly in reference to promotion and pay. An equal-pay-for-equal-work policy may not be acceptable to the politically dominant but racially minor group, even though the policy's strict application would mean job

[12]See Ann H. Nelson, *The One World of Working Women* (Washington, D.C.: U.S. Department of Labor, 1978); and *Social Indicators III* (Washington, D.C.: U.S. Department of Commerce, 1980).

fragmentation and thus lower pay per worker for the racial majority. In societies in which the dominant value system permits advancement of members in a numerically superior racial or ethnic group, but which is opposed socially by a higher status minority element, management may choose to phase out the latter as regular employees. This situation once prevailed in the copper mines of Zambia (formerly Northern Rhodesia), where the white minority dominated, but advancement of native Africans was permitted by the white elite and opposed by the middle-class whites. The breakthrough can be accelerated in some cases by an attractive pension system, by offering scholarships to children of the group who seek education abroad (thereby encouraging their emigration), and by similar measures that reduce the resistance of the recalcitrant group—in the Zambian case, the skilled white worker. Meanwhile, an intensified training effort to upgrade members of a racial or ethnic majority may be instituted. Optimum strategy rests on a careful assessment of relative costs during the relevant time period, including the risk of loss of assets as the racial majority gains political control.

A related but different problem is the employment of members of an ethnic or racial minority group considered outcast by the larger society. These enclaves are often differentiated by religion—for example, at various times in history, the Christian Armenians and Greeks in Turkey, Hindu Indians in East Africa, Jews in the Arab states, Muslim Arabs in Israel, Chinese Buddhists in Southeast Asia, or English Protestants in French Canada. Because these groups may not be fully accepted by the surrounding traditional society of the majority, they sometimes turn to nontraditional ways of securing power and status, often by commercial enterprise.

In virtually all traditional societies, commercial enterprise other than the sale of one's own handcraft and farm produce has been scorned as something not really respectable. Trafficking in the products of others for financial profit was traditionally not considered a prestigious occupation, and it frequently ranks far below military, administrative, religious, professional, or agricultural careers. Thus, the way was cleared for outcast minorities to dominate commercial enterprise. Indeed, financial power has been one of the few devices available to them to prove their importance to the majority community. The danger for the foreign firm is that it may employ a disproportionate number of ethnic-religious minority members in key positions and may become identified with the outcast groups. There is considerable pressure on a firm to employ them, for they frequently have a higher level of commercial-industrial skills, are more cosmopolitan in outlook because they are less nationalistic, more knowledgeable of the outside world, more likely to speak foreign languages useful in business, and are more aggressive in behavior (a response to the frustrations of their outcast social position). Thus, there is often a short-run cost advantage to the firm in employing such individuals, as well as a greater ease of communication. But the insulation of management from the host society by a wall of ethnic and religious outcasts can, in the long run, be disastrous. Relevant variables are the importance to the firm of government relations, the importance of internal markets (those outside the cosmopolitan centers), the size of the labor force recruited from the majority community, and the degree of area expertise within the foreign management itself.

Employment of Local Nationals

The laws of almost all countries require the employment of local nationals if adequate numbers of skilled people are available. Specific exceptions are granted (officially or unofficially) for contrary cases, as for Mexican farm workers in the United States, and for the influx of Italian, Spanish, Greek, and Turkish workers into Germany and the Benelux countries. Puerto Rican emigrants in New York City, Jewish emigrants of different national origins in Israel, Algerians in France, and the movement into the United Kingdom of West Indians, Hindus, and Pakistanis from the Commonwealth countries are special cases. In addition to these streams, substantial numbers of North Africans, Black Africans, Asians, and even Latin Americans have begun showing up in the European labor market.

As in many countries, the United States requires that all aliens intending to establish permanent residence enter with immigration visas, a prerequisite for which is a work certificate. Persons with professional training and other needed skills are given priority, as are persons with relatives living within the country. Work certification, which in the United States is granted by the Department of Labor, is given only if there are no qualified U.S. nationals available and willing to perform the work or if the foreigner's entry will not hurt the U.S. labor market. As an example, the United States limits the import of farm workers from Mexico (very largely without effect!) because this alien labor is seen as responsible for depressing U.S. wages and displacing U.S. labor. Generally, an immigration visa is not granted unless work certification has been given. At the request of a U.S. employer, temporary personnel may enter on a limited visa, although such visas are subject to renewal. There is conflict here in that some Treaties of Friendship, Commerce, and Navigation guarantee citizens of the signatory countries the right to establish business enterprises in the territory of the other and to employ their own professional personnel. In the United States, a foreign firm's right to discriminate in hiring and promoting in favor of its own nationals has been the subject of legal conflict in U.S. courts. It would appear the answer is that it may not.

The European Community countries are required by treaty to permit free movement of labor among themselves, although they may require work permits for nationals of non-Community countries, and in some cases, residence permits as well. A few countries have imposed special restrictions, such as those of Australia against Orientals (ended in 1973) and the Philippines against the Chinese. The less developed countries generally have stricter entrance procedures; in most cases enterprises are required to employ a certain percent of local nationals, and work permits are given only to foreign technical and managerial personnel when qualified nationals are not available. The legal requirement for the employment of local nationals ranges up to 100 percent after a stipulated time, which implies a transfer of skills via training. In some countries, employment is further limited by rather ambiguous definitions of who is a "qualified" national. In Indonesia and Malaysia, for instance, it is not clear how one defines a *prigumi* ("indigenous" Indonesian) or a *bumiputra* ("indigenous" Malay), in contrast to the ethnic Chinese. What of those of mixed blood?

It should be noted that of all the industrial countries, Japan has exhibited perhaps the greatest reluctance to admit foreign labor other than technicians and managers, despite the extreme tightness of the domestic labor market (roughly 3 percent unemployment as this book goes to press). There is reported to be real fear of the tensions and social problems that might arise if many foreign workers joined the Japanese labor force. Social discrimination and prejudice is an effective bar.

In the past, some of the more developed countries could meet their unskilled labor demands from the flow of people off the land. The Soviet Union is apparently still able to do so to some extent. Japan, on the other hand, has exhausted its supply of unskilled workers and has reluctantly admitted some Koreans, thereby releasing Japanese workers for more skilled, more pleasant, and more highly paid jobs. In the United States, it is the Hispanic-Americans who move to the bottom of the labor ladder, particularly the several million illegal aliens who have no legal recourse to force payment of even the legal minimum wage. European Community countries rely heavily on foreign workers to take less pleasant jobs. It would seem that a type of second-class citizen is developing in virtually all of the industrialized countries. Currently, only some of the more affluent and scarcely populated of the nonindustrial countries—such as Saudi Arabia—import large numbers of foreign labor.

Employment of nonnationals in a foreign enterprise, whether Greeks and Turks in West Germany or Mexicans and Puerto Ricans in the United States, may involve lower direct labor cost, but the indirect costs may be substantial, depending upon the responsibility assumed by public authorities for language training, vocational training, health services, community services, recruitment, and transportation to and from the workers' native countries. In any event, the firm incurs the costs of interpreters, translation of relevant documents, increased annual leave, transportation home in case of incompetency and/or ill health, and double holidays (local and foreign). Western European companies employing "guest workers" report that the following policies help lower indirect costs:

1. Accurate information on working conditions prior to the worker's departure from home (concerning hours, pay, nature of work, living conditions, social welfare, and pension benefits).
2. An understanding with the local unions about the position of foreign workers.
3. Reception of foreign workers by someone who speaks their language and is familiar with their culture.
4. Provision of adequate housing and community services at reasonable cost to the workers, national groups being housed together.

5. Employment of interpreters of the same nationalities as workers.
6. An initial guided tour of the plant with constant deemphasis of the complexities involved.
7. On-the-job training under foremen and skilled workers who do not look down on the foreign worker.
8. Initial assignment to work teams of mixed nationality, rather than to a team of single nationality.
9. Avoiding the use of **piece rates** as the standard for deciding norms for workers on hourly rates. (In order to achieve high levels of pay while abroad, foreign workers may produce at levels significantly higher than local nationals. They can do so because of their relatively short time horizon—often two years or less—while local nationals cannot produce at a comparable rate for an unlimited time without risk of damage to health. This problem has reportedly caused tensions in West Germany.)
10. Encouragement of foreign workers to participate in a local language course.
11. Maintenance of a balance between policies that appear to result in exploitation of the foreign worker and those seen by local nationals as giving preferential treatment to the foreign worker.
12. Establishment of a direct channel of communication between representatives of foreign labor groups and management.

4.5   Training and Development

Inherently, part of the recruitment problem is finding people who are adequately skilled to do the job demanded. The alternative is training internal to the firm, whether on the job or in school. Employment of those trained outside the firm is undoubtedly easier, particularly for the nonnational management, but not necessarily the least in cost to society in general. In-plant training can be focused on a specific task rather than employing the more generalized array of skills one trained externally is generally required to master, and for which demand, and cost, will be greater. A job may be broken down into relatively simple operations, with a skilled troubleshooter taking over whenever a problem develops. The worker with specialized skill has fewer opportunities for alternative employment. Also, literacy may not be required, but in hiring an externally trained worker the firm pays for literacy.

The general experience of firms operating in various parts of the world is that people who are relatively unsophisticated in a technological sense can learn adequate industrial skills with surprising ease. Difficulties may arise when the skill is related to an innovation associated with a deeply embedded traditional practice or device, such as putting lee boards on a native sailing craft or introducing an improved camel saddle in Arabia. The difficulty is much diminished when a completely new device is employed. Local military training of a technical nature may offer clues about the training methods most effective within the local culture, and also clues about motivation.

Motivation is of obvious importance in the training and development context, as is remuneration. Motivation may run the gamut from fear of inability to satisfy biological, social, or psychological determined needs (such as self-actualization), through habit (internalized values), to the lure of social gain (essentially nonfinancial). Social gain may be sought either for some definable group or identity such as family, community, region, nation, humankind, or for oneself vis-à-vis others, or for the promise of tangible financial or status gain for oneself or a group. Promising a worker a "clean" job may provide greater motivation than a promise of higher pay, if a clean job is important to one's social status, which is of course always a relative measure. Promise of promotion to a position in which one may engage in family or tribal nepotism may be of signal importance to the individual if collectivist values have high priority. Some people are highly motivated by the opportunity to achieve seniority or some other position in which they enjoy greater freedom or opportunity for self-actualization, such as longer vacation, financially secure retirement after a relatively short time, flexible work hours, and less authoritarian supervision.

Still common among larger Japanese companies is the seniority pay system (nenko seido). The wide variety of fringe benefits in Japan is part of this system, which guarantees minimum lifetime needs rather than linking pay and benefit directly in the short run with productivity, innovation, and responsibility. In Japan, wage increases for those in the same seniority group tend to move together with but slight variation for 20 years or so after entry. Japanese zeal is startling to the uninitiated. It may be that one's most direct reward for industry and creativity lies in the building up of esteem—and influence—within the relatively stable group within which one works. Lifetime employment and pay by seniority may work in the Japanese context because of their interaction and because of the existence of at least a third characteristic, consensus decision making, which differentiates the Japanese system from a truly paternalistic one. Alien management should realize that the whole system is highly integrated, and that one tinkers with pieces of it only with great care. That is, the decision-making system may operate well only if jobs are not threatened and direct interpersonal competition is avoided in the short and medium run, which are also conditions conducive to relatively open communications.

One of the essential pieces may be the Japanese tendency to hire unspecialized university graduates, start them in menial jobs on the factory floor or elsewhere, rotate them through several departments and functions, and eventually move them into management. (MBAs are almost never employed at entry level; there is only one officially recognized MBA program in all of Japan, and that one is quite new and very small.) Managerial salaries are a significantly lower multiple of blue-collar wages than is typically the case in North America or Western Europe. Even the company president may receive only seven or eight times the salary of an entry-level factory worker. Virtually all Japanese managers have spent time at lower levels in their own companies and have been active in the company or plant union. The result? There is less of the "we and they" attitude characteristic of industrial relations in the United States and Europe.

A great deal has been written about what motivates people to work productively and to improve and expand their capabilities. There is substantial reason to believe that no single strategy generates the highest levels of motivation under all circumstances. It is quite clear that in a highly traditional, relatively poor, socially stratified society, people are likely to respond to somewhat different strategies than those in a more modern, affluent, open society. For example, a study of workers' attitudes in Peru some years ago concluded that "in a highly distrustful society marked by authoritarianism, certain participation forms which involve man-to-group relationships will probably not be successful when they are initiated."[13] In short, one cannot generalize the validity of the more authoritarian Theory X of management or that of the more liberal Theory Y in terms of either human satisfaction, productivity, or creativity.

4.6   Pay Scales and Other Benefits

Closely related to the problems of training and development, and of identifying motivational priorities, are those associated with selecting the appropriate strategy in regard to pay and benefit standards for local labor. A number of options are open to the firm if law does not foreclose them. It may pay in cash or in noncash benefits. It may pay currently or defer payment of part of the remuneration. It may pay a fixed wage or incentive payments. Incentives may be personal (for individual piece work), based on group performance, or linked to enterprise results (profit sharing). National law and custom, of course, impact heavily on the choice.

Quite apart from these strategy options is the question, should management apply an international policy of equal pay for equal work? Should it pay the going local rates, something less than the local rates, or something above those rates? The last seems to be the most common practice for foreign-owned firms. In this calculation, of course, total labor cost should not be equated with direct labor cost, for the rate of direct to total labor cost may vary widely from one country to another, even from one region to another and from one ethnic group to another.

A firm's best strategy would probably be a function of (1) local law and government policy, (2) pay level required to recruit and *hold* competent workers, (3) union pressures, (4) vulnerability of the firm to charges of exploitation, (5) levels established by the firm in adjacent or similar countries, (6) political and economic significance of local business hostility

---

[13]Lawrence K. Williams, William F. Whyte, and Charles S. Green, "Do Cultural Differences Affect Workers' Attitudes?" *Industrial Relations*, Vol. 5, No. 3 (May 1966), p. 116.

directed toward a foreign firm not conforming to local pay scales, and (7) need for encouraging greater productivity and initiative than found in traditional local enterprises.

In order to minimize local criticism if the foreign firm opts to pay at a somewhat higher level than prevailing local standards, a larger share of the total labor bill may be dispensed through indirect compensation. For example, special training courses for upgrading technical expertise, employee scholarships, more liberal health insurance or retirement benefits than those required, interest-free loans to employees, educational benefits for employees' children, various free or low-cost benefits such as meals and work clothing, and special bonuses may be offered. This device may be particularly effective if the local labor union can claim at least some of the credit for winning these benefits. Immobilized earnings may, however, encourage nepotism, theft, and compacted living if the extended family system is operating. Cash can be divided up and distributed over space; many benefits cannot. The ratio of fringe benefits to total remuneration varies widely even within Europe. Likewise, note that the relationship between legally required and voluntary benefits varies widely among countries. In Japan, statutory benefits are relatively low. For example, although the Japanese government pays unemployment insurance to the jobless, the lifetime employment system makes this type of public assistance less important than in many other countries. The private sector is responsible for much social welfare, although this may be changing as the population ages.

As labor negotiations take on an international color, company negotiators may be faced with demands for a uniform package consisting of the relatively high cash wages of one country and the relatively high fringe benefits of another. Within the EEC, however, social welfare legislation of the member states has been converging, and wage differentials narrowing. There is also evidence that unit labor cost in U.S. and Japanese manufacturing is now converging with the European. Although difficult to quantify exactly because of national differences in payroll taxes paid by employee and employer, differing social welfare systems and lifetime earnings patterns, plus the vagaries of floating exchange rates, it appears that labor cost per unit of output in Germany, Sweden, and Belgium may actually have moved ahead of those in the United States. It should be noted that as rates of inflation persist at high levels, labor can be expected to assert pressure for the indexing of wages as in Brazil and, since 1975, in Australia.

Piece Rates

The piece rate is used widely, particularly for unskilled or semi-skilled labor. But there are several dangers inherent in the system. One, already noted, is that the norms should not be set on the basis of temporary foreign labor performance; they may be unduly high. Max Weber made an observation some years ago that speaks to the recent experience in Western Europe: **The simple fact [that] a change of residence is among the most effective means of intensifying labor is throughly established. The same Polish girl** who at home was not to be shaken loose from her traditional laziness by any chance of earning money, however tempted, seems to change her entire nature and become capable of unlimited accomplishments when she is a migratory worker in a foreign country. The same is true of migratory Italian laborers. That this is by no means entirely explicable in terms of educative influence of the entrance into a higher cultural environment . . . is shown by the fact that the same thing happens where the type of occupation, as in agricultural labor, is exactly the same at home. Furthermore, accomodations in labor barracks, etc. may involve a degradation to a standard of living which would never be tolerated at home.[14]

The real danger, of course, lies in angering domestic labor if the norms for piece rates are set high because of the short-term, unduly intense effort on the part of foreign labor. In some situations, management may wish to introduce job rates, that is, assign a task upon the completion of which the worker is free to leave. The competition is then in terms of time, not remuneration. In line with the drive for increased dignity of the individual on the shop floor, some firms have discontinued both piece rates and hourly rates by placing all employees on a monthly salary, subject periodically to merit bonuses. IBM pioneered this innovation in 1958 and currently claims to have few hourly employees anyplace in the world.

Annual Bonuses and Profit Sharing

In Italy, Japan, and certain other countries it is customary to add semiannual or annual lump-sum payments equal to one or two month's pay. Such payments should not be considered as profit sharing but as an integral part of the basic pay package. These bonuses are apparently preferred by employees as a sort of forced savings plan. In Japan, these payments may contribute substantially to maintaining the relatively high level of personal savings, so that the gap between income and consumption is sustained even though both increase rapidly. Some have observed that this is an essential part in the engine of Japanese economic growth. If Japanese authorities indeed have this perception, a foreign firm not paying the annual bonus might incur official displeasure.

Some companies have attempted some kind of **profit sharing** among their local employees overseas in order to create a greater area of common interest between management and labor. This scheme is appealing only if the enterprise is a profit center and the labor force is relatively stable. In any event, the time lapse between labor input and payments under many profit-sharing schemes is such as to reduce their effectiveness. Also, given the frequent lack of financial and accounting sophistication on the part of local labor, any payment is likely to be taken as due the beneficiaries regardless of the year's profit record. Any reduction may cause serious friction.

[14]Max Weber, *The Protestant Ethic and the Spirit of Capitalism* (New York: Charles Scribner's Sons, 1958), p. 19.

Nonetheless, it has become quite clear that there is a worldwide push in the direction of some form of profit sharing, ownership sharing, and participative management. Initially, both labor and management almost invariably oppose such schemes; it is the political sector that forces the issue in the interest of industrial harmony, increased productivity, and overall economic growth. Constant wrangling between labor and management over how a very slowly growing pie of economic goods is going to be served up becomes politically intolerable sooner or later. In Catholic countries, the notion of sharing has, of course, been encouraged by papal encyclicals to the effect that workers should share in the profits of the enterprises in which they are employed and become part owners. In practice, some socialist-communist countries such as Yugoslavia, Poland, Hungary, and, most recently, the People's Republic of China, have been trying to institute both profit sharing and management participation (with greater or lesser success, depending upon the basis used for judgment). Profit sharing is legally required for certain categories of industry in Mexico, Peru, Pakistan, India, Egypt, and formally Iran among the LDCs, and in France among the more developed countries. It may be legally encouraged in others (as in the United States, where delayed distribution of profits to employees is considered a cost for tax purposes, not a dividend), and is characteristic of the Scandinavian cooperative movement. The innovation of the Employee Stock Ownership Plan in the United States permits a firm to loan pretax funds to employees with which to buy the firm's stock.

In socialist enterprises of the Yugoslavian type, of course, all enterprise earnings (gross income less cost of materials and services bought, sales expenses, capital charges, and other legal and contractual obligations) are divided into four funds by decision of the workers' council (but satisfying certain legal minimums): the investment fund (depreciation of fixed assets, expansion), the social fund (for community and social welfare), the wage fund, and the business fund (the residual, equivalent to the nonsocialist notion of profit). The objective of the workers' council is to maximize the wage fund over a certain time horizon. It is reported that as the system has matured, workers' representatives have expanded their time horizons and see more clearly the relationship between foregone present income, investment, and larger income in the future.

Obviously, firms operating internationally encounter great difficulty when faced with national profit-sharing schemes. Tax, accounting, and control problems are compounded.

Bases for Determination and Allocation of Profit

It has been observed that labor-management relations can be of four basic models: (1) competition (collective bargaining from power positions), (2) arbitration, (3) sharing (based on a preproduction agreement to a formula for dividing profits generated by increases in productivity, however profits may be defined), and (4) cooperation (presupposes a convergence of rules and goals, since workers become owners and managers are merely specially trained workers). The first two types rest on a power relationship; in the short run, neither party need be fundamentally interested in increasing productivity. The latter two relationships, theoretically, are based on mutual interest in increasing productivity and sharing the product in such a way as to generate increased productivity. Where sharing and cooperation are the rule, collective bargaining makes no sense, nor do labor unions as economic forces.

In fact, significant problems remain in respect to determining the basis for dividing profit. First, who is going to participate? All employees or only those with certain seniority and/or rank and/or function? Second, what is the formula for sharing between employees (labor and management) and capital? A 50–50 split on the grounds that both factors are essential? (It is hard to support equal sharing in very labor intensive or very capital intensive plants.) Simply giving enough to employees to generate sufficient convergence of goals to minimize work stoppages, slowdowns, absenteeism, and idleness? (3) Finally, who makes the sharing decision? The board of directors? Management? A joint labor-management committee? Parliament? The executive branch of government?

If one assumes a significantly different level of income, education, and general sophistication between managers and labor, the marginal utility of additional income will differ between the two groups, as will time horizons. One would anticipate a tendency on the part of labor to demand that virtually all profit be paid out in current wage, and that reinvestment be kept to a bare minimum. In a situation where there is no obvious objective function to maximize, these differences will very likely be resolved through competition or bargaining based on relative power positions, or through arbitration by a political entity, which means that we have merely shifted the locale of the competition to the political sector. The political sector may specify a formula in law or authorize the executive branch to do so. Whoever has the greater political muscle will win the larger share. It follows that unions and employers' associations will tend to be highly politicized in such situations.[15]

Despite these conceptual difficulties, the international manager must relate effectively with a growing number and variety of national systems. These systems include simple profit-sharing (in the form of cash or deferred wages),[16] profit-sharing with or without ownership sharing, and either profit or ownership sharing with or without some form of participative mangement by labor.

In judging how well a system is working, there may be several significant signals to monitor. Among these: *trends* in the percentage of retained earnings, in the tenure of managers, in managerial wages as a ratio to

[15]In Yugoslavia, it appears that the minimum level of reinvestment, specified by regulation, is generally defined as that amount necessary to maintain the fixed assets and working capital of the enterprise. Some observers of the Yugoslavian system, which has been operating for over 25 years, seem to agree that in many enterprises the workers tend to be passive participants in the profit-sharing decision, which is dominated by management.

[16]Or possibly a shared savings plan in the case of a nonprofit organization or governmental department.

various categories of labor, in the work-years lost due to stoppages arising out of labor-management conflict and absenteeism, and *changes* in the role of unions. Curiously, there seems to have been very little hard research on the effectiveness in these terms of the various profit-sharing and ownership-sharing schemes around the world. It should be noted that the promise of mere economic award may not be very effective in certain economic and sociopsychological environments, as discussed earlier.

It seems quite clear from the foregoing discussion that it is unlikely that the best policy for labor relations is to apply the same strategies worldwide in respect to the scope of management responsibility, employee participation in management, local unions, recruitment and job assignment, training and promotion, and pay scales and other benefits. Implicit in this generalization is sensitivity on the part of headquarters management to the special conditions prevailing in various parts of the world and an information system adequate to monitor significant changes. For the firm operating internationally, local autonomy in choosing labor strategy is not wholly adequate because of the growing linkages among national trade unions and the increasing international flow of information relating to working conditions to which employees have access.

CHAPTER **5**

MANAGERIAL STRATEGY

area expertise specialized knowledge of a particular country or area in respect to its culture, economics, and politics.

cultural cluster a grouping of nations perceived as culturally similar along some set of dimensions (for example language, ethnic origin, belief system religion, level of development, or degree of industrialization), which leads to similarities in managerial style.

cultural distance the difference of one community or nation from another in terms of language, values, and institutions.

culture shock the disorientation and distress caused by the removal of familiar clues that give meaning to behavior, values, perceptions, and institutions.

human resources a nation's reservoir of human skills.

international base salary in corporate remuneration, a common scale of pay for all personnel regardless of nationality, with a variety of extras to compensate for specific costs incurred by employment overseas.

multiple pay scales salary structures that remunerate parent-country personnel at a rate comparable to their home pay and all other personnel at the relevant local rate.

national a citizen of a particular country.

Where a firm is establishing or running a business overseas, employees from the nation where the firm is domiciled are *parent-country* or **headquarter nationals**; employees from the nation where the new business is located are *local* or *host-country nationals*; employees drawn from elsewhere are *third-country nationals*. The term nonnational includes both parent-country nationals and third-country nationals. Both may also be called expatriates.

nationalize management the process of turning management of an enterprise over to local nationals.

off-shore income income that for tax purposes is not reported in the country where it was earned. Sometimes called split income in that only part is paid locally.

silent language the signals communicated by means other than words, such as spatial relationships, timing, movements, and sequences.

universalists those who believe that all managers share certain values and behavior regardless of their cultural milieu.

vertical consistency the degree to which managers at all levels within an organization use similar styles of decision making.

It is increasingly difficult to differentiate between management and non-management, labor if you will. As production becomes more and more technologically complex, no manager can possibly be expert in everything. Technological complexity forces decisions "downward," often to the level of the individual actually doing production work, whether on the factory floor or at an office desk. Continuity of decision making thus emerges, and there is a real question as to where labor ends and management begins.

Perhaps too frequently in some societies, "managers" are perceived as somehow more valuable, a cut above, and socially set apart from "nonmanagers." Managers are not infrequently paid 15, 20, or 50 times what a production worker receives. They are often socially segregated in closed offices, special dining rooms, executive washrooms, reserved parking, and distinct dress. Apprenticeship on the factory floor or at a clerk's desk may not be part of managers' preparation in the West. They frequently arrive with an MBA and are given a managerial function at the start, regardless of their production-level experience. Continuing communication and flow of advice is not seen as essential from nonmanager to manager, only the reverse. "What can *they* tell *me* about my job?" an executive commented to me recently. *They* were the nonmanagerial help in his office.

In some cases, however, that distanced relationship may be desirable. The most effective relationship between management and labor could be culturally determined to be the authoritarian mode.

The only generalization possible is that corporate strategies relating to **human resources** should be in harmony with the values, attitudes, and practices of the surrounding society. When that society lacks cultural homogeneity—as, for example, the United States—problems multiply. One has relatively few clear societal guidelines.

Conceptually it is difficult to separate strategy decisions in the labor and management areas; they impact heavily on one another, and should be seen as a continuum. However, we focus here specifically on those individuals perceived as occupying themselves largely with managerial functions—that is, decision making, supervising, directing, and controlling.

Given the communications and control problems involved, the selection, preparation, promotion, and remuneration of *international* managerial personnel become matters of signal importance; so likewise the selection of managerial style. Circumstances often compel overseas managers to operate more autonomously than their domestic counterparts, as expert staff assistance is not always immediately available. Their principal function in the long run may be to train rather than manage per se. At the same time they are part of an international communications system.

Despite so-called instantaneous communications, international communication is, in fact, often far from instantaneous, and frequently less than communication in the true sense of the word. In a single national setting, two parties need not make many relevant variables explicit; they are within the compass of the experience of both parties and are implicitly given similar values by both. Hence, their words are understood within a similar context. Not so for an international setting; much more must be made explicit, even the meaning of everyday words. In some societies the context impacts the meaning of words more heavily than in others. Anthropologists call these high context cultures. The Chinese and Japanese are examples.

To communicate by writing is time-consuming and tedious. Yet oral communication may lead to gross misunderstandings. The mind wanders for a moment; the thread is broken. A word is not understood; too late, the conversation goes on. A nuance is lost; a tone of voice, misinterpreted; puzzlement in a person's eyes, not seen. The probability of such events is multiplied if the conversation is over radio or wire. It is not happenstance that speaking in a foreign language on the telephone is more difficult than in face-to-face conversation.

An overseas manager occupies several roles: (1) representative of the parent firm, (2) manager of the local firm, (3) resident of the local community, (4) citizen of either the host state or of another, (5) member of a profession, not to mention (6) member of a family and all that implies. To the extent that these roles conflict, communication tends to be blocked. For example, if expectations created by the manager role cannot be realized due to the restraints imposed by the representative role, the individual is in a position of role conflict. The resident and citizen roles are similarly likely to conflict. Unless the parent management is sufficiently sensitive to these possible conflicts, the overseas manager's behavior may be inexplicable, and communications may become blocked or at least noisy.

Imagine that you are an executive of a U.S. firm sent to India for an extended period of time as financial manager of an Indian subsidiary. Over time you find yourself identifying emotionally with India and growing impatient with the financial restraint placed on the subsidiary by the U.S. parent. More rapid growth, which requires greater parent company financial commitment, is required if the enterprise is to live up to Indian expectations, which you see as an increasingly important objective in the broad context of supporting the more liberal approach to rapid national development. You make vigorous representation to the parent on behalf of the subsidiary, not necessarily on purely financial grounds; this becomes known in India and improves your status as one who understands the Indians' problems. But because your efforts produce no apparent increase in the parent company's commitment, you lose some authority within the Indian subsidiary itself. And your colleagues back home, knowing far less about India and identifying very little with its problems, refer to you as "unrealistic" and "soft." In addition, you yourself may realize that you are getting out of touch with domestic developments in your profession, as well as losing the contacts with professional colleagues that you kept up by attending periodic conferences and seminars. You begin to feel uncomfortable. So does your family, some of whom are perhaps reaching high school age. Even though the Indian subsidiary may be in critical need of your services, you may now engage in a homeward-bound strategy. You make decisions and recommendations for reasons other than the immediate financial profit of the corporation. Perhaps you should; that is not the issue. The point is that unless the parent company management is aware of the pressures and needs to which your various roles expose you, it may not be in a position to read your communications from India correctly.

If the firm substitutes a qualified local **national** in a case like this, it resolves some of these conflicts but intensifies others. For example, what if the financial manager were Indian, and the parent company had no process whereby nationals other than those of the parent company were considered for assignment to world corporate headquarters? If the Indian were ambitious and wished to develop international status in the field of financial management, he or she would either seek to increase autonomy for the Indian firm, or, failing that, leave the employ of the firm entirely. Whatever the action, it is likely that headquarters management will misunderstand the motivations.

The critical importance of overseas managerial selection is heightened by the greater difficulty in assessing performance and in finding replacements than in a purely domestic situation. Performance measurement is rendered difficult by the use of different technology, differential inflation and foreign exchange rate moves, time delays in reporting, and the external restraints embedded in intercompany relationships (such as pricing and financial decisions) over which local management has little control. Internal profit-and-loss accounting is thus unlikely to provide an adequate basis for judging managerial effectiveness. The replacement problem is often aggravated by personal difficulties involved in international moves and by the severe shortage of management skills in many parts of the world.

5.1   Selection of Overseas Management

Two decisions are involved in the selection of overseas management: choice of prerequisites and validation of those prerequisites. Let us consider the first.

Prerequisites of Nationality

If **cultural distance** (measured by difference in language, values, and institutions) is perceived as significant, the parent corporation may prefer to install its own people abroad. On the other hand, if the cultural distance is so great that its own nationals feel uncomfortable and unable to work effectively in the foreign environment, the nod may go to local nationals or third-country nationals. In either case, the problems of cross-cultural communications may be considerable.

Apparent national differences on this score may arise out of the fact that firms based in certain countries tend to be less evolved, or mature, internationally than those based elsewhere. There is evidence that the employment pattern varies with the stage of a firm's internationalization (Figure 5.1). Note that during the stage of initial foreign manufacture, the percentage of host country nationals is relatively low, possibly because the initial venture is in a culturally close country (for a U.S. firm, in Canada or England), and, in any event, the demand for managers overseas is small. As the period of foreign growth sets in, host-country nationals dominate; headquarters cannot supply enough managers. Subsequently, as the parent corporation gains experience and pressure for integrating overseas production mounts, the percentage of headquarter nationals employed overseas rises steeply, ostensibly to facilitate centralized control, and then drops off slowly as nationality loses its importance.

Two reasons are generally given for the employment of local national managers; lower cost and more intimate knowledge of the environment. A third possible explanation is the difficulty a **nonnational** may face in assuming either the highly paternalistic role vis-à-vis employees expected of him in a traditional society or the egalitarian or subordinate role required in some of the more collectivist societies.

Two obvious disadvantages to the employment of local nationals as managers are nontransferability (hence, local management may become frustrated, inbred, and nationalistic) and poor communications (unless there is someone in the parent firm sufficiently familiar with the local environment to be able to interpret signals to the rest of management). An alternative is the use of a third-country national, which implies assignment without regard to nationality, unless relating directly to managerial effectiveness. In some cases, of course, the denial of entry visas or work permits by a host government may require the firm to nationalize management over a specified period of time. In still other cases, it may be exceedingly difficult to use expatriate managers effectively because of cultural distance. Japan and China are both cases in point. In a number of LDCs, the development of local management may be legally required by the host government as a condition of entry. If some circulation of foreign national managers through assignments at corporate headquarters is anticipated, legal restraints imposed by the *parent* country can become important, such as visas and work permits.

Rules controlling entry for managers are sometimes modified reciprocally on the basis of a bilateral commerce, friendship, or navigation treaty or

Figure 5.1
Stage of Internationalization and Nationality
of Foreign Subsidiary Chief Executives:

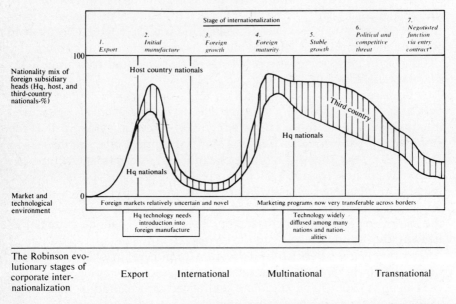

The Robinson evolutionary stages of corporate internationalization

| Export | International | Multinational | Transnational |

U.S. companies with low foreign product diversification
*Which may be explicit or implicit.

Source: Adapted from Lawrence G. Franko, "Who Manages Multinational Enterprises?" *Columbia Journal of World Business,* Summer 1973, p. 33. Franko's version did not include stage seven or use the Robinson classification system. For definitions of the latter, see Chapter Nine.

special convention. An example is the French-U.S. Convention of Establishment, which specifies that those French or U.S. nationals qualifying as "treaty traders" or "treaty investors" will be given permission to reside, to work in a salaried position, and to carry on a business in the other country. Qualifications consist principally of establishing nationality, a history free of bankruptcy, and creditworthiness.

Expatriate, Local, or Third-Country National?

The key question is what variables are relevant in determining the optimum strategy choice between employment of parent-country nationals, local nationals, or third-country nationals.

The use of parent-country nationals in key managerial roles may be justified in the following situations:

1.   The foreign enterprise is just being established (start-up phase).
2.   The parent firm wishes to develop an internationally oriented management for the headquarters (foreign assignments are seen essentially as management development).

3.   No adequate management is available from other sources.
4.   The parent firm has surplus managerial personnel toward which it feels responsible. (This reason, if relevant, should be examined with care if it implies pushing the least capable managers abroad.)
5.   The parent firm has no one sufficiently familiar with the foreign government to interpret communications from a nonparent country management, and therefore needs to develop area expertise.
6.   Virtually no autonomy is possible for the foreign enterprise because it is integrated so closely with operations elsewhere.
7.   Top management carries high-level technical knowledge and skill of a nature that cannot be protected legally (in a research-oriented service firm).
8.   The foreign enterprise is seen as short-lived.
9.* The host society is multiracial or multireligious, and a local manager belonging to one of the conflicting races or religions will make the enterprise politically vulnerable or lead to an economic boycott.
10. There is a compelling need for the firm to maintain a foreign image.
11. The parent firm will be serving largely other firms of the same nationality operating abroad, most of which are directed by parent-country nationals.
12.* It is felt desirable to avoid involving particular local nationals or families (former distributors or agents) in management, and the use of other local nationals would create dangerous animosities. (For example, U.S. executives are reported to be in demand in Europe to manage multicountry operations involving the supervision of managers of different European nationalities.)
13.* Local nationals are not mobile and resist foreign assignment.
14.* A parent-country national is simply the best person for the job, all things considered.
15.* Control is weak (see Section 9.6), and local nationals are highly nationalistic (patriotic) and more responsive to government appeals than an expatriate would be (but an expatriate may be less able to influence the government).

Several of these conditions are not persuasive in the long run, such as condition 1. In regard to condition 2, there is no reason for parent-country nationals to occupy the *top* roles.

Condition 3 may be limited in time; local nationals may be trainable. Unfamiliarity with individual foreign nationals may be a valid reason to send in known nationals for a period of time, though not indefinitely. After all, "adequacy" is in part a function of a perception of one's superiors; that is, personal confidence. For an individual not known intimately on a personal basis over a significant period of time, personal confidence is hard to come by. One way to build up adequate managerial skills in foreign nation-

*These items also show possible justification for employment of third-country nationals.

als is through extended assignment to corporate headquarters. Condition 4 is also a limited phenomenon; management can be sloughed off. Condition 5 will change over time as the parent-country nationals are rotated home. Condition 6 could be argued. Why should parent-country nationals perform more adequately than local managers in this situation? In either case, the manager's role should be carefully defined to avoid conflict of roles.

Condition 7 begs a question: Why should parent-country nationals be more trustworthy in this regard? In fact, given their greater ease in securing jobs with domestic (parent-country) competitors, the risk of loss of such knowledge and skill may be greater in the case of parent-country nationals. It might be argued, however, that the transfer of skills and know-how decreases a firm's external leverage against possible nationalization. Conditions 8 through 14 clearly seem to demand parent-country nationals under some circumstances. In the case of condition 15, the situation calls for a careful analysis of the source of weakness and the costs and benefits of enforcing greater control. What control is required and why is a parent-country national better able to control? Is this ability based simply on familiarity with both the local scene and the parent company? Very likely, in which case the key element here is a person who communicates effectively in both directions, as indicated in Figure 5.2.

Perhaps the alternatives shown in Figure 5.2 should really be thought of as representing a continuum over time as individual communication abilities develop—from channel one to channel two, to channel three, to channel four, to channel five. By the term "U.S.-trained Mexican manager," I mean a Mexican national who is able to communicate effectively with a U.S. management with no particular expertise in understanding Mexico or Mexicans. Channel five is characteristic of the multinational or transnational corporation, which has a cadre of international managers of different nationalities who can communicate effectively in all directions.

Because of the competition for such individuals, many firms may find it virtually impossible to move beyond channel three, which can be a perfectly adequate system of communications. The trouble is that the need for a person at headquarters who is knowledgeable of things Mexican is often overlooked. Words flow, and management is led to believe that it is communicating effectively with its Mexican management, when in fact it is not.

The danger is that the firm will opt for a policy of using parent-country nationals in foreign management positions by default, that is, simply as an automatic extension of domestic policy, rather than deliberately seeking the best utilization of management skills.

For a parent firm inexperienced abroad, the selection of foreign nationals, whether of the host or a third country, may be difficult. A variety of approaches are open: (1) recruitment from among foreign students or foreign alumni of domestic schools of engineering, business, and management; (2) recruitment from among students and alumni of recognized management development schools abroad, the number of which is growing rapidly (except in Japan); (3) application to the files of such organizations as

Figure 5.2
Alternative Channels of Communication between a U.S.
Firm and an Associated Mexican Enterprise

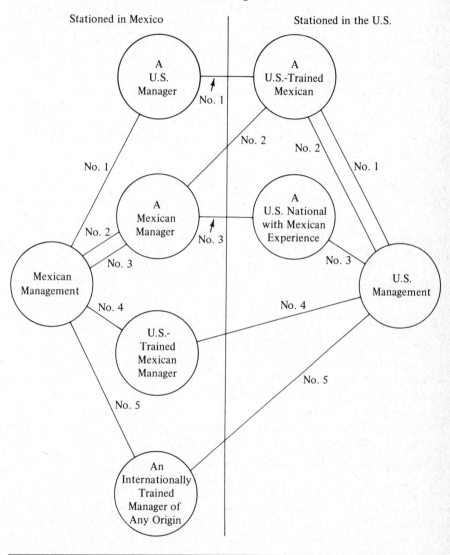

the Institute of International Education in New York City; (4) development of a company-sponsored management training program for foreign nationals; (5) reference to a home-country employment registry of foreign students, which in the United States is located at Tulane University; (6) utilization of one or more management recruitment organizations operating in the countries of interest.

An increase in management mobility has been noted in Western Europe, less so in Japan. There is a bothersome restriction in France and

Germany; nonstate employment agencies are prohibited legally from soliciting or maintaining files of either job seekers or companies in the market for personnel. Management consulting firms, however, are apparently not prohibited from giving advice in this area. In Japan, a foreign firm is normally forced either to compete for university graduates, or to pirate managers from Japanese companies. The latter is difficult for reasons already explored. In fact, an important reason to enter Japan via the joint venture route is to secure both labor and managers at lower cost than would otherwise be possible; the Japanese partner supplies the personnel.

In various parts of the world, people employed in business are not rated highly in relation to those in government service, medicine, law, teaching, or the military. Therefore, an unduly large proportion of the more qualified and achievement-oriented individuals may seek careers in these more prestigious professions, thus depleting the flows into private management. Nonetheless, because the cost advantage of a foreign, over a parent-country, national in a management position abroad is often substantial (frequently over 50 percent), a firm can justify considerable expense in finding and developing foreign nationals.

A firm can invest profitably in an individual's development only if he or she is likely to remain in the firm's employ for an extended period of time. This is an area, incidentally, in which the Japanese permanent employment system contains an advantage. In other societies with high job mobility among managers, whether due to a shortage of qualified people or other causes, the firm's interests dictate that it invest only in those managers committed to the company and likely to remain in its employment. Herein lies solid rationale for a hiring policy based on nepotism. Friends and relatives of owners and top executives are probably somewhat less likely to exploit the firm for training and development and then leave.

Enough for the pros and cons of the expatriate versus local national argument. What of other selection criteria for overseas managers?

Company Experience and Technical Competence

Assurance that an individual will be fully versed in company policies, procedures, and products is often felt to be of prime importance. It is sometimes claimed that a foreign manager, operating at greater distance from the home office and under a severe communications handicap, must have internalized thoroughly the way the company operates and the nature of its products. In fact, however, this may be the easiest prerequisite to satisfy by training and periodic conferences.

Technical competence is, of course, essential if by "technical" skills one refers to skills required to do the assigned job. Warning: the skill mix for a successful manager abroad may differ somewhat from the parent-country model. It is a truism that one of the elements most important in gaining acceptance for foreign management is demonstrated technical capacity. This quality is also important in providing the manager with the confidence necessary to overcome culture shock (see discussion in "Validation for Individuals"). A person must be genuinely self-confident, although not arrogantly so.

Language

Must a manager know the language of the host country? If we admit the validity of employing parent- or third-country nationals under certain circumstances, language may still impose a severe restraint on recruitment. A second language is most efficiently learned by children or mature adults when a specific language need arises. With concentrated effort, a *casual speaking* knowledge of any language may be acquired within 6 to 12 months by an intelligent adult. With but exceedingly rare exceptions, an adult with no prior exposure to a given language cannot become perfectly fluent in it. The two rare exceptions are linguistic genius or complete isolation from the mother tongue for a long period of time (as in confinement in a foreign prison). The major danger to management is that a person inadequate in the local language will nonetheless attempt to carry on as though he or she understands or is being understood at all times. The local community undoubtedly appreciates the foreigner's efforts to communicate directly, but these efforts should not be permitted to interfere with understanding. Pride should not stand in the way of employing a good interpreter.

For the novice in a language, there are at least three serious blocks to full understanding:

1. Inadequate knowledge of the culture and hence of the use and nuance of words. Many apparently equivalent words do not, in fact, carry the same meaning in different languages (e.g., "education," "management," "fair play," and "labor" may have no ready equivalents in a culture that does not share the same institutions, values, or attitudes that give them meaning).
2. Using one foreign word to carry all the meanings of the word that is its equivalent in only one sense. Concept clusters vary. Equivalency for a single meaning does not guarantee that the terms can be used interchangeably in all instances.
3. The difficulty of translating metaphors, similes, and analogies (e.g., "the sweater tickled her to death" may translate as "the sweater scratched her until she died"—hardly a complement).

Even the effective use of an interpreter requires an alertness to these difficulties.

Many nonlocal managers with no prior knowledge of the local language have been eminently successful. The skilled use of competent interpreters, plus coincidental study of the language to the point of being able to keep the interpreter on his toes, may be quite adequate. The pitfall here is the temptation to associate unduly with those speaking one's own language. In many non-Western countries, a manager may find him- or herself surrounded by English-speaking carpetbaggers, many of whom may not be ethnically or culturally part of the major community. One should be wary of becoming too closely involved.

Perhaps of greater importance than ability to use a given language is an awareness of the importance of language as a programmed thinking process. We are all programmed by language. The capacity and structure of a language to a significant degree determine our perceptions, thought, and emotion and, hence, behavior. Granted, a language changes over time, but for a given experience it is fixed.

Associated with this subject is that of the so-called **silent language,** only in the context of which a spoken language can be understood.[1] Essentially, silent language consists of signals communicated by means other than words—spatial relationships, timing, movements, sequences. What may be insulting in one culture may be complimentary in another. One characteristic of a good manager is a *capacity to communicate effectively.* How he or she does it is relatively unimportant, but awareness of silent as well as spoken communication will certainly ease the process.

Awareness and Expertise

As has been pointed out, an essential ingredient in effective communication is knowing one's *own* cultural bias.

The dynamic nature of cultural values works at both ends of an international assignment. The German manager brought up in the aftermath of World War II has different cultural values from the young German worker. A 28-year-old U.S. technician selected by a 45-year-old middle manager in the United States and sent to work for a 50-year-old manager in Germany, where the peer group is 28-year-old German technicians, is caught in a crossfire of cultural values before he starts. If he and the individual who selected him are unaware of cultural differences and cultural bias, the chances for a cultural clash are greatly increased.[2]
A cultural clash simply signals a breakdown in effective communication. Individuals are speaking and acting from different premises.

Another prerequisite often specified for the foreign manager is **area expertise**. Several points should be made. Firstly, prejudgment without personal experience can be very misleading. International communications are clogged with misinterpretation, bias, misinformation, propaganda, distortion, and outright lies. Secondly, experience has demonstrated that a person who has worked *successfully* in one national environment different from his or her own is very likely to operate with similar success wherever employed. Once a person has breached an international communications barrier and has felt the essential unity of human society, the likelihood of future failure is greatly reduced.

---

[1]The classic books dealing with this subject are Edward J. Hall, *The Silent Language* (Garden City: Doubleday, 1959; Anchor Press, 1973); and *Beyond Culture* (Garden City: Anchor Press, 1976).

[2]David H. Noer, *Multinational People Management* (Washington: The Bureau of National Affairs, 1975), pp. 47–48.

The last point needs expansion. By "essential unity of human society" I mean the fact that humans everywhere face similar needs and drives. But, given a different history and geographical environment, a community or nation develops particular institutions, patterns of relationships, personality types, and values. All are functional, that is, rational, within their social context. They are constantly changing as interactions slowly alter even historical traditions. Once people view human society in this manner, they always feel "at home" wherever they are. They realize that bargaining in the bazaar or elaborate rituals of politeness are not simply quaint old customs, but serve definite functions. This realization does not necessarily mean that one is resigned to the status quo. On the contrary, one is then in a position to deal with the cultural environment more effectively. For example, one knows what is likely to reduce the pressure to bargain.[3]

In short, the successful international manager is one who sees and feels the similarity of structure of all societies. The same set of variables are seen to operate, although their relative weights may be very different. This capacity is far more important than possession of specific area expertise, which may be gained quite rapidly if one already has an ability to see similarities and ask the right questions—those that will provide the appropriate values or weights for the relevant variables. Such an individual can very quickly orient himself on the sociocultural map.

It could be argued that managers' success in subsequent foreign environments after their initial success may not be because they have learned anything in particular but because they have developed a special set of qualities, perhaps most importantly a coherent identity and adequate ego strength. The counterargument is that identity and ego strength may be necessary conditions, but possibly not sufficient. It may be that the learning process in the initial experience shortens the time it takes to relate effectively to a foreign culture in subsequent experiences.

Personal Factors

Other than nationality, company experience, technical competence, and language and area expertise (communicative capacity), there are at least seven other prerequisites consciously or unconsciously used in selecting overseas management:

- health
- marital relations (and attitude of spouse)
- career plans and personal preference
- age
- social acceptability
- sex
- personality attributes

[3]Note that bazaar-type bargaining is functional when (1) customers differ greatly in wealth—from subsistence to affluence—the differences being known to the seller; (2) the selling unit is small so that profit and loss can be calculated almost continuously; (3) interest rates are high and turnover important and/or large margins are important; (4) the seller is the owner, or a close associate.

It has been noted by those experienced in this area that an individual's physical health is peculiarly relevant to success abroad. For example, the U.S. Foreign Service allegedly accepts only candidates with "*more* than average health." The health of one's family is also important. Adjustment to the different working and living conditions encountered abroad generates psychological and physical strain. Undue worry about one's health, or that of one's family, can well subvert managerial effectiveness.

Many analysts stress the importance of a strong and mutually reinforcing relationship between man and wife. In some circumstances, sending an unmarried person overseas can be risky, particularly in socially sensitive societies (for example, where the sexes tend to be segregated). In many cultures, a single person simply will not have the same access to families and homes as would a married couple, which may interfere with his or her effectiveness at work. Both husband and wife should have a positive attitude toward the proposed overseas assignment, though it must be an attitude based on accurate knowledge of the working and living conditions they can anticipate.

Individual career plans and personal preference cannot really come into full play unless overseas job opportunities are posted for all to see within the company, rather than communicated merely to selected individuals.

Influencing preferences for overseas assignment, of course, is the degree to which such assignments are seen by the individual as a necessary step on the ladder to the top. Is a foreign assignment considered preparation for promotion or is it a dead end? If the latter, the parent firm may push its undesirables overseas. Very frequently, U.S. firms with policies of employing local nationals in overseas management do not consider these managers transferable, either to third countries or to the United States. Therefore, their career horizons are limited to the local enterprises. A few U.S. firms now require foreign experience for promotion to corporate level. If this is the case, career expectations may be an essential prerequisite for selecting a manager for foreign enterprise. A tendency seems to be evident among U.S., European, and Japanese firms operating internationally to make foreign experience a necessary step up the ladder to a top corporate position.

Age may or may not be important to an overseas assignment. Should a Brazilian enterprise be run by a young or a senior person? Obviously, managing an enterprise far removed from headquarters requires great responsibility and maturity of judgment. Within a broad range, no one has demonstrated that these qualities are closely related to biological age. In more traditional societies, of course, age may be an important status symbol, which may then become relevant to selection of management. Age may also be relevant if an individual's overall management experience is considered to be a prerequisite for selection.

The list of prerequisites includes social acceptability, by which I mean the manager's reflection of those social characteristics identified with a "manager" by his or her local colleagues and subordinates in that society.

Particularly in a traditional society, where ascriptive factors, rather than demonstrated ability, predominate in establishing authority, care should be used to select someone who possesses at least some of the more valued characteristics, whether they be college degrees, knowledge of the fine arts, or manner of behavior. For a parent-country or third-country national, family background may not be important, but if a local national is involved, social status may be a relevant variable, however it may be defined in that particular society. Indeed, a more efficient organization may result than if management ignored such considerations and merely appointed the most *technically* qualified person.

Almost never mentioned in the literature is women's place in international business. In certain overseas managerial roles, particularly sales, a woman may have a distinct advantage. She is more likely to be treated with deference, may find it easier to gain access to distributors and customers, and may be more frequently invited into their homes. A case in point is the sale of pharmaceuticals in Western Europe and Latin America. This can vary, of course, with the area, the function, and the product. National differences in the degree to which women are active in business are remarkable. In some countries foreign business women are virtually banned from business roles (as in Saudi Arabia) or are not regarded seriously (as is frequently the case in Japan).

Even more seldom is race mentioned by researchers or practitioners as relevant to the selection of an overseas manager. For example, is a black American more likely to be effective in black Africa than a white American, or a nisei (American-born Japanese) in Japan? There seems to be little research on the subject, although some experienced observers express doubt. It is possible that such individuals would be viewed with more suspicion—if not hostility—than people who are not racially identified with the host-country population. It is known, however, that some Japanese firms established in the United States have employed nisei and that American-Chinese have been employed in developing the Chinese market.

Validation for Individuals

Having specified the prerequisites for overseas assignments, we still must validate certain of them for a given person. The problem arises particularly in the language and area expertise areas, which I have redefined in terms of ability to communicate and capacity to grasp the interrelationship of societies. How does one increase the probability of selecting an individual who will perform most effectively in a different culture, that is, one who will be least affected by **culture shock**?

Culture shock is induced by the removal of familiar cues. People are seen as behaving irrationally or stupidly; institutions, as not being functional. One is confronted by unexpected behavior and institutions and by different values and world perceptions. If expectations are not fulfilled, stress and dysfunction often follow. Stress, or culture shock, may be manifested in a request for a transfer, the desire to leave a job before completion, dissatisfaction and indifference to work, quarreling, undue criticism, blaming failures on inherent qualities of the local nationality, adulation of the home country, withdrawal from social relations with local nationals (the compound or enclave syndrome), alcoholism and/or poor quality work.

Methods for selecting individuals likely to be least upset by different value systems, and best able to work effectively, include formal tests, training, personal preference, and simple chance.

Formal tests are not widely used by companies to aid in the selection of personnel for overseas assignment, and there is some evidence indicating loss of confidence and decline in testing by former users. Those few firms employing tests do not seem to evaluate their predictability and so are not in a position to relate scores with on-the-job performance overseas. Various thematic apperception tests (TATs) may be useful in disclosing such characteristics as prejudice, a tendency to evaluate individuals by stereotypes (or generalities), and compulsion to see things always in terms of absolute universal values. These characteristics are generally undesirable among international managers who must deal with multinational situations, for they are likely to render them unable to see the cultural relativity of either personal behavior or corporate strategy.

Success in a special training course for a particular assignment, including language study, may be an indirect measure of ability to adapt and to relate oneself to a different culture, and may also provide an insight into motivation. Much, of course, depends on the quality of the training. The weight given to personal preference in the selection process depends on the reason for the preference; a keen interest in new and challenging social experience is very different from a mere desire for the glamour of the international jet set. One should be wary of those who speak of peoples and nations in broad generalities, who pass easy judgment on the acts of others, who "love to travel," who show little concern for their personal family responsibilities, or who are either extremely extroverted or extremely introverted.

The personality of the spouse and the quality of the husband-wife relationship are also of critical importance. There is evidence that many failures abroad are due to the wife's inability to adjust satisfactorily or of the marriage relationship to sustain the compression of isolation from the couple's own culture. (Eventually, cases of husbands' inability to adjust to their wives' overseas assignments may be recorded as well.)

All in all, there seems to be no substitute for the in-depth interview of both husband and wife by one or more persons intimately familiar with the problems of intercultural movement. Mobil's four-hour environmental interview is most revealing.[4] The Mobil interviewers first seek for above-average technical competence and a solid marital relationship. The interviewing process includes the presentation of a complete and accurate de-

[4]See William Alexander, Jr., "Mobil's Four-Hour Environmental Interview," *Worldwide P & I Planning* (January–February 1970), pp. 18 ff.

scription of the overseas work environment (from housing, schools, medical facilities, and food, to the availability of girdles), and the requirements of the job (family separation, work schedules, vacation). Interaction between husband and wife is observed in the process. To hurry the process would sterilize it; hence, the four hours. In addition, the applicant undergoes at least one functional interview confined to a job's technical aspects. The job offer is made after the lapse of a few days, and the applicant is permitted about two weeks to respond. The offer spells out the precise terms, such as base salary plus premium, less U.S. tax, and other relevant factors.

The organizations, business and otherwise, with long success records in recruiting for difficult overseas assignments have depended very heavily upon in-depth interviewing, not by professional psychologists but by people with first-hand experience of the sorts of problems the applicant will face overseas. A recent study reports a definite relationship between the rigor of the selection and training of expatriate managers and their ability to perform successfully in foreign environments.[5] A useful chart of the selection decision process is offered (in Figure 5.3).

5.2   Preparation for Overseas Assignment

Very few U.S. firms provide special training for managers slated for overseas assignment, not to mention their families. Many reasons are given for this situation; specifically, (1) the temporary nature of many overseas assignments, (2) lack of time because of the immediate need for the employee overseas, (3) the trend toward employment of local nationals, (4) doubt about the need for special training, and (5) parallel doubt about the effectiveness of existing training programs.

Training Programs

There are a few formal programs in the United States and elsewhere designed to improve the effectiveness of the international manager, whether posted to an overseas job or occupying a spot at headquarters within the international channels of communication. The best known of those in the United States are the American Graduate School of International Management in Glendale, Arizona; the Experiment in International Living in Brattleboro, Vermont; the Institute of the Business Council for International Understanding at the American University in Washington, D.C.; and the Monterey Institute of Foreign Studies in Monterey, California. In addition, such organizations as the Institute of International Education and Overseas Briefing Associates create tailor-made orientation programs on specific

[5]Rosalie L. Tung, "Comparative Analysis of the Selection and Training Procedures of U.S., European, and Japanese Multinationals," unpublished paper presented at the International Symposium on Cross-Cultural Management (Montreal, October 15–18, 1981), duplicated as a working paper by the Wharton School Multinational Enterprise Unit; and "Selection and Training of Personnel for Overseas Assignment," *Columbia Journal of World Business* (Spring 1981), pp. 68 ff.

Figure 5.3
Diagram of the Process for Selecting Overseas Managers

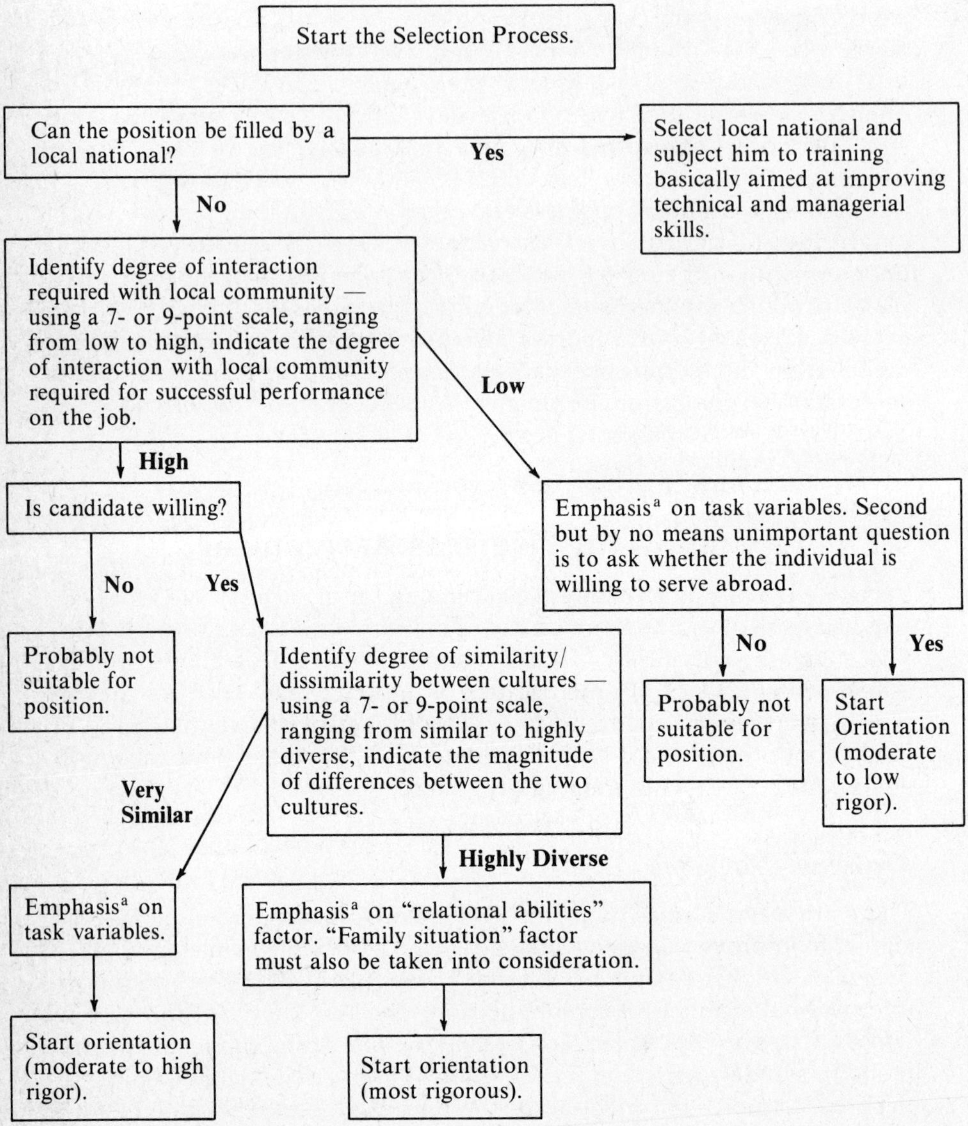

Start the Selection Process.

Can the position be filled by a local national? — **Yes** → Select local national and subject him to training basically aimed at improving technical and managerial skills.

No

Identify degree of interaction required with local community — using a 7- or 9-point scale, ranging from low to high, indicate the degree of interaction with local community required for successful performance on the job.

High

Low → Emphasis[a] on task variables. Second but by no means unimportant question is to ask whether the individual is willing to serve abroad.

Is candidate willing?

No → Probably not suitable for position.

Yes → Identify degree of similarity/dissimilarity between cultures — using a 7- or 9-point scale, ranging from similar to highly diverse, indicate the magnitude of differences between the two cultures.

No → Probably not suitable for position.

Yes → Start Orientation (moderate to low rigor).

Very Similar → Emphasis[a] on task variables.

Highly Diverse → Emphasis[a] on "relational abilities" factor. "Family situation" factor must also be taken into consideration.

Start orientation (moderate to high rigor).

Start orientation (most rigorous).

[a]"Emphasis" does not mean ignoring the other factors. It only means that this should be the dominant factor.

Source: Rosalie L. Tung, "Selection and Training of Personnel for Overseas Assignments," *Columbia Journal of World Business*, Spring 1981, p. 73.

countries for individual companies. The Asia Society, the Japan Society, the Middle East Institute, and similar organizations periodically mount briefing sessions for businessmen.

One of the more highly developed programs located outside the United States is the Institute of International Training and Studies near Fuji, Japan. Created by the Ministry of International Trade and Industry, the student body consists of young corporate executives who are sent by their respective employers for an intensive year-long, full-time course of study. It consists of intensive English language training plus U.S. area study, general management training, international management study, training in a second foreign language plus relevant area study, and, finally, a two-month study tour of some part of the world. Japanese industry is thus deliberately creating a trained cadre of international managers. Communication skills and the demonstration of the cultural relativism of management policy and practice receive full treatment. The major oversight of the program is that it isolates Japanese wives from this sort of preparation, although, if traditional Japanese practice continues, few will live overseas with their husbands in any event. Another well-known institution is the Center for Education in International Management in Geneva, Switzerland. One should also note the course on directing foreign operations offered by the Mangement College in Henley-on-Thames, England.

Training Needs

A study of 403 Americans working in Asia[6] found a high order of consistency in their ranking of training needs. The rankings of the first 10 of 15 needs (listed in Table 5.1) are shown in Table 5.2. On the hypothesis that Asians would rank these training needs quite differently, the researchers put the same question to 131 English-speaking Asian nationals with whom the Americans had worked. The rankings were identical for the first three, as can be noted in Table 5.2. The ranking of "orientation for service" reflected significant disparity. The author comments:

Apparently the motivation of Americans for working overseas appears somewhat more important to the Asian nationals than it does to Americans already overseas. The Asian nationals agree with findings of Cleveland, Mangone, and Adams that "belief in mission" is one of the five elements most relevant to success overseas.[7]

The relatively low rating by both groups of language ability should be noted.

An open-ended question asked the Asian respondents to identify the most needed areas of training in an orientation program for Americans preparing to work overseas. Typical comments were:

---

[6]Graduates of a five-month missionary orientation center program, one of the oldest orientation programs for Americans going overseas, and Peace Corps volunteers returning from service in Asia.

[7]Mary B. Johnston, "Training Needs of Overseas Americans as Seen by Their National Co-Workers in Asia," *IDR/Focus*, No. 4 (1974), p. 23. Reference is to H. Cleveland, G. J. Mangone, and J. C. Adams, *The Overseas Americans* (New York: McGraw-Hill, 1969). The five elements: technical skill, belief in mission, cultural empathy, a sense of politics, and organizational ability.

Table 5.1
Training Needs for Americans Overseas (N = 403)

1. *A sense for politics* (awareness of politial conditions in assigned country; alertness to political consequences of everyday behavior)
2. *Skill as change agent* (the ability to work toward change)
3. *Ability to keep records* (skill in keeping simple records and accounts)
4. *Human relations skills* (ability to work with others, based on understanding oneself and the structure and dynamics of human society)
5. *Teaching skills* (an understanding of and ability to apply the principles of learning and teaching)
6. *Understanding of mission* (having a sense of the purpose of and enthusiasm about one's job and organization)
7. *Technical competence* (ability to do the job: knowing the subject matter and techniques in one's field)
8. *Health knowledge* (an understanding of the principles essential for maintaining physical and mental health)
9. *Orientation for service* (an understanding of the value of all human life and potential, such that one is motivated to serve fellow human beings)
10. *Organizational ability* (ability to combine personnel and resources into dynamic self-sustaining enterprises: ability to "work oneself out of" the job by developing self-sustaining institutions and by training local national personnel to manage them)
11. *Ability to adapt* (flexibility: ability to adapt learning to unlike situations; ability to adjust oneself to change)
12. *Understanding of other cultures* (cross-cultural understanding; the skill to understand the inner logic and coherence of other ways of life, plus the restraint not to judge them as "bad" because they are different from one's own ways; cultural empathy)
13. *Understanding of American culture* (insight into Western values, mores, attitudes, behavior patterns)
14. *Language ability* (a growing ability to express oneself in, and to understand, the language of the adopted country)
15. *Sensitivity training* (self-insight, self-understanding, sensitivity to feelings of others)

Source: M.B. Johnston and G.L. Carter, Jr., "Training Needs of Americans Working Abroad," *Social Change*, (1972) reprinted in Mary B. Johnston, "Training Needs of Overseas Americans as Seen by Their National Co-Workers in Asia," *IDR/Focus* no. 4 (1974), p. 22.

Taiwan: Attitude of humility. The greatest hindrance to working successfully overseas is the attitude of intellectual, cultural, and religious superiority. Although Americans are sent out to help, and possibly to change the lives of other peoples, they should also be ready to learn, to receive, and to be changed.

Philippines: Americans must not confuse a sense of service to the people with the imposition of their way of life; i.e., the development of other peoples does not necessarily mean their Americanization. I find most Americans I have worked with technically competent (in the area for which they were asked to serve) but terribly presumptuous, carrying around with them a tragic sense of "know-it-all" or self-superiority. A deep sense of partnership with local people and fellow workers is essential in their preparation.

India: Change in attitude. Most of them behave as if they are superior human beings, although we do not believe they are. Some of them who are in the technical fields are not experts and they should be prepared to learn

**Table 5.2
Ranking of Training Needs for Americans Working Overseas
by Americans Abroad and Their Asian Colleagues
(most important = 1)**

Training need	Ranking by responses of Americans (N = 403)	Ranking by responses of nationals (N = 131)
Human relations skill	1	1
Understanding of other culture	2	2
Ability to adapt	3	3
Technical competence	4	6.5[a]
Sensitivity training	5	6.5
A sense of politics	6	12.5[b]
Language ability	7	9
Understanding of mission	8	5
Understanding of American culture	9	15
Orientation for service	10	4

[a]The two training needs that tied for sixth rank are both ranked 6.5.
[b]The two training needs that tied for 12th place are ranked as 12.5.
Source: Johnston, "Training Needs," p. 23.

from their colleagues . . . **Americans who are undergoing orientation courses should be made to believe that Indians are intellectual.**[8]
You may draw your own conclusion as to the relevancy of these findings to the expatriate business manager.

5.3   Promotion of Overseas Management

Three strategies are possible in the promotion of overseas management: national (limiting an individual's management career to national operations), binational (allowing promotion to parent corporate headquarters), multinational (individuals promoted without regard for nationality except where it is relevant to effectiveness). Valid considerations for the selection of an optimum promotion policy include:

1. Legal restraints on emigration and employment of aliens;
2. Family participation in ownership and management of an associated foreign enterprise, which may result in conflicting loyalty if family members are promoted to another associated firm;
3. Inability to set up a consistent worldwide remuneration strategy (see Section 5.4);
4. Degree of autonomy of associated firms (the parent may not be in a position to dictate career paths);

[8]Johnston, "Training Needs," *op. cit.*, p. 24.

5.   Preference on the part of key managerial personnel (if they do not wish to move physically, one must weigh the risk and cost of losing them versus cost of replacement);

6.   Relative cost per comparable management-year for the various options;

7.   Ownership of the parent firm (if owned in significant measure by foreign nationals, a multinational management may be compelled);

8.   Relative size of foreign and domestic market (if the foreign is relatively large and has been developed by foreign nationals, the pressure to promote them to top corporate positions may be irresistible);

9.   Direction of major flows of technical development and skills (a similar phenomenon may take place here if the flows are obviously from foreign to domestic; then the appointment of foreign nationals to corporate headquarters would appear desirable);

10.   Availability of parent-country nationals able to interpret communications from abroad (if there are none, clearly foreign nationals must be used in headquarters);

11.   Involvement in foreign legal problems requiring skills not available locally;

12.   Relative importance of foreign-source financing requiring special skills that perhaps only foreign nationals have.

Although admitted the subject has not been well researched, much subjective evidence suggests that in U.S.-based companies operating internationally a growing number of non-U.S. nationals are moving into top positions in corporate headquarters. This movement may or may not parallel comparable growth in non-U.S. ownership of the parent corporation and the appearance of foreign nationals on the parent's board. A few of the more mature U.S. companies with extensive international operations systematically rotate executives through foreign and domestic posts, and as a matter of corporate policy make it clear that only those with significant international experience will emerge at the top levels. The sheer dynamics of such a corporate policy leads to a greater multinationalization of management at headquarters. Overall, however, the number of Americans holding managerial posts abroad as a percentage of the total managerial cadre of U.S. firms overseas has dropped in recent years to less than 100,000.[9] Reasons for the relative decline in U.S. expatriate managers:

1.   Corporate policy to employ as many local managers as possible;

2.   Host government pressure;

3.   The fact that it costs a U.S. parent an average of $500,000 to support an American with an annual salary of $25,000 for a three-year period abroad (6.7 times aggregate annual salary);

[9]See study by Calvin Reynolds, "Careers: Hunting for a Job Overseas," reported in the *New York Times*, October 24, 1979, p. 19. By comparison, Japanese expatriate managers possibly number close to 400,000.

4. The increasing availability of managerial talent abroad, particularly in Western Europe;

5. A slowup in new investment and simultaneous maturation of U.S. business overseas, with reduced need to send Americans abroad as members of startup teams.[10]

The multinational promotional strategy is, of course, particularly difficult for Japanese-based firms. The realization of this fact may be one reason why the Japanese generally are internationalizing through the joint-venture and contractual route rather than through the creation of a family of centrally controlled and integrated subsidiaries. Noritake Kobayashi writes,

Despite the good will and intention to promote the locals in the overseas market, Japanese executives seem to experience a strong mental resistance when we discuss the stage of promoting the locals to managerial positions in their headquarters' organization. This is largely due to the closed culture of Japan and the resulting deficiencies of linguistic ability of many Japanese executives.[11]

My own first-hand impression is that Japanese executives do not expect any change on this score within the foreseeable future.

It is generally recognized that if the firm locks its foreign managers within their respective national firms, eventually one of three things happens: (1) as the maturity and stature of the local management increases relative to that in headquarters, it becomes increasingly difficult for headquarters to control, and local autonomy increases; (2) as competent, ambitious foreign nationals hit the promotion ceiling, they leave the firm; (3) the company breaks its nationality policy and creates a multinational management. This last process can be accelerated—if not made compelling—if parent-company equity is owned in significant amount by local nationals.

5.4 Remuneration

Although an exceedingly complex subject, strategies for remunerating international management are limited to two basic choices: (1) **multiple pay scales** (that is, parent-country personnel on a parent-country salary scale, all others on the relevant local scales), or (2) an **international base** plus a variety of extras. Common extras are a cost-of-living differential, an expatriate bonus to compensate for being away from home, and a number of personal adjustment payments (language training, moving allowance, children's education, home leave, entertainment, special health and accident insurance).

---

[10]*Ibid.*

[11]Noritake Kobayashi, "The International Manager Development by the Japanese Multinationals," unpublished manuscript (Tokyo, February 1976), p. 12.

It should be noted that the salary differential between expatriates and local national managers is likely to vary according to job level, narrowing as one ascends the managerial pyramid.

In some countries the cash salaries paid to management may be a relatively low multiple of the wages paid to labor. However, there may be a greater difference if all of the goods and services received by managers are taken into account, such perquisites as use of a car, large and well-located apartments, and access to luxury goods denied the ordinary citizen.

Problems

A special problem arises in the international area due to the need to pay expatriates enough (1) to induce them to leave the home country (or to return), (2) to maintain a home-country standard of living, (3) to facilitate reentry into the home country (by maintaining a home and professional updating), (4) to meet the requirements of children's education, and (5) to maintain social obligations to friends and family. The obvious cost of these many payments to already highly paid U.S. and Western European managers constitutes pressure toward the localization of management, or the employment of third-country nationals. It may be significant that Japanese managers in Japan, on average, are paid substantially less, and hence there is less economic pressure on Japanese firms to localize management abroad.

Almost inevitably, at some stage both parent-country nationals and foreign nationals, whether local or from a third country, are employed as managers within the same enterprise. There is a tendency now to limit the use of parent-country managers more and more to start-up teams or for troubleshooting, which means transfer from one foreign assignment to another. (Note the impact of a general economic slowdown and decline in new investment.) Finally, as enterprises and, correspondingly, their managerial personnel mature, nonparent-country nationals may be shifted as well, including periods of assignment to the parent country. A purely national wage policy thus becomes inoperative, for it makes the transfer of personnel difficult; they may refuse assignment to a post promising less total emoluments. Complicating the problem further are such factors as exchange controls and currency of payment (how much is to be paid in dollars, how much in local currency? what do the regulations permit?), national social security payments (benefits of which an alien national will never realize), exclusion from one's own social security system (by reason of prolonged absence), and diverse rates of taxation of personal income.

One Firm's Strategy

For illustrative purposes only, the compensation policy set up by one U.S.-based firm is described. *For U.S. personnel overseas,* this firm paid a base salary equal to the U.S. salary, plus an expatriate or overseas bonus (varying between zero percent of base salary for Western Europe to 35 percent for more remote and unpleasant posts), a cost-of-living adjustment (zero to 70 percent of spendable income, which was estimated to be that amount of total income deemed actually spent on normal living expenses excluding housing, utilities, taxes, and insurance, the adjustment being based on the U.S. State Department's Local Index of Living Costs Abroad), and several personal adjustment payments (two-month home leave every two years, education expenses for children under college level, transportation and moving expenses between assignments, social and business club memberships, income tax differential.)[12] American personnel were generally paid in local currency an amount equal to that paid to comparable local nationals, with the balance paid in dollars. In order to avoid foreign income tax, local social security taxes (which would not benefit U.S. nationals), and foreign exchange control difficulties when the U.S. nationals wished to pay dollar obligations or create dollar savings, a separate dollar salary was paid and not reported to the host government. *Local nationals* were paid the going local wage with no extra payment or dollar component. *Third-country personnel* were paid a base salary equal to that paid for a comparable position in the place where they were hired (not necessarily the country of national origin), plus a cost-of-living differential, for which the place of hiring was used as the base. Income in excess of comparable local salary could be paid in the currency of country of origin.

The problems inherent in such a system are manifold and include the following:

1.   It assumes that each individual's consumption preferences conform to the average.
2.   U.S. nationals may receive more for the same job than either third-country or local nationals. (A subordinate may receive more than his superiors.)
3.   Unreported **off-shore** (or **split**) **income** may well be illegal according to local tax authorities, which means that it cannot be shown as a cost against the local firm's taxable income. (Possibly not against parent company taxable income either.) Yet if the income were reported locally, it might be subject to foreign exchange control. Some people attempt to justify the split income technique on the grounds that part of an expatriate's salary is directly attributable to the work he or she does for the parent company and therefore is a valid cost to the parent and can be reported as such for tax purposes at home. At the very least, it is argued, a split income is justified to the extent that the manager travels outside of his or her base country.
4.   The value of off-shore income in the eyes of local nationals may be very great and can set up tension if the local is subject to foreign exchange controls.
5.   A uniform, company-wide pension scheme is difficult to institute.
6.   Once having enjoyed higher income elsewhere, employees may resist reassignment to a lower-income post, including their home country,

---

[12]If the foreign tax were less than the U.S. rate, the benefit was deducted from the cost-of-living differential.

even though costs may be lower (they may be taken with the illusion that money has an absolute value, forgetting the added financial and personal costs for which the higher salary compensated).

7. The necessarily arbitrary nature of expatriate bonuses and cost-of-living differentials sets up tensions.
8. Absence of local authority over salary structure may cause friction.
9. A company-wide profit-sharing system is virtually impossible.
10. Inclusion under the U.S. social security system must be considered.
11. Maintaining acceptable salary and benefit ratios among various levels of management and of labor may be desirable.

It is of interest to note that a few firms have a policy of reducing overseas allowances after a period of time. The assumption is that as time passes, the transferee approaches the buying habits and customs of the local inhabitants, thus rendering the initial cost-of-living allowance untenable.

A few firms follow a general policy of paying an international base salary without regard for nationality or place of hiring, plus whatever expenses are incurred by reason of employment with the company, including a cost-of-living differential (with the country in which the parent company is domiciled as the base). Each national enterprise may have its own pension plan, in which local nationals continue to participate regardless of where they may be assigned. The entire base salary and cost-of-living differential is paid in the currency of one's citizenship directly by the employing enterprise. In case foreign exchange controls operate, the local firm must negotiate with the host government for currency exchange by its nonnational employees of a certain portion of their respective incomes. Special adjustment payments may be made directly in the relevant foreign currency by the parent company. Thus, an international management cadre consisting of career foreign service executives is created. One suspects that as firms become truly multinational there is likely to be little or no distinction between foreign and domestic managers. Above a certain level, all will be placed on a global salary scale, subject only to cost-of-living and tax equalization allowances. Any pension and profit-sharing rights will be in respect to the consolidated corporate family. In poorer countries, of course, such a scheme has the effect of widening the disparities in income distribution.

5.5 Selection of Managerial Style

In the last chapter, we discussed McGregor's notion of Theory X and Theory Y types of organizations. Arnold S. Tannenbaum and others have expanded this simple dichotomy into four leadership styles (Table 5.3). Even that is very much oversimplified. I suggest that there are at least four significant dimensions to every managerial style and that each dimension represents a continuum.

Table 5.3
Four Styles of Leadership and Their Characteristics

	System 1	System 2	System 3	System 4
Leadership				
1. How much confidence is shown in subordinates?	None	Condescending	Substantial	Complete
2. How free do they feel to talk to superiors about job?	Not at all	Not very	Rather freely	Fully free
3. Are subordinates' ideas sought and used, if worthy?	Seldom	Sometimes	Usually	Always
Motivation				
4. Is predominant use made of (1) fear, (2) threats, (3) punishment, (4) rewards, (5) involvement	1, 2, 3, occasionally 4	4, some 3	4, some 3 and 5	5, 4, based on group-set goals
5. Where is responsibility felt for achieving organization goals?	Mostly at top	Top and middle	Fairly general	At all levels
Communication				
6. What is the direction of information flow?	Downward	Mostly downward	Down and up	Down, up, and sideways
7. How is downward communication accepted?	With suspicion	Possible, with suspicion	With caution	With open mind
8. How accurate is upward communication?	Often wrong	Censored for boss	Limited accuracy	Accurate
9. How well do superiors know problems faced by subordinates?	Know little	Some knowledge	Quite well	Very well
Interaction				
10. What is the character of interaction?	Little, always with fear and distrust	Little, usually with some condescension	Moderate, often fair amount of confidence and trust	Extensive, high degree of confidence and trust
11. How much cooperative teamwork is present?	None	Relatively little	Moderate amount	Very substantial throughout organization
Decisions				
12. At what level are decisions formally made?	Mostly at top	Policy at top, some delegation	Broad policy at top, more delegation	Throughout but well integrated

Table 5.3
Four Styles of Leadership and Their Characteristics (continued)

	System 1	System 2	System 3	System 4
Decisions				
13. What is the origin of technical and professional knowledge used in decision making?	Top management	Upper and middle	To a certain extent throughout	To a great extent throughout
14. Are subordinates involved in decisions related to their work?	Not at all	Occasionally consulted	Generally consulted	Fully involved
15. What does the decision making process contribute to motivation?	Nothing, often weakens it	Relatively little	Some contribution	Substantial contribution
Goals				
16. How are organizational goals established?	Orders issued	Orders issued with some chance to comment	Orders issued after discussion	Group action (except in crisis)
17. How much covert resistance to goals is present?	Strong resistance	Moderate resistance	Some resistance at times	Little or none
Control				
18. How concentrated are review and control functions?	Highly at top	Relatively high at top	Moderate delegation to lower levels	Quite widely shared
19. Is there an informal organization resisting the formal one?	Yes	Usually	Sometimes	No—same goals as formal
20. What are cost, productivity, and other control data used for?	Policing, punishment	Reward and punishment	Reward, some self-guidance	Self-guidance, problem solving

Source: Arnold S. Tannenbaum, Stane Mozina, Janez Jerovsek, and Rensis Likert, "Testing a Managerial Style," *European Business*, no. 27 (Autumn 1970), p. 64.

1. *Degree of subordinate participation;*
2. *Degree of calculation* (use of quantitative analysis) as contrasted with impressionism (use of intuition) based on experience;
3. *Degree of formality* (for example, the presence of formal *and* informal channels of communication from subordinate to superior, and to those horizontally equal in authority to the superior who may influence a subordinate's direct superior); and
4. *Vertical consistency* of these three dimensions in managerial style, from one level to another, or from one associated firm to another.

Participation of Subordinates

A continuum of subordinate participation in decision making would run thus:

1. Superior makes decision with no explanation and with little or no thought of subordinate (autocratic).
2. Superior makes decision with no explanation but with considerable thought of subordinates (paternalistic).
3. Superior makes decision, but with fairly complete explanation to subordinates so that they will be aware of why the decision was made (explanatory).
4. Superior makes decision with no explanation because of prior knowledge of (or feel for) the attitudes, values, and opinions of subordinates, which he or she has taken into consideration (empathetic).
5. Superior makes decision, but gives fairly complete explanation for the purpose of gaining the support of subordinates (supportive).
6. Superior makes decision, but gives fairly complete explanation to subordinates to indicate (1) that he or she has considered their known attitudes, values, and opinions, and (2) to gain their support (empathetic-supportive).
7. Superior makes decision after consultation with subordinates (consultative).
8. Decision is made jointly by superior and subordinates but is articulated by the superior to his boss (participative).
9. Decision is made jointly by superior (as leader) and subordinates and is articulated to the superior's boss as a group decision (collective or joint).
10. Decision is delegated to subordinates, but is subject to superior's influence (semi-delegated).
11. Decision is delegated entirely to subordinates (delegated).

Admittedly, styles 10 and 11 do not tell us how decisions are reached by the subordinates, who in turn may opt for any one of the styles listed.

The depth of management participation can be an important dimension. Participation may be limited to top management (chief executives, principal staff directors, division managers), upper-middle management (department heads and plant managers), lower-middle management (section chiefs), lower management (supervisors and foremen), or may be extended to include all employees (labor). The last form is discussed in Section 4.2. A closely associated subject, of course, is profit-sharing and ownership-sharing (discussed in Sections 4.6 and 6.2).

When one considers the variables that must relate in some circumstances to choice of decision-making style as defined by degree of participation (see Figure 5.4), it is obvious that there can be no universally valid superior style.

Figure 5.4
Development of a Decision-Making Style in
Relation to Degree of Participation

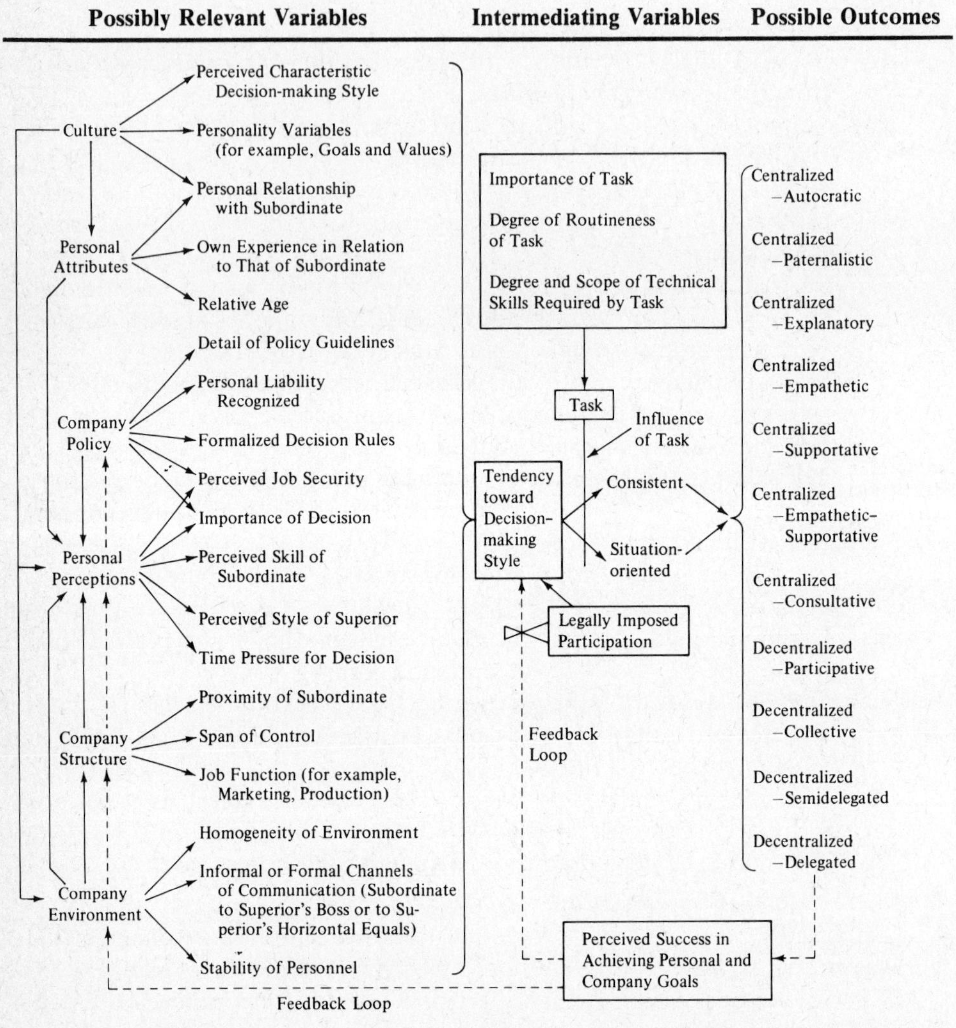

| Possibly Relevant Variables | Intermediating Variables | Possible Outcomes |

Feedback Loop

In reviewing all of the major research of a comparative nature relating to managerial attitudes and behavior, Gerald V. Barrett and Bernard M. Bass concluded:

We interpret ... the ... studies on superior-subordinate relationships to indicate that there are differences among countries in preferred style of leadership. These differences in leadership styles appear to be largely culturally based, and at this point of time it would appear naive to advocate one model of leadership style as being optimum for all cultural groups.

The widely-advocated American model of participative management may not be optimum for all cultures, and in fact may be dysfunctional in some.[13]

Degree of Calculation

There has been little research or writing in reference to the second dimension of managerial style, the use of statistical information in making decisions versus perception, intuitive assessment, or personal judgment; in other words, calculation versus impressionism. It has been observed that: **The American executive is number and fact oriented. This is often misleading in that facts and figures do not always contain all that is needed in making the "right" decision. The Latin American and European mind [are much better] . . . suited to the uniqueness of international business because they are humanistically oriented as opposed to the American factual orientation.**[14]

Alpander observed:

In developing countries, such as Mexico, executives need self-assurance, and they need to be quick in making their decisions in light of a rapidly changing environment. Therefore, expediency in decision-making by an intuitive approach is tolerated. This intuitive approach is not necessarily an asset in more developed countries like the United States, but it is definitely a characteristic that leads to success in environments like Mexico.[15]

It may also be true that the more quickly responsive intuitive decision-making style makes the introduction of more participative decision making difficult. Participation requires time. The greater the pressure of time, the less the degree of participation is likely to be. Some have observed that the relatively high degree of participative decision making in Japan, for instance, arises at least in part from the propensity of the Japanese to demand great detail prior to a decision. This propensity for detail is made possible, some argue, because Japanese corporations generally operate under less time pressure than their American and European counterparts, given their very different financial structures, which render quarterly and even annual financial statements relatively unimportant.

Formality of Communication

Very little can be said about national differences in respect to the degree to which informal channels of communication are open from subordinates to

[13]Gerald V. Barrett and Bernard M. Bass, "Comparative Studies of Managerial Attitudes and Behavior," Chap. 8 in J. Boddewyn, ed., *Comparative Management: Teaching, Training and Research* (New York: Graduate School of Business Administration, New York University, 1970), p. 194.

[14]Michael S. Werner, "Dealing with Governments in Developing Countries: Implications for the Multinational Enterprise," unpublished MBA thesis (New York University Graduate School of Business Administration, 1971), p. 68.

[15]Alpander, "A Comparative Study of Executives in Mexican Firms in Mexico," *Southern Journal of Business*, May 1971, p. 71.

superiors. Although the subject seems not to have been researched, some differences are apparent, in part a function of status-consciousness within a society and the degree to which voluntary, private associations are present. Who belongs to which clubs, associations (for example, Masonic lodges in some countries), churches, and political parties? The off-the-job social intercourse that takes place in such organizations may well influence the nature of the subordinate-superior relationship on the job and even the locale or forum in which decisions are made. If A knows that B, his subordinate, can talk freely and intimately with either C, A's boss, or D, who is on A's level, the relationship between A and B is likely to be affected, as is the decision-making style. It may be that really important decisions are not made in the office hierarchical context at all but within a more fluid group around the table at the club. In some cases, this circumvention of one's immediate superiors may be institutionalized, as reflected in the policy of some German companies previously commented upon, where, if a subordinate wishes to speak with someone above his superior, it is his right to do so, and an interview will be scheduled within a certain period of time.

Vertical Consistency

A fourth dimension of managerial style is **vertical consistency**, not only in respect to various forms of participation, but also to the degree of calculation and formality in decision making. To the extent that an elite upper management adopts a particular style that is inconsistent with managerial style at lower levels (whether induced by social, psychological, or educational differences), lack of communication may become a problem on the interface, at whatever level. An alien management from an industrially developed country operating in a less developed country may find itself precisely in this situation. If so, substantial inputs of patience, education, and training may be required to bridge the gap, or those functioning at the interface may have to adapt to the lower-level style. To date, there has been very little or no research bearing directly on this problem.

The Japanese System

The Japanese managerial style is identified by the phrase *ringi seido*, literally "the system of submitting a proposal to one's superior for approval." The initiative for a decision may be at any level of management, but the formal process starts with the preparation of a written proposal at the middle-management level. The proposal then works its way up both laterally and horizontally. If anyone objects along the way, a meeting is called and the problem talked out until there is a consensus. The process then continues to the top level, at which point the decision is articulated by the chief executive.

Four observations should be made about this system. First, though certainly time-consuming, this style of decision making means that everyone is fully aware of the details of a decision, and of his or her respective role in implementing it at the moment of articulation by the chief executive.

Hence, implementation is almost immediate. (Indeed, the elapsed time from the moment a project is proposed to actual implementation is about the same for a Japanese and a U.S. firm. The former takes longer to reach a decision; the latter, longer to implement a project after a decision has been made. Consequently, each may be critical of the other for delay.) Second, this system may only work effectively in association with two other characteristics of the Japanese managerial system, lifetime tenure and promotion by seniority. Third, a manager can through the *ringi* system be important without being president. Although many Japanese corporate chief executives are very important and much admired and respected men (virtually never women), one gets the impression that as *individuals* they are not as important in formulating decisions as, say, many of their U.S. counterparts. Fourth, in view of some evidence that decisions made in groups tend to be riskier than decisions made individually, it may be that the Japanese system is less risk-averse than the U.S. or European systems. In fact, however, it may be that the time taken for decision, the detail demanded prior to decision, the degree of participation, and the speed of implementation following decision, may only make it appear that the Japanese are less risk-averse. Their decision-making system may actually *reduce* risk. In any event, the individual does not bear the responsibility; the group does.

The idea of collective responsibility is related to a feeling called *shu-jo-nu-on* (gratitude to nature and other human beings for one's success). To conform to this concept requires abandoning the idea of individual power domination in favor of cooperative group action where no man's success may be attributed to his brains and the strength of his two arms unaided and alone. The great emphasis on harmony sometimes surprises Occidental visitors; a manager may describe with pride the spirit of concord prevalent in his factory, rather than the profits it makes, even where the profits are high.[16]

In Japanese, there seems to be no precise equivalent for the common phrase, "the self-made man."

5.6   Views of Managerial Behavior

The thrust of this discussion is that the present practice of many firms in regard to the selection, preparation, and promotion of international managerial personnel hardly seems to be the best. The remuneration problem is of a more tangible nature and, hence, has been given somewhat greater attention, but the interplay of conflicting laws and regulations and constantly shifting price levels and foreign exchange rates make the creation of an entirely equitable system exceedingly difficult without involving the firm in what would appear to be unnecessary cost. Finally, it is quite apparent that there is no universally best managerial style (in degree of participation,

---

[16]Van Zandt, "Japanese Culture and the Business Boom," *Foreign Affairs*, January 1970, p. 318.

use of quantitative calculations, or in terms of formality and consistency). This observation relates to the selection and preparation of international managers, for individuals with very different personality attributes, managerial philosophies, and calculative skills may all perform well, but in different environments. The problem lies in matching people to situations, which requires an ability to measure both with something more than random success. Obviously, the measures are imperfect, but such imperfection does not preclude effort or sensitivity to the problem.

This view is challenged by the so-called **universalists**, those who insist that there is a common set of values and pattern of behavior among all managers regardless of the cultural milieu in which they operate. Induced by the discipline imposed by modern industry, this common pattern is seen as a world managerial culture. Differences among managers are perceived as reflecting personal, situational, or organizational differences. It should be pointed out that this definition begs a question, for if there are *consistent* differences in personal behavior, situation, or organization, the impact of culture would thus be revealed.

A modification of the universalist view is that of the **cultural cluster** school, in which similarities of managerial values and behavior within multinational cultural regions are emphasized. Most frequent groupings are Nordic-European, Latin-European, Anglo-American, Japanese and Chinese, and the less developed countries.[17]

A third point of view is that managerial behavior is strongly influenced by key environmental or cultural characteristics, particularly the economy (for example, the levels of industrialization and wealth). Other possibly important factors: size of relevant markets, occupational mix, density of population, level of popular education, prevailing politico-economic ideology, social structure, and ethnic-religious homogeneity.

These views may not be as inconsistent as would first appear. That is, the technology of production and the competitiveness of the marketplace may impose certain pressures on the managerial team of an enterprise wherever located. However, given the general cultural environment of a region, managers within that region tend to react to systematic pressures in a similar fashion (the degree of regional commonality being a function of common history, language, and depth of social-economic-political intercourse). In societies that are truly unique along some combination of important dimensions (such as size, wealth, socio-economic ideology, population density, social structure), managerial values and behavior are likely to be distinctive. Therefore, I contend that any study designed to demonstrate *globally* either the universality or cultural relativity of managerial behavior will be inconclusive.

One difficulty in some studies directed to this subject is that they may not have homed in on the really key values and behavior patterns that

---

[17]For example, see M. Haire, E. E. Chiselli, and L. W. Porter, *Managerial Thinking: An International Study* (New York: John Wiley & Sons, 1966).

differentiate managers operating within different cultures. Also, the samples have to be picked with great care. For example, should public-sector managers be included in countries where public-sector industry is a significant part of the total? If they are not, the results of a comparative study could well be vitiated, for among the essential dimensions of managerial values and behavior are those having to do with managerial motivation and organizational goals. These can vary substantially between public- and private-sector enterprise; the fact that a society has opted for a greater activity in the public sector may be of signal importance. Another possibly relevant dimension is the occupational mix. Certain managerial values and behavior tend to be associated with specific activities (such as banking, accounting, mass assembly-line industry, high technology industry, and agrobusiness).

Barrett and Bass suggest seven variables in describing management behavior: (1) superior-subordinate relationship, (2) managerial needs or motivation, (3) interpersonal perceptions, (4) organizational goals, (5) perception of equity, (6) decision making under uncertainty, and (7) managerial values.[18] In respect to the first, the two authors, after surveying the literature of comparative organization, conclude that there are strong arguments against the view that the participative form of management has universal application throughout the world. Without being inconsistent, one can go on to claim that participative management may represent the most highly evolved form of management. That it is not immediately effective in large areas of the world is not surprising. Effective participative management may require that labor and management have consistent goals and similar time horizons, conditions implying a fairly high level of sophistication. It may also require material well-being and a sense of security on the part of all concerned—a fairly rare set of conditions.

Managerial needs and motivation, whether measured by a ranking of needs or of life goals, are remarkably similar around the world, although with some significant differences. In order to be more certain of these findings, however, one would have to know (1) whether managers are more similar than nonmanagers, (2) whether public-sector managers differ significantly from private-sector managers, and (3) whether there are significant occupational differences. Perhaps all that these studies tell us is that there is some hierarchy of human need that tends to be universal, at least among secularly educated people no longer directly concerned with daily survival. But these studies do not tell us how those needs are translated into personal or organizational behavior in a given environment.[19]

[18]Barrett and Bass, "Comparative Studies," *op. cit.*, p. 182.

[19]Some of the better known relevant studies not already listed in footnotes include: Mason Haire, et al., *Managerial Thinking: An International Study* (New York: John Wiley & Sons, 1966); Stephen H. Rhinesmith, *Cultural-Organizational Analysis: The Interrelationship of Value Orientations and Managerial Behavior* (Cambridge, MA.: McBer and Company, 1970); Richard W. Wright, "Organizational Ambients: Management and Environment in Chile," *Academy of Management Journal*, March 1971, pp. 65 ff; Desmond Graves, "The Impact of Culture upon Managerial Beliefs and Behavior in England and France," *Journal of Management Studies*, vol. 9, no. 1 (February 1972), p. 55; Richard B. Peterson, "A Cross-Cultural Prospective of Supervisory Values," *Academy of Management Journal*, vol. 15, no. 1 (March 1972), pp. 105 ff; J. L. Massie et al., eds., *Management in the International Context* (New York: Harper & Row, 1972); Frederick Harbison and Charles A. Myers, *Management in the Industrial World* (New York: McGraw-Hill, 1959).

In fact, there does exist an impressive array of empirical research purporting to demonstrate significant national (or cultural) differences among managers along many dimensions, including interpersonal perceptions, relative stress on efficiency and growth as opposed to security, willingness to innovate and assume risk, convictions as to the best supervisory style, and attitudes toward work rewards. For example, in at least some less developed countries, managers appear more inclined than those in the more developed countries to give smaller pay differentials for above-average performance and to give more weight to extenuating personal circumstances and job conditions when setting remuneration. In certain cultures—the Japanese, for example—the idea of a participant style of management may be culturally congenial. The notion of personal discipline, the "correct order" of things, and the idea of reciprocal obligations between individual and society may be ideas more compatible with a Confucian-based society than with many others. The impact of the surrounding culture on managerial values and behavior cannot be denied.

Finally, it should be pointed out that to say that the most *effective* style of management—however this may be defined—may vary with time and place is not to deny that there may eventually be a global convergence of managerial style. This evolutionary convergence is a legitimate problem for the organizational theorist, but the practicing manager must respond to the requirements imposed by the cultural milieu where he or she is working. The experienced international manager is well aware of the fact that what constitutes effective management varies as one moves geographically and over time.

CHAPTER 6

OWNERSHIP STRATEGY

affiliate a corporation 50 percent or less of whose voting stock is owned by another corporation.

competitive position the capacity of a firm to sell a product or service of a particular quality on terms (price, delivery, credit, etc.) relative to other firms selling in the same market.

entry agreement an explicit agreement between host government and alien corporation made upon the latter's entry through direct investment. Entry agreements commonly impose time limits on the alien's rights of ownership, schedules for phasing out alien employees from certain categories and for increasing local value-added, and include host government incentives as well as guarantees to honor alien rights for a given duration.

international contractual joint venture a contractual agreement by two or more legal entities of different nationality to supply certain assets to a joint undertaking, assume certain operational responsibilities, and receive earnings as defined by contract.

international equity joint venture an enterprise in which ownership is shared among two or more corporations (or owners) of different nationalities, each of whom contributes certain assets, shares risk to some extent, assumes some degree of operational responsibility, and receives a share of earnings via dividends.

minority-owned joint venture less than 50 percent but more than 10 percent ownership of a joint venture. Also called an *affiliate*.

mixed venture one in which a government is part owner, or in which equity is owned jointly by public and private interests.

obsolescing bargain the situation where a foreign firm's contribution to a project is perceived to be diminishing relative to its return.

100 percent ownership the equity position of owning 100 percent of the voting stock of an enterprise. An enterprise is normally considered *wholly owned* if the principal owner holds 90 percent or more of the voting stock.

portfolio investment investment with an equity position of less than 10 percent and with no managerial responsibility.

qualifying shares the minimum number of shares required by law in order to become a director of a corporation, or a distribution of shares to a given number of local nationals to qualify for incorporation.

subsidiary a corporation unambiguously controlled by another corporation via ownership (that is, over 50 percent ownership of the voting stock).

tied sourcing a requirement that certain goods or services be procured from the nation providing credit, or from the corporation providing technology or technical services.

transnational a corporation owned and managed to a significant degree by nationals of more than one country.

turnkey operation a project undertaken under contract to design and construct an industrial plant.

uninational involving or operating within the boundaries of one nation. A uninational enterprise is a business established, owned, and operated by the nationals of the country where it is located.
valuable rights the capacity to exercise options of commercial value, such as the right to buy or sell something; to license or to use trademarks, copyrights, patents, or commercial secrets; to receive dividends, fees, royalties, and other payments; to legally enforce one's decisions or preferences vis-à-vis another.

6.1   Varieties of Ownership

One of the most debated subjects in international business is the ownership of foreign assets. Discussion of the relative merits of **100 percent ownership**, versus joint venturing, versus contracting goes on interminably. The 100 percenters speak of conflict of interest in joint ownership and the need for control and integration of all operating facilities within a global corporate system. The joint venturers emphasize local contribution and the commensurate right of local nationals to share ownership. The contractors speak of minimizing risk and taking full advantage of one's monopoly position in regard to either market access or technology, or both.

Over the past three decades, the U.S. preference has been for 100 percent ownership, although there is some evidence of a shift toward greater tolerance for joint ventures and contracts. The Japanese have opted more frequently for the joint venture ownership strategy. European investors are someplace in between.

The joint venture strategy tends to be associated with a firm's early moves overseas, when it lacks expertise in the markets it is entering and has insufficient capacity and resources to build an internationally integrated production/sales system. That is, the joint venture strategy is most characteristic of export-oriented and international corporations, the latter being characterized by an international division and a dual decision-making and control system. As management accumulates international expertise and the capability of integrating its far-flung operations into a global *system*, there is a natural tendency to centralize control and to build a structure to facilitate doing just that. Hence, the firm moves away from joint ventures.

Technically, anything owned less than 50 percent and down to 10 percent is a **minority-owned joint venture**, or an **affiliate**. If the equity position is less than 10 percent and carries no managerial responsibility, the investment is simply a **portfolio investment**. An enterprise is normally considered **wholly owned** if the principal owner holds 90 percent or more of the voting stock. Because some national laws require that several entities— individuals or corporations—contract to form a corporation, a certain number of **qualifying shares** may be held locally simply to satisfy this legal requirement. So anything between an equity of over 50 percent up to around 90 percent implies a joint venture. Such enterprises, which are unambiguously controlled via equity by another firm, are said to be **subsidiaries** of the latter, as opposed to mere **affiliates**. In fact, of course, even an affiliate may be controlled in important ways by the foreign parent.

The pure international **equity joint venture** is an enterprise in which ownership is shared among two or more corporations (or owners) of different nationality, each of which contributes certain assets, shares risk to some extent, assumes some degree of operational responsibility, and receives a share of earnings via dividends. An international joint venture may also be of a **contractual** nature, in which case two or more legal entities of different nationality agree via contract to supply certain assets to a joint undertaking, assume certain operational responsibilities, and receive earnings as defined by contract. Such undertakings are normally limited in both scope and time, although not necessarily. Very frequently, they do not have separate corporate identity, but operate as branches of both partners. In either the equity or contractual joint venture, the assets contributed by the partners may be tangible (i.e., equipment, land, or cash) or intangible (i.e., skills, technology, or valuable rights).

Combinations of Contract and Equity

Most commonly, what we call international joint ventures are neither purely equity nor purely contractual, but a mixture of both. For example, let us assume a joint venture in which a U.S. corporation and a Swiss corporation each own 50 percent of the voting stock—a so-called 50-50 joint venture. Let us assume further that the enterprise is incorporated in Switzerland, and that the Swiss company supplies the managerial personnel, the U.S. company, the technology. In addition, the Swiss agree to market the joint venture's product everywhere except in the United States through their own international network. The U.S. partner, in addition to selling the product in the United States, agrees to provide the results of its R&D on an ongoing basis, plus the right to brand names that it owns. Both parent companies give the joint venture the exclusive right to use relevant patents owned by the two. The two companies also agree to supply specified raw materials and components to the joint venture. Additionally, the Swiss company is to supply some debt capital, either through outright loans or guarantees. Finally, the U.S. partner is to design and supervise construction of the joint venture facilities and train its operating personnel.

Let us also assume that both firms put up an equal amount of equity capital in cash (or the equivalent in land or hardware, i.e., machinery and equipment) and share equally in managerial control via a board of directors on which voting power is split equally. Even so, each firm will probably also enter into a whole series of contracts with the joint venture relating to managerial services, know-how, technology, marketing, use of patents and trademarks, supply, loans, design and supervision, and training. For each such contract, the contracting partner receives royalties or fees in some stipulated amount. These payments are, of course, recorded as costs on the joint venture books, which means that they constitute a reduction in earnings taxable to the joint venture and are deducted before any payment of dividends.

The sale of services or lease of assets by the parent firm to a foreign subsidiary in which there is local equity investment (that is, local nationals own a minority interest) is always a tricky business. Should the parent firm be compelled to provide services and assets at cost, which means that it will be dividing the profit derived therefrom with the local investors? Or should the subsidiary pay the full price (cost plus profit)? The latter would seem to be an acceptable policy so long as the price is a reasonable one. Because governments realize that they do not have adequate monitoring mechanisms, they usually simply outlaw these nondividend payments from subsidiary to parent. Unmonitored, these flows can, of course, move profit from one subsidiary to another or from subsidiary to parent at the whim of management and at the expense of local stockholders and tax collectors. This movement is one form of transfer pricing, pricing so as to reduce earnings in one firm and increase them in another.

To make the relationship even more complex, the U.S. company may have funded part of its equity investment in the joint venture, not in cash or hardware, but in shares of the U.S. company itself. In that case, either the Swiss partner or the joint venture may end up holding a percentage of ownership of the U.S. company, which in turn still owns 50 percent of the Swiss joint venture. The U.S. corporation has traded part of its equity for a foreign asset. Two examples are a 1969 exchange by Minnesota Mining and Manufacturing Company of its convertible preference stock for the common shares of its U.K. subsidiary in the hands of 30 percent minority owners, and a 1971 exchange by the Chrysler Corporation of Chrysler stock for an additional 20 percent of a Mexican firm in which it already had a 46 percent interest. (Japanese corporations find this strategy virtually closed to them because of a law preventing them from owning their own stock.)

Under some conceivable set of circumstances, any possible combination of contract and equity is possible, although as one approaches 100 percent ownership some of the contractual relationships become increasingly unlikely, and indeed may be forbidden by law. For instance, according to Brazilian law, if the foreign firm owns more than 50 percent of a local firm, that firm (technically the subsidiary of the foreign firm) cannot enter into license agreements for patents or trademarks with the parent, and can enter into agreements for know-how only for the first five years after startup. The Brazilian authorities wish to have profits repatriated as such, and not as fees and royalties, which are costed against the Brazilian subsidiary and thus paid out of pretax earnings.

Features of International Ownership

Many query the implicit assumption in the forgoing discussion that ownership across an international frontier is somehow different from the purely domestic. There are, I suggest, at least four reasons for believing that it does differ.

Resource Allocation.   Political commitments differ among nations because each nation assigns different priorities to what it considers the appropriate allocation of its resources, of its land, its waterways, its minerals, its manpower, its energy, its skills, its R&D effort, and its financial capital. The appearance of an alien business on the scene implies the use of some local resources. That is, a nation's allocation of resources is influenced by the firm's presence. The degree of penetration by an alien firm that a country tolerates is possibly related to:

1. The relative size of the two national economies;
2. Their historical relationship;
3. The size and importance of the foreign enterprise relative to the host economy;
4. The nature of the enterprise's local involvement (for instance, the degree of its public service, strategic and/or essential consumer content);
5. The nature of the international linkage, from complete alien control of decision making to virtually no control (as in the case of a simple sale and purchase agreement);
6. The nature and effectiveness of the political elite of the host nation;
7. The image and political effectiveness of the alien firm's parent country and of the alien firm itself.

Law.   One must consider international ownership differently from the purely domestic case because legal concepts generally differ more from country to country than within a single country, even those with a federal structure. Some nations do not even recognize the right of private individuals, whether domestic *or* foreign, to own certain types of (or any) real estate, mineral rights, buildings, productive machinery, or valuable intangible rights. For example, many nations of Spanish heritage deny the right of private persons to own underground mineral resources. Many countries (and some of the states of the United States) restrict alien ownership of real property. In socialist countries, the private ownership of certain types of real property is sharply restrained and, indeed, the derivation of private profit from real property may be a criminal offense.

Sometimes property rights vis-à-vis aliens are considered to be reciprocal ones. That is, if one country recognizes rights for nationals from another nation, the latter will recognize similar rights for nationals from the former. Some U.S. state and federal laws in the areas of banking, property, and mineral rights ownership are of this nature. In other cases, ownership may be considered in the nature of a lease or public trust—as in Yugoslavia, where the trustees are relatively autonomous working communities. Such a lease or trust may be subject to periodic revaluation and transfer if certain minimum conditions imposed by law are not met.

National Wealth.   A difference between international and **uninational** ownership may likewise appear because of differences in levels of national wealth. If the difference is great, the use of scarce resources (those that are underpriced for some reason) may be considered a matter of vital national interest. Given the vast disparity in time horizons between the decision-making political elite and the mass of consumers (who may be existing only slightly above subsistence level), market forces may not be perceived by the elite to be such as to achieve national development objectives. Hence, a responsible elite (responsible in terms of trying to promote maximum, long-term national development) may use measures for evaluating alien use of scarce local resources other than internal, financial profit and loss. Some of these measures may be balance-of-payments, national income, public revenue, long-run growth, or allocational effects.[1] Thus, the reception an alien proposing to establish a local enterprise should anticipate may differ substantially from that accorded a purely domestic venture.

In a less-developed country, because the consumer (the ultimate buyer and user of goods) frequently has one time horizon and the governing elite another, which is generally much longer, there can be no single set of mutually acceptable prices. In a more highly developed market economy, these two time horizons tend to converge; prices are assumed to have some relation to relative contribution to national development. For instance, the consumer in the more-developed countries is willing to pay a great deal for education. A village farmer in a traditional society may not be. In general, in the more-developed countries, people are more likely to approve of government expenditures designed to stimulate long-run growth (e.g., education and R&D), although it means taking money out of their pockets to do so. In a developing country just moving off the subsistence level, this is not a

---

[1] For a more complete discussion of this aspect, see R. D. Robinson, *International Business Policy* (New York: Holt, Rinehart & Winston, 1964), Chap. 3; and *National Control of Foreign Business Entry* (New York: Praeger, 1976).

popular thing for politicians to attempt. For these and other reasons, the price system may not allocate resources in a way that maximizes long-run economic growth.

If price cannot be assumed even to approximate the priorities desired by the elite in allocating resources, then the private property system cannot be permitted to operate. Why, one may ask, are we concerned only with an elite? Simply because it probably represents the greatest force for modernization and creativity; for investment in education, public health, and economic growth; and, eventually, for economic integration and, hopefully, one day, political integration as well. The mass of people living in highly traditional communities at near subsistence level cannot, in the near future, be expected to demonstrate the sort of sophisticated and untraditional behavior that leads to modernization through a free market or liberal political system.

Monetary Systems.   Difference in monetary systems and wealth levels dictates a further disparity between international and domestic ownership. Assuming that the alien interest is of U.S. origin, profits must be repatriated in dollars or something of value ultimately convertible to dollars (with which dollars may be purchased). Because of the forced-draft development (a deliberate effort by a government to capture savings and force investment in productive capacity at higher levels than would normally be the case) that a widening international disparity in per capita national wealth induces in many poor countries, sooner or later development-committed political elites may be inclined to enforce their own consumption preferences over that of the masses. One way of doing this is for a government to husband scarce resources, including scarce foreign exchange (foreign currencies) such as dollars, and to allocate them through administrative procedures to high-priority imports. Hence, the exchange rate (the rate at which dollars may be purchased with local currency) is not market determined, but "pegged," which means that scarce foreign exchange is periodically undervalued; that is why it is scarce. The local currency buys more dollars, or the dollars buy fewer local currency units, than would be the case if the conversion rate were determined by a free movement of exports and imports. (Wherever there is a foreign exchange control system in place, this must be true. If not, there would be no need for the control system, for its purpose is to capture undervalued foreign exchange and ration it according to a government-determined priority of use.) Therefore, an alien firm repatriating profits at the pegged official rate may receive more dollars than its local currency earnings really justify, in that the marginal value of those dollars to long-term development is likely to be very much greater than that implied in the official exchange rate. Even free exchange rates would be set by relatively few commodities being traded internationally within a limited range of time, which might or might not clear the market at a rate equal to the relative marginal value of the two currencies to long-run economic growth. At best, it would be a lucky coincidence if the two values (of a free exchange rate and of a marginal value to development) converged.

Also, inflation rates periodically tend to move ahead of the rate of change in an exchange rate. Say 100 pesos buy a dollar at the official rate. Prices in the peso-area then move up, say, 50 percent, and the exchange rate (pesos per dollar) is increased by 25 percent. Now 125 pesos buy a dollar, but they are worth only 83 of the previous pesos. The dollar is now of less value than before in terms of local goods and services according to the official rate, but, in fact, it probably is not; rather it is worth more if one relates it to economic growth. The point is that the dollar can purchase foreign capital equipment and skills which, in combination with local resources, can maximize the productivity of those resources.

All of these national pressures generated by disparities in politically determined resource allocation, legal system, level of per capita wealth, and monetary system, in turn generate a distinctive nationalism. This nationalism becomes relevant to the international manager when it leads to restraints on alien ownership of commercially valuable assets located within the national territory, or on profits (through special taxes, artificially high costs, or controlled prices), or on the repatriation of earnings generated by such assets. Therefore, international ownership can be, and usually is, very different from uninational ownership in terms of how ownership is perceived and valued by the relevant authorities, which in turn may be equated with different sets of restraints imposed on alien ownership.

Further Restraints on Alien Firms

The question arises whether under the circumstances described a firm is well advised to invest at all in the *ownership* of physical assets located elsewhere, particularly in a less-developed country. One suspects that there may be, in fact, relatively few instances in which such investment is advisable on a long-run basis. For such investment to be attractive, the investing company must feel relatively certain that it can recapture its investment, plus an appropriate return, within a period of time during which it can demonstrate that its ownership is in the interest of the host society, both as presently perceived and in reality. (The corporate planner must assume that these two images of national interest will become similar over the planning horizon.)

Various measures may be used, explicitly or implicitly, by host governments in evaluating what foreign business interests do locally. For the corporation, long-run security of market position and business assets is anchored in the capacity of its management to think in similar terms and so structure overseas enterprises as to identify with the *perceived* interests of host societies. Relevant economic measures are net-value-added, balance-of-payments, public revenue, and growth-generating effects—the last being a combination of allocational and innovational effects. It seems quite clear that the political vulnerability of a given enterprise is a function of all four of these measures, taken separately and in concert, plus certain essentially noneconomic measures of political impact that relate to (1) a firm's operational policies, (2) the structure of the enterprise, (3) the size of the enterprise, and (4) the nature of the product.

Aside from avoiding political hostility, the foreign investor maximizes return by limiting investment and ownership to those rights and assets productive of the greatest return, which, in the long run, should be precisely those of greatest value to the associated local business interests and the host society. On occasion, the foreigner may feel compelled to protect that profit stream by retaining ownership of certain rights and assets. For example, a strategy of majority ownership may be selected in order to assure continued purchase of intermediary goods from the parent firm, or to assure a management contract or the purchase of technical assistance. Obviously, however, if a firm feels it necessary to capture its profit stream in this manner it must likewise feel that, in the eyes of foreign associates or host governments, the value of what it is contributing may not measure up to what it is extracting. The firm is thereby admitting its vulnerability. The assumption that either contractual rights or equity ownership can be supported when the firm's impact is contrary to the interest of foreign associates and/or the host society has only short-run validity, if that. For example, if a firm has been securing an adequate product for its market through contract manufacturing undertaken by a locally owned firm—or could do so—then the establishment of a foreign-owned manufacturing establishment may be considered unwarranted and, therefore, be opposed by both the host government and local business community, unless there is some more attractive alternative employment for the local resources concerned.

The point is that, looked at from the side of the local society in which an alien-owned enterprise is embedded, the level of earnings and other costs imposed by its activity on the host economy should be of lesser value than the inputs or contributions made by the alien parent corporation. Some of these costs to local society are obviously very difficult to quantify, such as the amount of local enterprise growth being blocked. But the stream of earnings paid out by a society *is very visible*. To minimize risk, these returns should, if possible, be adjusted periodically as the perceived cost/benefit ratio for the local society shifts, as it almost certainly will over time.

Typically, though admittedly not in all cases, as the foreign firm transfers resources and skills over time, its continuing contribution relative to its return will become less and less. Some have dubbed this situation the **obsolescing bargain**. In such event, one can expect mounting host government pressure in the direction of reducing the outflow of earnings to the foreign parent—perhaps to zero. Some research indicates that a firm may be willing to limit its initial entry in a foreign market relative to a new product to a license or joint venture. However, as the product matures (that is, as the relevant product and/or production processes become routinized and part of general industrial knowledge), the firm may try to protect its position through a 100 percent owned enterprise. At this point, product differentiation, heavy promotional effort, and production specialization become critical, all of which push in the direction of centralized control and the elimination of any local partners. Such a policy may very well lead to maximum political vulnerability.

It has been precisely this inflexibility on the part of Western business in readjusting benefits derived from a foreign venture *so as to accord with the benefits received by the host country* that has induced many countries to introduce the **entry agreement**. This phrase refers to an explicit agreement between host government and corporation, made upon the latter's entry through direct investment. This system was first introduced in the early 1950s by India for certain ventures and more generally by Indonesia in 1956. The idea is now quite widespread among LDCs. The essential elements of such an agreement are: (1) a time limit on the right of the alien corporation to occupy and use industrial properties, most frequently 20 to 30 years, but often extendable under certain conditions; (2) a host government guarantee that it will not expropriate the alien-owned enterprise limited to the same period; (3) a schedule for phasing out alien employees of various categories; and (4) a schedule for increasing local value-added over time. Most commonly there are provisions for the phased spinoff of foreign ownership, say 30 percent in 10 years, 100 percent in 20 years. Furthermore, approval may be given only to those projects meeting certain tests, such as employment, capital commitment, foreign exchange earnings, exports, production, and location.[2]

An entry agreement, to all intents and purposes, means that rights arising from ownership are of a contractual nature. Only so long as the alien firm lives up to its agreement are those rights valid. In that a government, in entering into such an agreement, specifically states that the terms of such an agreement are in harmony with its national interests and development plans, the element of uncertainty from the corporate view may be reduced. And, of course, it forces the corporate negotiators either to justify or modify their relationships to conform to such interests and plans. A few countries (Indonesia and Malaysia) have given these agreements the coloration of international contracts by binding themselves to arbitrate disputes arising under such agreements before the International Center for the Settlement of Investment Disputes. Others (Chile) may give the alien owner the right to sue the government locally in event of alleged breach of contract.

The relative power position of the corporation tends to shift downward once it is locked in the embrace of a government. In the case of an international **mixed venture** (one in which the host government is part owner), the embrace is more real than vicarious. However, were the firm to restrain its participation and earnings to that fraction of the total local enterprise representing continuing externally derived inputs (those not available locally), then its leverage should continue to be great. This strategy requires a continuing cost/benefit analysis. If, however, management's attitude is that joint venturing dilutes control, and somehow this is seen as apart from any

[2]See Robinson, *National Control of Foreign Business Entry,* for a detailed study of entry agreements and other entry conditions.

comparative profit calculation, then it should be made explicit that management is maximizing power, not profit.

Basically three questions are involved in a choice of ownership strategy:

1.   In what should the domestic (parent) firm hold ownership? Possible choices: equity (zero to 100 percent), debt, intangible assets (such as patents, copyrights, trademarks, trade secrets), managerial knowledge and skills, technical knowledge and skills, distribution networks, physical assets (machines, land, resources), other contractual rights (such as a lease).
2.   In what should the associated foreign business interest hold ownership?
3.   What type of foreign associate(s) should the firm select? Possible choices: the general public, the host government, a limited number of identified private persons, a business entity, a nonprofit organization (e.g., a labor union).

6.2   Rights and Assets Owned by the International Firm

Reasons advanced by parent managements for insisting upon 100 percent ownership of foreign ventures fall into these categories:

1.   Unpleasant past experience with joint ventures;
2.   Lack of confidence in the integrity and/or ability of foreign business groups;
3.   Uncertainty regarding the identify of those to whom the locally held equity may be transferred in the future;
4.   Difficulty in maintaining equity;
5.   Conflict of interest between the parent company and the foreign partners (e.g., in such decisions as intercompany pricing, profit distribution, rate of growth, personnel policy, pricing, quality control);
6.   Desire to integrate the operation with the total corporate system in respect to export, production, marketing, and financial management.

It will be noted that reason one above is a matter of chance, and reason two, possibly a function of the first, reflects a generalized distrust. Not a few experienced international business executives have observed that the general level of integrity is not significantly different across international frontiers. Dishonesty cannot be associated with nationality, only the form it takes. Levels of competence obviously vary, but training is always possible. The absence of any effort to develop a local management, given the frequently great cost advantage, throws one back to reasons one or two. In any event, a management contract need not be associated with participation in equity. The future transfer of locally held shares to "undesirables" may constitute a serious problem, although in some cases transferability can be limited. Equity can be maintained in a joint venture through special stock-holders' agreement, if possible under local law. Conflict of interest, on the other hand, is a very real issue, although many areas of conflict can be eliminated by working out operating policies ahead of time. One firm actually staged a "war game" simulating the conflicts of setting up a joint venture with its prospective foreign partner, the result of which was 90 percent agreement. The 10 percent area of disagreement was worked out by compromise and committed to writing. Profit channels need not be the same for all participants; different classes of stock may be possible, special bo-nuses may be paid, and a minority interest represented on the board of directors may hold a veto power in certain decision areas. Such contingency planning may be very important in avoiding costly conflict.

Forgetting for the moment personal preferences on the part of decision makers and the extent of a firm's resources, five factors are possibly relevant to the ownership decision: (1) competitive position, (2) availability of accept-able associates (or consumers), (3) legal constraints, (4) control require-ments, and (5) benefit/cost relationships. These are diagrammed in Figure 6.1. I shall consider each in the order indicated.

Competitive Position

Competitive position refers to a firm's capacity to sell a product or service of a particular quality on terms (price, delivery, credit, guaranties, etc.) relative to other firms selling in the same market. If the firm's good or service is, in fact, uniquely superior or effectively differentiated (by brand name) and has commercial value, it may well opt for 100 percent ownership, if this rela-tionship will better protect the uniqueness of its product (or its name) than would lesser ownership and some contractual relationship. And the host government may be forced to accept it. If, however, another alien firm—or local firm—offers a comparable product or service at a lesser cost in terms of scarce inputs (such as foreign exchange), the initial firm may find itself under pressure to reduce return, either by selling some or all of its equity to a local firm and relying on a contractual relationship that generates an appro-priately reduced income or, if already linked by contract, by reducing the percentage fee stipulated therein. The latter is often easier to accomplish, particularly if forced upon the firm suddenly. Reducing a royalty or fee is relatively easy; spinning off ownership is not. For that very reason this strategy (choice of contractual relationship) may be avoided. The host gov-ernment's attitude toward private property (for example, an ideologically based commitment to protect property rights) may tend to restrain it from forcing a readjustment in ownership, such as expropriation. In the short run, it may be much less restrained in forcing renegotiation of a contract, for the life of a contractual relationship is limited in any event. In the long run, however, ownership may be in greater jeopardy because of the rigidity implicit in the idea that ownership runs forever so long as certain conditions are fulfilled (such as payment of taxes).

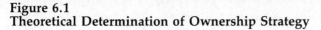

Figure 6.1
Theoretical Determination of Ownership Strategy

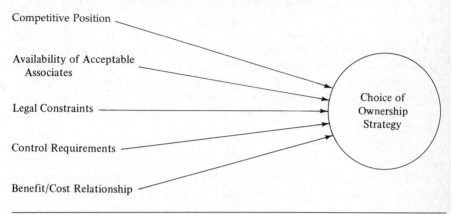

Of course, most firms fall in between a pure monopoly position (whether based on a unique product, unique process, unique access to market, relevant skills, or capital) and a perfectly competitive situation. They must be willing to meet competing offers in respect to ownership and contractual relationships. A flexible ownership policy is thereby indicated in the international case. Indeed, the entry agreement, even though it stipulates a spin-off equity over time, may provide maximum stability.

Availability of Acceptable Associates

Whether a partner, contractee, contractor, licensor, licensee, supplier, or customer, the availability of acceptable associates obviously imposes a restraint. Even if a firm can find suitable associates, how does it know that they will retain that interest and not transfer it to others who may be less than acceptable? In any event, everyone dies sooner or later. What of the next generation? Here, local laws of inheritance and the possibility of imposing legal restraint on stock or contract transference may be of critical importance. Barring this problem, and in the absence of an immediately available associate acceptable to the parent firm, the latter must consider the cost of finding and developing appropriate local nationals. Consequently, one perforce gets into a benefit/cost analysis, which is anchored in one's expectations of what the local associate will contribute to the enterprise.

Legal Factors

Next, one might appropriately consider laws bearing directly on the matter of selecting an ownership-contracting strategy. Certain legal restraints have already been touched upon, specifically, inheritance law, law on restricting transfer of ownership, entry controls, and recognition of private property rights. A variety of other legal factors bear on the choice of ownership strategy. I give only a few to illustrate the point, largely from a U.S. point of view.

1. Foreign tax credit. For example, for U.S. firms to credit foreign income and wealth taxes paid by associated foreign firms against U.S. tax liability, the U.S. firm must own at least 10 percent of the equity of a first-tier foreign subsidiary, which in turn must own at least 10 percent of the second, and the second at least 10 percent of the third. But in no case may the U.S. interest be less than 5 percent.

2. Tax liability. For example, if a U.S. firm owns more than 50 percent of the voting power of a foreign corporation, it is a controlled foreign corporation and some or all of its income may be taxable currently in the United States even if not repatriated.

3. Reduction of withholding tax. The withholding tax imposed abroad on dividends paid to a domestic firm by an associated foreign firm may be reduced if the foreign firm is owned to a significant degree by the domestic. For example, the French withholding tax is reduced from 15 percent to 5 percent if a U.S. firm owns at least 10 percent of the paying French firm.

4. Withholding tax and local ownership. The withholding tax imposed abroad may be reduced if local ownership is permitted. For example, the Canadian withholding tax on dividends is reduced from 15 to 10 percent on those paid by a Canadian subsidiary to a foreign parent if Canadians are permitted to participate in the equity and voting rights of the Canadian subsidiary to the extent of at least 25 percent.

5. Tax exemption and ownership. Some countries impose a low tax or no tax on dividends received from foreign subsidiaries if a minimum ownership test is met. For instance, if a Canadian parent corporation owns 25 percent or more of a foreign subsidiary, dividends received from the latter are exempt from Canadian tax.

6. Liquidation. For example, the redemption or sale of stock in, or liquidation of, a U.S.-controlled foreign corporation (in which more than 50 percent of the voting power is owned by U.S. persons or entities) may result in ordinary income, not capital gain, and be taxable as such.

7. Investment guarantees. For example, in order to qualify for a guarantee issued by OPIC, a U.S. corporation must be over 50 percent owned by U.S. entities. In order for an investment made by an associated foreign firm to qualify, the latter must be at least 95 percent owned by U.S. interests. Other capital exporting countries have different ownership tests in order to qualify for their respective schemes.

8. Social security. In the U.S., for a firm to include U.S. citizens employed overseas under U.S. social security and in a qualified deferred compensation plan, it must own at least 20 percent of the voting stock of the foreign corporation employing those citizens and, if they are employed by a second-tier corporation, the 20 percent owned foreign corporation must own at least 50 percent of the second tier.

9. Treaty rights. To take advantage of certain treaties among foreign countries (such as those relating to right of establishment, national and most-favored-nation treatment, access to local courts, double taxation, patent protection, and reciprocal dividend tax exemption), nationality tests in terms of ownership may be imposed.

10. Selling rights. To sell in certain restricted markets (e.g., government defense procurement, NATO, and projects financed by the Agency for International Development (AID)), the firm may be required to meet nationality tests, including ownership. For example, Sulzer, the Swiss manufacturer of diesel engines and other products, was compelled to limit its equity in a French enterprise to 50 percent because, according to French law, the subsidiary had to be majority French-owned in order to qualify as a supplier of diesel engines and other products to the nationalized French industry, navy, and armed forces.

11. Restrictions on ownership. The host government may restrict the percentage of foreign ownership. For example, for many years Japan banned majority foreign ownership of Japanese enterprises except in special cases. Mexico, Yugoslavia, and Turkey specifically limit alien ownership, generally to 49 percent. Of the socialist countries, Poland, Rumania, Yugoslavia, and Hungary permit 49 percent foreign ownership in joint ventures with local enterprises. The People's Republic of China requires at least 25 percent foreign participation in a joint venture. Many countries bar firms more than 49 percent foreign-owned from owning real estate or engaging in importing, exporting, local distribution, publishing, and trade-related services. In general, most countries, including the United States, restrict foreign ownership in certain types of strategic industries. Typically, these include internal communication, domestic transport, coastal shipping, lease of government land, agriculture, insurance, banking, and sometimes mining. The Andean countries prohibit direct investment in activities adequately covered by existing investments. Particularly vulnerable to entry restraints on foreign ownership are *acquisitions of existing enterprises*. The laws of many countries discriminate in this fashion.

For further treatment of these and other legal considerations, see Chapter Eight.

Control Requirements

In discussing our fourth critical variable relative to choice of ownership strategy, it is important to make explicit the implicit assumptions held by those who simply equate equity ownership with control. These assumptions are:

1. Ownership rights resting on equity are, in the long run, less likely to be disturbed by a foreign government than purely contractual rights. (Empirically, this does not seem to have been the case.)
2. Total control by the international headquarters is necessary to accomplish corporate objectives, whether they be defined in terms of maximization of corporate profit, return on investment, cash throw-off, growth, geographical spread, or market share. (May or may not hold true in a particular case.)
3. Adequate control without equity ownership is impossible. (This assumption implies that contractual rights cannot be enforced. Experience does not support this assumption.)
4. Total control by an international firm of a foreign enterprise is legally possible on the basis of majority or 100 percent ownership. (In fact, local law and regulation may seriously restrict freedom of decision in respect to personnel policies (such as wage rates and hiring and firing, negotiation with unions, nationality of management and of labor), transfer pricing, product pricing, profit repatriation, local borrowing, contracting with the associated domestic firm or entering into tying agreements, market restraints, expansion of plant, reinvestment of earnings, purchase of materials, degree of local manufacture, import of further capital, use of external services, and plant location—to mention a few areas.)

Possibly it needs pointing out that equity-based control can be maintained with substantially less than a majority interest, if the balance of the equity is held by a large number of unorganized individuals or entities. There are other ways of diluting majority ownership. One is to use a nominee or nominees (literally strawmen) which, for one reason or another, will do as the minority owner decides. Some national laws prohibit this practice—Mexican, for example. Another form of dilution is the destruction of bearer shares, where bearer shares are legal, to elevate the minority interest to a de facto majority. Still another method is to put the majority ownership into a trust that the minority owner controls through his control of the trustees. Again, local law may or may not recognize the trust as a separate legal entity for this purpose. Finally, local law permitting, one might issue different types of stock—voting and nonvoting, with the majority of the voting stock retained by the minority owner.

The need for controls arises in anticipation of conflict of interest. Possible conflict areas are:

1. *Ownership* (the sale or transfer of equity to third parties);
2. *Dividend policy* (distribution versus reinvestment);

3. *Borrowing* (acceptable debt/equity ratios);
4. *Plant expansion* (what and where)
5. *Research and development* (level, purpose, location);
6. *Production processes* (degree of integration, degree of capital-labor intensity);
7. *Source of supply* (external or internal, transfer prices);
8. *Quality standards* (domestic or absolute, international standards);
9. *Product mix* (diversification, competitive exports);
10. *Reinvestment* (dilution of equity held by a minority);
11. *Terms of sales* (credits, servicing, pricing);
12. *Market area* (restricted or open);
13. *Market penetration* (choice of channels, promotional effort);
14. *Labor-management relations* (degree of paternalism, union recognition and negotiation, national versus international negotiation, levels of remuneration, profit sharing);
15. *Management selection and remuneration* (nationality, skills required, number, salaries, decision-making style—see Section 5.5);
16. *Politics* (honesty, company-government relations, degree of sensitivity to political decisions such as desired allocation of national resources); and
17. *Image*.

The relevant query here is, given these possible conflict areas, what controls are needed to maintain a tolerable benefit/cost relationship for the firm? These controls may rest on the leverage the firm can mount by reason of:

1. *Ownership* (control over the election of boards; hiring, development, and firing of managers; and/or determination of financial structure and profit distribution);
2. *Market access* (control over channels, trademarks, brand names, and/or ownership of import licenses or business permits);
3. *Technology* (control of patents and relevant R&D flow);
4. *Finance* (ability to provide low-cost debt and equity and/or working capital, such as commercial credit);
5. *Personnel* (ability to provide scarce skills at relatively low cost—including management—and/or relatively cheap labor);
6. *Political assistance* (greater ability to deal effectively with governments in preventing restraints or gaining largesse; and/or to gain customer or market acceptability);
7. *Supply* (limitation of source for the associated firm);
8. *Physical assets* (control over sites; specialized transport, power sources).

In each case, the cost is that which would be incurred by the firm (firm A) if the relevant contribution of the associated firm (firm B) were to be interrupted. Hence, the ability of firm A to shut off any one of these flows is a control device, and the ability of firm B to do likewise, a restraint.

In summary, a firm should determine what it proposes to do and where, define the essential elements of control relevant to accomplishing

Figure 6.2
Possible Contributions by Participating Firms to a Joint Enterprise*

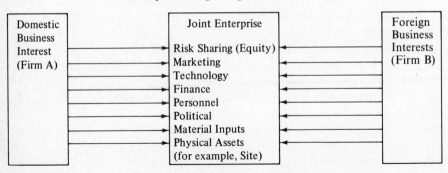

(i.e., costs)
*The term "joint enterprise," it will be recalled, is used to avoid confusion with the equity-sharing concept inherent in the term "joint venture."

that purpose, and then decide upon the best means of assuring that control. The often-hidden cost of maintaining long-distance control through equity should be included in this analysis. Otherwise, the benefit/cost analysis will be invalidated and corporate objectives not be achieved.

Benefit/Cost Analysis

Costs for a domestic firm and its associated foreign business interests may be seen as two sets of flows converging on a foreign entity, which, in the terminology used here, is always a joint enterprise. It is joint, not necessarily in an equity sense, but always in the sense of sharing common interests and responsibilities, whether explicitly recognized or not, with foreign business interests.[3] These costs, or contributions (from the point of view of the joint enterprise), may be classified generally in terms of assistance in marketing, technology, finance, personnel, politics, supply, and/or physical assets (see Figure 6.2). It is important to distinguish here between a one-time contribution (or transfer) and one that continues over time.

On the other hand, the benefits accruing to the domestic and foreign business interests may flow through a number of channels, as illustrated in Figure 6.3. These benefits (costs from the point of the joint enterprise) should likewise be viewed over time. Some flows, however, may be of a one-time nature, such as in a simple sale or a **turnkey operation**.

It is relevant to ask at this point: Is there agreement as to who contributes what, for how long, and who receives how much, by what route, for

[3]May be partner firm or firms, suppliers, contractors, contractees, or customers.

Figure 6.3
Possible Benefits Flowing to Firms Associated in a Joint Enterprise

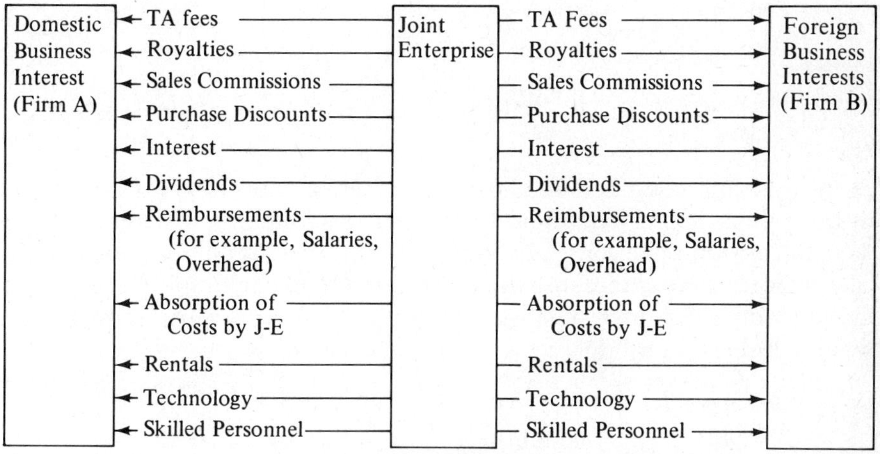

Domestic Business Interest (Firm A)		Joint Enterprise		Foreign Business Interests (Firm B)
← TA fees ───────			─ TA Fees ──────→	
← Royalties ─────			─ Royalties ──────→	
← Sales Commissions ──			─ Sales Commissions ─→	
← Purchase Discounts──			─ Purchase Discounts─→	
← Interest ───────			─ Interest ──────→	
← Dividends ──────			─ Dividends ─────→	
← Reimbursements─── (for example, Salaries, Overhead)			─ Reimbursements────→ (for example, Salaries, Overhead)	
← Absorption of ──── Costs by J-E			─ Absorption of ────→ Costs by J-E	
← Rentals ───────			─ Rentals ──────→	
← Technology ─────			─ Technology ─────→	
← Skilled Personnel──			─ Skilled Personnel ─→	

how long? In other words, what are the expectations? As skills are transferred from the international firm, the flow of management contributions in terms of personnel and development of local nationals may dry up. Is this anticipated by both parties? How soon?

To simplify this discussion, let us assume two individuals, Mr. A and Ms. B. Presumably, they would combine their resources in a joint undertaking only in the event that they both perceived that their respective benefits flowing from a combined effort would surpass those anticipated in an individual effort. A split in benefits is proposed, say, 50-50. In the first instance, Mr. A will look at the benefit/cost ratio as he perceives it, that is, the self-perceived value of what he will contribute. This will be discounted by his ability to measure these flows and his confidence in the measure. In order to assure this flow, he should anticipate the need for some degree of control over the joint operation, which effort will encounter some restraints by Ms. B (that is, negative controls so far as Mr. A is concerned), who is trying to do the same thing. If it is possible to reduce potential conflict of interest and dissatisfaction to a level that would leave the appropriately discounted flow of benefits still acceptably greater than the flow of contribution (that is, significantly greater than that anticipated in a one-person enterprise) for both parties, a joint enterprise should result. If not, it is because of the inability of Mr. A or Ms. B, or both, to adjust the expected flows of contributions and benefits, to design better measures for the flows, to develop a heightened confidence in them, or to shift the cost of control.

To avoid a critical level of dissatisfaction, Mr. A's self-perceived benefit/cost ratio must be approximately equal to, or exceed, the ratio he perceives for Ms. B. The reverse must likewise be true. Each must perceive his or her own ratio as approximately equal to or exceeding that of the other.

Hence:

self-perceived   other-perceived

$$\left(\frac{\text{benefit}_A}{\text{cost}_A} \right) A \geq \left(\frac{\text{benefit}_B}{\text{cost}_B} \right) A, \text{ and} \tag{6.1}$$

$$\left(\frac{\text{benefit}_B}{\text{cost}_B} \right) B \geq \left(\frac{\text{benefit}_A}{\text{cost}_A} \right) B. \tag{6.2}$$

Note that this condition implies nothing about the vertical or diagonal relationships. In fact, one should expect that over time, A's perception of B's benefit/cost ratio will converge on B's self-perceived ratio, for both A and B should learn how to measure the flows better, and communications should be less subject to manipulation by either. Thus, a long-run equilibrium would require that:

self-perceived   other-perceived

$$\left(\frac{\text{benefit}_B}{\text{cost}_B} \right) A = \left(\frac{\text{benefit}_B}{\text{cost}_B} \right) B, \text{ and} \tag{6.3}$$

$$\left(\frac{\text{benefit}_A}{\text{cost}_A} \right) B = \left(\frac{\text{benefit}_A}{\text{cost}_A} \right) A. \tag{6.4}$$

These relationships imply further that

self-perceived   other-perceived

$$\left(\frac{\text{benefit}_A}{\text{cost}_A} \right) A = \left(\frac{\text{benefit}_B}{\text{cost}_B} \right) B. \tag{6.5}$$

If the self-perceived benefit/cost ratios vary significantly, a potential conflict of interest is hidden in the situation. It is translated into overt dissatisfaction as one or both of the parties becomes aware of this disparity even though the initial conditions [equations (6.1) and (6.2)] were met. Note that there is no mention of the actual benefit/cost ratios, only the self-perceived and other-perceived ratios, for reality is only relevant as it is perceived.

No method suggests itself for quantifying these factors in any precise manner, least of all those relating to determining the tolerable limits of conflict. But many firms do not even consider the range of possible benefit/cost relationships, instead rush into all overseas adventures according to some fixed ownership policy. Even for the level of conflict that will be tolerated, it is useful to try inserting carefully considered subjective values and to consider at what point conflict is likely to bring about significant added restraints and to force a firm to incur added costs to maintain tolerable controls. A costing of various types of controls vis-à-vis possible losses (or gains) in terms of achieving corporate objectives may be useful.

The point is that this sort of exercise leads one to ask the relevant questions, such as, which of the contributions that firm A can make to the joint enterprise (costs to A) will firm B accept at the same, or higher, value as that assigned by A? Presumably, this will result in the maximization of the benefit/cost ratio for A within an acceptable level of conflict. Hence, the relevant questions for a firm are:

1. What value does the firm (firm A) place on what it proposes to contribute?
2. What value does firm B place on A's contribution?
3. What value does firm A place on the benefits to accrue to it?
4. What value does firm B place on the benefits to accrue to A?
5. What value does firm B place on the benefits to accrue to it?
6. What value does firm A place on the benefits to accrue to B?
7. How certain is A of its measure of resources received and resources contributed?
8. What restraints does A anticipate?
9. What are the likely costs to A of these restraints?
10. What controls does A perceive to be necessary to reduce the effect of these restraints to a tolerable level?
11. What is the cost of maintaining these controls?
12. How will the value of all these factors shift over time?

The importance of the final query lies in the fact that, if any of the values shift significantly, mounting pressure toward a comparable shift in the flows of contribution and benefit should be anticipated. By anticipating such shifts, they may be made with minimum friction and cost, in both psychological and physical terms.

Assume that the domestic firm, say, a U.S. company, supplies from sources outside of the host country, say Peru, virtually all of the technology, managerial skills, financing, and marketing services for the 80 percent of the product that is exported. We shall assume that comparable services and assets are not available from alternative sources, local or foreign. Given this set of relationships, 100 percent U.S. ownership of the Peruvian enterprise is perhaps justified. As time passes, several things happen: (1) the relevant technical and managerial skills are transferred to local nationals; (2) the market becomes essentially an internal Peruvian one rather than an export one; (3) local finance (debt plus reinvested earnings) sustains the operation; and (4) other firms are willing to supply the equivalent of the few remaining parent company inputs under contract. At this point, the parent firm is contributing little or nothing that would justify continued ownership.

Under these circumstances, although a 100 percent or majority ownership may be optimum for the first period over time, a subsequent reduction in foreign ownership to a minority position or only to a contractual relationship seems reasonable. In other words, the marginal utility to host country economic growth of the dollars being repatriated by the parent company becomes greater than the marginal utility of the current contribution of the parent company. One measure of this change is the willingness of others to do the same thing for less return. Such a consideration is particularly appropriate where the host country has been experiencing or anticipating a persistent balance-of-payments deficit because of asymmetric economic relationships between the host country and the domicile of the parent firm, an asymmetry inherent where wealth levels, growth rates, and political regimes are widely disparate.

It is precisely this logic that pushes countries in the direction of limiting alien ownership in time. Such pressures have the effect of pushing the foreign firm to a greater utilization of local resources so as to be in a preferred position to sell by contract those external inputs still required, such as new technology and access to an international marketing network.

6.3   Rights and Assets Owned by the Local Firm

Here we have the reverse situation, with the same devices for transferring **valuable rights** being employed. In the transfer, however, the firm should exercise care not to lose unwittingly the assets from which such rights emanate by failing to secure valid local protection abroad (see Section 8.4). For example, trade secrets, although recognized by the laws of some countries as a valid form of property giving rise to recognizable rights, may not be so perceived elsewhere. To assume, however, that an American management is any more trustworthy in this regard than a management consisting of foreign nationals, begs a large question.

The point can be made and defended that conflicts of interest in an international joint venture are probably unavoidable so long as there are significant differentials among nations in respect to tax level, commercial policy, monetary stability, remittance restriction, and resource allocation priorities. Maximization of profits at the joint-venture level may not be consistent with maximum profits for an internationally integrated enterprise. Therefore, as we have already seen, the firm operating internationally tends to develop profit centers quite apart from many of its individual overseas ventures through transfer pricing.

On the other hand, without local participation in the profits generated by the employment of local resources, the conflict between the parent firm and the host government may be insurmountable. The latter is probably desirous of maximizing the balance of payments, income, public revenue, and growth effects of the local enterprise. Although the parent firm may wish to hold profits down in certain enterprises for legal and monetary reasons, it may find it difficult to establish mutually acceptable prices for goods and services moving among related enterprises. Also, the allocation of marketing areas among subsidiaries, and between them and the parent, becomes awkward. If security of market position and assets depends on the extent of perceived mutual interest between an international firm, its foreign associates, and the host government, then the optimum long-run strategy may well be the transnational approach achieved through merger—that is, an exchange of ownership or the exchange of its own equity for ownership in a new, jointly owned enterprise. With repeated international mergers, of course, a firm becomes truly **transnational**—that is, it is owned and managed to a significant degree by nationals of more than one country—in that it loses virtually all national identify except that thrust upon it legally by its

selection of a place to incorporate headquarters. Herein lies an odd dilemma, which may constitute the most important single problem facing
international business.

It can be demonstrated that in order to quiet nationalist political pressures, to maximize the employment of local resources, and to minimize cost
and expense, many firms operating internationally feel mounting pressure
to withdraw all parent-country management personnel from foreign ventures and to share ownership in these enterprises with local interests. But if
the ultimate form of much of international business is of the transnational
variety, as seems possible, how does one move from this highly localized
(nationalized) structure to the transnational, where both ownership and
management of the parent corporation are shared among the nationals of
many countries? Indeed, how does one recruit management personnel able
to operate effectively in a transnational entity, if relatively few parent-
country executives are getting any real management experience in foreign
environments? It seems likely that without such experience, few managers
will achieve the ability to divorce themselves intellectually and emotionally
from their native national identities long enough to make national bias-free
decisions.

The Japanese, more than others, may encounter a real obstacle in
making such a transition because of the unique managerial behavior and
financial structure of many Japanese firms.

6.4   Selection of Foreign Associates

Quite apart from selecting an optimum strategy in regard to the ownership
of assets and valuable rights, the choice of the foreign associate—whether a
joint owner, contractor, contractee, or agent—can be of critical importance.
The degree of criticalness depends upon the duration of the association and
the ability of the parent firm to mount adequate leverage against the foreign
associate in event of behavior injurious to the interests of the parent. Of
course, the foreign associate looks at the parent firm in precisely the same
light.

Options in respect to selection of foreign associates are threefold: (1)
sector (public or private), (2) dispersion (limited to named persons, named
institutions or firms, the general public), and (3) nationality (local nationals,
parent-country entities or nationals, multinationals).

Some firms have realized that the possible disparity between the
values assigned to the flows (benefits and costs) in the system described by
the two associated firms and those assigned by the host government may be
virtually eliminated by entering directly into an arrangement with an entity
of that government; hence, the international mixed venture. Of course, the
foreign firm may be left no choice. In either case, the risk inherent in any
significant disparity between private and official valuations placed on the
flows of benefits and costs can be reduced to almost zero by joining in a
mixed venture.

Public versus Private Sector Associates

In this age of the professional manager, of development banks, economic plans and regulations, large-scale government buying, and monetary and fiscal control, it is often difficult to differentiate meaningfully between public and private economic institutions. For present purposes, I suggest that state-dominated institutions can be of two varieties: (1) those in which decisions are dominated by internal profit considerations and (2) all others. Clues about the nature of a given institution are its legal basis (special statutes or ordinary commercial law), auditing authority, terms of office for directors, frequency of turnover of top management, political stature of directors and top management, disclosure of financial statements, degree to which the product is subject to distribution and price control, and degree of official protection awarded (legal monopoly, tax and credit advantages, and so forth). The relevance of the distinction is that a *mixed venture*, in the sense of joint ownership of equity by public and private interests, assumes a certain area of mutual interest in generating an internal financial profit within the relevant time horizon. If the state-owned equity is concerned primarily with external economies or political power, then dividends should not be relied upon as the major profit route by the private partner. This does not mean that the foreign firm cannot find a profitable relationship through contracted sale (or purchase) of services and/or product, whether or not associated with debt or equity financing.

In some instances, the enterprise may be considered by the government to be a development or pioneer industry whose prime purposes are training, development of supply (for example, agriculture-based industry), and market expansion. If that is the case, the private partner may wish to retain an option to secure equity when skills, supply, and market reach levels adequate to support an internal profit. Indeed, at that point, the government may wish to spin off the entire enterprise into private hands. This move is possible if the state ownership is not seen as part of an ideological commitment but simply as a manifestation of a pragmatic policy. There is mounting evidence in many countries that the commitment to socialist ideology is weakening in favor of more pragmatic economic policies. Here, then, is a critically important variable.

But there are others. Consider the possible rationales for placing an economic activity in the public (government) sector, and the types of public sector enterprise possible. The rationales could include:

1. Inability to internalize profit (social overhead and infrastructure type of enterprise, such as education).
2. Tendency to monopoly, which is a function of the limited size of many national markets, and which in turn transforms many industries into decreasing cost industries; that is, there is only room for one plant, if that.
3. Need for pioneer industry, which implies an inability to internalize profit over a long initial development period (the school-factory and regional development concept).

4. Inadequacy of private resources, in that by the very nature of a sociopolitical system a greater reservoir of capital, entrepreneurial capacity, and managerial and technical skills may appear in the public sector, thereby draining the private sector.[4]

5. Need for public revenue with which to finance social overhead and infrastructure.

6. Need for public control, as in defense-related industries, in industries whose output is inherently dangerous to public health or safety, and in activities involving an exhaustible resource (minerals).

7. High risk due to uncertainty in respect to the timing and amount of the pay-out for a particular investment, such as space exploration. (It should be noted that in a small country, individual private enterprises are likely to be small and, hence, the level of risk that can be tolerated is less. Therefore, there is greater pressure to spread risk by placing an investment in the public sector.)

The types of public sector enterprise can be characterized by:

1. *Legal status* (government department, autonomous government agency, specially chartered corporation, corporation established under general, that is, private, commercial law).

2. *Exclusiveness* (closed or public corporation).

3. *Scope of operation* (multinational, national, regional, provincial, municipal, communal).

4. *Goal* (internal financial profit, external socioeconomic benefit, general or regional economic development, personal prestige and power, employment).

5. *Economic status* (monopoly or oligopoly, competitive with private).

6. *Philosophy* (ideologically based, pragmatic).

Turning to choice of foreign associates in the private sector, one sees quite clearly that international firms most frequently limit their associations to either named persons or to specific legal entities. This is obviously required for contractual relationships. However, in the case of joint venturing through equity, the international firm has the option of a few or many local partners. Assume that an important reason for moving into a joint venture is either the purchase of a local management, which is available only if that management participates in ownership, or the need for a special relationship with suppliers, customers, competitors, distributors, government, and/or financiers. The firm will usually opt for limiting the issue of shares to named persons or institutions, whether the shares are in the local or parent international firm. However, if the overriding reason for joint venturing is the need to effect maximum dispersion of foreign operations (hence, a need for local financing), to create a larger area of common interest

---

[4]This may be due to the relatively high status of military bureaucrats, the traditional low status of private business because of identity with racial or religious minority groups or a tendency to monopolize in a small market, or the appeal of the public sector (including the military) to those without the right family connections and to those more committed to long-run national welfare.

with the host society (because of the utilization of local resources in generating profit), or simply to satisfy legal requirements, then the international
firm may well decide to seek a public sale of equity. The ability to do so
successfully rests on the reputation of the firm and its access to a local
securities market.

A serious problem in limiting local partners to named persons or
institutions is that one can never be certain into whose hands the equity will
fall in succeeding generations. Local law determines whether it is possible to
limit the transferability of shares. In the United States, limitation is possible
under certain circumstances. This problem need not arise for contractual
relationships, which always can be limited in time and assignability. Therefore, the legal ability to limit the transferability of shares may determine the
wisdom of joint venturing where public sale is neither possible nor desirable.

On some occasions, firms have seen fit to go into joint ventures abroad
with other companies or financial interests of the same nationality. It is
common, for example, for a Japanese manufacturing company to join a
Japanese trading company in a joint venture abroad, which often includes a
significant local equity interest as well. This domestic joint venture approach
appears most commonly in response to pressure from an important domestic customer or supplier, the need for foreign area expertise (including access
to the market) not available in the company, the desire to gain financing, or
the desire to spread risk. Warning: a U.S. firm joining a domestic U.S.
competitor in a joint venture abroad may be vulnerable to U.S. antitrust
prosecution. Economic justification seems to be no bar. Multinational participation is becoming more common with the development of international
financial consortia and the **tied sourcing** of such international entities as
NATO.

In summary, the only valid generalization is that a fixed policy in
regard to ownership or choice of foreign associates, regardless of the circumstances, is very likely to lead to something less than the best strategy.
Firms insisting generally on 100 percent owned enterprises abroad and
favoring local national ownership of the parent, or insisting on limiting the
association to contracts, are equally vulnerable to the charge that they are
not really maximizing their return on investment. The same can be said of
firms that refuse to associate with a government entity under any and all
circumstances. It all depends on which entity, and where. It seems likely
that the best approach is a situational one, not conformance to a general
ownership policy. Indeed, as national entry laws become more restrictive,
the firm operating internationally may be required either to withdraw or to
bend its policy.

CHAPTER 7

FINANCIAL STRATEGY

attachment a legal device by which property is officially seized as security for payment of a claimed debt.

convertible exchange a currency that may be sold for other currencies and over which there are relatively few exchange controls imposed by the issuing government. Also called *hard currency*.

debt a contractual obligation to pay a defined amount of money at a given date or dates (maturity) plus a specific interest.

devaluation the loss of value of one currency in terms of another currency.

Edge Act corporations domestic subsidiaries of U.S. banks incorporated under the Federal Reserve Act to engage in international banking and to finance foreign projects through long-term debt and equity.

Eurodollar dollar accounts banked outside of the United States.

evaluation the increase of value of one currency in terms of another currency.

exchange rate the price one pays in one currency for another, expressed as a ratio (at five pesos for one dollar, the dollar/peso exchange rate is 5; the peso/dollar exchange rate is .20).

foreign exchange financial claims that one nation has on the goods and services of another. These claims are in the form of the currency of the other country, often held as foreign bank accounts.

foreign reserves a government's holdings of foreign exchange, gold, and IMF drawing rights, all of which the government may use to pay its international obligations.

IMF drawing rights the capacity of a government to borrow the equivalent of foreign exchange from the International Monetary Fund which can be used to pay obligations to member countries.

intangibles valuable rights (e.g., patents, copyrights, trademarks) and nonmaterial assets (such as reputation, image, goodwill).

investment center the locale of investment decisions.

leverage the debt/equity ratio.

liquid assets holdings convertible to cash in a relatively short time.

parallel financing an arrangement by foreign borrowers (governments and businesses) with a consortium of banks in different countries to float largely identical bond issues in each country at the same time, each in the currency of the issuing country.

participating debt a negotiable security that bestows on the holder rights in the form of profit participation up to a given percentage of annual net profits distributed. It is always callable by the holder and is not considered part of a corporation's capital.

profit center the place in an organization where profits are legally recorded. Full financial *consolidation* means the parent firm is the sole profit center; full financial *integration* means that profit centers are located wherever there is an advantage to be realized, although they are under central financial control of the parent firm.

transfer prices the prices at which goods, services, and funds move among related companies.

unit-of-account financing financing in securities denominated in several different currencies held in fixed relationship.

Financial, legal, and control (administrative) structures should not be confused. Particularly in the international field, the three may diverge widely. The flow of funds may not coincide with the legal or control relationships, and legal entities may have virtually no relevance to the channel of authority. For example, a firm may opt to organize its management on a regional basis, with offices in Europe, North America, Latin America, and the Far East. Each regional headquarters may be virtually autonomous in a variety of ways. However, certain of the European subsidiaries, along with a number of Latin American subsidiaries, may be owned by a Panamanian holding company, thereby deriving a possible tax advantage. The funds accumulated in Panama, on which very little tax has been paid, may be used for investment in, say, India, where the subsidiary receiving the funds as a loan is owned directly by the parent firm, although its management is a responsibility of the Far Eastern regional headquarters. Each of these strategy sets, financial, legal, and control, though related, are distinct.

Essentially, there are eight questions facing management, the answers to which determine the firm's financial strategy:

1. Where are profits to be taken (location of profit centers)?
2. By what routes are profits to move to the profit centers?
3. Where are investment decisions to be made (location of investment centers)?
4. What type of financing is to be used?
5. What is to be the substance of investment?
6. What is to be the source of financing?
7. What legal instrumentality should be used?
8. How are claims to earnings streams to be made secure?

Although one might ask similar questions about a purely uninational operation, the nature of the relevant variables, their weighting, and the range of options differ when one deals with international transactions. Indeed, there may be profound political consequences to the strategies a firm selects internationally. For example, the *liquid assets* in the hands of private U.S. companies and banks probably amount to several times the size of the U.S. government's foreign reserves. Obviously, the larger firms operating internationally, if they acted more or less in concert, could bring great pressure to bear on the countries in which they do business by moving liquid assets in and out, thereby causing powerful inflationary or deflationary pressures. In many cases, there is little that the affected nations could do. A firm operating internationally must be sensitive to the general economic and political implications of its financial strategies if it is to avoid political hostility and eventual exclusion from a national market.

7.1   Choice of Profit Center

Within a family of enterprises interrelated by ownership, the profits recorded by any one are based on a number of arbitrary decisions regarding **transfer prices** (the prices at which goods, services, and funds move among related companies), inventory policy and accounting, depreciation policy, cost allocation, assignment of production and sales, speed in effecting the collection of receivables, dividend pay-out, and debt repayment. In theory, the parent company may influence profit to the extent that it can affect the activities and costs of associated firms. In practice, the range of that influence is restrained by (1) the efforts of internal revenue authorities, abroad and at home, to collect taxes levied on corporate profits, transactions, and payrolls; (2) pressure exerted by local shareholders, if any, in foreign subsidies to maximize their return; and (3) the desire of local foreign managers to increase their autonomy and, hence, their power.

A **profit center** is the place in an organization where profits are legally recorded. This can be, for example, a function, product, division, subsidiary, or the entire corporation. Obviously, it is in the interest of the parent company to generate a maximum profit—and hence locate its profit center— where it is owned 100 percent by the parent, where tax rates are the lowest, where funds may be held with least restriction, and in currencies or securities freely convertible at predictable exchange rates to the currency of the parent country. Factors such as a legally enforced right by labor to see the firm's books (as in Italy) may be relevant because unduly high profits may generate agitation. If funds in a profit center are to be used to finance operations elsewhere, as is often the case, a further consideration is the relationship between the profit-center country and potential host countries in respect to double taxation, withholding taxes (on dividends, interest, fees), investment guarantees, and political boycotts (such as the Arab attitude toward Israeli-sourced financing, or the U.S. attitude toward Cuba). It should also be noted that if a subsidiary's profits are reduced through transfer pricing, its capacity to borrow locally may be reduced.

A firm may opt to define a profit center by function (such as marketing or production), by product line, enterprise, or geographical area. A critical variable may be the administrative or control structure of the firm, for if that structure coincides with the system of financial reporting, a single accounting system may serve both a financial and a control purpose.

If profit centers are defined by enterprise, they will coincide with individual business entities (thereby leading to financial autonomy of these subsidiaries). Defining the parent firm as the profit center is the equivalent of full global financial **consolidation**. Profit centers may be located wherever there is an advantage to be realized, which implies full financial **integration,** in the sense of central financial control. A word of caution: if profit centers are located in order to achieve maximum *global* profit on a consolidated corporate basis, profit and loss statements of local firms cannot be used as a measure of managerial effectiveness, nor for the purposes of internal control. For the latter purpose, a second set of books must be kept showing "true costs," a practice that may be exceedingly dangerous from a legal (that is, a tax) point of view. In fact, where exchange controls operate and inflation is rapid, any measure of *local* profit may be very misleading (see Section 9.5).

7.2   Profit Route

Quite apart from the profit routes of dividends and capital gains (the sale of a capital asset gives rise to a capital gain), profits may be shifted from enterprise to enterprise by creating interenterprise costs, such as sales commissions, fees for contracted services (technical, managerial, entrepreneurial, distributional), salaries, interest, rent, purchase premiums or discounts (that is, special transfer prices), and royalties (on copyrights, patents, trademarks). Although tax and foreign exchange control systems invariably impose restraints on such devices, substantial latitude is often possible.

Although a firm may thus have some choice among profit routes, it must nonetheless be ready to defend its choice to tax authorities. The best defenses are consistency over time and geography, a business (i.e., nontax) justification, or recording similar profits/sales ratios for comparable enterprises elsewhere, unless special conditions can be demonstrated. It should be noted that the capital gains route may be used for the sale of intangible property, including commercial or industrial secrets of a patentable nature. Equity may be taken in lieu of payment. Even direct payment, in lump sum or installment, may be considered a capital gain instead of income for U.S. tax purposes *if* the sale is to a foreign corporation not controlled by the U.S. firm. A capital gain is usually taxed at a lower rate than that applied to income.

Transfer Pricing

Pricing is not of major importance to many companies in moving profits from one incorporated entity to another to minimize taxes and/or customs duties. First, there is no significant tax differential between the major industrialized countries among which the bulk of trade and investment takes place; hence, there is little advantage in artificially shifting profits from one country to another. Second, the use of a tax haven holding company located in a country such as Switzerland, Liechtenstein, Panama, Liberia, Bahama, and the like (see Section 8.7) to siphon off profits from higher tax countries simply does not work to the extent that it did a decade or two ago. The U.S. and many other industrialized countries have fairly effectively plugged this loophole. Tax haven countries are well known to tax collectors worldwide, who are inclined to scrutinize very closely the prices of goods sold to, or purchased from, associated firms located within them. Third, artificially high prices often mean high customs duties, as customs duties are most frequently levied on the value of the product. Conversely, artificially low prices mean low customs duties but increased profits and profit-based taxes. Fourth, even if a firm could accumulate profits in a low-tax country through transfer pricing, this is an advantage only so long as those profits remain abroad. The real gain may be limited to the interest-free use of funds that would otherwise be paid out in taxes. Fifth, there is a real risk of double taxation arising from transfer pricing. Artificial pricing necessarily means that reported profits are too low in one country, too high in another. The tax collector in the latter is not likely to object, but in the former he or she is likely to, and at some later date to reallocate income, thereby increasing the taxable profits within that country. Bear in mind that these profits have already been taxed in the other country. If there is no tax treaty between the two countries, there may be no relief at all. Even if there is a treaty, recovery may be slow and uncertain. Sixth, effective transfer pricing assumes a degree of centralized corporate control which simply may be inoperative. Significant transfer at distorted (i.e., nonmarket) pricing means that subsidiary companies cannot operate as profit centers without incurring the substantial risk of keeping two sets of books, one based on the artificially contrived prices and one reflecting the true state of affairs. Subsidiary managements are likely to be very jealous of their managerial prerogatives, and there is a natural tendency to try to make their profit performance look as good as possible, unless local managers are being evaluated and rewarded explicitly on some basis other than local reported profit.

It should be noted that only two or three hundred U.S. firms account for something like 75 percent of U.S. merchandise exports and imports and that close to half of this trade is intrafirm, that is, it represents direct transfers between U.S. firms and their overseas subsidiaries. The opportunity for transfer price manipulation for U.S.-based companies is great. The same opportunity undoubtedly exists for European and Japanese-based corporations.

One sees only the tip of the iceberg. Why are the prices of certain goods manufactured by a given company so much higher in one market than another? Why, when ownership rights are forcibly spun off to a local interest, does a firm then say that its transfer prices must be increased, say by 30 percent (which one U.S management claimed would be the case if its equity in a Venezuelan subsidiary were lost)? Why do many U.S. firms impose no charge on their Canadian subsidiaries for R&D performed in the United States or for internal consulting services delivered to them by the parent U.S. firm? In many cases, one suspects, such unrealistic transfer prices are not deliberate, possibly not even realized, on the part of management until the transactions are externalized for some reason. That is, the sales or purchases are with entirely independent entities.

As noted in Chapter Three, the perceived gaps in per capita economic well-being between the industrial and resource-rich less-developed countries on the one hand and the poorer LDCs on the other seems to be widening. It is only reasonable to expect that the poorer countries, the "Group of 77," will continue pressure for redistribution of income and wealth. In that private corporations are the most visible vehicles for the international transfer of capital, goods, knowledge, and services, one can anticipate the attacks on them will intensify. To the extent that these corporations maintain centrally controlled, integrated production and sales systems, they remain suspect to many people. Many of the prices attached to funds, goods, knowledge, and service moving internationally are artificially determined—and necessarily so. The relevant markets are too imperfect for them to be otherwise. Where markets are imperfect and entry barriers high, oligopoly pricing is possible, which means that the firm may increase its profits by restricting output and selling at higher price. In such circumstance, the firm becomes vulnerable to charges of exploitation because of the "unjustifiably" high rents on the goods or technology it controls. In an economic sense they are unjustifiably high only so long as the beneficiary corporation contrives to restrain or eliminate competition through essentially nonmarket forces (e.g., meaningless product differentiation based on brand names unrelated to superior quality, deals with governments whereby investment rights are traded for protection, illegal payments, massive lobbying for special legislative treatment, and limiting access to knowledge by buying up inventions and patent rights that are subsequently not used). Otherwise, the high prices do not constitute exploitation; the firm is merely reacting to a market condition created by the unique nature of the goods or services it is offering for sale.

7.3 Investment Centers

The **investment center** (the locale of investment decisions) may or may not coincide with the relevant profit center. The former may be located within the parent corporate headquarters; the latter in a foreign subsidiary or in a regional headquarters. A question arises as to why investment decisions should be centralized if decisions relevant to profit maximization are not. One reason lies in the need to know the cost of capital of different types and sources (internal and external, local and foreign).

From the point of view of a subsidiary operation, the *perceived* cost of capital may well be limited to its own or the parent's domestic cost of capital. The subsidiary management may not perceive the third-country alternative, which implies a cost of capital equivalent to the corporate family's *worldwide* cost. Furthermore, a subsidiary management may not have the expertise to operate in this fashion, which requires moving through different currency barriers and utilizing different hedging devices, both of which carry important costs.

7.4   Type of Financing

Given the availability of both domestic and foreign financing, an international business has a wider range of types of financing from which to choose than does the purely domestic business. In addition, a variety of specialized devices for financing exports have been developed by many countries. In general, the strategy lies among these choices: **debt, participating debt,** convertible securities, and shares in equity. But there are many variations.

First of all, debt includes short-, medium-, and long-term *export* financing[1] through a variety of instruments, many of which are described in the appendix to this chapter. Long-term *capital* debt is quite another matter, in that it becomes part of the capital structure of the enterprise. Short- or medium-term borrowing for working capital needs is another category.

Several types of multinational debt financing are of relatively recent origin: **parallel financing, unit-of-account financing,** and the Eurocurrency loan. You should be familiar with all three in order to speak the language of international business.

Parallel financing involves an arrangement by foreign borrowers (governments and businesses) with a consortium of banks in different countries to float largely identical bond issues in each country at the same time, each in the currency of the issuing country. Each bank takes a part (a *tranche*) of the proposed loan and sells it locally. Interest rates and maturities are the same, but the issuing price and, therefore, the yield (issuing price times interest rate) may vary from country to country.

Unit-of-account financing involves securities denominated in several different currencies held in fixed relationship, sometimes in terms of special drawing rights or European Currency Units.[2] The investor pays in one of the

---

[1]"Short-term" is generally defined as debt with a maturity of less than two years; "medium-term," from two to five years; "long-term," anything over five years (or indeterminate). For purposes of discussing export financing, however, "short-term" refers to maturities up to 180 days; "medium-term," 181 days to five years.

[2]The special drawing right (SDR) is an international reserve asset, a paper money, created by the International Monetary Fund and allocated to members in accord with agreement among them. SDRs may be used only for intergovernmental transactions and between the IMF and governments. The value of the SDR is set in terms of a basket of major currencies, weighted roughly by each country's share of world exports. The IMF calculates the value daily. The European Currency Unit (ECU) is a basket of

currencies (currency may be stipulated by the borrower), receives interest in any one of the currencies, and redeems in any currency desired.

A Eurocurrency loan is one designated in a currency other than that of the country in which the debt contract is executed. The use of a Eurocurrency permits both lender and borrower to escape national controls. It should be pointed out that any difference in interest rates between a Eurocurrency loan and a domestic currency loan reveals market distortions. In that there is little or no intervention in the Eurocurrency markets, the divergence in rates reveals an intervention at the national level. The international firm is in position to exploit these market distortions much more easily than a uninational firm.

The preeminent Eurocurrency has been the **Eurodollar**, which simply refers to dollar accounts banked outside of the United States, which constitute an important source of financing for both international trade and investment. The Eurodollar arose because of the inadequacy of gold production, the relatively large U.S. gold supply, the size, diversity, and productivity of the U.S. economy, the easy convertibility of the dollar, the relaxation of exchange controls in Europe and Japan, and the U.S balance-of-payments deficit. The latter means that dollar obligations are created outside the United States for which there is no immediate demand for use in purchasing U.S. goods, or services. Many international loans are denominated in Eurodollars, loans in which the creditor has no intention of utilizing the dollars directly. Any convertible currency can exist in a "Euro" form by simply being deposited in a bank in a country (not necessarily European) to which the currency is not native.

Participating debt, a type of debt not common in the United States, is the *partes beneficiaries* peculiar to some civil-law countries. This is a negotiable security, always callable by the holder and not considered part of a corporation's capital, that bestows on the holder rights in the form of profit participation up to a given percentage of annual net profits distributed. A sinking fund provision is generally required, because the security becomes convertible to equity shares at the option of the holder when it is redeemed (i.e., paid). The redemption price is determined at the time of the issue, although it may be represented as a multiple of average annual earnings over the last five years or so.

Closely associated with participating debt is the convertible debenture, a device that has grown more popular in international business as a device to counter inflation. This is essentially a bond that can be converted to equity shares. A variation is the bond with attached stock warrants, the security being purchasable in one or more currencies to be decided by the purchaser at time of issue. Thereafter, the currency of the bond remains fixed. The

---

the currencies of the nine member countries of the EEC. The amount of each currency in the basket corresponds to the economic importance of each country. The value of the basket is calculated each day by the EEC Commission on the basis of quotations on the relevant national foreign exchange markets. All EEC central banks hold 20 percent of their gold and dollar reserves in the form of ECUs. The official ECU can only be held and used by the central banks of the Community. However, the private market denominates a variety of transactions in ECUs in that it has greater stability than any individual currency. The weighting of each currency in the basket has remained fixed since the initiation of the ECU in March 1979 up to this writing, but it must be changed at the latest at the end of 1985 when the Greek drachma will be included.

purchaser of the bond also acquires the right to buy a given number of shares of the issuing company within a specified time. The purchaser exercises that right by converting the bond into shares without additional cash outlay.

Finally, shares in equity can be sold. Such shares carry one or more rights, such as voting, preemption, preference, cumulation, participation,[3] and divident payment in a specified currency. Regulations governing public issue vary, of course, from country to country in respect to such matters as disclosure, fees and taxes, and minimum size and legal status of the issuing firm. In the United States, a quoted company (one whose shares are traded on a public exchange) must be very circumspect in its management if it is to avoid legal trouble. A quoted company, on the other hand, can raise money more cheaply through debt and rights issues. It can also use its paper to take over other concerns more easily than if it had to use cash.

In countries where corporate securities cannot be transferred physically to foreigners (Japan, for example), a foreigner can hold them only by appointing a proxy and having them held locally. In the United States, the problem is solved by issuing American depository receipts (ADRs). An expansion of the ADR, the international depository receipt (IDR), is designed to stimulate the international sale of corporate securities. Because an IDR is owned in bearer form and is not registered with the U.S. Securities Exchange, it may not be used within the U.S. market. An example of IDRs' utility: Say a Frenchman wishes to buy shares in a Japanese steel company. He goes to his local bank and advises those handling securities transactions that he wishes to buy 1,000 shares in bearer form—that is, in IDRs issued by a bank doing business in IDRs. This bank (we will call it Bank X) places an order for 1,000 shares of the Japanese steel company to be deposited with Bank X's custodian in Japan against authorization to Bank X for the issue of the IDRs. Bank X then delivers the IDRs to the French bank from which the order originated, for delivery to the French buyer.

Securities Regulation

Since 1965, U.S. law has required that any corporation with at least 300 American stockholders must meet Securities Exchange Commission requirements regarding financial disclosure, proxy solicitations, and the like, whether or not the foreign firm sought to sell its shares in the United States. The SEC has, however, waived certain disclosure requirements from time to time when they would be at odds with foreign law or practice.

The Securities Exchange Law of 1934 introduced fairly rigorous control over the public sale of corporate securities in the United States. The extraterritorial reach of that law has been expanding in order to protect the

---

[3]*Preemption* refers to the right of first refusal in relation to the issue of additional stock by a company; *preference*, to shares with a claim on profit before distribution to common shareholders; *cumulation*, to a preferred stock that—if the specified dividend is missed—must be paid in arrears before any dividend may be paid on common shares; *participation*, to preferred shares that participate, beyond the fixed rate, with common shares in the distribution of earnings.

U.S. purchaser of foreign corporate securities, although Congress did not provide the courts with any clear indication of the intended scope of application. There is no apparent problem with fraudulent action within the United States that affects the value of corporate securities listed in the United States, even if the corporation is foreign-domiciled. The circulation of untrue information to potential American investors, for instance, is clearly illegal.

The application of U.S. law in this field has generated substantial conflict, for the degree of corporate disclosure required as a precondition for public sale differs substantially from country to country, despite some recent convergence. The problem is that some nations regulate the securities market by means other than full disclosure. For example, disclosure requirements in the United Kingdom and Belgium are somewhat less exacting than in the United States. However, these two, like many other European countries, impose severe limitations directly upon the conduct of corporations listing their securities on national exchanges. The Belgian authorities, for instance, have required the reorganization of a company's internal operations before permitting the marketing of its securities. The London Stock Exchange has been known to demand the removal of particular officers from a firm before permitting it to sell its securities publicly. In other cases, the authorities may require detailed information not revealed to the public. The result is that the investor may be better protected in the United Kingdom or Belgium than in the United States.

Even so, a trend toward greater disclosure is discernible for publicly traded shares. Firms whose shares are traded on the London Exchange are now subject to reasonably strict disclosure rules. Canada, France, and West Germany have recently adopted securities laws that are closer to those of the United States than were their previous laws.

The strategy choice between types of financing, whether debt or equity, obviously rests on relative cost (availability), optimum **leverage**[4] (given projected inflation and profit rates), legal restraints (including the maximum debt/equity ratio permitted by the parent government), foreign exchange controls, the degree to which risk may be spread, the relative utility of different currencies to the firm, and the ease of repatriation.

7.5   Substance of Investment

An investment may be in the form of cash, capital equipment, depreciated machinery, inventories, services, intangibles, or real estate. Real estate, including buildings, would represent a cash investment insofar as an alien is concerned.

---

[4]"Leverage" refers to the debt/equity ratio. In a period of rapid growth and/or inflation, increased debt may lead to higher returns on equity (to owners) than would otherwise be the case. This situation can hold whenever the cost of debt is less than the return on equity.

The particular problems here for international business lie in the valuation of assets for the purpose of capitalization in a foreign enterprise. Which **exchange rate** should be used, a free rate or a controlled rate? The former creates more local currency value, but often obligates the investor to repatriate earnings likewise at the free rate in the future. Should capital equipment and inventories be valued at their foreign or local values? Under what circumstances should depreciated machinery be used? Problems of local acceptance, maintenance, and operating cost may arise. In any event, the investor can expect a demand for independent expert appraisal and authentication by consular officials of the government involved. How does one establish a reasonable basis for capitalizing services and intangibles? Should one shoot for a maximum capital base in view of the facts that (1) the repatriation of annual profits may be limited to a percentage of capital, (2) the local corporate tax based on percentage of capital may be progressive within a certain range, and (3) certain advantages (e.g., a tax reduction) may accrue if the foreign investment exceeds a specified minimum capital investment? On the other hand, the large foreign-owned capital base may so dilute earnings as to make local participation unappealing, assuming that such participation is otherwise held desirable by the foreign owner. Bear in mind that in some cases, local participation may be legally required, a subject already discussed in Chapter Six. Property taxes may also be relevant. In the event of forced sale, understatement of value for tax purposes may constitute a trap, for that value may be used to establish the level of compensation.

7.6 Source of Financing

The basic strategy choices here have to do with (1) national origin—local (to the associated foreign operation), parent country, third country, or a mix of these (multinational)—and (2) the choice between debt and equity in each case. Appropriate considerations include exchange controls, availability of investment guarantees at the source,[5] tax treatment (level of withholding tax, tax credits, tax deferral), ability to denominate debt and equity in the source currency or one freely convertible to it (whether local, foreign, Eurodollar, or unit-of-account), differential rates of inflation, possible changes in exchange rates, and parent-country balance-of-payments problems. Obviously, this sourcing decision is exceedingly complicated and demands high-level skills and high-quality information.

One approach is to select the currency that appears to be weakest in the long run, but which is presently **convertible** to the end-use currency. Let us assume an American firm contemplating a domestic U.S. venture. If sterling were available and the firm were willing to speculate that the pound would be **devalued** over the next 15 years while the dollar remained relatively

---

[5]Some governments, the United States included, provide investment "insurance" against such risks as expropriation, nonconvertibility of profits, and war and insurrection.

stable, it might borrow in sterling and then convert to dollars for its U.S. investment. Earnings would be in dollars. With a subsequently devalued pound, the firm could pay the loan back, converting from a relatively more valuable dollar (in terms of sterling) than was originally acquired. The profit would be roughly equivalent to the amount by which the pound had been devalued. This device, of course, assumes convertibility at maturity from dollars to sterling. On the other hand, should the pound remain stable and the dollar be devalued, the devaluation would result in a corresponding loss. The point is that capital-cost considerations must be modified to take these uncertainties into account.

Elimination of exchange risks by financing in local currencies seems to be a significant factor pushing U.S. companies into borrowing overseas at interest rates substantially above those in the United States. If the proceeds of long-term borrowing are for use in, say, Brazil, and the firm's earnings are derived largely from Brazil, then the Brazilian cruzeiro would seem to be the best currency in which to borrow—that is, the least costly. But such is not always the case.

Consider the choice between foreign and local debt financing—that is, the determination of relevant cost. Assume a two-country situation in which Country A is the domicile of the parent corporation and Country B that of the subsidiary corporation. Where is it cheaper for the subsidiary to borrow? The answer depends upon three factors: the interest rates in the two countries, the exchange rate, and taxes. For the moment we shall ignore taxes. The relative rates of inflation do not matter when one currency is converted into another in the future. Presumably, comparative inflation rates are already incorporated in the estimates of the future exchange rates. A foreign loan will be repaid in inflated local currency, as will a local loan.

First, if the exchange rate does not shift, which is the cheaper source to borrow, Brazil or the United States? Obviously, it is where the relevant interest rate (the cost of debt) is lower. In either case, the Brazilian subsidiary has the same earnings out of which it must repay the debt, plus interest.

Second, if the exchange rate does shift, then the lower cost of debt depends upon whether the change in the exchange rate more than compensates for the lower interest rate. Assume that the loan is denominated in dollars and that the Brazilian cruzeiro is depreciated relative to the U.S. dollar. The Brazilian subsidiary may or may not have to expend more cruzeiros to repay principal and interest. It depends on the interplay between the interest rates in the two countries and the change in the exchange rate.[6]

The limit of debt a firm can incur is usually measured against equity in the form of maximum leverage or debt/equity ratio, which in itself implies an inexplicable discontinuity. One can understand why risk might increase as

[6]For those interested in the mathematical solution of this problem, see "An Update and Corrections" (December 1981) to Richard D. Robinson, *International Business Management: A Guide to Decision Making* (Hinsdale: Dryden Press, 1978).

the debt/equity ratio increases and, hence, why both debt and equity might become more costly. But why a financial institution should impose a ceiling, equivalent to an infinitely high cost, is not easily understood. Such a limit is reinforced if the taxing authorities likewise recognize a ceiling. That is, if the ceiling is exceeded, interest may not be considered a cost to the taxpayer, and repayment of principal may not be considered tax-free income to the payee (if it is likewise an owner). What needs underscoring is the fact that permissible debt/equity ratios may vary substantially from country to country, from perhaps 2:1 for the United States to 10:1 in Japan. The higher acceptable debt/equity ratio in Japan may suggest to a U.S. firm the wisdom of pursuing a joint venture strategy in Japan (perhaps on a minority basis) so as to profit from the higher leverage, provided it could do so without running the risk that financial institutions in the United States might consolidate Japanese debt and equity with that held by the firm domestically, and either impose a lower debt ceiling or increase cost of additional debt.

If the firm opts for local financing abroad, then it has the choice of public institutions (government-owned entities), private institutions (private banks), a local business firm, specific persons, public sale of securities, or internal financing (reinvested earnings). The criteria are, of course, availability (relative cost), the degree to which financial disclosure is felt desirable, and ownership and legal strategies preferred by management for reasons other than financial (see Chapters Six and Eight).

The financing decision becomes somewhat more complex, of course, when the options are expanded from local and foreign loans to include (1) retained earnings, (2) equity external to the firm, and (3) intersubsidiary equity (ownership by one subsidiary of shares in another).

Of special concern to the international executive is the existence of blocked funds, liquid assets that may not be immediately exchangeable into usable foreign currency, but that may be remitted through the export of goods on deblockage lists[7] or invested locally under certain circumstances. Care must be exercised that such investment be considered foreign investment, the proceeds for which are subject to eventual repatriation. Blocked funds to be invested in productive enterprise (associated perhaps with newly imported capital) should be considered sunk cost.

Of growing interest is the development of organized security markets in an increasing number of countries, including several in the less-developed category. It is quite clear that more and more firms operating internationally have been listing their shares on foreign stock exchanges. A few companies have a policy of offering their stock for sale in any country in which the firm has significant investment in fixed assets. In some instances, firms have swapped stock for participation in a joint venture abroad, thereby creating a mutuality of interest.

---

[7]Lists of goods that may be exported, the foreign currency proceeds from which (in whole or in part) may be retained by the exporting firm for the purpose of reimbursing itself for funds that otherwise would have to be held in local currency, or "blocked."

A specialized institution now common around the world is the development bank or corporation.[8] Quasipublic entities, these institutions
channel both private and public capital into local projects deemed to have a
high priority from the point of view of national or regional economic development. **Foreign exchange** resources have been made available to many
of them by their respective governments and international financial institutions. Under some circumstances, debt and equity capital may be available
to a foreign-owned enterprise through this channel. The circumstances
frequently include a requirement that the enterprise be a joint venture with
local capital, that local management and technical personnel be developed,
and that there be complete financial disclosure, including transactions with
the associated foreign firm.

Many countries, political subdivisions thereof (states, provinces,
cities), and regional groupings (as the European Community) offer special
financial incentives if the firm invests within their respective jurisdictions,
within certain areas (such as economically depressed or less-developed
areas), or in certain types of activities (R&D, approved projects, those
generating foreign exchange). These inducements may run from tax holidays and low-interest loans to outright grants and permission for a larger
share of foreign ownership than would otherwise be allowed.

On the international level are several public institutional financial
sources, most notably the International Bank for Reconstruction and Development (World Bank), the International Development Association
(IDA), the International Finance Corporation (IFC), the Inter-American
Development Bank (IADB), and the Asian Development Bank (ADB).
General requirements for financing often include evidence that normal
commercial financing is not available, acceptance by the host government,
and demonstration that reasonable benefits will accrue to the host country
from the contemplated investment.

Within the United States are a number of financial sources specializing
in international operations, including such public institutional investors as
the Export-Import Bank, the Overseas Private Investment Corporation, and
such private institutional investors as "agreement corporations," **Edge Act
corporations,**[9] and investment houses and mutual funds concentrating on
foreign securities. The Edge Act authorizes equity financing in foreign
enterprises by U.S. banks through special Edge Act subsidiaries, which are
U.S. entities. Very frequently, these institutions require a convertible debenture or an option for stock interest from a borrower. Inasmuch as an

---

[8]The more important public agencies and development corporations are the European Development Fund (EDF), the British
Commonwealth Development Corporation (CDC), the German Development Corporation (DEGO), the Dutch Financial
Corporatin for Development (FMO), the French Central Fund of Economic Cooperation (CCCF), the Danish Industrialization
Fund for Developing Countries (IFU), the U.S. Overseas Development Corporation (ODC), and the Japanese Overseas
Economic Fund (OEF).

[9]Agreement corporations and Edge Act corporations are domestic subsidiaries of U.S. banks incorporated under the Federal
Reserve Act to engage in international banking and to finance foreign projects through long-term debt and equity. Authorized
in 1916 and 1919, respectively, such corporations are, unlike domestic banks, permitted to make equity investments and to
have branches outside their own state. As a consequence, many non-New York state banks have Edge Act subsidiaries in New
York City through which they do business overseas, including acting as a holding company for the bank's direct investments in
foreign banking institutions.

Edge Act corporation rarely desires control (other than in financial institutions), the borrower may frequently buy back these rights after a period of time. Although legally barred from making equity investments, OPIC is perceived as an important financial intermediary between U.S. investors and enterprises within developing countries in order to increase the flow of capital and technology. As a wholly owned government corporation, OPIC has no authority to increase its reserves by selling equity or borrowing in private capital markets or from the U.S. Treasury; any increase depends upon specific congressional appropriation. OPIC can, however, make direct loans through its direct investment fund and sell participations on the market. OPIC direct loans are limited largely to project loans in "friendly" LDCs for the purchase of U.S. goods and services.

In addition, of course, funds for overseas investment may be generated by a parent firm itself either through guaranteeing credit opened on behalf of a foreign associate or by loaning internally generated assets, namely, earnings, surplus machinery, services, and intangibles. As already indicated, one device is to sell parent-company securities abroad and use the proceeds to loan to an associated foreign enterprise, or to exchange equity with a foreign joint venturer. A large and attractive foreign firm, including one in which a parent foreign firm has a direct interest, may, of course, tap the parent firm's home securities market directly.

Not to be overlooked is the possibility of using funds from third-country sources, particularly export credit facilities and commercial banking facilities in such places as Switzerland and London. For reasons of tax considerations, it may be useful to utilize the funds of an associated firm in a third country, thereby delaying repatriation of earnings to the parent country, where they may become taxable. (For U.S. corporations, the Revenue Act of 1962 seriously restricted such operations. See Section 8.7.) Also, joint ventures with either associated or nonassociated third-country firms may be a desirable financial strategy when those involved will provide a flow of valuable assets or services.

7.7   Legal Instrumentality to Be Used

A recent innovation by the larger U.S. corporations operating internationally is to set up financing subsidiaries incorporated either abroad (typically in Luxembourg, Liechtenstein, or the Bahamas) or domestically (in New York or Delaware). These subsidiaries provide finance in their own name either with or without parent-company guarantees and conversion features. The general purpose of a financing subsidiary, either foreign or domestic, is to avoid payment of the U.S. withholding tax imposed on interest and dividends flowing to foreigners that the U.S. parent would have to pay if it issued the securities itself. There may be a secondary purpose of interposing a corporate shield to protect parent-company assets from direct liability. Various tests are applied to determine the tax consequences (see appendix to Chapter Eight, item 6).

7.8   Protecting Claims on Earnings Stream

A major issue in international business is the management of risk. Like a purely domestic corporation, the corporation operating internationally attempts to maintain a reasonable balance between the risks it takes and the profits it expects to earn. Thus, in evaluating any business decision, whether it involves investing in new plant and equipment in a particular country or the choice of invoicing sales in the home or the customer's currency, risk should be traded off against expected return, either implicitly or explicitly. In structuring transactions, for example, the firm must decide which risks to take on and which risks to impose on the firm or individual with which it is doing business. Although the final result is often based on bargaining between the two, it nonetheless involves making risk-return tradeoffs. Once the firm has made a decision that exposes it to risks, it must then decide whether to "self-insure" these risks, thereby passing them through to its shareholders, or to transfer the risks to a third party in the form of insurance or other risk-bearing financial contracts.

Conceptually, there is no difference between this problem and that faced by the purely domestic firm. However, the firm operating internationally does face a greater variety of risk. Further, more risks may be of the type lying outside the influence and/or experience of management, the type better dealt with by someone else. Finally, and one suspects this is a major factor in international decisions, many risks faced overseas involve unknowns to management, which leads it to overreact. In such cases, management may seek costly forms of insurance, even though within the home market it would readily self-insure risks of much greater magnitude.

Hence, a major problem in international business lies in reducing risk (loss of claims on a stream of earnings) to reasonable proportions as measured against expected return. A variety of devices are available, the choice of which depends upon the nature of the assets giving rise to the stream of earnings (physical, intangible, liquid), the nature of the risk (expropriation, dilution of control, destruction, dishonesty, inflation and devaluation), and the management's time horizon. In each case the firm may either avoid the risk (by not going into a project or transaction), self-insure, transfer the risk, or moderate the risk by its own behavior.

In order to protect earnings arising out of physical assets, the firm may self-insure through geographical dispersion or large size; it may take out commercial insurance policies; utilize the investment guarantee schemes offered by certain governments; rely upon the specific guarantees of the host government; depend upon the leverage provided by a continuing flow from abroad of essential commodities and/or services (essential in the sense of not being available locally or from other international companies at comparable price); depend upon a high level of identity with the economic and political interests of the host country; employ company police; or it may offer special gratuities.

The risks themselves can be classified as commercial and casualty, political, and currency-related.

Commercial and Casualty Risk

Commercial risk as used here includes both the risk inherent in future—and hence unknown—market conditions, as well as normal casualty risk. Text-books seldom cover the conditions under which ordinary casualty insurance coverage (for fire, explosion, theft, liability) is available in various parts of the world. The major problems are either the absence of any coverage at reasonable cost or coverage in an inconvertible currency, even though the assets involved can only be replaced from a convertible-currency country. One may, of course, take out so-called "unadmitted insurance"—that is, insurance issued by a foreign insurance company not legally authorized to do business in the country in which the insured assets are located. The premiums paid out by such a company are frequently not recognized as legitimate business expenses and, hence, must be paid out of *post-tax* earnings, which often considerably increases cost. For example, in France unadmitted insurance is prohibited without governmental approval. Purchase of such insurance may be considered technically as tax evasion, and penalties can be imposed. In Chile, unadmitted insurance is permitted for exports and imports. Otherwise, it is subject to a tax amounting to 60 percent of the premiums that would have been charged in the Chilean market. In Guyana, unadmitted insurance is not prohibited except for compulsory insurance, and premiums may be taken as a local tax deduction. So it goes; national laws vary and are constantly changing.

In protecting one's tangible overseas assets, the employment of company police (a device that modifies casualty risk), may be fraught with political risk in the less mature LDCs. Risk may be particularly high if the enterprise is identified as being essentially foreign. A much better solution is, if necessary, to subsidize the local government to the extent of the cost of providing special police protection. You should note that the payment of special gratuities for protection is exceedingly hazardous, particularly in a politically unstable situation, unless the time horizon of the firm is very short indeed.

One reason to set up a wholly owned domestic subsidiary to enter into contracts with foreign clients, execute foreign sales, and hold equity in foreign enterprises is simply to shield the corporate assets of the parent against adverse—and possibly politically dictated—decisions of foreign arbitration and judicial bodies. In the United States, the parent company is generally permitted, and often required, by the Internal Revenue Service to consolidate the earnings of its *domestic* U.S. subsidiaries. The existence or nonexistence of a domestically incorporated international subsidiary has no direct relevance to the administrative control structure of the firm.

By far the best insurance against loss of one's assets overseas, whether tangible or otherwise, is the leverage the foreign firm can develop through the flow of services it maintains (managerial, distributional, technical, financial) that are not available locally. If the enterprise is also perceived by the host government as having a relatively strong positive effect on net national product, balance of payments, public revenues, economic growth, and political development, the firm has little to fear. As the uniqueness (that is, the value) of what the firm contributes to the host society diminishes over time, the relationship between the firm and the associated foreign enterprise should likewise be altered, as noted in Chapter Six.

In the case of liquid assets, special precautions are necessary. Some alternative policies are personal bonding, external audits, the use of anonymous accounts, and the deposit of funds or securities where attachment is difficult. Given the time delay almost inevitable in controlling the flow of liquid assets overseas by an international parent firm, fiscal authority must be delegated. And given distance and isolation, the uncovering of irregularities may be delayed. Hence, it becomes doubly important to bond those with disbursing authority and to have periodic, though not necessarily regular, external audits by a reputable auditing firm. Several of the large auditing firms based in the United States and Europe have worldwide coverage.

The only legitimate reason to use anonymous or confidential bank accounts (for example, a numbered account in a Swiss bank) is to prevent capricious **attachment** of the firm's liquid assets by a disgruntled foreign government, client, customer, partner, or stockholder. This risk is considered to be a real one, particularly by those in the contracting business, where performance may always be questioned and damages claimed. Although Swiss law makes disclosure of the ownership of a numbered account by a bank official a penal offense (and permits recovery of damages through civil suit), writs of attachment are relatively easy to obtain in Switzerland. The only problem lies in serving them on the right bank because of the difficulty of learning the location of deposits. Serving writs on all of the leading banks is likely to include the right one, in which case the confidential nature of the account is no defense. The funds may remain attached until final judicial decision, which may be several years off. Writs of attachment are also relatively easy to come by in the United States. A recent court decision has held that funds on deposit with a *foreign* branch of a U.S. bank may be reached by attachment served on the U.S. parent. The best protection against capricious attachment is gained by depositing funds in a bank in the United Kingdom, where a reasonable cause for the attachment must be demonstrated *prior* to the blocking of an account.

Political Risk

Most of the capital exporting countries offer foreign investment guarantees or political insurance. U.S. foreign investment guarantees (administered by OPIC) are available for risk of expropriation, nonconvertibility of profits, and loss due to war, insurrection, and civil disorder in respect to new investment approved by the host government, but only in countries defined as less-developed countries with which the United States has a guarantee agreement. These "specific risk" guarantees may be packaged with usual *commercial* risk insurance (covering defaults, bankruptcy, and so on) in the form of an "extended risk" guarantee. Guarantees may be issued to any U.S.

entity, or to a foreign entity that is owned 10 percent or more by a U.S. entity. Contractual arrangements, which embody some form of investment (such as withheld earnings or a performance bond) may likewise be covered. For this purpose, three years is generally considered to differentiate investment from sale.

National investment guarantee schemes vary in respect to coverage (term, type, and country limitation), cost (and, hence, level of subsidy), the requirement of prior host government approval, differentiation of an investment from a sale, and the nationality test of the applicant. For example, because some national schemes are more extensive in their coverage than is U.S. coverage, it may be important for a U.S.-based corporation to qualify through a subsidiary for a guarantee under, say, the West German scheme. No one guarantees the rate of exchange applying in the case of blocked earnings other than the current rate. Average premiums run about 1 percent ($\pm$ 0.5 percent), depending upon the type and amount of coverage. As in the case of export credit insurance (see appendix to this chapter), an investment guarantee insurance policy may make an otherwise unacceptable project into a bankable proposition.

A persistent question is whether national schemes may, in the long run, cause more difficulty than they avoid by increasing risk. Offering investment guarantees to corporations may tend to reward the traditional manner of conducting international business—namely, direct equity investment on a majority or wholly owned basis, with control centralized in the parent company headquarters. This traditional pattern stands in opposition to a movement out of ownership of the local firm into a set of contractual relationships that, by their very nature, possibly tend to render the firm more sensitive to the interests of the host society and also tend to reduce risk by associating specific inputs with specific benefits. This pattern is shown in Figure 7.1. It would appear plausible that the availability of investment guarantees for financial investment tends to discourage the type of relationship envisioned here and, thus, sets companies (and the guaranteeing parent governments) on a collision course with host foreign governments and business interests.

The protection of national investment guarantee schemes has, however, been available only for a small portion of companies' total overseas investments. Restrictions written into the various schemes limit the countries for which coverage is offered and the assets that can be covered (for instance, frequently only new investment, not reinvested earnings). The resulting gap has prompted the creation of a London-based private market, organized around Lloyd's, for political risk insurance offering complementary coverage. Since the basic premise of this private market is to spread risk, the insurer generally requires that a company insure its entire overseas assets against expropriation, including those located in low-risk countries. The Lloyd's scheme covers virtually every country in the world, including those socialist countries where international joint ventures are possible. The amount of insurance available in each country, however, is limited and is sold on a first come, first served basis. Availability is deter-

Figure 7.1
Relating Specific Costs and Benefits vis-à-vis a Foreign Entity via Contract

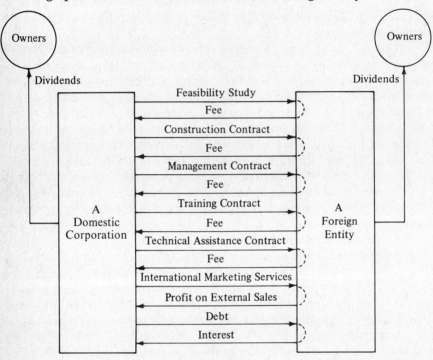

mined by three factors: national origin of the investment, the country of investment, and the industry. This allocation of available coverage, a device to spread risk, is made because the risk of expropriation is not the same for all nationalities, all countries, or all industries. Fees range from 0.2 percent to 10 percent per annum per country, depending upon the perceived risk in each case, which is based on the same three factors as determine the allocation of coverage.

Currency-Related Risk

Of special concern to the international business manager are the devices for the protection of earnings flows against devaluation and inflation effects; that is, currency-related risks. The appropriateness of each device depends upon the legal restraints, relative costs, availability of local financing, price controls, export potential (and legal capacity to retain export earnings), and the relation between relevant price movements and changes in the exchange rate. In addition to a variety of tax tools (such as accelerated depreciation), the principal devices are listed below. The first eight are essentially *risk-modifying*, numbers nine and ten are forms of *self-insuring*, and the balance are devices for *risk-shifting*.

1. Developing exports   Provided that the firm can retain any of the foreign exchange earnings.

2. Increasing prices   Assumes the absence of price controls.

3. Revaluating assets   Important only if profits are linked to capital base for purposes of taxation or repatriation, or if it is a joint venture in which the foreign equity is measured and recorded in foreign currency. Otherwise, asset revaluation is only of accounting significance. (An Italian firm assured itself that it would maintain its 50 percent ownership of a Brazilian joint venture by inserting in the charter a provision that the value of its initial investment would change parallel to the effective exchange rate; that is, a devaluation would trigger an increase in value.)

4. Reducing import requirements   Eliminating products with a high foreign exchange content and reducing inventories of imported components (through use of air transport and better control). Useful if management expects that the rate of increase in revenue to the local firm will lag behind the rate at which the exchange rate used for the relative imports increases. (If the exchange rate increases less rapidly, the local currency received by the firm gains in strength vis-à-vis the foreign currency and its imports cheapen in terms of local currency. In such case, the firm might well opt to increase the imported component.)

5. Unit-of-account financing   Or invoicing (see Section 7.4).

6. Concentrating on the production of goods with high margins   Should not be done blindly; one should look at the risk-reward trade-off.

7. Accumulating maximum credit abroad   On behalf of the foreign firm through the accumulation of fees, dividends, royalties, profits on intracompany sales or purchases.

8. Incurring local debt   Running up payables in relation to receivables. (A reduction of receivables may be accomplished by "factoring."[10] By altering their fiscal years, some firms have been able to borrow tax funds through a one-time deferment of taxes.) The point is that by borrowing locally, the firm can reduce its net foreign exchange exposure. After a currency devaluation, the debt translates into fewer foreign currency units.

9. Manipulating leads and lags   Involves the prepayment for imports or the early receipt of export proceeds (leads), or the postponement of import payments or a delay in the receipt of export proceeds (lags). In the first case, the length of the transaction is shortened in anticipation that the currency

---

[10]Essentially, the sale of a receivable to a bank or other financial intermediary.

being received will soon devalue or that the currency being paid will soon revalue. In the second case (lag), the length of the transaction is lengthened in anticipation that the currency received will soon revalue or that the currency being paid will soon devalue. Leads and lags may be limited by regulation. For example, France, as of early 1975, limited export lag to 180 days and import lag to one year, and permitted any export lead but ruled out import leads (other than a 30 percent downpayment on imported capital goods).

10. Netting   The offset of payables and receivables between related companies so that only the net balance is actually transferred. Netting may be multilateral, in which case there is a complete analysis of all intracompany liabilities, and actual payments are made only to the *net* creditors of the group. Not only does netting reduce the transfer costs associated with the movement of funds, but it also provides a mechanism for timing the clearing process to take advantage of anticipated shifts in exchange rates between major currencies, either by triggering clearance or postponing it. National regulation may limit a company's freedom in this regard.

11. Purchase of futures   (Forward cover or a forward contract), which refers to a commitment to buy a foreign currency at a given time in the future for a stipulated amount. The cost of such a contract can be interpreted as the cost of insuring against a possible loss due to currency fluctuations.

      Typically, textbooks define the cost of a forward contract as the difference in the exchange rate between two currencies on the date the contract is agreed upon (the "spot" rate) and that on the date the contract matures. A definition leading to better management decision is that the cost of locking into a future exchange rate is the difference between the forward rate and the spot rate one anticipates for that date. In a sense, the former definition involves an accounting illusion. For example, assume that a U.S. firm purchases a machine from an English firm for a given number of pounds sterling, payable at a future date. To avoid speculating on the value of the future pound in reference to the dollar,[11] it may wish to fix the number of dollars needed to buy the pounds

[11]"Speculation in the foreign exchange market takes place when an individual has an amount of assets (a future inflow) different from the amount of liabilities (a future outflow) in a given currency. If there is a change in the value of the currency in question, the value of the net holdings of the individual in that currency will change. In this case, the individual or institution has a "net position" in that currency. This position is called "long" if there are more assets (future inflows) than liabilities (future outflows). The net position is called "short" if there are more liabilities (future outflows) than assets (future inflows). A net position is called *outright speculation*." Rita M. Rodriguez and E. Eugene Carter, *International Financial Management* (Englewood Cliffs: Prentice-Hall, 1976), p. 107.

at that future date. The annualized cost of such a forward contract may be represented thus:

$$\left(\frac{360}{n}\right)\left(\frac{X_f - X_s}{X_s}\right) \tag{7.4}$$

where n = the number of days to maturity of the forward contract

X_f = the forward rate of exchange of pounds per dollar

X_s = the spot rate of exchange of pounds per dollar.

Say the obligation is for £1000 payable 90 days in the future, that the spot rate quoted for the British pound is \$2.40 and the 90-day rate \$2.30. The *annualized* cost of a forward contract would be calculated thus:

$$\left(\frac{360}{90}\right)\left(\frac{2.30 - 2.40}{2.30}\right) = (4)\,\frac{-.10}{2.30} = 4(.0435) = -.1743$$

(or 17.40% discount).

In this case, the market is anticipating a devaluation of the pound in reference to the dollar. If the firm does not buy forward cover, and it has no receivables in pounds, it is "short" in pounds and is involved in outright speculation. It may find that when it is actually obliged to buy the £1000 90 days later, that it must do so at either a higher or lower rate than that anticipated in forward contract. If the pound 90 days out actually sells for \$2.20, instead of \$2.30, the firm gains \$.10 per pound or \$100 in our example by *not* buying a forward contract. If the actual rate 90 days in the future turns out to be \$2.35 per pound, the firm will have lost \$.05 per pound, or \$50, by not buying a forward contract. If, on the other hand, the firm buys a forward contract, it will have lost \$100 it otherwise would have gained in the first case, or gained \$50 it otherwise would have lost in the second case.

As can be noted in the example above, the U.S. firm pays 4.35 percent less for the pounds 90 days in the future than it would have if it had purchased the pounds at the time of the purchase commitment. Therefore, it gains by this amount; in our example, \$18.11. Gains of this sort are usually taxable. If, on the other hand, the firm were buying Deutsche marks 90 days in the future, it might well have to pay a premium. In this case, the firm incurs a cost, which is usually treated for tax purposes as a deduction from taxable income. Therefore, the net *annualized* rate on a forward contract to the company buying the contract would be represented thus:

$$\left(\frac{360}{n}\right) \quad \left(\frac{X_f - X_s}{X_s}\right) (1 - t) \tag{7.5}$$

where t = the effective rate on the forward contract gain or loss in the country in which the forward contract is sourced. (It may vary depending upon whether X_f or X_s is the larger.)

There is a strong market force that tends to make the cost of forward cover equal to the difference between the rates of return available in low-risk, short-term securities of the respective countries. The process that underlies this market force is as follows: If the annual rate of return on treasury bills were 8 percent in the United States and 10 percent in the United Kingdom, the cost of forward cover would tend to be a 2 percent premium for U.S. residents investing in U.K. securities and purchasing a forward contract simultaneously in order to avoid the currency fluctuation risk. If it were less, for example 1 percent, then U.S. residents could invest in equivalent risk securities in the United Kingdom with a 10 percent return, pay a 1 percent premium for a forward contract, and receive a net 9 percent yield as compared with an 8 percent yield on U.S. Treasury bills. The rush to take advantage of this return differential would tend to increase the cost of forward cover and/or the rate of return in the United States, or decrease the rate of return in the United Kingdom. Thus, the cost of forward cover is strongly influenced by the rates of return on short-term securities in the various countries. However, in that the interest rate differentials among countries appear to be very much influenced by the policies of the respective governments, the cost of forward cover may only coincidentally reflect the risk perceived by the market of future currency fluctuation. So although the cost of forward cover represents the cost of insuring against loss due to foreign exchange fluctuation, it may be a poor indicator of the perceived risk of the occurrences being insured against.

12. Swaps   A parent firm loans dollars (possibly interest-free) to a foreign bank, which in turn makes a local currency loan to the firm's local subsidiary. After the stipulated period, the subsidiary repays the loan, and the bank repays the dollars to the corporate parent abroad. Note that the local firm gains so long as the expected local currency return on the loan invested in the business is greater than the interest on the loan from the bank. The parent firm gains only if the cost of the swap (i.e., the rate of dollar return on a comparable direct investment at free-market rates in its associated foreign firm or on an investment elsewhere, whichever is greater) is less than the gain realized by the associated foreign firm at the swap rate.

13. Export swap   A parent firm pays dollars to a foreign bank, which in turn transmits the foreign currency equivalent to a local firm, the latter being given the privilege of repaying the dollars through export proceeds accumulated over a specified time.

All of these devices imply some cost. When is the incurring of cost justified? Three considerations arise: (1) how to predict a shift in an exchange rate with some reasonable degree of accuracy,[12] (2) how to determine the extent of a firm's net exposure to such a shift, and (3) how to determine the optimum hedging moves—that is, the extent to which a firm should shift risk, and how.

According to the rules of the IMF established at Bretton Woods in 1944 and continued up to the Smithsonian Agreement of December 1971, member countries[13] were not supposed to shift the exchange (or parity) value (defined in terms of gold) of their respective currencies more than plus or minus 1 percent around parity without prior consultation. Thus, up to mid-1971, IMF members attempted to maintain fixed (or pegged) exchange rates. Parity rates were changed only by government decision and by discrete amounts.[14] A few countries maintained for periods of time floating rates (market determined and varying), notable cases being Canada in 1970 and the United States (and its major trading partners) for a short time in 1971. Some countries tried to adjust their currencies by a "creeping peg," which refers to many frequent, small, discrete changes in the parity rate.

By 1971, the pressure on this relatively inflexible system forced a change. Coinciding with the suspension of gold convertibility of the dollar (permitted to foreign governments) and with a reduction in the gold value of the dollar, the Smithsonian Agreement of 1971 permitted fluctuation of exchange rates of plus and minus 2.25 percent around parity. This spread was the so-called band, the end points of which were the intervention points at which a country's central bank or stabilization fund was required to start buying or selling foreign currencies. But in March 1973, even the idea of a band was terminated, and since that date currencies have been floating, some fluctuating by as much as plus or minus 20 percent. In fact, IMF members employ a variety of exchange rate techniques. The currencies of many major countries are floating, but with substantial government intervention (the so-called "dirty float"). Moreover, the majority of countries have pegged their currencies in some way to other currencies, or to certain

---

[12]A firm should only attempt to outguess the market if it is dealing in a currency subject to foreign exchange control and only if it feels that it has superior information. In a completely free market situation, such that the purchasing power of the two currencies is expected to maintain parity, there is no need for the firm to outguess the market, or hedge.

[13]Some 115 countries, including all the significant noncommunist nations other than Switzerland, which nonetheless cooperates.

[14]In fact, during this period of fixed rates under the Bretton Woods agreement, there were more than 150 official parity changes among IMF countries, *not* including the Latin American currencies.

composites, such as the special drawing rights or trade-weighted baskets of currencies. In addition, a varying number of Western European countries have endeavored to keep their respective currencies within a specified plus or minus percent of a stated central rate, the so-called "snake."

Forcing this greater flexibility in exchange rates were perhaps a number of factors, among them being changes in the relative productivity of various national economies, which set up persistent balance-of-payments pressure. Others: lack of confidence in the United States economy (due to rising unemployment, accelerating inflation, and slowed economic growth rate), a shift of liquidity from central banks to private hands (hence, a growing ability of corporations to shift large amounts of funds rapidly), and more rapid dissemination of information. The last means that it is virtually impossible for a central bank to intervene effectively in the market to control foreign exchange rates because the market can anticipate such intervention in ways already described. For example, if the market feels that a government is about to devalue its currency, everyone who can do so will buy foreign currency and, after devaluation, sell it back for local currency. One result is that it makes it difficult for a government to know what the equilibrium rate is.

Most observers seem convinced that the system of floating rates is here to stay. Curiously, their advent does not seem to have had an appreciable impact on the volume of trade and investment. One explanation is that for every currency movement there is a winner and a loser. Admittedly, however, floating rates do make planning difficult. There is some indication that the impact of floating exchange rates on a firm operating internationally is to centralize decision making, eliminate fixed price lists, change the currency in which bills are rendered, and shift sources of supply.

The corporate treasurer obviously has a problem every time the probability of a devaluation of a currency in which the firm has a net exposed position seems significant. The treasurer's problem is really three-fold: (1) how to monitor each national system important to the firm so as to affix a probability of a change in parity rate, and the extent of that change, with reasonable accuracy; (2) how to determine the firm's net exposure in a devaluation-prone currency; and (3) how to combine the probability of a devaluation and the level of the firm's net exposure with the cost of various hedging devices to achieve the lowest cost situation given the firm's propensity to assume risk. Consider the first problem.

In an efficient foreign exchange market, changes in relative prices of two countries correspond to changes in the exchange rate between their currencies. This phenomenon is known as the purchasing power parity theory, the validity of which increases the longer the time period we look at. Some deviations over short periods have been attributed to monetary, as well as nonmonetary, factors. The latter include changes in people's tastes, changes in technology, and sudden discovery of a natural resource. Nonmonetary factors affect a country's balance of payments, which in turn puts pressure on the exchange rate. From the empirical evidence, however, it appears that over a period of five to six years, the difference in the relative inflation rate is an approximately unbiased estimator of the change in the exchange rate between two countries.

Over a very long period, the purchasing power parity theory would operate even in situations where there was heavy government intervention in the exchange market. However, this long-run tendency may or may not be of value to management, for the long run may fall well beyond its decision-making time horizon. Meanwhile, we are left with the task of anticipating short-run shifts in parity rates among currencies.

Signals Forecasting Shifts in Exchange Rates

There seems to be no real agreement among either scholars or practitioners as to the signals upon which one can forecast shifts in exchange rates. There are, however, certain phenomena that are always associated with such changes. Although there is no a priori way of establishing which factor or factors will precipitate a change in a particular situation, the presence of one or more increases the probability of change. The list, stated in terms of pressures toward a devaluation, follows. Contrary trends would tend to signal a revaluation.

Exchange Market Signals

1. *Increase in selling pressure in forward exchange*   A forward exchange rate, say a three-month rate, is the rate at which an exchange contract, a forward contract or futures, is negotiated for the sale and purchase of a given currency three months hence. Obviously, the actual rate may turn out to differ from the contracted rate. The advantage to the nonspeculating businessperson foreseeing the need for buying or selling one currency for another is that he or she may thus stabilize the rate at which to buy or sell the foreign currency; in other words, "cover." The other party is betting that the actual rate three months out will be such that it can either sell the currency involved at a higher-than-spot rate, or buy a currency at a lower rate, thereby making a profit. Thus, selling pressure on the forward exchange (when the forward rate for a currency falls in value relative to another currency) means that those dealing in exchange futures are expecting a change in the parity rate. If there were no perceived risk of change, the discount or premium between a spot and forward rate would be simply the difference in the interest rates realizable in the two currencies.

2. *Widening of margins between buy and sell quotations*   in both spot and forward transactions, which simply means that there is either a selling or buying pressure. That is, the market anticipates a shift in parity rate.

3. *Widening of profit margins on interest arbitrage*   (Interest arbitrage refers to the movement of short-term funds between international centers as borrowers and lenders try to take advantage of differences in interest rates.) If the margins widen, it means simply that those involved perceive a risk of

parity shift and are trying to cover themselves by responding only to greater interest-rate differentials.

4. Increase in the degree of official intervention in the exchange market (either buying or selling of a foreign currency by a central bank or exchange stabilization fund). This would be indicated by the sudden arrest of a downward trend, and by continuing ability of the market to absorb a volume of exchange sales out of proportion to estimated government and commercial needs.

5. Inception of, or growth in, gray or black exchange markets A black market refers to illegal transactions; a gray market is illegal, but is tolerated by a government even though aware of it.

6. Increase in volume of transactions in the foreign exchange market, especially just before weekends (when markets are closed) and other short dates, demonstrating a general perception of higher risk of a parity rate change.

A phone call by the corporate financial manager to the foreign exchange department of the firm's bank will quickly provide adequate information on all of these exchange market trends. The better financial newspapers such as the *Wall Street Journal, Japan Economic Journal*, and the *London Financial Times* provide enough trend warning to trigger a responsive manager to make the call.

National Economic Signals

1. Weakening reserve position in gold and hard currencies.
2. Introduction or tightening of trade or exchange controls.
3. Export goods becoming less competitive in world markets because of changes in price, technology, or taste.
4. Decrease in exports or imports.
5. Increasing or chronic balance-of-payments deficit.[15]
6. Growing foreign debt or weakening ability to service foreign debt (e.g., an increasing debt service/export earnings ratio).
7. Reduced availability of foreign credit, signified by excessive interest rates on foreign borrowing.
8. Increasing or chronic excessive government budgetary deficits.
9. Increasing internal rate of price inflation.
10. Disproportionate increase in volume of money in circulation or in volume of credit.
11. Increasing occurrence of "figure fudging," indicated by discrepancies between statistics issued by different governmental agencies.

[15]A nation's balance of payments is essentially the record of a nation's annual cash flow (movement of liquid assets and liabilities) in relation to the rest of the world, balanced by an increase or decrease of the nation's international monetary reserves. The reserves consist of claims against foreign countries (i.e., foreign exchange balances), gold, and IMF drawing rights.

The financial manager will find the IMF monthly *International Financial Statistics* gives excellent information on all of the above except competitive position of exports, interest rates on foreign borrowings, and figure fudging. The competitive position of exports is a condition, not a quantity, and can best be estimated from reports on trade in such publications as *Business International, Wall Street Journal* and the *London Financial Times*, as well as bank information services. Figure fudging is difficult and time-consuming for a manager to identify, but bank economists regularly track this down through their work with many governmental agency reports. An occasional telephone call to one or two of them will be quite adequate to keep the manager abreast of this phenomenon.

Financial Signals

1. Rise in domestic interest rates relative to other countries', especially for short maturities.
2. Reduction of foreign-owned domestic bank balances, indicating a general anticipation of a devaluation.

Both of these phenomena are covered in the monthly IMF *International Financial Statistics*.

Political Signals

1. Decreasing political stability.
2. National demoralization.

These phenomena are conditions, not quantities, and are best gathered from personal contacts within the country in question, as well as from commentaries in the media.

Production Signals

1. Increasing labor-capital disunity.
2. Increasing wage demands and production costs.
3. Increasing obsolescence and inefficiency of means of production.

Other than deriving a general feel for these phenomena from reports and commentaries in the media, a closer examination can be made through statistics developed by the U.S. Department of Commerce, by many foreign ministries of trade and labor, special country reports by banks, and, when noteworthy developments or trends occur, by such services as *Business International*.

Commercial Signals

1. Domestic importers and exporters lengthen leads and lags on transactions denominated in foreign currencies, while foreign importers and exporters shorten leads and lags on transactions denominated in the domestic currency.

2.   Increased forward coverage by foreigners of balances and receivables denominated in the local currency, and increased hedging of their currency invesments.

One is hesitant even to include these commercial phenomena in the list, simply because they are so difficult to determine. However, they are so important and potent that even a little information about them goes a long way. The foreign exchange departments of a corporation's banks represent the most likely source of information in this area for the financial manager, outside of a review of his own company's receipts and disbursements for transactions with the country in question to spot lead or lag tendencies.

International Signals

1.   Adverse developments abroad which, by the domino principle, can affect a country in a variety of ways (e.g., a change in the parity of the currency of an important trading partner).
2.   Adverse action by another country or countries specifically directed at the country in question (such as trade sanctions).

The news media provides sufficient information on overt developments of this nature, while banks and special services adequately cover the more subtle moves.

This list of signals of an impending change in an exchange rate is fairly long, but most of the items on it can be monitored relatively easily with a limited set of information sources and an equally limited expenditure of time. When one or more of these phenomena become apparent, it is important for the manager to determine whether they are dominating the system. He or she is then in a position to affix the probability of a change and to estimate its most likely magnitude, as well as the minimum and maximum magnitudes. The next step involves a calculation of company exposure.

Calculating Net Exposure

Net exposure is simply the difference between a firm's exposed assets and exposed liabilities, with exposure being measured in terms of the effect of a devaluation on the value of the assets or liabilities.

Exposed assets include accounts receivable, local currency bank deposits, and other current assets denominated in local currency. (The larger the exposed assets, the greater is a possible devaluation loss—that is, the greater the firm's "negative exposure.") Exposed liabilities include local bank loans, accounts and notes payable in local currency, and local taxes payable. (The larger the exposed liabilities, the greater is a possible gain from devaluation—that is, the greater the firm's "positive exposure.") Inventories may be anywhere between 100 percent positive and 100 percent negative exposure. The percentage of inventory exposure depends upon the ratio of possible inventory gain or loss (the difference between the change in the market value of inventories and their replacement value) to the total replacement value times the expected devaluation (expressed as a percentage). The formula for determining inventory exposure is:

$$e = \frac{M - R}{ID} \tag{7.6}$$

where

e = percentage of inventory exposure
M = change in dollar* *market* value of inventories after devaluation
R = change in dollar* *replacement* value of inventories after devaluation
I = *total* replacement value of inventories prior to devaluation
D = expected devaluation (percentage).

The situation is somewhat more complicated when the corporation is concerned with its *worldwide* net after-tax exposure in each currency, which is an algebraic sum of its exposed assets, corrected for taxes, everywhere. Since the advent of floating exchange rates, this problem is no longer subject to "back of the envelope" calculation. Major international banks offer computer models that permit a company to evaluate its worldwide exposure in either accounting terms (translation exposure) or economic terms (transaction exposure). Normally, such a model requires indication of the most likely, most optimistic, and most pessimistic forecasts in relation to currency evaluation or devaluation for each time period being evaluated. The model then indicates the expected loss or gain in each currency from the spot rates prevailing on a particular day. It may also quantify the riskiness of the exposures by indicating the maximum possible loss or gain that could be incurred at various confidence levels.

Having determined the probability of a parity rate change (and of its amount) and the firm's net exposure, the final question is: What is the best hedging policy? The answer is that there is no *single* best policy, but, rather, an infinite set of options—from minimum risk to maximum risk, and from maximum cost to minimum cost. The two taken together generate an efficiency frontier. The best choice depends upon the risk a firm wants to avoid (or assume) at what cost. A model can make the trade-offs explicit, but it does not determine objectively which is best, for that depends upon the firm's subjectively determined risk preference.

Because of the diversity of strategy options in the financial area, many of which are not available or relevant to purely domestic business, it is likely that one of the more important competitive advantages of the large firm operating internationally lies in its capacity to make efficient use of its financial resources.

Greater efficiency, however, is realizable only if management is sensitive to the benefits to be derived from a sophisticated and continuing

---

*Or any currency against which the devaluation is expected and which can be used to purchase the imported inputs.

analysis of where profits should be taken, of the most productive profit routes, of where investment decisions should be made, of the range and cost of various types and sources of financing, of the best legal instrumentalities to use, of how to minimize risk by enhancing the security of assets, and of the risks and costs associated with maintaining the value of assets in a world characterized by shifting exchange rates and differential rates of inflation and deflation. All of these considerations push in the direction of centralized financial control.

Indeed, the arguments for centralized control are strong. Local executives can rarely know the liquidity position of the entire global organization, nor can they analyze with accuracy the exchange exposure of the corporation as a consolidated entity. A central financial office draws on information from many financial institutions and can formulate a broader decision on the probable nature of financial events and devise measures of protection against them.

APPENDIX **7A**

EXPORT FINANCING

As indicated in Section 7.4, debt includes short-, medium-, and long-term export financing. Various methods are used for the debt transaction, specifically, open-account, cash-against-documents, sight draft, time draft, banker's acceptance, letters of credit, consignment, factoring, undisclosed non-recourse financing, and cash in advance. These are described below, arranged in the order of descending risk from the point of view of the exporter. In addition there are the highly specialized methods sometimes used to finance East-West trade, which were described in Chapter Two.

It should be noted that related to the export financing decision are three questions: (1) In what currency is the sale to be made? (2) Where should the sale be booked (by what national subsidiary)? and (3) Where is the risk to be taken (by the firm, by an external agency, or in part by both)? The risk to which we refer really breaks down into the risk of default, a foreign exchange risk, and political risk (government intervention). If the sale is to be made in a foreign currency, one must then be aware of the fact that the firm has set up a fixed foreign currency flow at some point in the future. If the export financing is denominated in another currency, one must anticipate the foreign exchange rate that will prevail at that time in order to determine the true cost of the financing.

1. Open-account (sale of unsecured credit) in which the seller ships goods and subsequently bills the buyer.

2. Cash-against-documents   in which cash payment is made once shipping documents have been delivered to the buyer through a commercial bank. This is a common method of payment in East-West trade.

3. Draft   an unconditional order written by the seller (an exporter in our case) directing the buyer (an importer) or its agent (such as a bank) to pay a specified amount of money at a specified time. Sometimes called a bill of exchange, a draft may be either a *sight draft*, which is payable immediately, or a *time draft*, which is payable upon the lapse of a specified amount of time (normally, 30, 90, 120, or 180 days). A time draft directed to a bank can become a *banker's acceptance* if the bank has in fact accepted the draft as a valid claim. Such a draft becomes negotiable and may be sold at an appropriate discount.

4. Letter of credit(L/C) a document issued by a bank upon request of a buyer (the importer) stating that it will honor drafts drawn against it by a specified party (the exporter) if the terms and conditions set forth in the L/C are satisfied. In return, the buyer promises to pay the bank the amount of the L/C, plus fees, according to mutually agreed upon terms. Once the proper documents proving shipment of the goods (bill of lading) have been delivered to a corresponding bank abroad by the exporter, it will be sent payment. The L/C is said to be a *confirmed L/C* if the corresponding bank adds its own confirmation to the L/C. In such case, if the importer does not pay its bank, both banks are nonetheless obligated to pay the exporter. In the unconfirmed case, only the bank initially issuing the L/C is liable. An L/C is said to be "revocable" if neither bank has guaranteed payment, in which case the exporter has no assurance that the L/C will not be revoked by the importer at any time prior to payment. These differences are summarized below:

	Revocable L/C	Unconfirmed Irrevocable L/C	Confirmed Irrevocable L/C
Who applies for L/C?	importer	importer	importer
Who is obliged to pay?	no one	issuing bank	issuing and confirming bank
Who reimburses paying bank?	issuing bank	issuing bank	issuing bank
Who reimburses issuing bank?	importer	importer	importer

5. Consignment   in which the seller ships the goods to a second party but retains title. The second party simply sells the goods on behalf of the original seller according to mutually agreed upon terms.

6. Factoring   involves the outright sale to a bank of accounts receivable without recourse to the seller, the bank thus assuming the entire risk so long as the seller avoids disputes relating to the delivery and quality of its merchandise. The factor charges a fee for making the collections and assuming the risk. Also, cash advances to the maturity of the factored accounts carry an interest rate often somewhat above the usual rate. A variation of this case is *undisclosed, nonrecourse financing*. Here, the factor turns around and appoints the seller of the accounts receivable as the agent to complete the sale and make collections in due course on behalf of an undisclosed principal (the bank). In some instances, an exporter may induce a commercial bank to take the earlier maturities of its foreign customer's obligations (with recourse) if the exporter assumes the later maturities. In this way a firm may extend longer credit terms to its buyers.

7. Cash in advance.

In some countries, there are private firms willing to insure against insolvency, sometimes against default or delayed payment as well. Private banks and companies do not, however, insure on their own account against such noncommercial risks as war, confiscation, civil disorder, inconvertibility, and other politically decreed costs. To fill this gap, national export guarantee systems have been established, whose guarantees have the effect of creating a bankable risk.[1] The U.S. export financing is offered jointly by the Export-Import Bank (Eximbank) and the Foreign Insurance Credit Association (FICA). The Eximbank and the Private Export Funding Corporation (PEFCO, in which some 50 major banks participate) maintain an agreement under which the Eximbank guarantees the principal and interest on debt obligations that are issued by foreign purchasers of U.S. products and services by PEFCO. PEFCO thereby acquires a portfolio of Eximbank—guaranteed paper that can be used as the basis for raising funds in the private market.

The Export-Import Bank of the United States, and comparable banks elsewhere, are designed to overcome deficiencies in private financial markets. Such deficiencies include the lack of adequate long-term export financing, limited knowledge of foreign markets and foreign buyers among the smaller banks and many exporters, a generally exaggerated assessment of the risk of financing foreign transactions, as well as the nonavailability of private cover for noncommercial (i.e., political) risks. Significant variations in national systems are listed below:

1. Type of organization offering export credit and/or guarantees. Possible alternatives: a private company acting on behalf of a government; a governmental department; a state agency; or a government corporation, alone or in cooperation with private banks and insurance companies.

2. Categories of exports eligible for coverage: consumer goods, capital

[1]Those known to have export credit insurance systems include Canada, the United Kingdom, France, Germany, Belgium, Austria, Hungary, Ireland, Switzerland, the Netherlands, Sweden, Denmark, Norway, Italy, Spain, Japan, Australia, India, Israel, Pakistan, Republic of South Africa, United States, and Yugoslavia.

goods, services (feasibility studies, marketing, engineering, architectural, construction, management).

3. Risks that may be underwritten:
Commercial. Insolvency of the buyer, arbitrary nonacceptance by the buyer not due to the fault of the seller, buyer's failure to pay local currency deposit on due date.

Political. Cancellation of an export license (not due to fault of exporter), cancellation of a contract by a public buyer, cancellation of an import license, transport or insurance charges due to diversion of shipment caused by political events, currency inconvertibility and transfer delays, outbreak of war or civil commotion preventing delivery or payment by the buyer, requisition or expropriation or other government intervention that prevents payment.

Other. Inflation risk (exporter generally absorbs the first few percentage points and may or may not get 100 percent coverage); exchange rate losses (above a certain percentage per annum on contracts over a given length); losses from performance bond guarantees.

4. Type of export credit policies offered: specific (by transaction, such as ordinary supplier's credit), comprehensive (covers all of a firm's export business for a specified time), selective (covers only transactions designated by the firm within the overall total), restricted (covers transactions only with certain countries), single-buyer (covers only transactions with a particular buyer), project (covers shipments to a designated project), commercial risk guarantee (covers only commercial risks), political (covers only political risks), extended (covers both political and commercial risks).

5. Types of export credit offered: fixed-rate, preferential fixed-rate (less than market rate, that is, subsidized: sometimes offered only for long-term credit, sometimes for medium-term as well), preshipment, postshipment, short-term (up to two years), medium-term (two to five years), long-term (over five years, sometimes up to 15 years), direct loan (to foreign buyer), concessionary or "mixed" credits (for certain LDCs, mixing developmental aid with export credit), government-to-government line of credit, local cost financing, discounting of commercial bank credit.

6. Content: local origin rules (often 80 percent or more by value must be produced in issuing country), local financing (some countries will finance the purchase of local, that is, foreign goods and services associated with an export).

7. Terms: market interest rate, preferential rate, grace period (before repayment starts), duration (up to 15 years on some long-term loans; some countries define short-term as anything up to 18 months rather than two years).

8. Fees charged: for commitment, stand-by, management and legal services.

9. Rates: may be given in a standard scale or set for each transaction (possible variables: risks covered, duration, types of goods, country of destination, credit standing of buyer).

10. Deposit requirements: such as the U.S. FICA requirement that the buyer make a payment of 10 percent.

11. Exclusion: for example, the U.S. Eximbank is prohibited by the Trade Act of 1974 from extending export credits, export guaranties, or investment guaranties directly or indirectly to any nonmarket economy that denies its citizens freedom of emigration. Since the act does not apply to any nonmarket economy country that enjoyed most-favored-nation tariff treatment when the act was enacted, Poland is exempt. In addition, Romania was subsequently exempted from the provision when Congress approved a trade agreement with Romania in 1975.

12. Timing: the point at which an export credit guarantee may be issued. Possible variations: guarantee issued upon receipt of an order but prior to or during production (prefinancing insurance), at time of shipment, after shipment (normal export credit insurance).

There is a continuing effort to harmonize national practice in respect to export credit, although why international competition in this area is considered bad has never been made clear. Since all national systems have some degree of government involvement, the competition is not between subsidized and nonsubsidized systems.

CHAPTER 8

LEGAL STRATEGY

dual taxation the taxing of both corporate profits and stockholder dividends.

know-how contract a contractual agreement to transfer technology that is not covered by patent, copyright, trademark, or secrecy. The subject matter is considered to be in the public domain. Payment is designated as a *fee*. Also called *technical assistance contract*.

license a contractual agreement to permit another to use a functional or design invention protected by patent, a unique literary or artistic expression protected by copyright, a unique identification protected by trademark, or technology and/or skills of a secret nature. Payment is designated as a *royalty*.

neutral tax a tax that neither stimulates nor depresses particular types of income, forms of business organization, location of production, or seat of control.

Paris Union the popular name for the International Convention for the Protection of Industrial Property, which provides that if a patent application is filed in one member country, the applicant may file in other member countries within one year, with priority running from the date of first application. Also called the *Paris Convention*.

per se violations business practices deemed to be illegal under the antitrust laws without proof of any adverse effect on competition; the harm is assumed.

private arbitration resolution of disputes by use of private intermediaries according to rules and procedures provided ahead of time in the parties' underlying commercial contract.

registered user someone other than the owner of a patent or trademark who is recorded as such and who has use of the patent or trademark, but in the latter case only after scrutiny has determined that adequate quality control will be exercised by the owner over the manufacture of the goods by the licensee.

tax haven a country with no tax or a very low tax rate on foreign source income and accumulated earnings; popular domicile for subsidiaries that act as holding companies for corporations domiciled in high-tax countries.

tax holiday a commitment by a taxing authority to waive payment of a tax for a specified period that would otherwise have to be paid.

trademarks words, phrases, or symbols identifying certain products, services, or individuals and whose use is legally restricted. There are four varieties of trademarks: *true trademarks* identify a product with a specific manufacturer or source; *service marks* (tradenames) identify the services of an individual or a corporation; *certification marks* indicate that a product is of a certain quality, is manufactured in a specific location, or bears some other factual characteristic; *collective marks* indicate membership past or present, in an associaton or organization of some sort.

unitary taxation the taxing of only corporate profits, differentiated from dual taxation (see above); also used to refer to a system of taxing a corporation's income on the basis of the ratios of its local sales, local assets, and local employment to its global sales, assets, and employment

Webb-Pomerene association an association of U.S. firms who are authorized to use joint facilities, fix prices, and allocate orders. The association must engage solely in export trade, and is subject to numerous other restrictions.

Many firms start with legal strategy in structuring international operations. Sales, production, management, finance, ownership, labor, and control strategies are made to conform. In doing so, one loses sight of the fact that the firm's basic need is to determine the best strategy for generating a profit over the relevant time horizon, not to gain maximum legal security per se. Legal counsel should be employed in a consulting capacity, not as the final architect of a business relationship. Therefore, the relevant question one should ask is: *Given a set of strategy choices in the business area, what is the best legal strategy?* In the final analysis, some of the nonlegal strategy choices may have to be modified, but rarely should they be determined *solely* by legal rationale.

The legal strategies considered here fall into three general categories:

1. The preferred legal character of the entity representing the principal domestic interest vis-à-vis the foreign interest.
2. The preferred legal character of the entity representing the associated foreign principal.
3. The preferred legal nature of the relationship between the two parties.

In each case, the entity representing a principal may be the principal itself (a domestic or foreign corporation or a branch of either), its subsidiary, its representative (a third party not controlled by the principal interest except in a limited contractual sense), or an affiliate jointly owned with other interests.

8.1   Corporate Legal Organization

The range of possible legal forms is similar from country to country, but far from identical. In civil-law countries (continental Europe and its former colonies, Latin America, and Japan), a corporation is considered to be a contractual relationship, and a minimum number of stockholders is required, always more than one. Directors do not stand in a fiduciary or trust relationship to stockholders, as in the common-law countries, but in an agent relationship in that they are subject to a supervisory audit initiated by the stockholders. Hence, theoretically, the stockholders are in a stronger position vis-à-vis the board than in a common-law country like the United States. Major corporate control in civil law countries rests with an executive committee or general director (or managing director) selected by and from the board. Thus, there is no real distinction between officers and directors. Corporate nationality may be determined by place of actual management, rather than place of incorporation.

In common-law countries (United Kingdom and its present and former colonies, including the United States), a corporation is a legal person, and a single individual may incorporate. Directors have only a fiduciary responsibility to the stockholders, and major control rests with a president elected by but not necessarily a member of the board. Corporate nationality is often determined by place of incorporation.

Depending upon local law, alternative types of legal organization and their distinguishing characteristics are:

1. *Individual entrepreneur.* Personal ownership, personal liability.
2. *Branch.* Legally indistinguishable from principal; liability runs to principal; may require a capital allocation if the principal is foreign.
3. *Partnership.* Personal and joint liability; participation limited to named partners (individuals, partnerships, or corporations); called a consortium if corporations or partnerships are the partners.
4. *Limited partnership.* Silent partners with liability limited to their share or quota and full partners with unlimited liability; limited to named partners.
5. *Limited partnership with shares.* Same as four above, except that shares of silent partners are transferable.
6. *Cooperative.* Liability may or may not be limited; occupational limitation may be imposed on transfer of shares; profits may be distributed according to shareholders' participation in business of firm as producers, suppliers, employees, or customers.
7. *Closed corporation.* A limited liability company, or private corporation; participation may be limited to a given number of stockholders (often 50); transferability of shares is limited; no public issue.
8. *Public corporation.* Limited liability, unlimited shareholding in regard to both number and identity of shareholders; public issue possible.
9. *Business trust.* Organization in which one or more trustees (may be self-perpetuating) manage assets for specified purposes in which others have a beneficiary interest but no control other than that spe-

cified in the trust deed and in law. Ownership may be evidenced by transferable shares.

It should be noted that, technically, a branch is indivisible from the parent corporation, even though located in a different country. Not infrequently, however, local law requires that in establishing a local branch, the foreign parent provide certified copies of its own articles of incorporation and by-laws, evidence of reciprocity (i.e., evidence that the country—or state in the case of the United States—in which the parent is domiciled permits branching by corporations of host-country nationality), and of the board decision to establish the branch. The foreign corporation may also be obliged to designate or provide a responsible local representative, a special power of attorney to a local counsel, and in some cases even allocate capital to the branch. Also, the books of the parent may be open to scrutiny by local tax officials.

The various corporate forms are defined in commercial codes, generally at the national level, but sometimes at a lower level as in the United States, where commercial law is largely a matter of *state* jurisdiction. In some countries, there are organizational forms not generally available in the United States, particularly those standing between a corporation and partnership, for example, the limited partnership. In Brazil, the *limitada* is very popular because it requires no minimum capital, the number of owners may be unlimited, and no publication of financial statements is required.

In civil-law countries the minimum number of incorporators is frequently five or seven. Therefore, if a foreign firm is setting up a subsidiary, local qualifying shares are required. A problem may arise in this area because it may not be possible to transfer those qualifying shares to the parent once the subsidiary has been created. Hence, 100 percent ownership by the parent becomes impossible.

Treasury stock (stock authorized but not issued) may be very narrowly limited, if permitted at all. A corporation may not be permitted to buy its own stock, and even if it is, the capital of the corporation may have to be reduced accordingly. There may also be voting limits on stock. For example, in Colombia, no one shareholder may vote more than 25 percent of the stock of a corporation. The stock in a subsidiary must therefore be held by different affiliated entities if ownership-based control is to be maintained, and sometimes not even that is permitted.

Some other consequences of the choice of legal form, but upon which law differs from country to country, are as follows:

1. Degree of public control exercised (audits, reports, disclosure, and so on).
2. Degree of organizational flexibility.
3. Taxation.
4. Ease of borrowing.
5. Treatment under foreign exchange control regulations.
6. Transferability of equity.

7. Ability to engage in certain types of activities (professional services, utilities, banking, mining, and so on).

8. Degree of personal liability.

9. Access to local courts (in Japan, for example, a foreign company cannot be a plaintiff, though its local subsidiary can).

10. Types of shares or financial participation permitted (common and preferred stock, voting and nonvoting shares, voting power proportional to shares held or one vote per shareholder, bearer[1] and registered shares, cumulative and noncumulative shares,[2] convertible and nonconvertible securities, redeemable and nonredeemable shares, participating and nonparticipating preferred shares, mortgages and debentures, founders' shares such as *partes beneficiares*).

11. Paid-in requirements.

12. Minimum capital requirements.

13. Debt-equity ratio permitted.

14. Ease of dissolution, merger, and dedomiciling (i.e., moving a company's legal seat, or domicile, from one country to another).

15. Location of decision-making authority (for example, shareholders, board, officers).

16. Degree to which assets are exposed.

17. Number of shareholders required.

18. Antitrust vulnerability.

19. Basis for determining nationality (hence, the applicability of various national laws).

20. The requirement to share management in some manner with employees.

21. The requirement to share profit with employees.

22. A requirement that a given percentage of board and/or executive members be local nationals.

One other point should be made in respect to the differences in legal approach between civil- and common-law countries. In the former, contracts tend to be rather lean in that many of the contractual conditions are embedded in law and need not be repeated in the contract. By contrast, contracts in common-law countries often contain many pages of "boilerplate," spelling out definitions, precise relationships, liabilities, and the like. One accustomed to the common-law approach should be wary of a civil-law contract unless thoroughly familiar with the relevant law.

Corporate law around the world is constantly changing. Typical recent changes were reported from Japan and Europe in late 1982. At that time a new commercial code became operative in Japan, for the first time permitting stockholders in Japanese corporations to make proposals to manage-

---

[1]Reasons for bearer shares are anonymity and ease of transfer and, hence, of negotiability.
[2]See Section 7.4, note 3.

ment. Previously, they had been allowed only to vote "yes" or "no" on proposals made by management at stockholders' meetings. Nonetheless, the "unit stock" system continues, which means that only those stockholders owning a minimum number of shares—most frequently 1,000—are permitted to attend stockholders' meetings. Meanwhile, the European Community has been wrestling with the notion of requiring all corporations—both public and closed, foreign parent and European subsidiary—to make more complete disclosure of their European operations than had previously been the case. U.S.-based parents are up in arms.

8.2   Legal Character of the Domestic Principal

A business interest wishing to develop a continuing relationship with a foreign market needs to determine which legal form best suits that relationship. In many cases, some forms will clearly be impossible. The following list gives the full range of conceivable options for the domestic firm as to its legal entity on the international interface:

1. An individual domestic entrepreneur.
2. A domestic partnership.
3. A closely held or personal holding company.
4. The stockholders of the domestic firm.
5. Two or more domestic firms (a joint venture agreement or consortium).
6. Principal domestic firm itself, alone (including domestic branches and agencies).
7. A domestic subsidiary of the firm (a domestic holding company).
8. The domestic subsidiary of two or more firms (a joint holding company).
9. An associated foreign enterprise, which in turn may take any one of the forms listed above.

Major factors relevant to the choice of legal strategy in this regard include the ownership structure of the principal domestic firm, the degree of liability risk running from the foreign enterprise to the domestic, antitrust considerations, the protection of property rights, and tax law.

In respect to the first two strategy alternatives listed above (those in which an individual or partnership may be used on the international interface, note that in some jurisdictions *unincorporated* entities cannot take credit, against domestic income liability, for foreign income taxes paid by a foreign corporation in which equity interest may be held.[3] This is the case in the United States. For a large, publicly held corporation, alternative four would be awkward. If the risk of liability is considered high, the domestic

---

[3] They can, of course, take foreign taxes as a cost, thereby reducing taxable income.

principal (as well as its stockholders) may desire to insert a domestic or foreign corporate subsidiary between itself and the principal foreign interest or to operate through a domestic representative. Possible risks to be considered in this respect are damage suits for alleged nonperformance, personal injury, errors and omissions, and default or bankruptcy on the part of the foreign interest. On the other hand, a reputable international firm that considers itself in a foreign market to stay is unlikely to permit a foreign subsidiary, agent, or representative to destroy the firm's image of reliability and quality. But it has been known to happen.

8.3 Legal Character of the Associated Foreign Principal

Within the limitation of local law, the alternatives listed in Section 8.2 are available for the foreign associate as well. If the associated foreign business equity is completely separate from the domestic firm in terms of ownership and management control, the legal character of the foreign associate is, of course, a given insofar as the domestic firm is concerned. It has no choice. Even so, the domestic firm may have a choice of associating with several different foreign entities or may exert some influence on its selected associate in the direction of encouraging it to establish a subsidiary or a partnership of jointly owned subsidiaries on the part of two or more foreign firms. There are a number of business reasons making such structures attractive. One is the possession of necessary services to exploit the target market by more than one foreign firm. Another is inadequate financial resources in a single foreign firm. There may also be a need to isolate the projected enterprise from other involvements of the associated foreign firm in order to establish a desired equity or control position. Further, there may be a need for the foreign business entity, with which the domestic firm is to enter into relationship, to be located in a jurisdiction different from that of the foreign principal. This poses the danger, however, that the foreign subsidiary or partnership (if limited) may have no tangible assets and, hence, may carry little real liability.

8.4 Choice of Relationship between the Two Parties

The legal relationship between associated firms on the international interface may take a number of forms, specifically:

1. Informal "understanding" between parties (maintained by continuing communication).
2. Agreement on basic goals of policies (cartel, conference, conscious parallelism in operations).
3. Representation (one firm acts for another vis-à-vis third parties but is liable for its own acts).

4. Distributorship (one firm contracts to buy another firm's goods and services and sells to third parties).
5. Agency (one firm buys nothing from the other firm—its principal—but acts on its behalf as defined by agreement, with liability running to the principal).
6. Contract (for management, management prerogative,[4] personnel recruitment, technical service, cooperative research, license, lease, manufacturing, purchase and sale, design, technical consulting, construction, turnkey, turnkey-plus).
7. Branch relationship (an executive agency or direct operation with a permanent place of business).
8. Partnership agreement.
9. Limited partnership agreement.
10. Participation in a limited partnership with shares.
11. Co-ownership of a closed corporation.
12. Co-investment in a public corporation (one whose shares are bought and sold by the public).

Relevant to the choice are such management policies as the degree and type of control deemed necessary, one's time horizon, the anticipated volume of business, financial requirements, and the attitude of the associated foreign management. In addition, there are three areas of law where faulty legal judgment can introduce significant, unnecessary costs; namely, antitrust, protection of valuable rights, and taxation. In no case should a firm enter into an international business relationship without the advice of legal counsel experienced in these matters.

8.5   Antitrust Law

In the United States, antitrust implications may arise whenever two or more firms are involved. Because U.S. antimonopoly law is probably the most developed and has the broadest application of any to international business transactions, the practitioner in any way involved with U.S. firms or the U.S. market must be guided to some degree by its restraints.

U.S. antitrust proceedings may be initiated either by the federal government or by private parties (domestic or foreign) alleging injury due to illegal acts. In a government case, possible remedies are a consent decree (essentially an out-of-court agreement by the firm to do, or not to do, certain things) or a judicial decision calling for termination or modification of the offending practices or agreements, divestiture of certain assets, compulsory licensing, creation of a competing firm, forfeiture of property, denial of trading rights, deprivation of patent protection, fine, and/or imprisonment

---

[4]A contract under which a firm has the right to exercise managerial control over another firm in the event of certain specified eventualities, such as dropping below a minimum sales volume or profit level.

of responsible executives. Action initiated by private parties alleging injury (often after a finding of guilt in a government-initiated case) can result in an award of treble damages. A U.S. court has jurisdiction over a foreign party if it has assets in the United States (including patents), conducts any business in the United States, or has officers present in the United States.

Of relevance in this discussion are the foreign trade provisions in the Sherman Act (1890) and Clayton Act (1914), as amended by the Robinson-Patman Act (1936) and augmented by the Federal Trade Commission Act (1970). The first renders the following to be misdemeanors: (1) any agreement restraining commerce among the states or with foreign nations, and (2) any attempt to monopolize any part of interstate commerce or trade with foreign nations or with U.S. possessions. The Sherman Act permits various penalties to be imposed and declares that the injured private parties may recover "threefold the damages by him sustained." The Clayton Act declares as illegal (1) tying agreements (a sale or purchase conditioned in some way on an agreement not to deal with a competitor) which may "substantially lessen competition" or "create a monopoly in any line of commerce" within the United States; and (2) the acquisition by one corporation engaged in commerce of stock in another corporation if the effect is "substantially to lessen competition, or to create a monopoly of any line of commerce" in any section of the country. The Robinson-Patman Act defines certain specific practices as illegal, such as price discrmination between different buyers and the paying of rebates, but the restraint must be felt within the United States. In effect, such domestic practices are **per se violations** (i.e., inherently illegal because the adverse effect on competition is assumed).

Various business arrangements are exempted from attack under antitrust law either by executive decision or by statute. For example, the executive power has been used to shield U.S. oil companies operating jointly abroad, although in the absence of legislative authority empowering the executive branch to make such exemptions, some experts doubt their legality. The general rule, according to court decision, is that joint-venturing overseas by firms competing in the domestic market implies a conspiracy to restrain trade either in the United States or in the foreign commerce of the United States. Some of the businesses granted *statutory* exemptions are:

1.   Regulated industries (those under the jurisdiction of such agencies as the Federal Maritime Commission, Federal Communications Commission, Federal Power Commission, and Civil Aeronautics Board);
2.   Activities granted specific legal exemption (agricultural cooperatives, export associations (**Webb Pomerene associations**,[5] and export trading companies (if given prior clearance)).

---

[5]The Webb-Pomerene Act (1918) authorizes joint facilities, price fixing, and allocation of orders among members of a certain kind of association. Members may be required to export through the association, but the association must engage solely in export trade (joint foreign manufacturing facilities are not covered, nor is the export of capital). An association may not engage in domestic business; it may not restrain nonmember exports; it may not enter into agreement with foreign companies that are illegal for independent U.S. firms. There are very few operative Webb-Pomerene associations.

3.   Those in the defense industry that can be granted immunity by the executive under the Defense Production Act of 1950. (Approval of the Attorney General is required.)

4.   Certain small businesses that qualify under the Small Business Mobilization Act of 1953. (Approval of the Small Business Administration is required.)

The following is a reasonable statement of the major risks that international firms run in respect to U.S. antitrust law and regulation. In each situation the actual degree of risk (that is, likelihood of prosecution) rests on (1) the visibility of the firms involved in terms of dominance of a sector and/or geographical area; (2) sheer size of the firm; (3) the possibility of demonstrating an actual or probable restraint on U.S. trade; (4) the willingness of a foreign government to act to protect the allegedly illegal act by interposing its own law or diplomatic representation; and (5) the ability of the U.S. government to obtain jurisdiction over either the assets, employees, owners, or valuable commercial rights of the firms. In cases involving monopoly or attempted monopoly, an important question always is, what is the relevant market, both in geographical terms and product terms? For example, are hand-held and electric razors in the same market? Is a nickel producer a potential competitor in the battery market? U.S. courts have defined the market as "the area of effective competition," which is not exactly clarifying in that all but the most essential goods and services compete for the taxpayer's disposable income.

Legal Vulnerability of Corporate Practices

Practices that *appear* to be vulnerable to U.S. law in at least some circumstances, given judicial rulings, are:

1. Joint venturing overseas by firms in competition within the United States, even by members of a Webb-Pomerene Association (unless it can be shown that the only effect is to reduce competition among the parties in a foreign market).

2. The acquisition of a foreign firm by a U.S. company, if that acquisition significantly reduces actual or potential competition within the United States or in U.S. foreign trade.

3. Participation by a U.S. firm in a foreign cartel that operates in such a manner as to reduce competition within the United States or in U.S. foreign trade (either importing or exporting), unless the cartel is enforced by foreign law.

4. Agreements between a U.S. firm and a foreign firm to divide markets and fix prices, that is, not to compete (particularly if the U.S. firm has a noncontrolling equity interest in the foreign firm). (Restraint of a firm's *own* trade may be considered illegal).

5. The acquisition by a foreign firm of a competing U.S. firm if the acquisition results in a significant reduction of competition within the United States or U.S. foreign trade. (It appears that the acquisition of a *potential* U.S. competitor may likewise be a violation unless it can be shown that the acquiring company had no alternative feasible means of entering the U.S. market and that the acquisition is likely to lead to ultimate deconcentration of the market, the so-called "toe-hold" doctrine.)

6. The merger of two foreign firms, each of which has competing subsidiaries in the United States.

7. The use of technical assistance or other agreements not associated with a patent, copyright, trademark, or trade secret, to divide markets, force the purchase of the contractor's parts, or fix prices. (A simple condition prohibiting the recipient of the technology from selling the relevant products in specified markets may be all right if not for an excessive period of time, if production of the product depends on the technology, and if the agreement stands alone and is not part of a web of such agreements.)

8. The use of patent pooling or cross-licensing or mutual exchange of technical assistance as instruments for effectuating a general conspiracy to divide markets, if there is an effect on U.S. trade.

9. Restriction of a foreign manufacturer, who is the recipient of nonproprietary technology, to sell only outside the United States or to sell only in its own country.

10. Agreement with a foreign manufacturer, who is to receive nonproprietary technology, that the U.S. firm will not export to the home country of the licensee.

11. Imposition of a restriction on any licensee to the effect that it will not use any other trademark during the life of the agreement.

12. Discrimination between domestic and foreign sales when such discrimination is for the purpose of restraining a competitor's trade, or is not based on differences in quantities purchased, cost of delivery, competitive conditions in a particular locality, or grade and quality (such as tying clauses to the effect that a second party must purchase the licensor's parts or services exclusively).

13. The merger of two or more foreign firms, or the acquisition by one foreign firm of another foreign firm, if the effect in the U.S. is to reduce competition (which would be the case if the firms had been competing in the U.S. prior to the merger or acquisition).

14. Imposition by the foreign owner of a U.S. patent on its U.S. licensee of a requirement that it abide by certain practices that have the effect of restricting competition beyond the patent monopoly (e.g., a requirement that a particular antibiotic drug be sold only in dosage form and that prior approval must be obtained from the licensor before selling it in bulk form).

15. Adherence by a U.S. corporation to an international boycott that has the effect of restraining other U.S. companies from competing as subcontractors (that is, refusal by a corporation to deal with blacklisted subcontractors).

16. Acquisition by a U.S. company with a foreign operation of another U.S. firm that also has a foreign operation, where the foreign operation of the acquired firm is a potential competitor within the U.S. of the acquiring company's foreign operation.

Practices probably safe under U.S. law include (1) the granting of an exclusive patent or trademark license for a country (but if more than one complete, that is, nonexclusive, license is given in a country, the trademark or patent may be lost); (2) giving exclusive technical assistance or know-how agreements (if not part of a larger pattern of restriction, such as a contract between two dominant companies to refuse a technology to anyone else); (3) the fixing of prices to be charged by licensees on patented products; (4) the allocation of territories and setting of prices by a parent corporation in respect to majority-owned foreign subsidiaries (or those in which the parent has enough stock to maintain effective control); and (5) joint holding by two or more firms competitive within the U.S. market in a single foreign project (a "one-shot deal").

The first of its kind, an agreement was signed in June 1976 by the United States and Germany providing for cooperation regarding restrictive business practices, thereby formalizing preexisting informal cooperation. The agreement provides that the antitrust authorities in the two countries will assist each other in connection with antitrust investigations or proceedings, studies related to competition policy, and activities related to restrictive business practices undertaken by international organizations in which both are members. An earlier U.S. agreement with Canada simply assures the Canadian government that it will be notified prior to prosecution of an antitrust case affecting Canada and will be given an opportunity for its views to be heard. A similar Australian-U.S. agreement was signed in mid-1982. One can anticipate more.

Since the early 1970s, both foreign and American firms have been able to seek an informal, unofficial opinion from the U.S. Justice Department of the legality of a proposed merger or acquisition under the business review procedure. A favorable review states only the enforcement intention of the Department of Justice at the time of review and does not bar the Department from future action. In practice, no criminal actions have been brought against companies that availed themselves of this procedure and made full and accurate disclosures of all of the relevant details at that time. It is quite clear, however, that many firms do not undertake such inquiries in order to avoid drawing attention to their activities, particularly since the business review procedure does not produce a binding opinion that would constitute a shield against subsequent prosecution.

Even an impartial observer might be led to conclude that steps should be taken to reduce the uncertainty of U.S. antitrust law, both as to its content and its enforcement, and to eliminate the notion of per se violations, which can render any test of reasonableness irrelevant. Insofar as international policy harmonization is concerned, one can already sense a certain tendency for antitrust law in the European Community, Japan, and the United States to converge. A number of countries, until recently critical of the long arm of U.S. antitrust law, have themselves begun to introduce laws on competition that seem vaguely familiar to a U.S. observer.

It should be kept in mind that there are two general situations in which antimonopoly law of the U.S. type does not have a great deal of relevance. The higher a firm's fixed cost ratio, the less likely it is to be able to restrict output. Rather, there is a great internal pressure to grow and, depending upon the market response to price changes, to grow by reducing price and expanding output. Under these circumstances, a monopolist or oligopolist may behave very much as though in a truly competitive market. This situation also means that the government does not have to police the system as rigorously—which may be a necessary, if not sufficient, condition for the close identification of Japanese business and government. Much of Japanese industry is of the nature just described by reason of its very high fixed cost/total cost ratio due to the lifetime employment system and the typically high debt/equity ratios.

The second situation rendering the importance of antitrust regulation substantially less is a small national market. A relatively small market makes many industries into decreasing-cost industries over the relevant range, and hence into natural monopolies. That is, they are able to reduce unit cost by expanding volume. In other words, there is only room for one plant if it is to produce at anything approaching its minimum average cost. In this situation, an antimonopoly law makes little sense, although price control sometimes constitutes a pressure for pushing monopolistic enterprises into the public sector. It is of interest to note that Article 37 of the Rome Treaty (which established the European Economic Community) requires member states to "progressively adjust any state monopolies of a commercial character in such a manner as will ensure the exclusion, at the date of expiry of the transitional period, of all discrimination between the nationals of member states in regard to conditions of supply and marketing."

International Antitrust Regulation

It appears that governments generally are becoming increasingly concerned about the anational politico-economic power of the larger firms operating internationally. An obvious reason for this governmental interest is the growing concentration of world business. But growing concentration can mean more intense competition internationally. The automotive industry is a case in point.

Many of the developed countries have indeed been tightening their antitrust laws, particularly in reference to takeovers by foreign corporations. Canada has a commission empowered to issue appropriate remedial orders where serious anticompetitive effects are found. In 1973, the Foreign Investment Review Act was passed by the Canadian Parliament, and the following year, the Foreign Investment Agency appeared. A major purpose of the latter was to block the foreign acquisition of Canadian business enterprises unless supported by significant benefit to the Canadian economy. Additionally, one purpose of the Canadian Development Corporation is to help Canadian companies withstand attempted alien takeovers. In Germany, the Federal Cartel Office has been given wide powers to intervene in cases of misuse of dominant position, anticompetitive mergers, or similar concentration moves. There are many cases in which European governments have apparently prevented a merger of a national company with a foreign company, or a takeover by the latter of the former, and one can reasonably anticipate continuing European and Japanese opposition to both the mergers of large dominant corporations and their acquisition of national companies. In many instances such acquisitions or mergers specifically require prior government approval. European Community antitrust law has been interpreted recently to include the possibility of blocking an acquisition or merger if it can be demonstrated that misuse of dominant market position is involved (e.g., forcing the acquisition).

In the European Economic Community, Articles 85 and 86 of the Rome Treaty constitute the basis for the antitrust regulation. The first prohibits interenterprise agreements that are likely to affect trade between the member states and that have as their purpose the prevention, restriction, or distortion of competition within the Common Market (in general, price fixing, restrictions on production, market sharing, price discrimination, and tied conditions). But such an agreement may be exempted (granted "negative clearance") if: (1) it has been registered with the EEC Commission; (2) it has the effect of improving production, distribution, or technology, and users receive an equitable share in the profit resulting therefrom (the beneficent cartel concept); or (3) competition is not substantially reduced. Consequently, there are no per se violations except those defined by precedent. Article 86 has to do with the misuse of dominant position by one or more enterprises within the Common Market or within a substantial part of it. Presumably misuse of such position within a single country would not fall afoul of Article 86. Misuse seems to be established by unjustifiably high prices, price discrimination among countries, and refusal to deal in a commodity or raw material. Where violations are established, remedies run from declaring an agreement null and void to heavy cash fines. The underlying philosophy of the EEC law is to prevent the division of the community market on the one hand, and on the other to encourage the development of larger business units of a transnational nature so as to be more competitive with the U.S. corporate giants. The two objectives sometimes conflict.

Although EEC law does not require a company to sell its goods at the same price throughout the Community, it does require that an EEC buyer be able to buy wherever the prices are the lowest and take the purchase back to its own country for resale. An important unresolved question is to what extent patent rights can be invoked to restrict exports within the Community. Can a firm holding patents on a given product in two or more Community countries limit competition among its licensees within the Community either by contract or by legal action against third parties who buy from one licensee and reexport to another member country? It is hoped that the new Community Patent Convention will resolve this problem (see Section 8.5).

Major differences between the U.S. and EEC approaches include the absence of per se violations, the notion of a beneficient cartel, the absence of any criminal sanctions, and the process of prior notification and clearance in EEC law. In addition, the EEC Commission had issued group exemptions covering two categories of agreements, exclusive distributor agreements and certain types of specialization agreements (joint research agreements and undertaking for other joint functions among small or medium-sized firms), which means that notification of such agreements to the commission is not required.

8.6 Protection of Valuable Rights

The relationship between two firms operating under different legal systems almost invariably involves the protection of valuable rights that are transferred from one to the other. These can be the right to use patents, copyrights, trademarks, or trade secrets, plus the enforcement of contractual obligations of all kinds. The protection of valuable rights afforded by the judicial system of a host country depends upon the ease with which the judiciary feels able to take jurisdiction, the degree to which the process is insulated from political pressure, and the time and cost of litigation.

International Dispute Settlement

Systems of law vary, and the international executive should not assume that what appears "reasonable" is, in fact, the law. Indeed, a firm may have no legal standing at all if it is not held "to be in business" in the country where it seeks to bring action. Further considerations have to do with the effect of litigation on a continuing business relationship and the ability to enforce a court award and secure assets of value to the claimant. If gross denial of local justice can be shown, it is sometimes possible to bring suit in one's home courts and secure attachment of the defendant's property present in the country (for example, a shipment of goods, a vessel, or a bank account). As noted in Section 7.8, a purely *commercial* entity of a foreign government may likewise be sued in a number of countries without being blocked by the doctrine of sovereign immunity, which holds that a sovereign may not be sued without its permission. In the United States, it would appear that the courts will undertake adjudication in cases involving acts of a foreign government if those acts are of a commercial nature.

There is no international legal forum now available to private persons unless their cause is espoused by their respective government before the International Court of Justice. However, private firms do have recourse to the mechanism established under the auspices of the World Bank in 1966, based on the "Convention on the Settlement of Investment Disputes between States and the Nationals of Other States." This convention applies to situations where a foreign firm enters into a contract or agreement with a signatory government (or a subdivision) and the agreement includes a provision that disagreements will be resolved either by arbitration or conciliation in the International Centre for the Settlement of Investment Disputes (ICSID). In such cases, that agreement is considered binding and may not be unilaterally withdrawn even if the state involved subsequently withdraws from the Centre. In that the Centre is a member of the World Bank "family," there may be some force to reach an agreement; capricious withdrawal or refusal to enforce an award could conceivably have an impact on a nation's credit standing. The consent of a government may be qualified by its requiring prior exhaustion of local administrative or judicial remedies. Consent may be restricted by prior agreement to conciliation, to arbitration, or to conciliation followed, if necessary, by arbitration.

Many firms attempt to insert into international agreements a clause subjecting them to their own nation's laws. It should be borne in mind, however, that domestic law may be more restrictive than the foreign. One has to check. In any event, the reach of one's own judicial processes to foreign persons or corporations is problematical. The rule upheld in U.S. courts has been that, given a good faith effort to obey, compliance with a U.S. court order is excused to the extent that it would violate foreign law. Further difficulty may arise if one's domestic law is to be applied, but it turns out that the foreign party must be sued where it is domiciled. Requiring a court to apply a foreign law may lead it to demand proof of the relevant law, which may involve delay and expense. Also, a court may disregard the foreign law requirement if it is deemed to be contrary to its own national policy.

Of increasing importance in the resolution of private international business disputes is **private arbitration**. Its advantages lie in its relatively low cost and speed and in the ability of the two parties to determine ahead of time the rules or system of law that will govern and the place of arbitration. Various arbitration organizations (most notably the American Arbitration Association and its foreign counterparts, the International Chamber of Commerce, and the various commodity arbitration systems for traders in textiles, rubber, and so on) offer standard contract clauses, which set into motion a specified set of procedures once a dispute arises. The arbitration rules developed by the UN Commission on International Trade Law are a possible alternative. A typical arbitration clause in an international commercial contract might read:

The parties agree that if any controversy or claim shall arise out of the agreement or the breach thereof and either party shall request that the matter shall be settled by arbitration, the matter shall be settled exclusively

by . . . the International Chamber of Commerce, Paris, France . . . All arbitration proceedings shall be held in Paris, France, and each party agrees to comply in all respects with any award made in any such proceeding and to the entry of a judgment in any jurisdiction upon any award rendered in such proceeding. The laws of the State of Illinois, U.S.A., shall apply to and govern this agreement, its interpretation and performance. Paris and Illinois are used for purpose of illustration only. A corporation frequently seeks agreement to apply the law of the state or country in which it is domiciled to resolve conflict, as this is the body of law with which it is most familiar. Whether a company is correct in preferring its domestic law depends on the substance of the relevant law. Interpretation according to foreign law may be more favorable. The stipulation of Swedish law and arbitration in Sweden, for example, has become increasingly popular over recent years.

A major problem relative to arbitration lies in the enforceability of foreign awards. U.S. bilateral commercial treaties often provide for the enforcement of arbitration agreements and awards in disputes between nationals and corporations of the respective countries. The recognized U.S. principle is that enforcement cannot be denied solely for the reason that the award was rendered in another country or that the nationality of the arbitrator was not that of the party concerned. But such clauses do not assure enforcement. Ratification by the United States of treaties or international conventions recognizing the validity of foreign arbitration awards has been difficult because of possible conflict with state law. Nonetheless, the United States has acceded to the UN Convention on the Recognition and Enforcement of Foreign Arbitral Awards. Adherence to this convention binds a nation to compel arbitration when the parties have so agreed, and to provide judicial recourse for citizens and corporations of other adhering countries to secure recognition and enforcement of voluntary foreign arbitration agreements.

A number of countries, some of which have had an unfortunate past experience with international commercial arbitration, have banned the submission of any dispute within their respective territories to foreign arbitration. Among such countries are Saudi Arabia and the members of the Andean Common Market. In the latter case, the ANCOM regulations specifically prohibit nonnational arbitration. The Latin American countries generally adhere to the Calvo principle (named after a Venezuelan jurist) which denies the validity of any adjudication outside the national territory.

Patents, Trademarks, Copyrights, and Trade Secrets

The only existing international conventions constituting enforceable international law in respect to protecting property rights internationally are those relating to patents, trademarks, copyrights, and trade secrets.

Patents Patent protection is available in approximately 120 countries; trademark protection, in 140. National laws all differ to a certain extent. U.S.

patent protection is valid for 17 years; 5 to 20 years is common elsewhere. Substantial registration fees are imposed in some countries, plus an annual tax. Some countries exclude certain fields, such as chemicals and phar- maceuticals. Others may permit processes but not the products themselves to be patented (e.g., Italy in the case of pharmaceuticals). Possible policies for a U.S. firm in respect to patents and trademarks are: (1) file only in the United States, (2) file in the United States and Canada, (3) file in all countries where the company manufacturers, (4) file in all countries where manufac- ture is possible or likely. Reasons for registration abroad are threefold: as the substance for foreign investment, as a subject for licensing, or to protect a market.

Approximately 90 countries (since early 1965, including the USSR) adhere to the International Convention for the Protection of Industrial Property (the **Paris Union** of 1883, subsequently revised six times), which provides that if a patent application is filed in one member country, the applicant may file in other member countries within one year, with priority running from the date of first application. There is no protection offered prior to the original filing. A serious difficulty with this system is that the commercial value of the patent may not be ascertained within one year. The applicant secures protection by filing in a member country before receiving a parent-government patent (which in the United States usually takes three to five years from the date of application), provided that there has been no publication or public use anywhere, including the applicant's home coun- try. (In some countries only publication or public use in that country consti- tutes a bar to filing.) Therefore, after a patent has been issued in one country, it is no longer possible to obtain valid protection in many of the most important foreign countries, with some exceptions in Latin America. U.S. law permits the filing of a valid patent application any time within one year from publication or public use of the invention. Elsewhere, publication or public use prior to filing may act as a bar. Therefore, a firm should avoid public use or publication before U.S. filing.

Some countries require local manufacture—by a "registered user"—of patented products sufficient to meet reasonable local demand. In the ab- sence of such local supply, the patent may be subject to compulsory licens- ing if someone wants it and is willing to pay a reasonable royalty. Local manufacture is generally not required for the first three years, and indeed, under the Paris Convention compulsory licensing may not be required for the first three years. Thereafter, one often has two years to **license**. In Argentina, Cuba, and Venezuela, the patent owner must take steps to interest third parties in taking a license under the patent, or it becomes void. (To avoid the ambiguity of some of the literature on valuable rights, the specific meaning of "license" should be noted. A license is a contractual agreement to permit another to use a functional or design invention pro- tected by patent, a unique literary or artistic expression protected by copy- right, a unique identification protected by trademark, or technology and/or skills of a secret nature. Payment is designated as a **royalty**.)

In the USSR, a Soviet inventor may opt to obtain either an inventor's certificate or a patent. In the former case, the patent is assigned to the government, which thereby incurs an obligation to see that the invention is put to use. Payment to an inventor holding a certificate depends upon the savings realized by the invention's use up to a specified maximum. If the invention is not perceived as useful, a certificate is not issued. A Soviet patent is very similar to patents elsewhere in that the owner has the exclusive right to use, sell, or license the patent to a second party. That is, Soviet industry is not permitted to use the invention unless it is sold or licensed to it. The Stockholm Convention, a 1967 amendment to the Paris Convention, gives patent status to an inventor's certificate in establishing priority of filing rights in signatory countries.

In some countries design patents are available. Generally more limited in duration than the normal patent, a design patent has to do with the appearance of an item rather than its function.

There are national differences in respect to the enforceability of patent rights against alleged infringers. For example, it is very difficult in the U.S. to secure a preliminary injunction to halt the production and sale of a contested product without going through a trial. In any event, a very high proportion of such infringement cases are lost. Elsewhere, as in the United Kingdom, it may be easier to secure a preliminary injunction, for example, the Polaroid injunction against Kodak in the United Kingdom in 1975.

Facilitating the international filing of patents are three relatively recent international agreements: the European Patent Convention (EPC), the Community Patent Convention (CPC), and the Patent Cooperation Treaty (PCT). The EPC was signed in 1973 by 16 countries (the nine EEC members plus Austria, Greece, Liechtenstein, Monaco, Norway, Sweden, and Switzerland). Operational in 1977, the convention provides that on the basis of a single application made to the European Patent Office (EPO) in Munich and searched by the International Patent Institute (IPI) at the Hague, a single patent may be issued for as many of the convention countries as the applicant desires. Such a patent is equivalent to national patents in the contracting states. The CPC, signed in 1975 by the nine EC members, is not yet in full force as of this writing. Under the CPC, a single application to the European Patent Office is to lead to a single Common Market patent subject to EC law. Community patent protection will be at least equivalent to that offered by the national laws of member countries. The use of the Community patent is optional, the alternative being an EPC patent which, as stated, gives the same protection as *national* patents. Later, it is expected that anyone using the EPC patent route to secure patents in the EC will be obliged to take out a Community patent. The point is that one of the aims of the new EEC patent system is to abolish territorial limits for the marketing of patented goods, so that the division of the EEC into nine separate markets on the basis of patents will no longer be possible. Both the Community and the European patents are valid for 20 years from the date of filing, and both are open to nonresidents.

The Patent Cooperation Treaty became operational in 1978. It makes possible a single application for designated member countries. It is not a patent system, only an application system, as is the Paris Convention system. Protection is accorded by national patents and lasts only so long as the national patent is valid. However, unlike the Paris Convention, the PCT makes possible a *single* application covering as many member states as the applicant desires, a single search and preliminary examination procedure, and provides 20 months (not 12 as under the Paris Convention) for the applicant to determine which national patents are desired. The World Intellectual Property Organization (WIPO) in Geneva acts as the central administrative agency. IPI and several of the more industrialized countries (including the United States) have activated their respective national parent offices for the purpose of acting as international searching or preliminary examining authorities. The patent offices of all signatory countries accept the search and preliminary examination report (dealing with an invention's novelty, nonobviousness, and commercial value) prepared by the authority (either the IPI or a designated national patent office) to which initial application is made.

In ratifying the Patent Cooperation Treaty, the United States made two important reservations. First, the United States retained the right to reject the preliminary examination rights made by other countries and to undertake its own search. Second, the United States did not accept the treaty's provision that information in applications should be published within 18 months from the priority date (even though no patent had been issued by that time) because this provision conflicted with the U.S. principle that applicants have the right to keep their inventions confidential until they actually obtain patent protection.

Understandably, many of the LDCs have had serious second thoughts about the value of a full-fledged patent system to them, given the fact that the overwhelming percentage of all patents issued are owned by individuals and corporations domiciled in the industrialized countries. Even a country such as Canada, noting that 95 percent of all patents issued in the country are based on inventions by foreigners, is becoming suspicious that the patent system may be serving as a brake on Canadian industrial development. A number of proposals have been made in Canada, including reducing the period of patent protection from 17 years to 9 (with an added 5 years for those actively working their patents in Canada), requiring greater disclosure of information by patent holders, changing from a "first to invent" system of priority rights to a "first to file" system, and allowing imports of a patentee's product made outside Canada to be marketed freely in the country, thus discouraging noncompetitive pricing in Canada. One result has been the introduction of compulsory licensing. A number of countries have declared that certain products (or processes) are not subject to patent protection.

Major objections on the part of many LDCs to the traditional notion of a patent are:

1. The guarantee of national treatment to foreign patent holders. Some have suggested that foreign-owned patents should be treated differently from locally developed patents in respect to duration of protection and compulsory licensing requirements. The rationale advanced for the difference is threefold: R&D allocation in the industrial countries is not influenced by patent protection in the LDCs and, hence, does not provide incentive for innovation;[6] most patents issued by the LDCs are never worked; and many patents are simply used to exclude competitors from LDC markets.

2. The nonuse of patents. Under present laws, even where compulsory licensing is enforced, it takes too long to compel licensing (one year priority for local filing, plus three years during which the compulsory licensing rule is not enforced, plus another two to three years to establish liability for not working the patent, plus perhaps another two years before a local court finally orders compulsory licensing). By that time, the life of the patent is at least half over.

3. A patentee's right to exclude imports of a nonlicensed manufacturer in respect to a patent protected locally even though there is no local production. Some have urged that such protection should be limited only to the areas of actual production.

4. The fact that no criteria are considered in issuing a patent related to the contribution of such patent protection to economic development.

5. The feeling that the covering of such essentials as pharmaceuticals and food products by patent is intolerable from the point of view of the public welfare.

6. The licensing of a patent by a foreign parent corporation to a local firm over which it exercises control, in which case the extraction of royalties is seen as simply a device to drive down local profits and, hence, taxes.

The patent issue has entered the North-South dialogue, and the World Intellectual Property Organization has urged a number of revisions in the Paris Convention along some of the lines suggested above.[7] In these discussions, some have argued for the abolition of patents altogether. But if there were no patents, inventions could be kept secret—and hence, proprietary— much longer, and thus could not be used by others as a basis for further research. Once a patent is issued, and often before, application or patent

---

[6]Very clearly not the case. In the absence of patent protection in the LDCs, Kodak, for example, could have taken Polaroid's technology and built a plant, say in Brazil, and from there exported a virtual replica of the Polaroid camera to much of the world.

[7]See Edith Penrose, "International Patenting and the Less Developed Countries," *Economic Journal* (September 1973), p. 768 ff; and Constantin Vaitsos, "The Revision of the International Patent System: Legal Considerations for a Third World Revision," *World Development*, Vol. 4, No. 2, 1976, p. 85 ff.

documents describing the technology in detail are generally available to anyone for a nominal fee.

Trademarks   Trademarks fall into four general categories: **true trademarks** identify a product with a specific manufacturer or source; **service marks** identify the services of an individual or a corporation (e.g., SRI for Stanford Research Institute); **certification marks** indicate that a product is of a certain quality, is manufactured in a specific location, or bears some other factual characteristic (e.g., Underwriters Laboratories, the Seal of Approval of Good Housekeeping Magazine); and **collective marks** indicate membership in an association or organization of some sort (e.g., Massachusetts Institute of Technology).

Trade names and trademarks are protected in all Paris Union countries without the obligation of filing or registration, and countries of the Union are obliged to provide protection against false designation or origin for nationals of member countries. Goods bearing illegal trademarks, trade names, or false origin are subject to seizure at the time of importation into countries of the Union.

Use and registration of trademarks in the United States provide no protection elsewhere, although registration in the United States may be necessary as a basis for registration in some countries. Use in most foreign countries provides little or no protection except in common-law countries, but even then a trademark can be lost through lack of continuous use. In the United States all federally protected trademark rights arise from use, in that registration becomes possible when a mark is used in interstate commerce or when continuous use elsewhere can be demonstrated. Only in the United States, Canada, and the Philippines is use a precondition to registration. In most countries protection arises only through registration, and prior use need not be shown. Trademark protection varies from 10 to 20 years, but is subject to renewal. Barring rejection by any member state within 12 months of application, the Madrid Agreement (1891) on trademarks automatically extends trademark protection to signatory states (most of Europe, but not the United States or Scandinavia). Registration in one member state is considered to be registration in all.

In that the United States is a member of the Paris Union, the owner of a U.S. mark is given six months for filing elsewhere after the date of filing in the United States. National treatment is afforded U.S. nationals and entities in most Latin American countries through the General American Convention for Trademark and Commercial Protection. Also, trademark protection is often included on a reciprocal basis in friendship, commerce, and navigation treaties, sometimes on a most-favored-nation basis. Some countries require local use of a trademark within a given time after registration. Otherwise, it may be subject to cancellation.

Four important problems may arise in regard to trademarks: (1) protection in countries other than those adhering to the Paris Union may be difficult, unless reciprocal protection has been written into a treaty; (2) penalties for infringement are often too light to be effective; (3) someone may succeed in registering a generic term; (4) a trademark may become a generic term in the local language and its identify with a given make of product lost, in some cases legally so. Now-common words which were once registered trademarks include nylon, zipper, escalator, cellophane, shredded wheat, trampoline, linoleum, thermos, brassiere, cola or coke and aspirin—to name a few. In the United States the Federal Trade Commission has the legal authority to challenge the continued validity of a mark on the grounds that a word has become generic, or that it has come to denote a product rather than the producer. The "Monopoly" trademark was lost in 1982 to Parker Brothers for the latter reason. A U.S. management should be aware that law prohibits importation into the United States of articles bearing marks confusingly similar to, or conterfeit of, trademarks registered in the Patent Office. The Customs Bureau is required to prohibit importation of foreign-made goods bearing marks registered in the Patent Office by a U.S. citizen or entity if a copy of the certificate of registration has been filed with the Treasury Department. (Curiously, however, there is no law excluding the import of articles that infringe on U.S. patents.)

Many of the British Commonwealth countries derive their trademark laws from the British Trade Marks Act of 1938, which created a statutory procedure for recording **registered users.** The act defines a registered user as someone other than the owner of a trademark who is recorded as such and who has use of the trademark, but only after scrutiny has determined that adequate quality control will be exercised by the owner over the manufacture of the goods by the licensee. Use of a mark by a registered user is deemed to be use by the owner. If the licensee is not a registered user and, in fact, does not use the trademark for a certain number of years, the owner may lose his rights to the mark. In some countries, a mark may be lost if it can be demonstrated that the owner does not exercise some sort of quality control over the licensee.

Policy decisions relating to trademarks concern the option for developing local marks for each major national or regional market or for devising standard international marks. In each case, they may or may not be similar to those used in one's domestic market. Some U.S. marks cannot be used because of prior use elsewhere, such as the AMF triangle by the Australian Military Forces. General international acceptability must also be tested carefully. Development of important marks in one's home market without protection elsewhere makes the firm vulnerable to extortion by pirates abroad who watch trade literature and move quickly to secure local registration for important trademarks.

Copyrights Copyrights are protected internationally under the Berne Convention of 1886 for the "protection of literacy and artistic works." The Convention gives automatic protection similar to that extended to local nationals in all adhering countries. Protection is the author's life plus 50 years. The United States is not a member. But the United States is a member of the Universal Copyright Convention of 1954, along with some 50-odd other countries, including the Soviet Union since 1974. Hence, the works of

American authors first published in a UCC country are subject to copyright protection in each member country, and vice versa. Under the convention, certain formalities are eliminated for members' nationals in obtaining protection in other member states. Duration of copyright protection varies by country and by the nature of the protected work (books, photographs, architectural drawings, computer programs, etc.).

Trade Secrets The laws of many countries give protection to trade secrets similar to that accorded patents, but only so long as the secrecy is maintained. Companies may not choose to patent for a number of reasons, such as the time and cost involved in patenting, the difficulty of monitoring patent infringement and enforcing patent rights against alleged infringers, and the uncertainty of patent validity. It has been said that well over half of all patents issued in the United States are ultimately declared invalid. Coca Cola is an example of a company that has gone the trade secret route in protection of its "ingredient X." Over 20 U.S. states have laws that impose criminal sanctions against the unauthorized taking of valuable secret information. However, in a 1973 decision, a U.S. court held that valuable secrets that have not been patented, but that might have been appropriate for patent protection and have been in commercial use over a year, cannot be protected legally even against wrongful appropriation through breach of obligation of confidence. (Unlike patents, there is no statutory provision at the federal level in the United States for the protection of trade secrets.) Under this ruling, foreign companies are likely to think twice before licensing unpatented trade secrets in the United States, since their licensees cannot be held accountable for a breach of confidentiality, and a licensee's employees might be hired away by a competitor. Likewise, a U.S company is unlikely to enter into many licenses based on trade secrets with foreign firms if the latter know that by hiring away key employees from the U.S. firm they can capture the secrets without committing themselves to paying royalties. There is also the possibility that U.S. firms may be tempted to transfer R&D activity to foreign subsidiaries in countries with strong laws protecting trade secrets, such as Canada, Japan, and much of Europe.

In protecting trade secrets, companies rely upon employee secrecy agreements, such as nondisclosure and nonuse clauses in employment contracts. Whether a company requires all employees to sign contracts containing such clauses, or only designated categories of employees, is a matter of company policy. In France, for example, collective labor agreements within a particular industrial sector may contain provisions prohibiting employees from committing trade secret abuses.

Management problems arising out of the international patent, copyright, and trademark systems include:

1. The need for an early evaluation of the commercial value of a patent in that the first party to apply for a patent in one Paris Union country has only one year of grace before applying for protection in other member states. The applicant has priority against others during that year. (One can, of course, apply later if no one else has applied in the meantime, so long as publication has not occurred. The actual issuance of a patent anywhere is equivalent to publication.)

2. The need to set up a system to assure continuation of patent, trademark, or copyright validity. Payment of an annual fee may be required. In case of patents or trademarks, use may be required. In the case of a trademark, application for renewal may be required.

3. The need to set up a system to monitor important markets for infringement and to prosecute infringers.

4. The need to decide whether to develop a universal trademark or a series of national or regional marks. If the former, the problem of avoiding legal restrictions and unpleasant connotations in every country is a formidable one requiring substantial research.

5. The need to decide who is going to own the proprietary right—the parent company or subsidiary. If the parent, the subsidiary must be licensed to use. But such licensing of subsidiaries is not legal under all systems. If the subsidiary is 100 percent owned, the only difference is that between a dividend (posttax earnings) and a royalty (a pretax cost). If it is a joint venture, the local partner may not take kindly to payment of a royalty (which is a cost) to the parent firm, particularly if the level of the royalty is determined by the parent. On the other hand, if a proprietary right is sold to, or capitalized by, a subsidiary abroad, the parent must assure itself that the right is not lost to it if ownership of the subsidiary changes hands.

6. The need to have continuing access to a legal counsel expert in international trademark, copyright, and patent law.

7. In that prior use is not a requirement in many countries for registering a trademark and the United States is not a member of the Madrid Agreement, it may be useful for a subsidiary of a U.S. firm in one of the countries signatory to the Madrid Agreement to register the trademark. In such cases, the subsidiary must own the trademark, which introduces the problems suggested in item five above.

8. Desirability of relying on patent protection (which constitutes publication) or maintaining secrecy (hence, denying knowledge to competitors).

8.7 Tax Law

Possibly the most complicated and important legal factor of all in designing the relationship between two enterprises of different nationality is taxation.

National tax systems vary along important dimensions. Some of the more important are:

Aggregate level of tax income. As a percentage of GNP (Denmark is among the highest with close to 50 percent; the United States is moderate, about 30 percent; Japan is low, a little over 20 percent. The LDCs are generally low, an example being Turkey at less than 20 percent).

Burden on the firm. Corporate tax rates run from a high of 46 to 52 percent in the United States and Europe to around 30 percent in many LDCs. Switzerland, with a rate of less than 10 percent, has among the lowest of the industrialized countries.[8] Distributed and undistributed profits may be taxed differently, although not in the United States. In continental Europe, distributed profits are taxed at a lower rate, and not infrequently the shareholder can take credit against his tax liability for his pro rata share of corporate income taxes paid on his dividends. In Mexico, reinvested corporate earnings are not taxed.

Taxation of capital gains. Runs from 28 percent in the United States down to zero percent for many European countries. Other differences relate to the definition of a capital gain and evaluation of the basis (initial value).

Type. Income, wealth or property, consumption or sale, transaction, value added, capital gains, dividend, withholding (a tax withheld at the source of a stream of income—interest, dividends, royalties, wages), import or export (duties). The preeminence of certain types will determine whether the overall impact of a tax system is progressive (higher percentage imposed on the more affluent), regressive, or neutral.

Progressiveness of corporate tax. From a flat rate regardless of income, to a five-tiered system (as in the United States) or a multiple-stepped progressive tax (often tied to a profit/capital ratio, as in several Latin American countries), sometimes called "schedular."

Dual corporate taxation. The taxation of all corporate profits *and* the taxation of dividends to stockholders, as in the United States. Some countries tax only corporate profits (**unitary**); others permit the dividend recipient to take a credit for all or some of the pro rata share of the corporate tax.

Purpose. Revenue, control, stimulation of growth, direction of economic activity. For example, in Japan, as a device to promote the export of technology, firms have been able to deduct from taxable income 70 percent

---

[8]The Swiss federal tax varies from 3.63 to 9.8 percent, depending on the ratio of profits to net worth, but each canton imposes its own income tax (which varies from 5 to 40 percent).

of the income from **know-how sales** and 20 percent of the income from **technical service fees** earned abroad.

Inobservance. Some tax systems are notorious for noncompliance, cases in point being Spain and Italy. In Italy, a firm may be faced with the imposition of a "presumptive tax" based on the tax office's estimate of what the profit of the firm should have been. The firm then tries to negotiate it downward to what it considers to be a reasonable level. Other countries are prone to give **tax holidays** for specified periods.

Basis for jurisdiction. By domicile or legal seat, permanent establishment, nationality, seat of control, the conduct of an active trade or business, treaty.

Jurisdiction claimed. Over worldwide income (as in the United States) or over local source income only (as in several European countries). Some countries impose a lower tax on foreign-source income, as Canada does. (Canada exempts dividends entirely if the foreign firm paying the dividend is owned at least 25 percent by the Canadian firm.)

Recognizing costs (i.e., defining taxable income). Transfer prices,[9] depreciation allowances, investment allowances (i.e., deduction in excess of total depreciation), investment tax credit, credits for foreign taxes paid, allocation of overhead expenses from headquarters to subsidiary. (An example: After 1958 the United States permitted no deduction—as a cost—against taxable income for payments made to officials or employees of a foreign government if the payment would be unlawful under U.S. law.)

Timing of tax. Payment to be made in the period earned or only as remitted from subsidiary to parent. (In some cases, the right of tax deferral may be lost, as in the United States since 1976, by participating in an "illegal boycott" or by making "extraordinary payments" abroad.) Tax deferral permits the use of **tax haven** countries; that is, the accumulation of earnings in a holding company domiciled in a country that imposes no tax or a very low tax on foreign source income and on accumulated earnings.

Tax sparing. Recognition by a firm's parent government of a certificate issued in lieu of payment of tax by a foreign government to the firm's local subsidiary, possibly as part of a tax incentive scheme (i.e., tax holiday) to attract foreign business. In some countries, the parent can use this certificate as a credit against its own tax liability (a scheme specifically rejected by the United States, but practiced by Japan and several European countries).

---

[9]Methods of calculation used by the U.S. taxing authorities are: arm's length or comparable uncontrolled price method; resale price (resale price less profit); cost plus reasonable profit; proportionate profit and rate of return on investment. A reallocation of income can, of course, lead to double taxation.

Degree to which a tax system adheres to the principle of tax neutrality. Unless specifically intended to do otherwise, a **neutral tax** does not stimulate or depress particular types of income, forms of business organization, location of production, or seat of control. Internationally, there are two types of mutually inconsistent tax neutrality: (1) imposition of the same total tax burden on income received by a country's firms, whether derived abroad or domestically, (2) imposition of the same total tax burden on a country's firms as that borne by their foreign competitors.

Recognizing tax exemptions. For profits derived from exports (Ireland), income generated from the export of technology and skills (Japan), income having its origin in certain countries (Singapore in respect to neighboring Southeast Asian countries), and for certain types of business enterprise (the partnership).

Flexibility. For example, the capacity to adjust depreciation allowances to pace inflation or to adopt appropriate inventory accounting practice (last-in-first-out, LIFO, as opposed to first-in-first-out, FIFO).

Providing tax incentives. For investing in certain sectors or regions, investing more than a certain amount, or employing a certain number related to the capital invested (such as a full tax holiday, investment tax credit, accelerated depreciation, or an investment allowance).

Number of jurisdictions claiming taxes. For example, a firm operating a national chain of outlets in the United States may be subject to the income, franchise, property, license, network, sales, and use taxes in 50 states, in addition to both federal and local (county and municipal) taxes. All told, it may have to file over 1,000 tax returns and reports each year, a significant cost item.

Taxation of contractors. In some countries (as in Mexico), a contractor can negotiate a clause in his contract to the effect that he will be reimbursed for any corporate taxes levied on him within the country. In others (as in Venezuela), such a clause is illegal; the contractor's only recourse is to anticipate the tax and include it in his fee. The more restrictive Venezuelan approach seems to be becoming more common.

Taxation of foreign source income. The method used in taxing foreign source income (see Table 8.1) can have a significant effect on the total tax paid.

Taxation of Foreign Source Income

The last item in the list is complicated by the fact that a country may tax income coming from certain countries, such as designated LDCs, at a reduced rate. Normally, a tax credit is given only for foreign wealth and

Table 8.1
The Five Methods of Taxing Foreign Source Income

	Exemption	Tax Reduction	Crediting Foreign Taxes	Expensing Foreign Taxes	Double Taxing
Taxable Income Abroad	$100	$100	$100	$100	$100
Foreign Tax (assume 40%)	40	40	40	40	40
Dividend to Parent	60	60	60	60	60
Tentative Parent-Country Tax (assume 50% in the full case, 10% in the reduced case)	0	10	50	30	50
Tax Credit	0	0	40	0	0
Tax Liability to Parent Country	0	10	10	30	50
Total Tax Paid	$ 40	$ 50	$ 50	$ 70	$ 90

income taxes (in proportion to the dividend remitted to total taxable earnings), which gives rise to a definitional problem. Does a tax on *gross* income qualify? Does a royalty on gross income—on the full value of oil received, for example—qualify? What of the oil delivered under a production sharing contract? A country also has the option of taxing foreign source income only when remitted (tax deferral) or when earned, even though not remitted. In the latter case, problems can arise if the exchange rate changes between the time the tax is assessed and the time the earnings are actually remitted. Should a further tax be extracted if the rate shifts in favor of the corporation (i.e., an evaluation of the foreign currency in reference to the parent-country currency), or a tax rebate be given if the rate shifts in the opposite direction? Such a system would add enormously to the complexities surrounding taxation, but to deny such adjustments could lead to substantial inequity.

Few countries, if any, require their corporations to expense foreign corporate income or wealth taxes in calculating taxable income, nor do any simply ignore foreign taxes as implied under the double taxing case. Most countries appear either to exempt foreign source income from domestic taxation or to impose a reduced rate. The United States uses the tax credit system, although there have been strong pressures to apply the expensing concept. One suspects that the Japanese and Europeans would be very pleased if the U.S. Congress in its wisdom did so and thus rendered U.S. corporations noncompetitive in many parts of the world where foreign firms are virtually compelled, for economic and legal reasons, to process or manufacture locally. As it is, by not recognizing the tax-sparing principle, contrary to many other countries with the tax credit system, the U.S. government penalizes U.S. corporations that are encouraged by foreign governments' tax holidays. To the extent that corporate earnings are remitted to the United States, a tax holiday simply transfers earnings from the foreign treasury to the U.S. Treasury. Fortunately, the United States still recognizes tax deferral in most cases, so that the benefits of a foreign tax holiday can be realized so long as earnings are held overseas.

Table 8.2
Residency and Domicile for Tax Purposes

Residence	Legal Domicile[a]	
	Foreign Corporation (alien)	Domestic Corporation[b] (national)
Nonresident (not engaged in business locally, no permanent establishment)	Nonresident Foreign Corporation[c] (nonresident alien)	Nonresident Domestic Corporations[d] (nonresident national)
Resident (engaged in business locally, has a permanent establishment)	Resident Foreign corporation[e] (resident alien)	Domestic Corporation (local nationals)

[a]May be either where incorporated (U.S. case) or where the seat of management is located; i.e., fiscal residence of those who have final authority in all major decisions (as in the case of Germany and the United Kingdom).

[b]Even though 100 percent owned by nonresident aliens and/or foreign corporations.

[c]For example, a foreign corporation that sells into the United States through independent representatives.

[d]For example, a personal holding company that does no business in the United States and has no permanent establishment in the United States.

[e]For example, a foreign corporation with a permanent establishment in the United States, or conducting business in the United States, i.e., through a branch (as opposed to an incorporated subsidiary).

To further one's understanding of international taxation, a few further definitions are in order. One needs to appreciate the importance of residency and legal domicile. Essentially, there are four possibilities, as indicated in Table 8.2.

In the United States, there is a 30 percent withholding tax imposed on interest, dividends, royalties, and rents paid to nonresident foreign corporations and nonresident aliens, except as reduced by treaty. There is no federal tax imposed on sales income. A resident foreign corporation, like a resident alien, pays full U.S. (corporate) income tax on U.S.-source income. Domestic corporations and nationals—whether resident in the United States or not—pay full U.S. tax on worldwide income even though not remitted to the United States, with some exceptions. In both cases, corporations can credit foreign wealth and income taxes paid, but for individuals (nonincorporated entities) such taxes are merely deductions from taxable income.

One can see that many definitional problems are introduced here which can only be resolved by tax regulation and/or tax treaty, such as the definitions of "legal domicile," "permanent establishment," "being engaged in business," "residency," and "source of income," to mention only a few.

The last term is of particular importance because of the latitude a firm may have in manipulating transactions to generate profit in desired locations, often in a relatively low-tax area. It then is in a position to use those profits for investment purposes. Instead of having only 54 cents of the profit dollar, which would be the case if those earnings had been fully taxed in the United States, the company may have 70 or 80 cents of the profit dollar for reinvestment.

Monitoring transfer prices that give rise to the movement of profits other than through the dividend route is administratively very difficult. Hundreds of thousands of invoices and contracts have to be studied and prices compared to arm's length prices which is often difficult because the goods or services may be unique to a particular firm or enjoy substantial brand name price premium because of allegedly superior quality.

An alternative is to allocate corporate income, as many states within the United States do. The bulk of the income of an interstate firm operating within the United States is apportioned by a formula based on a state's share of the firm's total economic activity. The latter is usually defined in terms of payroll, property, and sales. Ordinarily the formula contains all three factors, but sometimes two, depending upon state law. With a three-factor formula, a particular state taxes that fraction of the firm's income equal to the average of the state's shares in the payroll, property, and sales of the firm. Some states have applied this so-called "unitary" principle on worldwide income, which has given rise to a number of legal challenges. Some have suggested that many problems would be eliminated if the same system were adopted internationally. Of course, unless all countries were to use the same method for measuring total and local payroll, property, and sales, the result could be either under- or overtaxation. By far the most troublesome problem, if the U.S. experience is any guide, lies in affixing the source of income from sales. First, what proportion of a company's income should be judged to be from sales for those goods and services produced in one country and sold in another? Second, what is the source of sales income? The country in which title is passed, the country of destination, or the country in which the sale is negotiated? Finally, of course, each country would have to tax the corporation as a single entity on the basis of a single consolidated set of financial statements, which introduces currency translation problems.

In part to offer some needed definitions on the international level, there exists a web of bilateral tax treaties or conventions for the avoidance of double taxation with respect to taxes on income and capital. Each treaty varies somewhat, but characteristically a tax treaty includes provisions relating to:

1. The definition of what constitutes local source income, residency, permanent establishment, and being engaged in business.
2. A mutual reduction of withholding taxes levied on dividends, interest, and royalties paid by a domestic firm to a firm located in the other country, frequently restricted to firms owned to some given percentage by the recipient firm.
3. The taxation of capital gains realized by a citizen or enterprise of one country within the territory of the other.
4. A reduction or elimination of taxes imposed on specific income streams originating in the other country and taxed there.
5. The allowability, as costs, of certain expenses, such as royalties and fees, paid by a foreign subsidiary to its parent, and recognition of a parent-country investment credit for an investment made by a qualified foreign subsidiary.

6.   The rules covering the taxation of citizens of each contracting state
      residing or working within the other.
7.   Exchange of information between the taxing authorities of the two
      countries and a mechanism for resolving any conflicts.

As noted, some countries tax foreign source income only when remitted (the tax deferral notion); others tax such income under certain circumstances whether remitted or not (as the United States). Under a full tax
deferral system, or if the parent country does not tax foreign source income,
a company can make use of a tax haven holding company, which is simply a
subsidiary corporation located in a country that is appealing from a tax point
of view.

The ideal tax haven country also enjoys monetary stability, maintains a
modern banking system, enforces banking secrecy, places no controls on
the foreign exchange market, has a stable government and economy, enjoys
good international communications, has a web of tax treaties that reduce
withholding taxes in both directions, and has favorable corporation law. By
"favorable" I mean law that permits the maintenance of records and offices
outside the country, permits unlimited foreign stock ownership, imposes no
restriction on the nationality of officers and directors, requires only the
presence of a statutory representative, and permits quick and inexpensive
incorporation. Popular tax haven countries include Panama, Liechtenstein,
Liberia, Luxembourg, Switzerland, Monaco, and the Netherlands.

For parent corporations domiciled in countries taxing only local source
income or not taxing foreign source income until actually repatriated (the
U.S. situation prior to 1963), the tax haven holding company can be very
attractive. To the extent permitted by the taxing authorities, goods and
services may be invoiced to the tax haven company at minimum prices and
sold by it at maximum prices. Paying perhaps no taxes on foreign income
within the country of domicile, the tax haven company can accumulate
virtually untaxed money for investment or to use as working capital elsewhere, possibly even to loan to the parent company.

Asymmetries among national tax systems can cause difficulty. According to the General Agreement on Trade and Tariffs, indirect taxes (excise,
sales, value added taxes) should be levied in the country of destination.
Hence, such taxes may be rebated on exports, and such rebate is not deemed
an export subsidy. The importing country, if it also levies indirect taxes, may
impose its own taxes on the imported goods. On the other hand, direct taxes
(income, wealth, property, or profits taxes) should be collected, according to
the GATT, in the country in which the income originates. Therefore, relief of
such taxes on exports constitutes a subsidy, and import duties to compensate for direct taxes not paid abroad are unacceptable. The point is that the
GATT forbids export subsidies. A problem arises when a country relying
heavily on indirect taxes, such as the value added tax in Europe, exports to a
country relying heavily on direct taxes, such as the income tax in the United
States. In such cases, the exporting country may rebate the indirect taxes
imposed on the exported goods, but the importing country may not com-

pensate by burdening the imported goods by imposing a direct tax. Therefore, the exports enjoy a competitive advantage.

There is another asymmetry between national tax systems that can lead to a conflict of interest. If a country has a dual corporate income tax that imposes a higher tax on retained earnings than on distributed earnings, that country is likely to want to place a relatively high withholding tax on dividends paid to foreigners. The point is that the purpose of the dual tax is to encourage the payout of earnings to *local* shareholders, but not necessarily to *foreign* shareholders. In contrast, a country that permits a shareholder in a corporation to credit his share of the tax paid by that corporation against his own tax liability is likely to be neutral on the issue. It makes no difference whether corporate earnings are paid to local residents or foreigners.

Indirect taxes paid abroad are always expensed, never credited against parent-country tax liability. Hence, if in the course of negotiating a project abroad a corporation can trade off indirect taxes for direct taxes, it may gain even if it agrees to pay somewhat more taxes to the host country.

The most complicated tax system in the world, barring none, is that of the United States, particularly if one includes the taxes imposed by states, counties, and municipalities. The general principles relating to the federal taxation of foreign source income are outlined in the appendix attached to this chapter. The reader should be forewarned not to use this outline in lieu of expert counsel. There are legions of exceptions and complications.

In fact, along with other reasons, the increasing burden of U.S. taxation on foreign source income, with the elimination of tax deferral and tax credit in a number of situations, plus the cost inherent in the sheer complexity and many uncertainties in the U.S. system, has led a number of U.S. corporate executives at least to speculate upon the costs and benefits of dedomiciling their corporations. This term refers to the process of transferring ownership of most corporate assets to a parent corporation legally domiciled outside of the United States, making the U.S. operation a subsidiary of a foreign corporation. (Pressure for dedomiciling, other than out of a desire to reduce taxes, could originate from the internationalization of corporate ownership, accelerated by issues of convertible Eurobonds.) In any event, this development could well trigger partial spinning off of assets to parallel parent companies in other countries where sizeable segments of total corporate profits originate. Although no U.S. cases of dedomiciling have been reported, Canada has lost a number of corporations.

As we have in noted this chapter, the corporate strategist examines the various legal forms the two business interests might take, the advantages and disadvantages of each, and the legal implications of the relationship between the two. Particularly relevant to the last of these are such matters as antitrust vulnerability, maintaining adequate protection of valuable rights, and minimizing tax liability. The strategist then moves on to develop an adequate fit between the legal and control requirements.

APPENDIX 8A

U.S. TAXATION OF FOREIGN INCOME

General Principle

All income of U.S. citizens, domestic corporations, and resident aliens, regardless of source, is taxable at the full U.S. rate during the year earned. Rates: *personal*, 0–50 percent; *corporations*, 16 percent on the first $25,000, and progressively higher rates on the next three $25,000 increments, with the top rate of 46 percent applicable to earnings over $100,000; *corporate dividend received deduction*, if a dividend is paid by one domestic corporation to another, it is 85 percent exempt from taxation (with the balance taxed at normal corporate rate) and 100 percent exempt when the dividend is paid by one domestic corporation to another in an affiliated group (i.e., a parent and its at least 80 percent owned domestic subsidiaries); *corporate capital gains*, 28 percent; *personal holding companies* (corporations in which 50 percent or more of the value of the stock is held by 5 or fewer persons and at least 80 percent—60 percent in the foreign case—of its income is passive, that is, dividends, interest, royalties, and rents, which income is taxed to stockholders as personal income), 70 percent if not distributed; *nonresident aliens*, 30 percent withholding tax on U.S. source income.

Exceptions in Respect to Foreign Source Income

Test of source: where title passes for goods, where services are performed in the case of services. (Since 1981, all expenses for R&D conducted in the United States are allocated to U.S. source income.)

Exceptions for Persons

The exclusions from U.S. taxation for U.S. citizens resident abroad were increased by the 1981 Tax Act to $75,000 from the previous range of $20,000 to $25,000. This amount is increased in four annual $5,000 increments to $95,000 of foreign earned income[1] in 1986. In addition, reasonable housing expenses in excess of $6,059 (varies depending on government salary scales) can also be deducted or excluded. To qualify for these benefits, the individual must be a resident of a foreign country for 330 full days during any period of 12 consecutive months. For nonresident aliens with a gross income not over $15,400 and not doing business with the United States, the rate continues to be 30 percent (or lower treaty rate) on certain U.S. income, but from 1977 on, bank interest has been included.

Exceptions for Corporations[2]

Tax deduction, which is the same as treating foreign taxes (including corporate wealth and income taxes) as expenses against taxable income of a foreign subsidiary. This occurs unless the U.S. taxpayer claims a foreign tax credit. The election to deduct or credit is an annual election. Because the foreign tax credit is subject to limitations based on U.S. tax liability and upon the ratio of foreign source income to worldwide taxable income of the U.S. corporation, it may be advantageous under certain circumstances to elect to *deduct* all foreign taxes rather than to claim a credit. This situation arises when there is more foreign source loss than income. For example, assume that a U.S. corporation reports $100,000 U.S.-source income, $100,000 income from Country A (with a 40 percent tax), and a loss of $120,000 from Country B. We assume that the U.S. tax is 50 percent. Table 8A.1 shows the calculated tax.

Tax credit for income and wealth taxes (but not for taxes on gross income or any indirect taxes) paid to foreign governments by a foreign corporation in respect to dividends or earnings remitted to a U.S. corporation owning 10 percent or more of the voting stock of the foreign corporation. Credit may also be taken for such taxes paid by second- and third-tier foreign corporations, if the first tier owns 10 percent or more of the voting stock of the second tier, and the second owns at least 10 percent of the third, so long as the indirect ownership does not fall below 5 percent (which is simply the multiple of the percentage of ownership traceable back to the parent at all three levels). This rule embodies the "deemed paid" concept. The first-tier corporation is deemed to have paid the taxes of the second and third tier corporations in proportion to ownership held. Excess taxes may be carried

---

[1]In calculating taxable income, no foreign bribe is deductible. A bribe refers to a payment to a foreign government official if such payment would be illegal in the United States. Such a bribe is considered a "deemed dividend."

[2]Not treated here are investment tax credits and tax incentives for R&D expenditures made within the United States.

Table 8A.1
Calculation of Tax on Foreign Source and U.S. Income

	Deduction Elected		Credit Elected
1. U.S. Source Income	$100,000		$100,000
2. Country A Income	100,000		100,000
3. Country A Tax (40%)	40,000		40,000
4. Country B Income (loss)	− 120,000		− 120,000
5. Taxable Income in U.S. [1 + (2 − 3) + 4]	40,000	(1 + 2 + 4)→	80,000
6. Tentative U.S. Tax (50%)[a]	20,000		40,000
7. Foreign Tax Credit	—		0[b]
8. U.S. Tax Liability	20,000		40,000
9. Total Tax Paid (3 + 8)	60,000		80,000

[a]Assumed to be 50% to simplify the example.

[b]Can take no tax credit because it is limited by the ratio − 20,000/80,000, which would result in a negative credit, the − 20,000 being the total foreign source income (i.e., 2 + 4).

back two years and forward five years for credit purposes. The formula for calculating a foreign tax credit (indirect) is illustrated in Table 8A.2. (Again, assume the U.S. tax rate is 50 percent.) Starting in 1977, this method is applied to foreign source income from developed or less developed countries earned after 1977. (Direct credit is taken for withholding taxes imposed abroad, subject to the limitation discussed below. That is, the U.S. tax liability is reduced directly by the amount of the withholding.) Subsequently, of course, when the $15,000 reinvested profit in A is remitted to the United States, the U.S. tax would be applied and a foreign tax credit calculated in the same way. The gain to the taxpayer is the interest that would otherwise have had to be paid on the $15,000 of additional tax.

Limitation on the tax credit:

1. Overall limitation; that is, total credits are limited to the U.S. tax attributable to foreign source taxable income (interest income excluded). The formula for determining the overall limitation on the foreign tax credit is:

$$\left(\frac{\text{Foreign source taxable income}}{\text{Worldwide taxable income [including domestic]}}\right) \left(\begin{array}{l}\text{Amount of U.S. tax} \\ \text{liability before} \\ \text{tax credit}\end{array}\right) =$$

Maximum total credit.

2. International boycott factor. The ratio of a firm's operations in, or related to, countries associated in carrying out an international boycott against a friendly country (e.g., Arab countries against Israel) to the

Table 8A.2
Calculation of the Foreign Tax Credit

	A With Reinvestment	B Without Reinvestment
1. Foreign Source Income	$100,000	$100,000
2. Foreign Tax (25%)	25,000	25,000
3. Profit	75,000	75,000
4. Reinvested Profit	15,000	0
5. Remittance to United States [3−4]	60,000	75,000
6. Tentative U.S. Tax (50%)	$ 40,000[a]	$ 50,000[a]
7. Foreign Tax Credit	20,000[b]	25,000[b]
8. U.S. Tax Liability	20,000	25,000
9. Total Tax Paid (2+8)	$ 45,000	$ 50,000

[a] $(\text{U.S. tax rate}) \left[\text{Remittance} + \left(\dfrac{\text{Remittance}}{\text{Profit}} \times \text{Foreign tax} \right) \right]$

[b] $\dfrac{\text{Remittance}}{\text{Profit}} \times (\text{Foreign tax})$

firm's worldwide operations (excluding the United States), if the firm participates in the boycott. The unit of measure is the sum of sales, purchases and payroll. That ratio is applied to foreign tax credits, hence the limitation may be represented thus:

$$\left[1 - \frac{(\text{Boycott-related sales} + \text{purchases} + \text{payroll})}{(\text{Worldwide sales} + \text{purchases} + \text{payroll})} \right] \left(\begin{array}{l} \text{Foreign tax} \\ \text{credit} \end{array} \right) =$$

Maximum permitted credit.

In addition, tax deferral is denied to such income. One of the problems is that the law seems to imply that *all* of the income of the foreign subsidiaries deriving income from business with boycotting countries may be denied tax credit or deferral treatment unless the tainted income is clearly identifiable. If, however, the income is coming to a subsidiary located in a country with which the United States has a tax treaty, this treatment may be contrary to the treaty.

Tax reductions:

1. Investment credit. For certain LDCs, on the basis of treaty, U.S. firms may receive a specified investment tax credit for qualified investments. This credit may be used as a credit against U.S. tax liability.
2. Capital gains. Taxable at 28 percent. Payment received from the transfer of intangible property, defined as patents, copyrights, trademarks, secret processes, and information in the general nature of a patentable invention, may, under certain circumstances, be considered a capital gain and not income for tax purposes, whether received as a lump sum

or installments.[3] But, if the transfer is to a controlled foreign corporation (see below), the gain is taxable as ordinary income.

Tax exclusions:

1. U.S. possessions corporations. A domestic corporation whose gross income is 80 percent or more derived from U.S. possessions and 65 percent or more derived from active conduct of trade or business (which excludes dividends, interest, royalties and fees—called passive income). U.S. source income is included in the gross income of its U.S. shareholders. Such a corporation is taxable on worldwide income at the usual rate, but a full foreign tax credit of 46 percent is given for its business and qualified investment income within the possession regardless of whether any taxes have been paid to the government of the possession. No taxes paid to a foreign country are creditable, nor is a consolidated return with the parent permitted. The special credit is effective for ten consecutive years. Tax-free distribution of earnings with or without liquidation is permitted.

2. Foreign-owned corporations (those not incorporated in the United States):
    a. Nonresident foreign corporations pay a 30 percent withholding tax on certain gross income received from U.S. sources, interest, dividends, rent, and so on. Frequently reduced to 15 percent by treaty (see tax deferral, below).
    b. Resident foreign-owned corporations pay the normal U.S. tax on all income from U.S. source income. (Residency equals a permanent place of business and/or location of decision-making authority.)

Tax deferral.   Refers to postponing of tax on income until the income is actually remitted to the United States. Note that there is no tax deferral in respect to income of foreign branches of a U.S. entity, for income is automatically consolidated during the current year. Deferral occurs only in the case of an incorporated foreign subsidiary, and then only if certain conditions are satisfied.

1. Foreign corporations (i.e., those incorporated outside the United States) *other than* foreign personal holding companies and U.S.-controlled foreign corporations, are not liable for any U.S. corporate income tax until earnings are repatriated to the United States *except* for

---

[3]To avoid the general rule that royalty income is ordinary income, and thereby open up the capital gains route, one must *not* be in the business of selling patents. Also, the transfer must be of a complete and indivisible interest. (That is, it must convey the exclusive right to manufacture, distribute, and sell on a national basis for the life of a patent, or, if unpatented, indefinitely. Any retention of a substantial interest will defeat the purpose, but note that know-how and a patent are considered two separate pieces of property.) Additionally, one must hold the asset for at least six months (running from the date of patent issue or the date on which an invention was actually reduced to practice). A continuing royalty is permissible as a sales price for a capital asset, likewise a minimum royalty. Know-how seems to be transferable as a capital asset if there is no time limit on the transfer. A country-by-country transfer is acceptable, but not a subnational transfer (e.g., for northern Italy). The right of termination by the licensee is permitted, but not the right of termination by the licensor.

income derived from support of a boycott against a friendly country or related to an illegal payment made abroad, in which cases the tax deferral option is lost. In the case of the foreign personal holding company and the controlled foreign corporation, certain income is taxable currently to the U.S. owners whether distributed or not.

a. Foreign personal holding company (a firm in which more than 50 percent of the stock is held by 5 or fewer U.S. citizens or residents). If 60 percent or more of the income is personal holding company income (rents, royalties, interest, dividends not earned in the active conduct of a real estate, service, banking, or insurance business), all undistributed income is taxable currently to the stockholders as ordinary income.

b. Controlled foreign corporation (CFC) (a foreign corporation in which at least 50 percent of the total equity is owned by U.S. stockholders, each of whom holds 10 percent or more.)[4] Upon liquidation, any capital gains realized by reason of earnings after 1962 are taxable as income.

i. *Subpart F income* is taxed to the U.S. shareholders owning 10 percent or more of a controlled foreign corporation, whether or not such income is distributed during the current year. Subpart F income is the total of U.S. insurance income, illegal bribes paid to foreign government officials, and *foreign base company* (FBC) income. FBC income is the total of (1) FBC holding company income (see above) received from outside the country of incorporation; (2) FBC sales income, that is, purchase of tangible property from, or sale of same to, a related entity *and* production or use of the property outside the country of incorporation; (3) FBC service income, that is, services performed for or on behalf of a related entity and performed outside the country of incorporation;[5] (4) FBC shipping income, which is income derived from the use of aircraft or vessels in foreign commerce and directly related ser-

[4]Although the law uses the voting power test of control, later regulations interpreted the statutory language as referring to "actual control," whatever the percentage of formal voting power might be. Tests of control: (1) Do non-U.S. shareholders have nominal voting power disproportionate to their share of corporate earnings? (2) Do non-U.S. shareholders fail to exercise their voting power fully or independently? (3) Is the principal purpose of the arrangement to avoid classification of the corporate entity as a CFC? It appears that an affirmative answer *only* to test number three is inadequate to attack a decontrolled CFC.

[5]The Revenue Act of 1962 specifically provides that any gain realized from the transfer of patent rights to a controlled foreign corporation is to be taxed as ordinary income, even though such a transfer leads to a capital gain under other circumstances. If the transfer were made for stock, according to subsequent rulings, the gain is still treated as ordinary income, not capital gain, unless the patent rights are employed in the subsidiary's own manufacturing operations and there are adequate business purposes in having a separate manufacturing facility. In any event, prior IRS approval is needed, which is not forthcoming if the foreign subsidiary is going to engage in the granting of sublicenses outside of the country in which it is incorporated. However, it is clear that if the foreign subsidiary enhances the value of an invention acquired from its parent through its own R&D, then the royalties derived from licensing the improved invention to unrelated companies is not part of the subsidiary's subpart F income. Also, royalty income derived through a sublicense within the country within which the CFC is located is excluded, so likewise technical service income derived from the CFC's own licensing program regardless of where the income is derived. But if the U.S. parent conducts a licensing program, the technical service income of the subsidiary constitutes subpart F income. If, on the other hand, the technical service is performed by the subsidiary for an unrelated party in connection with the purchase by the unrelated party of goods manufactured in the United States (even if by the U.S. parent), the income derived from the service by the CFC is not subpart F income. In addition, the Tax Reform Act of 1976 imposed a 35 percent excise tax on certain transfers to foreign operations, trusts, or partnerships. The tax applies to transfers of all types of property (securities included), but only to the extent that no gain is recognized by the transferer at the time of the transfer. No tax applies when the transferer establishes that the transfer has no tax avoidance purposes.

vices; (5) funds derived from the withdrawal of income previously invested in shipping operations and any increase in earnings invested in the United States, that is, in tangible property in a U.S. corporation related to the parent, in the right to use U.S. patents developed in the United States, and so on, but not deposits in ordinary bank accounts nor portfolio investment in unrelated U.S. companies; and (6) income derived from illegal payments.

ii.   Exclusions from subpart F income are: (1) shipping profits to the extent that they are reinvested in shipping operations; (2) the 10-70 rule, which says that if FBC income is less than 10 percent of the income of the controlled foreign corporation, none is taxed until distributed, but if it is over 70 percent, all is taxed as subpart F income; and (3) income of a CFC that does not have as one of its significant purposes the substantial reduction of U.S. tax.

2.   Domestic international sales corporation (DISC). A domestic corporation, 95 percent of whose receipts are from qualified export sales of goods and services[6] and 95 percent of whose assets are in qualified export-related forms. If the DISC's goods are manufactured with foreign components, the value added in the United States must equal or exceed 50 percent of fair market value. Proceeds from the sale of export assets qualify as export income, as do dividends from foreign selling subsidiaries.[7] Export-related assets include service and sales facilities, inventories, working capital, and producer loans to the parent for use in modernizing or expanding export facilities. For such corporations, tax is deferred on 50 percent of the export income exceeding 67 percent of the annual average for a 3-year base period, lagged by 5 years. The deferral lasts until such income is paid to the parent,[8] but may be deferred even so if made available as a "producers loan," which is used in the financing of export production. A parent company is permitted either (1) to price goods and service to its DISC so that it earns 4 percent on qualified export receipts plus 10 percent of its export promotion expenditures attributable to the sale, or (2) to allocate to the DISC up to 50 percent of the combined taxable income of the DISC and of the parent derived from an export sale plus 10 percent of the promotional expenses attributable to the sale. DISC benefits may be curtailed if the DISC or its parent or affiliates participate in an international boycott.[9]

[6]Excludes any natural resources subject to depletion other than timber unless U.S. *processing* is equal to or greater than 50 percent of the export value, and excludes one half of the taxable income attributable to military sales made after October 2, 1975.

[7]That is, if the DISC owns more than 50 percent of the voting power of a foreign international sales corporation (FISC, a foreign corporation, 95 percent of whose receipts are from qualified export sales and 95 percent of whose assets are in qualified export-related forms), owns less than 10 percent of the voting stock in an associated foreign corporation, or owns more than 50 percent of the voting stock of foreign corporations whose only function is to hold real property for the exclusive use of the DISC.

[8]Although the federal government may defer taxes on 50 percent of a DISC's income, the state wherein it is chartered may not. One is generally better off in those states where laws defer state corporate taxes on DISC income, as in Florida, Utah, and Delaware.

[9]DISCs have been attacked abroad as constituting a discriminatory export subsidy; and—as of this writing—they may be phased out. An export trading company may not be set up as a DISC.

Withheld tax. A U.S. corporation must withhold a 30 percent tax on interest and dividends paid to nonresident aliens and foreign corporations not in business in the United States. The paying corporation is exempt if over 80 percent of its gross revenue is derived from foreign sources. Since 1969, the following have been treated as foreign source income: (1) interest earned by a nonresident alien or foreign corporation on U.S. bank deposits not effectively connected with a U.S. business, and (2) interest received by a nonresident alien or foreign corporation from the U.S. branch of a foreign bank. This change meant that there would be no withholding on such income and, in effect, it would not normally be taxed at all in the United States.

Despite the nondeferrability of tax of foreign branch income, operation through foreign branches may be desirable in certain cases:

1.   For mining enterprises, in which depletion allowances and the inclusion of intangible drilling costs as current expenses, rather than as a capital investment, are important. The U.S. provisions on these subjects do not apply to foreign corporations, even though wholly owned by U.S. nationals or by a U.S. corporation.
2.   If foreign law requires no capital allocation for a branch operation (in the sense of depositing funds or valuable securities locally) and such a situation is deemed by management to minimize risk—and, hence, cost. (On the other hand, in a branch operation the host government may demand access to the records of the parent company and allocate taxable income as it deems equitable. Also, liability runs directly to the parent's assets, unless a domestic or third-country corporate buffer lies between the two.)[10]

It should be noted that the tax haven holding company is attractive to the U.S. firm only under two circumstances. These two cases are: (1) avoidance of the controlled foreign corporation classification, by placing majority ownership in the hands of non-U.S. nationals, or by holding each U.S. shareholding to less than 10 percent; (2) maintenance of subpart F income at a level under 10 percent of the total taxable income of the controlled foreign corporation.

In organizing a new corporation, its U.S. founders might incorporate the *parent* in one of the tax haven countries, so long as it can avoid the category of a foreign personal holding company or of a controlled foreign

---

[10]By using an incorporated *foreign* entity as its agent for entering arrangements with other foreign enterprises, either through contract or investment, the U.S. principal may lose the advantages of U.S. law, such as reciprocal treaty rights between the United States and country in which the other enterprise is incorporated in respect to reduction in withholding taxes and double taxation and in situations where regional authorities, including the United States, tend to limit purchasing from member states (e.g., NATO). In certain cases, tax credits and the right to OPIC contracts and investment guarantees, FICA facilities, and Export-Import Bank loans may be lost, as well as official U.S. representation on one's behalf. For example, in 1967 there was a ruling to the effect that suppliers not maintaining a regular place of business in the United States were not eligible to participate in many purchases financed by U.S. foreign economic assistance. This ruling specifies further that title must be passed within the United States from supplier to foreign buyer. However, by contract, many firms have to sell through distributors and sales subsidiaries and for that reason cannot pass title at the shore line. Similar regulations can be found within the foreign economic assistance activities of other countries.

corporation. This device is called the parent base company. To spin off assets of an existing U.S. parent to a foreign subsidiary requires the prior approval of the Internal Revenue Service, which is extremely hard to obtain unless one can demonstrate compelling business reasons for the spinoff. *Tax avoidance is not considered a valid business reason!* Apparently, companies based in other countries have similar problems in initiating such a spinoff.

CHAPTER **9**

CONTROL STRATEGY

centralization the retention of authority at the center, usually with the top-level management of the parent corporation.

control the relationships and devices designed to assure that strategy (or policy) decisions are made by designated authority in conformance with corporate goals, that tactical (or operating) decisions conform to the selected strategies, and that actual operations are in accord with decisions.

corporate culture the rules, as perceived by corporate employees, which describe behavior within the organization; often unwritten and not formally articulated.

export-oriented a firm where international interest and expertise are limited to a staff department and restricted to searching for and developing *export markets only*, but with decision-making authority remaining within largely domestically oriented divisions.

international a firm where international interest and relevant skill are in an international division, but with most functional expertise remaining in domestic divisions and domestically oriented staff departments.

multinational a firm where international interest and expertise are located throughout the firm, but which is owned and managed preeminently by home-country nationals and which operates internationally essentially through subsidiaries, the latter constituting an internationally integrated production system. (See also definition in Chapter One.)

multinational association a group of locally owned firms of different nationalities linked by contracts with a central firm that supplies a variety of services.

socialization the internationalization of values and rules of behavior by employees of a corporation.

supranational a firm not legally domiciled within any national state but whose operations are governed by an international convention. Hence, its management is free structurally, psychologically, and legally to allocate resources on a global basis in conformance with corporate goals insofar as they do not conflict with the international political regime controlling the corporation.

transnational a firm in which ownership and management is multinational (see definition, Chapter Six), and whose members develop loyalty of a sort that transcends national identity, thus eliminating covert or psychologically based national bias in decision making.

transnational association a multinational association in which the central firm is owned, at least in part, by the local firms linked to it by contract.

Control may be defined simply as the relationships and devices designed to assure that strategy (or policy) decisions are made by designated authority in conformance with corporate goals, that tactical (or operating) decisions conform to the selected strategies, and that actual operations are in accord with decisions.

Clearly, corporate administrative structure should be looked at from the point of view of establishing and maintaining adequate control over the firm's activities at least cost. Administrative structure can be viewed as the network of channels through which authority flows, together with the feedback generated, plus the network of informal flows. A distinct but related subject has to do with the *nature* of the flows within the system and the devices used to assure against unintended changes in the flows.

Therefore, in considering alternative control strategies, several key questions present themselves:

1. Where should decision-making authority reside in the firm in respect to strategy choices; that is, the global allocation of corporate resources?
2. Where should the relevant tactical decision-making authority be located?
3. By what methods should operating performance be reported?
4. By what means should decisions be communicated?
5. What measures of performance (conformance of strategy decisions to goals, of tactical decision to strategy, of actual operations to tactical decisions) should be used?
6. How can decisions be enforced; that is, how can control be maintained?

You might well ask whether there are problems in this area unique to the firm operating internationally. A listing of differences between domestic and international control systems might include the following:

1.   Currency differences require a more careful approach to pricing, working-capital management, and selection of funds sources, as well as great care in interpreting the meaning of overseas balance sheets and earnings statements.

2.   The foreign manager may have little control over many important decisions made by the parent company, which may seriously affect his or her operating performance.

3.   Economic data and historical and industry comparisons are often harder to obtain, even occasionally nonexistent, in the foreign environment, which makes budgetary goal setting more difficult.

4.   Internal performance data for the foreign subsidiary occasionally is difficult to obtain in the form desired, due to the unfamiliarity of many foreign-educated managers with management accounting techniques in the country of the parent.

5.   Informal communication between foreign managers and headquarters tends to be less frequent than between domestic manager and headquarters, possibly causing greater reliance on the data from the formal system.[1]

Overseas managers often complain that: (1) they feel out of touch with the mainstream of the company; (2) it takes an inordinate amount of time to get information from headquarters; (3) headquarters insists on making decisions that can be better made by those in the field who are closer to the situation; and (4) visits by headquarters' personnel are often "junkets" that waste valuable time for those in the field.

On the other hand, those at corporate headquarters often complain that: (1) it takes too long to get information from the field; (2) managers in foreign subsidiaries make decisions without consulting headquarters; (3) overseas executives become too "localized" to function at peak efficiency when they return from their international assignments; and (4) site visits abroad often waste valuable time because the overseas executives have not adequately prepared for them.

One could argue plausibly that these conditions are found in all large, complex organizations. Complaints regarding headquarters-field information barriers, and headquarters interference in local decision making are certainly not limited to international firms.

Some companies, however, maintain more effective communication links between headquarters and overseas operations than others. Possible characteristics of the better communicators are (1) greater involvement in foreign markets, (2) greater tenure of both headquarters and overseas managers, (3) more headquarters experience by overseas managers, (4) less

---

[1]Adapted from John J. Muriel, "Evaluation and Control of Overseas Operations," in *Management Accounting* (May 1969), p. 37.

formal control by headquarters personnel over overseas subsidiary operations, (5) greater headquarter willingness to accept decisions made by subsidiary management, and (6) greater sense of teamwork between headquarters and subsidiary managers. What we have described here are several of the ingredients of a strong **corporate culture**, that is, a general internalization of common values and rules of behavior by those in its employ. The more effective this internalization—or **socialization**—process, the less need for formal rules to be articulated and disseminated and the better communications are understood by all concerned. The contexts out of which they are transmitted and received tends to be very similar; there is a corporate "language."

As communication is the key to effective control, it is important to reflect on some of the necessary, though perhaps not sufficient, conditions for maintaining an effective international communications network. Figure 9.1 plots some of these conditions and how they relate, including some of the positive feedback loops. The variable that may dominate the system of corporate communication is reflected in the following observation.

The extensive management development programs that some multinational enterprises maintain appear designed to create an elite cadre of men who all know one another and who share operating experience in different types of managerial activity. The purpose of creating these elites is to foster an environment in which men who are physically distant at any one time can communicate easily and informally. If men share common experience and perceive themselves as having similar status in the hierarchy, they generally cooperate more readily than they would in other circumstances. Informal links among the members of the elite help to compensate for the absence of many formal reporting relationships and reduce the demand for specialized staff.[2]

It follows from this discussion that companies in which the tenure of the relevant managers is relatively long and in which they are promoted by seniority (that is, an age group moves up together) would, all else being equal, lead to the most effective international communication network. The corporate culture would tend to be strong and the process of socialization of those within it, relatively effective. The Japanese system, in which there are few intercompany transfers of managers and in which there are personal ties of long standing, suggests itself as an example. Indeed, the impression one gets is that the international communication network within an established Japanese corporation is so tightly drawn that it is virtually impossible for new managers to be introduced into the system effectively, whether they are Japanese or non-Japanese. Much of that communication network is informal. The socialization process is so effective that relatively few formal standard operating procedures need be transmitted. Managers know what is expected without being explicitly directed. A result is that as Japanese

[2]John M. Stopford and Louis T. Wells, Jr., "Ironing Out the New Relationships," *Worldwide P & I Planning* (May–June 1972), p. 35, reprinted from Stopford and Wells, *Managing the Multinational Enterprise* (New York: Basic Books, 1972). Should one presume that the authors meant to include women as well?

Figure 9.1
Some Factors Enhancing International Corporate Communications

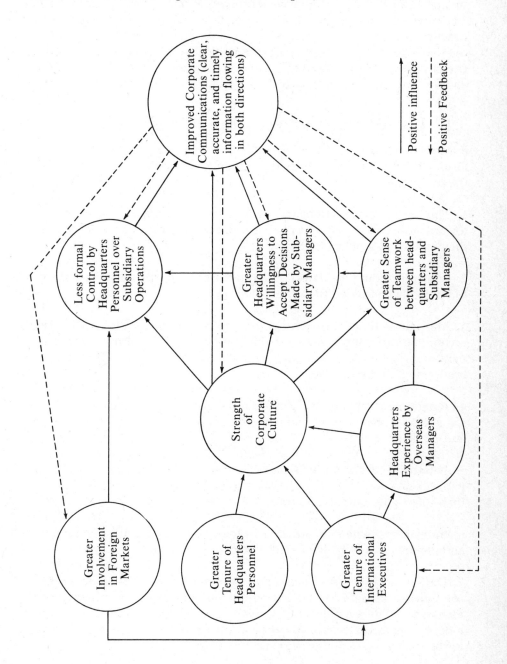

nationalize the managements of their foreign subsidiaries, the communications problem becomes exceedingly difficult. As much of the local and Japanese management try to have it otherwise, one suspects that the local non-Japanese manager has a feeling of facing a tightly knit monolithic structure into which any real access is denied the outsider. Frustration is very likely to lead to an erosion of communication and of effective control. This situation perhaps suggests one reason the Japanese have developed the trading company approach, which is discussed in a later section.

9.1   Location of Authority for Strategy Selection

It is probably true that the degree of decision making retained in corporate headquarters in practice is related to a number of factors, among which are the following:

1. **The nature of the industry.**   Companies in certain industries tend toward more centralized control—for example, drug manufacturers because they require product consistency.

2. **Function of the subsidiary.**   Manufacturing subsidiaries are more likely to be tightly controlled than marketing units.

3. **Managerial function.**   Finance tends to be centrally controlled, likewise accounting procedures, sales reporting, executive appointments and compensation, sourcing of materials, quality control, patent and trademark monitoring, and advertising.

4. **Range of a subsidiary's products and markets.**   Those with a wide range tend to be more autonomous than affiliates with uniform products and markets.

5. **Number and size of affiliated companies in a given market.**   Companies with a few large subsidiaries in a region tend to exercise less control than those with many small units.

6. **Subsidiary ownership structure.**   Joint ventures are likely to be more autonomous than wholly owned subsidiaries.

7. **Date of acquisition of subsidiary.**   A newly acquired affiliate which continues to manufacture its old product lines under the former management tends to have greater autonomy. Also, control is seldom constant over time; during early stages of affiliation, control may be very loose, but tighten as the foreign operation grows—up to a point.

8. **Degree of personal interest and expertise in corporate headquarters.** The greater headquarters' interest and relevant expertise, the less autonomy a foreign affiliate may enjoy.

9. Distance from corporate headquarters. Distant subsidiaries tend to have greater autonomy, particularly if located in countries with unfamiliar environments—the "cultural distance" factor.

10. Priority of corporate goals. If the principal goal is power maximization, extreme **centralization** may be optimal; if market share maximization, extreme decentralization; if rate-of-return maximization, somewhat more centralized control. If one holds other factors constant, the priority of corporate goals could perhaps be implied by the level of centralization.

11. Corporate ownership. For example, if ownership of the corporate parent is in the hands of a family, the family of stockholders may exercise close surveillance over strategy choice in regard to ownership, management, and finance, thereby forcing corporate headquarters to retain control in these areas.

12. Headquarters confidence in the affiliate's management. As confidence grows, decision making tends to move into the hands of the affiliate.

13. Perceived success of affiliate.

14. The volume of interdivision and interregion transactions. Corporations with a great deal of intrafirm movement of goods and services tend to maintain a higher level of headquarters control.

15. The relative importance of the foreign market. If there is a high degree of headquarters confidence in the subsidiary's management and it is perceived in headquarters as successful, this factor could lead to greater autonomy; if not, to less autonomy.

In addition, there are several critically important intervening variables, which tend to make these factors more or less important—such as various legal constraints, the quality of the corporate communications network, corporate structure, and the nature of the planning process. We shall look at the last two in some detail later in the chapter.

In the final analysis, corporate control over strategy should be maintained only in those functional areas where a suboptimization problem is likely to arise between the division (whether international, regional, product, or functional) and the entire corporate family, or between subsidiary and division. Such problems may appear when important economies of scale arise in the joint utilization of scarce resources, including high-cost specialized personnel. Even in that situation, however, specialized personnel at the corporate level may be used only in an advisory capacity to division or subsidiary managements in determining strategy. Of course, centralized control is also fully justified where the internal corporate market is seen as more efficient than external markets in respect to international flows of goods and services.

Figure 9.2
Types of Firms by Location of Authority over
Associated Foreign Enterprise

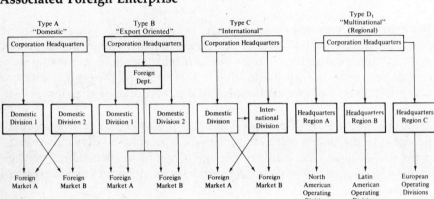

Note: Heavily lined boxes indicate source of effective line authority in respect to foreign operations.

Strategy decisions relating to the development and servicing of foreign markets may be made in the domestic operating divisions; in a domestically oriented corporate headquarters assisted by a staff office specializing in exports; in an international division; or in multinational, regional, product, or functional headquarters. These variations in corporate organization are outlined in Figure 9.2. Bear in mind here that we are really concerned with the reality of the decision-making structure, not in an empty organizational or legal shell.

In types A, B, and C, the domestic divisions may be defined by geographical area, product, function, process (for example, mining, smelting, refining, shipping), or customer (government, industry, consumer). In type C, the international division is, by definition, regional. In type D (only one form of which is diagrammed in Figure 9.2), the first layer of organization under corporate headquarters, whatever it may be called (headquarters, division, group, or coordinating committee), may likewise be defined by geographical area, product, function, process, or customer (as indicated in Figure 9.3). Hence, D_1 is a regionally organized multinational firm. Let it be noted that in this text, the terms export-oriented, international, multinational, and transnational are *not* used interchangeably.

Also possible are Types E and F, firms that, insofar as the flow of authority goes, look the same as Type D, but that in fact are quite different. Type E, the **transnational**, is a firm owned and managed multinationally (that is, by nationals of different countries). Type F, the **supranational**, is a firm that is not domiciled within any nation state but is governed by international convention, as the IBRD and the International Telecommunications Satellite System (INTELSAT). In such case, management is free structurally, psychologically, and legally to allocate resources on a global

Figure 9.3
Variations of the Multinational Corporation

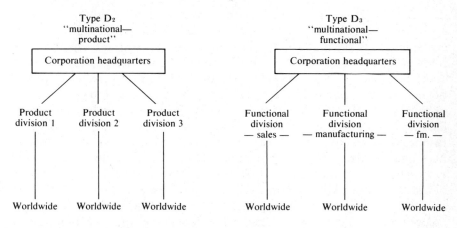

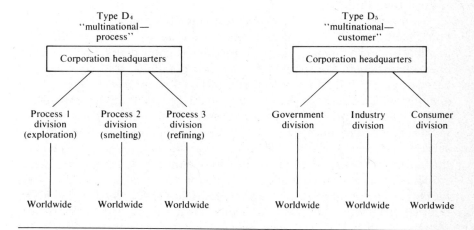

basis in conformance with corporate goals, insofar as they do not conflict with the international political regime controlling the corporation.

A word about the definition of the multinational corporation is in order here. The multinational corporation (MNC), technically defined, is characterized by four factors:

1. Ownership and management of a parent corporation essentially by the nationals of one country.
2. An integrated international production system (i.e., centralized control of production).
3. Equity-based control (i.e., the centralized control is based preeminently on ownership except where local law blocks alien ownership).

4. A legal domicile within the country with which the preponderance of parent-company owners and managers identify.

If one changes any one of these four dimensions, a different type of enterprise emerges, from which one can expect different behavior. For example, if one postulates ownership and management of the parent corporation by the nationals of more than one country to a significant degree, one has a *transnational* corporation (Figure 9.4). A firm becomes transnational when its member develop loyalty to the firm of a sort that transcends national identity, thus eliminating covert or psychologically based national bias in decision making and making possible a better allocation of corporate resources, insofar as national law permits. Key decision makers may, in fact, no longer reside in the parent country. Several transnational firms have emerged within Europe. Figure 9.5 details the structure of three of the oldest. Temporary transnational ventures are likewise to be found, such as those related to the implementation of various NATO projects. One is diagrammed in Figure 9.6. (A major problem associated with this type of transnational lies in its temporary nature. Managers assigned to the ventures anticipate returning to their parent firms, and, hence, are in a position of great role conflict.)

If the corporation is not managing an integrated international production system, then it is simply an *international holding company* of some sort, possibly based on financial linkages and some vaguely defined policy guidelines, characteristics of some *international* corporations. If its control is not based on equity, but rather rests on contracts, we have an *international service company*, which can range all the way from the general trading companies of Japan, which essentially sell marketing services (and other services ancillary to that central function; see Figure 9.7), to the company marketing a specific service, such as engineering, construction, and the like. And if one changes the fourth part of the definition of the MNC, either by domiciling the parent corporation in a country with which neither owners nor top managers identify, or by permitting the parent corporation special legal status under international convention (so that legally it is not domiciled in any nation-state), one either has the *dedomiciled multinational* or, in the latter case, the *supranational corporation* of which we have only public (International Bank for Reconstruction and Development) and quasipublic (International Telecommunications Satellite System, or Intelsat) examples. (See Figure 9.8.)

One of the difficulties with so much of the research in the international business area is that it has not seen the nature of the international enterprise itself as an important variable. For example, much data has been collected on "multinational corporations" which in fact includes information on many firms that are not multinational as defined above. Only rarely is such data classified by type of corporation. One might derive data for corporations with or without international divisions, but it is exceedingly important to distinguish between those corporations that *have had* an international division in the past, and dissolved it in favor of a true multinational structure, and those firms that have never evolved far enough beyond export to have

Figure 9.4
A Transnational Corporate Model

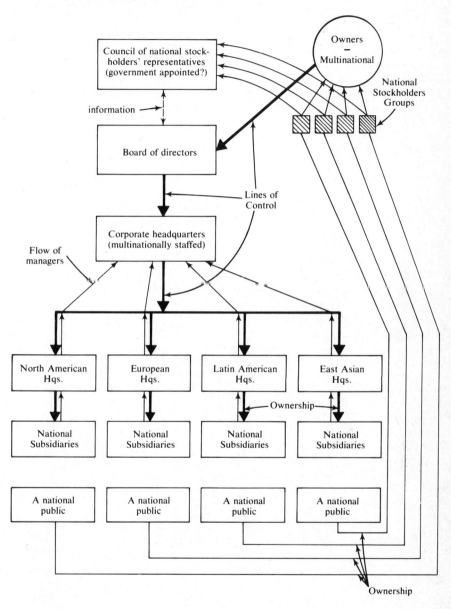

Figure 9.5
Transnational Firms

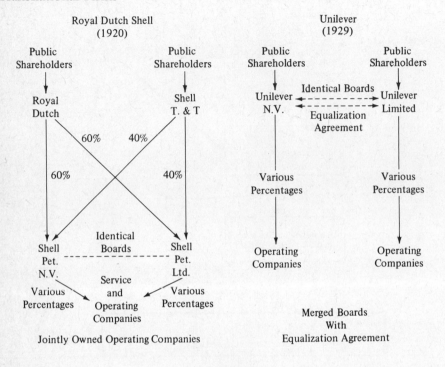

Royal Dutch Shell
(1920)

Unilever
(1929)

Jointly Owned Operating Companies

Merged Boards
With
Equalization Agreement

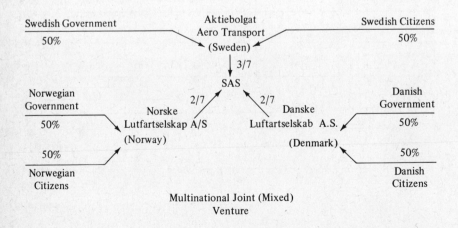

Scandinavian
Airlines System
(1951)

Multinational Joint (Mixed)
Venture

Figure 9.6
A Transnational Venture of a Temporary Nature

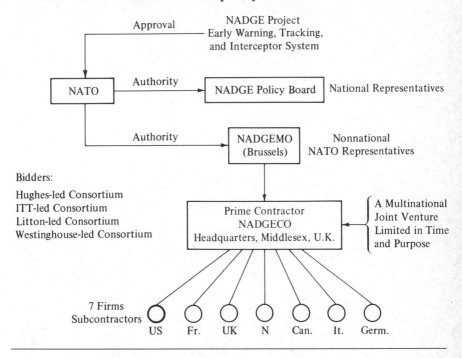

Note: Conditions: fixed price; prime contractor responsible for system integration; and B/P provision (2 percent margin. That is national contribution should equal local spending ± 2 percent).

created an international division. In some instances an international division may be retained *after* multinationalization, simply as a staff-support, planning, and/or integrative unit.

The problems of classifying international corporate form have been further compounded by the United Nations' insistence on using the term "transnational" to cover all firms operating internationally. Given the definitions used here and elsewhere in the more technical literature, the term "transnational," as used by the United Nations, includes export-oriented, international, multinational, and transnational firms, plus international service companies, international holding companies, and dedomiciled multinationals. The point is that each type of corporation gives rise to different public policy issues. For example, if the multinationals are in greatest conflict with host-country governments, one might argue that the transnationals are likely to be in greatest conflict with parent-country governments. It is important to make these definitional distinctions because it seems very likely that they impact on corporate behavior (for example, the degree of national bias in decision making) and, hence, on public policy. Curiously, there has been virtually no research on how the internationalization of the firm, and subsequently its multinationalization and transnationalization, affect the nature and quality of corporate decisions.

Figure 9.7
An International Service Company, or Transnational-
Multinational Association Model

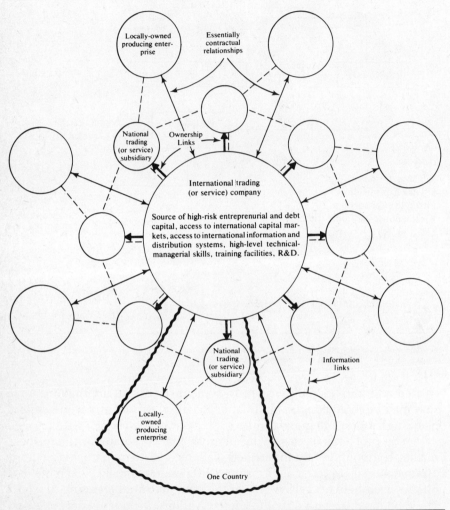

Note: If the international company is owned and managed essentially by local nationals, it is a *multinational* association; if owned largely by the associated firms and managed at least in part by them, it is a *transnational* association.

9.2   Evolution of the Firm

In speaking of the evolution of the firm in its international dimension, one must superimpose two related but distinct processes. There is, first, the pattern of geographical dispersion of corporate resources and, second, the pattern of functional and organizational development as the perceived corporate market internationalizes.

Figure 9.8
Structure of Intelsat

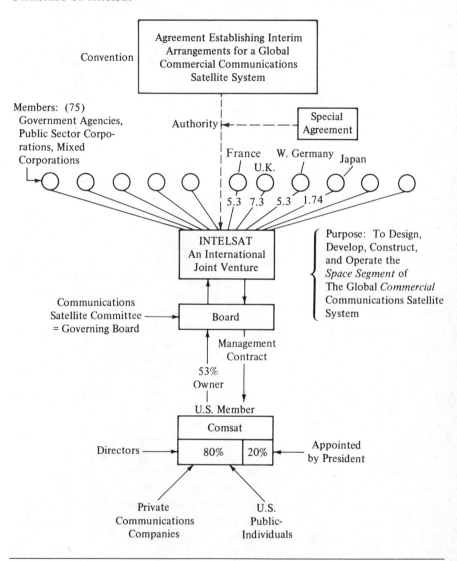

Carlson observed:

As long as the survival of a firm is not threatened, its primary objective is to grow. Its immediate goal is to increase its sales, with the qualification that it can at the same time reach a certain profit level, a certain level of financial stability, etc. If these conditions cannot be fulfilled in its present operations, it starts to search for new alternative activities. But since new alternatives generally seem more uncertain than old ones, we assume that this search will be directed to alternatives which are as similar as possible to those with which it is already familiar.[3]

Carlson goes on to point out that the uncertainty the firm feels during such a search is due to four factors:

1. Lack of knowledge of the existence of possible new alternatives.
2. Lack of knowledge of the conditions, internal or external to the firm, which will determine the consequences of a new alternative.
3. Lack of knowledge of what consequences these conditions, even when they are known, may have for the firm.
4. Lack of knowledge of how these consequences may be expressed in relevant terms of goal fulfillment.[4]

Uncertainty increases with the time that elapses between decision and outcome and with the degree of unfamiliarity in respect to the place of that outcome, that is, its "degree of foreignness." Carlson adds the uncertainty associated with what he dubs "frontier problems," such as the variety of laws and regulations relating to the cross-border movement of goods, money, and people. Export experience reduces both elements of this uncertainty over time, and hence usually precedes any major commitment of corporate assets to the purchase of fixed assets abroad. In any event, the accumulation of new information sufficient to reduce uncertainty bears a cost. The information must be collected, transmitted, and interpreted.

Carlson uses the notion of "cultural distance," which he defines in terms of the difference between home country and foreign market in respect to level of development, education, business language, everyday language, cultural differences, and the extent of the connection between the two countries. Various Swedish studies reported by Carlson, his own included, seem to establish that buying preferences of Swedish firms correlate negatively with cultural distance, as does the degree of corporate commitment in exploiting foreign markets, although once a firm has progressed to the point of establishing a sales *subsidiary* in a particular country, it seems to be more influenced by size of market than by cultural distance. Finally, another Swedish study reported by Carlson concluded that Swedish firms

start to establish subsidiaries in culturally nearby countries before they do so further away, but there seems to be a certain difference in the chronological order as between different periods, different branches of industry, and different sized firms. Firms that produced technology-intensive products seemed to be more influenced by cultural distance than other firms, and small firms were more influenced than large firms.[5]

These studies support the observation that, historically, U.S. firms very frequently move assets first into Canada, then into the United Kingdom and

[3]Sune Carlson, *How Foreign Is Foreign Trade?* (Uppsala, Sweden: Acta Universitatis Upsaliensis, 1975).

[4]Carlson, *How Foreign,* p. 7. Carlson gives attribution to E. Hornell and J. E. Vahines, "Information vid etableringsbeslut," in Jan Johanson, ed., *Exportstrategiska problem* (Stockholm, 1972), p. 96.

[5]Carlson, *How Foreign,* pp. 14–19.

Table 9.1
Characteristic Business Patterns of Firms
at Various Evolutionary Levels
(foreign activity as a percent of the corporate total)

	Foreign Sales	Product Value from Foreign Manufacturing	Foreign Assets in Manufacturing	Foreign Profits
A. Domestic (no specialized export effort)	0–10%	0	0	0–15%
B. Export (specialized export effort)	10–20	0–5	0–5	15–20
C. International (Export bias eliminated, emphasis on foreign market entry by any strategy)	20–40	5–30	5–20	20–40
D. Multinational (Discontinuity between domestic and foreign decisions minimal)	40–60	30–60	30–50	40–70
E. Transnational (Elimination of all national bias in decision making except that legally imposed)	60–80	60–100	50–90	70–95

other English-speaking countries, even before the firm becomes either multinational or international in structure. It is often true that these first investments come about as the result of some personal relationship or interest at the top, not as the result of a global scanning process.

If the evolution of administrative structure is viewed alongside growth of foreign sales of the firm (in relation to domestic sales), types A, B, C, and D tend to follow one another in time for a given firm (see Table 9.1).

Type A (Domestic)

In type A, each division handles its own foreign sales, which arise initially in response to largely unsolicited orders from overseas. If the potential foreign market is small, if divisions are organized on a product basis, and if divisions are relatively autonomous and large, type A may be appropriate. One problem is that the foreign market potential from the point of view of each division may be seen as relatively small, in which event no one in the firm develops sufficient interest to examine the potential of various foreign markets and to combine corporate resources for full exploitation. Nor are experts employed who are capable of realizing such foreign market potential, nor specialists capable of facilitating product movement into such markets (such as documenters, linguists, freight forwarders, customs expeditors, credit and insurance negotiators, foreign exchange transactors).

Type B (Export-Oriented)

In part out of realization of this deficiency, the firm may move to type B, in which case authority for foreign market development is centralized in corporate headquarters within a foreign or export department. (An intermediate step may be the employment of an independent export managing firm; see Section 2.5). The ease with which this move may be made is very largely a function of the perceived relative profitability of the foreign business by top corporate management. That is, if profits derived from foreign sales are greater than average, the attention of the chief executive is attracted. The export or foreign department is likely to appear first as a staff office, but subsequently gains more and more line authority in respect to overseas activities, thereby causing friction with the operating divisions. Also, the foreign department may have difficulty inducing the product divisions to fill export orders promptly or at all. Meanwhile, sooner or later, top management will perceive that a better entry strategy in respect to one or more foreign markets is through licensing, contract, manufacturing, or direct investment, not exports. A decision-making process that is not functionally biased (in favor of exporting as against contracting or direct investment) requires individuals whose careers do not rest on a record of successful exporting and who have some knowledge of production, as well as of sales in the foreign context. These sources of friction, plus the need for line control over foreign operations by qualified people, push a firm to introduce a type C structure, the characteristic hallmark of which is the international division.

Type C (International)

Ideally, an international division[6] should be so organized and staffed to facilitate a functionally and geographically bias-free search for the most profitable opportunities abroad, whether via exporting, importing, licensing, selling technical assistance or managerial services, contract manufacturing, investing in a manufacturing subsidiary or joint venture, or providing debt capital. It should also have the capacity to recruit corporate resources to take advantage of perceived opportunities, to start up operations overseas, and to control overseas operations. In each function, specialized skills are required in such areas as negotiation, law, finance, marketing, personnel,

---

[6]Whether an international division is set up as a domestic incorporated subsidiary is irrelevant to our discussion unless one assumes that managers are fooled by the "legal illusion" that the "international corporation" has greater prestige and, hence, command over corporate resources. Somehow, setting up a separate corporation seems to insulate what is initially a relatively weak division from the internal politics of the corporation. It may be given its own capital and be permitted to reinvest earnings without referral to the corporate investment center. Separate corporate identity may give greater autonomy, facilitate overseas expansion, and provide a better arm's length relationship. Technically, all of this could be achieved, of course, with a division setup, without separate incorporation.

accounting, R&D, and the firm needs line management with *manufacturing* competence. Note that virtually all the *technical* skills required for establishing and maintaining a manufacturing facility are likely to be found in the domestic divisions, and embodied in people with little or no foreign experience and typically with an exaggerated notion of the superiority of their own nationality, national business system, and technical competency.

As the foreign part of a firm's business achieves a significant percentage of the total, certain frictions are likely to develop within the firm. The international division may find it difficult to attract competent operating personnel from the domestic manufacturing divisions, to induce corporate staff departments to develop the relevant expertise and interest (say, in international legal and financial matters), or to stimulate R&D in reference to products and processes so as to be more responsive to differing market environments. The domestic divisions may assign their least competent, most expendable personnel to overseas projects. If a division manager is being evaluated on the division's profit and loss, why should he or she do otherwise unless participation in the overseas project somehow contributes to division profit?

This last consideration has on occasion induced a system of interdepartmental administrative credit memos. The international division might negotiate with a domestic division for certain technical assistance and personnel, say for plant construction, startup, and training of foreign personnel. For such assistance, the domestic division may be awarded a contract (e.g., with a minimum fee plus a percentage of the gross sales of the foreign activity and/or a participation in net earnings). But, over time, such a system can create an onerous and costly international accounting problem. Also, profit expectations may not be realized (indeed, a particular operation may not be seen as a profit center at all later on). In any event, the R&D and staff problems remain, as well as those inherent in the ethnocentric attitude of many of the managers and technicians. The result is that there is a demonstrable tendency for an international division eventually to start building up its own staff. It can do so more easily, of course, if it is physically separated from corporate headquarters.

The type C structure thus tends to create divided loyalties (international versus domestic) and to isolate virtually all interest and expertise in foreign operations within the international division. Even in the formation of the international division, those with special knowledge or interest in international business were probably pulled out of corporate headquarters and the operating divisions. The upshot is that overseas projects are likely not to be given the same attention as comparable domestic projects by the corporate staff or those on the strategic decision-making level. And risk attached to overseas projects tends to be exaggerated. All of these problems are compounded if the international division is located physically apart from corporate headquarters. The influence of the internationally oriented managers on the rest of the firm may be reduced if their division is isolated from headquarters.

Characteristically, a type C firm initially tends to expand its overseas operations rapidly. If the international division is relatively isolated from corporate headquarters, and if it is perceived by top management as a distinct organization, a discontinuity in decision making may appear, which facilitates this rapid growth. A capital budget may be established for the division, which means that so long as it does not attempt to capture *more* corporate resources, decisions relative to overseas expansion can be made very largely on the division level. And for a time, there may be an understanding that the division earnings can be retained for investment. Given this new willingness to commit resources through a wider band of strategies to develop important overseas markets, the firm is very likely to enjoy a sudden spurt in overseas business. Pressure for expansion, plus division management's desire to prove itself (a desire restrained by a lack of foreign environmental expertness in the division) may well lead to a willingness to enter into joint ventures and contractual arrangements.[7]

At this point, there is little awareness of the possible advantages to setting up integrated production and marketing systems regionally or globally. Indeed, the company has usually not developed foreign markets sufficiently at this point to make integration across borders an attractive proposition. Hence, there is little pressure for centralized control except over purely technical and financial matters.

However, as the system builds, as market penetration goes deeper, and as foreign environmental expertise builds up in division headquarters (i.e., control capability), control over production and marketing is very likely to become more centralized. A corollary is that an increasing number of domestic nationals are dispatched abroad to manage foreign manufacturing and marketing subsidiaries. And an effort begins to buy up any local equity held in the corporation's far-flung enterprises, so that the newly centralized control can be exercised with less resistance from joint venture partners or minority stockholders. The advantages in exercising some flexibility in transfer pricing become apparent, which provides further reason to avoid joint venturing wherever possible. (The movement of profit by means other than dividends is awkward if one has local partners.) We now have what might be dubbed "the mature international corporation," one that is ripe for evolution into the multinational phase.

Until that move is made, however, a distinction remains. Decisions relating to the allocation of corporate resources overseas continue to be made largely in the international division. If it wants to grow at a rate faster than retained earnings permit, the division faces a challenge from internal corporate politics. Its demand for a greater allocation of the corporate pie is likely to face the opposition of equally ambitious domestic division managers, who probably outscore the international division management in numbers and seniority within the corporation.

---

[7]It has been suggested that the relatively high propensity for joint venturing on the part of Japanese firms is due at least in part to the fact that relatively more Japanese firms investing abroad are *new* international corporations than is true of U.S. and European firms investing abroad.

The international division is possibly appropriate if (1) sales outside the United States remain a small part of the total corporate sales (and are significantly less than sales of the largest domestic divisions), (2) the firm has activities in a very limited number of countries, (3) there are few internationally experienced executives within the firm, (4) the firm has few product lines, and (5) the products are of such a nature that the environmental influences on sales and production strategy vary little if at all from one national market to another. The last is likely to be more true of capital intensive, technologically complex products sold to sophisticated markets.

If any one of these conditions fails to be satisfied, pressures are very likely to develop within the firm, pushing it toward the mutlinational form, or type D structure. Over time, as foreign markets continue to grow, one or more of these conditions will, in most cases, fail to be satisfied. The level of foreign sales, if it is roughly equal to those of one of the larger domestic divisions, may be the critical level psychologically in bringing about a change in corporate structure. It will then be perceived by top corporate management that the international division lacks the leverage within the corporation to capture adequate corporate resources to service the expanding foreign market opportunities.

It may be, however, that at least two variables of significance intervene between a firm's perception that its market is internationalizing and its structural response; specifically, the levels of the technologies and cultures involved. If one is dealing with a relatively static technology in relatively advanced societies, the firm may drop the international division structure more slowly in favor of some form of global management than if it were involved with a more dynamic technology in less-developed countries. In the latter case, an international division would probably be unable to compete effectively for corporate skillls in exploiting the rapidly changing technology internationally, nor would it be able to exert sufficient pressure to effect environmentally inspired product and process changes.

In any event, the ease with which the transformation from international to multinational can be made obviously varies enormously. Great size, an existing *regional* organization, a strong corporate headquarters, and personal interest and expertness in key places obviously facilitate matters greatly.

Type D (Multinational)

In the case of the regionally organized multinational, it would be useful to know more about where firms tend to site their regional headquarters, the reasons for the choice, and the magnitude of the benefits flowing to the host country. Brussels is a common choice for the European headquarters of U.S.-based multinationals, in part because of the need to interface with the European Community bureaucracy. Many U.S. multinationals have located their Latin American headquarters in Coral Gables, Florida, in part because of the ease of communicating with Central and South America from that point. One suspects that as a group of corporate regional headquarters becomes situated in a particular site, for whatever reason, others are attracted. And of course, the greater the number, the more pressure can be exerted on telecommunications and airline companies to improve service. Elsewhere the pattern is not so recognizable. In Southeast Asia, a number of countries are competing for corporate regional headquarters by offering relief from certain taxes and work permit requirements for foreign personnel. The Philippines and Malaysia have offered special facilities. In France, there is a special official at the Finance Ministry charged with attracting foreign headquarters. Brochures promoting the selection of France as the site for European regional headquarters have been circulated, and residence permits for headquarters' employees have been expedited.

Some MNCs have moved their regional executives into corporate headquarters. The reasons given: need to improve communication between regional staff and upper corporate management at headquarters; the realization that, technically, intraregional communication is no better than that between the parent country and the region; plus the need to reduce cost. One cannot help but speculate that the physical presence of foreign regional management in the U.S. headquarters facilitates the upward mobility of foreign managers into top corporate management, thereby facilitating the transformation of the corporation into a transnational.

As was the case of the international corporation before it, the multinational corporation has built into it the seeds of its own destruction. It is not in equilibrium either with itself or with the environment. Point one: although corporate personnel are given multinational responsibilities, characteristically, few have had international experience and relevant technical-professional training. Point two: being members of a corporate headquarters peopled almost entirely with fellow nationals, the executives with new global responsibilities possess a set of values and a world perception that is very likely to bias their decision making. Although they may possess a *willingness* to allocate corporate resources optimally on a global basis, in fact, they are *psychologically* and *legally* incapable of doing so. The legal inability arises because a multinational is a creature of national law and its decision makers are obliged to observe that law (e.g., tax, antitrust, export licensing, foreign exchange control personnel, etc.) Point three: given the unavailability of headquarters personnel equipped to operate effectively overseas, and the lower cost of employing *local* national managers abroad rather than home country expatriates, plus the rapid rate of expansion often characteristic of the multinational stage, the firm mostly employs local nationals to manage its new foreign facilities. It may also continue to enter into a number of joint ventures, which may be legally required in the LDCs. Hence, headquarters may lack the capacity to maintain really effective central control. It depends upon how "mature" the international division had become prior to the company's transformation into a multinational.

Although perhaps initially inclined for these reasons to grant substantial autonomy to their associated foreign firms, the multinationals, as they mature and gain international experience at the center, eventually begin to accelerate the centralization process. The benefits to be derived from integrating the worldwide movement of corporate resources become increasingly apparent as the contribution to corporate profits from overseas activity mounts and as the skill to effect such integration appears in corporate headquarters. MNCs then begin to try to capture control at the center and to buy up whatever partially owned affiliates remain.

This process is very likely to generate powerful internal conflicts. On the one hand, we have competent and now experienced local national managers moving upward toward the promotion ceilings of their respective national subsidiaries. On the other hand is the fact of increasingly centralized control within corporate headquarters. Local managers may respond by pushing for greater autonomy of their own operations, which is often signaled by a breakdown in communication between subsidiary and headquarters, an exaggerated importance given to environmental factors in subsidiary decision making, and continued inability of the firm to maintain effective control. Or the local manager may simply leave the employ of the firm. Host governments tend to support the local manager's desire for greater autonomy, for increased external control, implicit in centralization, over the allocation of domestic resources sooner or later becomes politically unacceptable. The local environmental factor (i.e., social, political, economic concerns) does in fact become blown up; so, likewise, the loss of key manpower.

Eventually, the multinational headquarters may perceive the cost inherent in the communications breakdown, loss of control, mounting political pressures, and possible loss of key foreign managerial personnel. As it does so, nationality barriers are removed, and foreign nationals are likely to begin appearing in responsible managerial spots outside their respective national subsidiaries, first in regional headquarters if there are such, then in corporate headquarters itself.

Type E (Transnational)

This is where the European and American model begins to diverge from the Japanese. It is almost inconceivable that non-Japanese managers could work effectively at high levels within the corporate headquarters of a Japanese corporation, particularly when one considers the system of permanent employment and relatively permanent work groups still characteristic of large Japanese corporations. How can the non-Japanese manager be thrust into such a situation horizontally and be expected to relate effectively? Commenting somewhat along the same line, the Chairman of the Investment Bank of Zurich observed:

European communities have long . . . understood the importance and efficiency of having on their boards nationals of the countries where they export, or manufacture for that matter. U.S. companies were completely closed to non-U.S. board members until some years ago, but they now have

begun to open up. But Japanese corporations seem to stay very reluctant [to participate] in that evolution.[8]

Returning to our non-Japanese model, you should note that several forces combine over time to multinationalize the *ownership* of the multinational corporation. Among these are the attraction of swapping parent company stock for foreign assets, the foreign sale of debentures convertible to parent company stock, and the listing of parent company stock on foreign stock exchanges. For the European-based multinationals, the relatively small size of the local capital market pushes in the direction of multinational ownership, including the appeal of cross-border mergers and/or repeated joint venturing among multinationals. As already noted, several European transnationals have appeared, although national corporate law makes the true merger difficult. There have been, however, several thousand "common undertakings" by European firms of different nationalities which, over time, look very much like transnational enterprises. One also suspects that repeated participation in transnational ventures of a temporary nature could lead to more permanent association.

Both in the more- and less-developed countries, a firm may be compelled to recognize host society demands—often translated into political pressures—for a share in the profit derived from its market. It is even conceivable that an LDC government, rather than compelling the spinoff of ownership in the local subsidiary, might opt to trade MNC access to local market and resources in return for parent company stock of equivalent value, plus some sort of representation at the top level of the corporation. Although not yet actually proposed, the idea has been discussed among some LDC decision makers.

The degree to which corporate ownership has in fact been multinationalized is an inadequately researched subject for which we have no empirically based trend line. However, the impression of knowledgeable observers in Europe, Japan, and the United States is that the ownership of locally based corporations has become increasingly multinational. Many firms are undoubtedly now in this transitional state between the multinational firm and the truly transnational firm. The latter is simply a corporation that has lost its national identity except insofar as legal restraints may shape its decisions and operations. It is owned and managed by the nationals of more than one country. It is possibly true that in the long run a necessary, if not sufficient, condition for maximum corporate growth is multinational ownership and management at all levels. Thus, the transnational corporations may eventually grow more rapidly than the multinational.

Transnationals with annual gross sales of upward of $50 billion may become relatively common. Some pundits predict that there will soon be a few hundred such corporations controlling a very large part of the fixed industrial assets of the free world. But will they? Their sheer size, and the

---

[8]*The Japan Economic Journal*, No. 583 (February 26, 1974), p. 4.

absence of all national loyalty inherent in their multinational ownership and management, may bring such corporations into a collision course with the nation-state. Indeed, there is considerable evidence that even though governments may be promoting or permitting *national* mergers and industrial concentrations, increasingly they are resisting mergers and arrangements among the giant multinationals and transnationals. As noted elsewhere, it is U.S. antitrust policy to prevent mergers, wherever they take place or whatever the nationality of the merging companies, if the effect of the merger would be to reduce competition significantly within the United States or within the foreign trade of the United States. The European community seems to be setting precedent in barring the further acquisition of important national companies by large multinationals or transnationals. The Japanese have been restrictive in this regard for some time, and one sees no reason why they should shift direction.

To achieve effective political control of giant multinational and transnational firms requires new international institutions, particularly in regard to the dedomiciled multinationals and transnationals because of their even greater growth potential and absence of national loyalty or bias. No national government, or even an international regional agency such as the European Community, can claim the right to determine the law under which a multinationally owned and multinationally managed corporation, with resources strewn around the world, should operate. This rationale will be particularly relevant to corporations operating beyond the reach of any national sovereignty—on the deep ocean bed, in arctic regions, and in space. In the final analysis, what one faces is the management of global resources.

Type F (Supranational)

Therefore, the next stage in the evolutionary process may be the appearance of the *supranational* firm. The existence of such entities necessarily rests on special intergovernmental agreements or treaties, which in each case provide the legal basis for a governing body. One can expect two further developments in the near term: (1) the emergence of a European corporation chartered and controlled—if not taxed—under European Community law, and (2) the appearance of an international seabed authority, which would charter, control, and possibly tax corporations operating on the bed of the deep sea. Various proposals have been made for a *general* international convention, under which some sort of commission would be created for the chartering, controlling, and taxing of corporations satisfying certain conditions in respect to multinationality of ownership and management, but this seems far off.

For the very large firms, continued rapid growth is obviously a short-run phenomenon. Their growth rate cannot long exceed that of the world's economy. Once their limit has approached, it will not be the large firms that will be growing, but the smaller ones. It is entirely possible that many of the super-firms of the near future will break up because they will be unable to attract resources, particularly skilled people. A relatively slow growing organization may be less appealing to many.

In the meantime, the very size of these multinationals and transnationals is likely to be viewed by nation-states as politically intolerable. The degree to which economic power may become concentrated in the hands of decision makers virtually unreachable by any government could render it impossible for any single nation-state, or even regional group, to regulate these firms. The common interest of nation-states almost compels them to participate in an effort to harmonize national policy in regard to antitrust, taxation, corporate law, and restraint on resource allocation.

The common interest becomes irresistibly compelling if one adds the mounting pressure to internationalize political decision making as we approach the finite limits of our global environment. Obviously, the rate of resource usage, energy consumption, and atmospheric and oceanic pollution can only be regulated effectively on a global basis. Finally, there is no evidence leading one to believe that the giant multinational or transnational corporation will voluntarily incorporate any mechanism rendering it socially responsible other than through the marketplace, which, even within the United States, is perceived as inadequate in respect to the protection of consumer, investor, worker, and the general welfare. It would appear that either the nation-states in concert will dominate the giant multinationals and transnationals or the reverse will occur. Bear in mind that the former implies an international convention creating a body of basic law and a representative body with adequate resources to control these corporations. International corporate law might specify, for example, that national shareholders will be represented in the corporate board by a government appointee approved by those shareholders. Given such a system of international law and control, the possibility of a truly supranational corporation appears.

If nations find it impossible to collaborate to this degree, they are very likely to act to restrain further transnational corporate growth, first by forbidding further mergers and acquisitions, and, if this is seen as an inadequate impediment to further growth, then by expropriating local assets. Most vulnerable, of course, would be integrated plants in mature industries that serve primarily the local market and that belong to transnational corporations in which there is little or no local equity involvement.

Multinational Associations

Or it may just be that the pattern apparently emerging in Japan and elsewhere, for some of the reasons already suggested, will prove so profitable that the large multinationals and transnationals based in North America and Western Europe will be induced to change their structure. What seems to be developing in Japan is the **multinational association,** one form of which is the general trading company (see Figure 9.7). At the center is a Japanese-owned and managed corporation, which is linked internationally by a web of contractual relations with largely locally owned and managed associated firms. The center supplies capital intensive, scarce resources, such as new technology (R&D, plus the training of local nationals), management and managerial training, international marketing services, purchase and sale contracts, debt capital, and possibly initial high-risk (entrepreneurial) equity that is later withdrawn. The associated, eventually largely locally owned and managed, firms produce goods for trade. Such an association becomes transnational if the central corporation is owned by the associated foreign firms.

Many pressures combine to push multinationals to evolve more in the direction of the multinational association than into transnationals. First, managements are learning—in part through experience in East-West trade, which is necessarily limited to contract in most cases—that the sale or lease of capital-intensive inputs (particularly technology and high-level skills) can be very lucrative, often more so than the return on direct investment. No only may the rate of return on committed corporate assets be heightened but the risk of costly adverse political acts may be significantly reduced. The corporation has few fixed assets in place subject to expropriation or restricted use. In most cases, payment for services provided under contract parallels the delivery of those services. Hence, the corporation has greater flexibility; it can walk away from an unpleasant (costly) situation more easily than if it had fixed assets in place for which it hoped to earn a return through dividends spread over several years. Second, experience shows that most host countries under balance-of-payments pressure are inclined to make foreign exchange available for the payment of fees, royalties, imported goods, and interest before permitting the remittance of earnings in the form of dividends. The host country can easily perceive the quid pro quo in the sale or lease of a particular item or service for a specified price. It can see the value of that for which payment is made. Not so in the case of a dividend, particularly if the investment has been in place for any period of time. Increasingly, the host country may see those remittances as representing "unearned" foreign profit derived from the local market, local labor, locally available technology (transferred technology), and local capital (reinvested earnings). Under exchange pressure, dividends are invariably the first to suffer.

Third, the contract route also permits a systematic periodic renegotiation as the benefit/cost ratios shift, which, for instance, would be signalled when another firm is prepared to provide comparable inputs at less cost. Increasingly, LDCs are unwilling to accept alien ownership of a local enterprise without a specific date for withdrawal of that ownership. Hence, even ownership is taking on the coloration of a contractual relationship. Fourth, these reasons, plus the apparently growing attraction of public sector enterprises, profit-sharing enterprises, and management-sharing (self-managed) enterprises, suggest that this pattern of governance may indeed be the wave of the future, that the multinational and transnational corporation as presently conceived will prove to be relatively short-lived transitional forms. The point is that the degree of international integration, hence centralized control, required for multinationals and transnationals may become unrealistic in view of mounting pressures for *local* control.[9]

Briefly, management of an integrated international *marketing* system may prove to be the most profitable and least risky form of international business. In fact, there is some evidence that it is the most rapidly growing. Although figures in this area are slippery, it appears that the average growth of multinationals and transnationals is in the range of 10 to 15 percent, and of the large general trading companies, 20 to 30 percent. A more refined monitoring of the rates of growth of various types of international business activity is needed as a guide to the future.

One is thus driven to the conclusion that either a mechanism is created for providing international political control over the giant transnational firms, which would constitute an important next step in the long road to effective world government, or the Japanese model of multinational associations is very likely to dominate. As these associations become transnational in nature, at which point the Japanese may find themselves at a disadvantage, the need for some form of international political control will again arise. Such control is also dictated by the environmental problem and the global resource allocation process it implies. So, following either route, the pressure of world business is likely one day to force the nation-states into a posture of cooperation thus far unknown.

To summarize, the control of corporations differentiates them into six types:

1. In type A (domestic) firms, no particular interest or expertise is engaged in searching for and developing foreign markets. Decision making is prejudiced against any commitment to overseas activity and is responsive only to external pressures, not to an internally generated search process.

2. In type B (export-oriented) firms, international interest and expertise are limited to a staff department and are restricted to searching for and developing *export markets only*. Operating decisions are made in the domestic divisions and domestically oriented staff departments. Hence, such decisions have strong *national bias*.

---

[9]Another point should be made. As trade liberalization moves forward, international economic integration accelerates. As this happens, the need to move national resources constantly into new sectors and uses requires state leadership and influence (if not control) over the flow of internal resources. Unless the state itself moves into production, state intervention means ever closer government-business relations, including government-backed guarantee of continuous employment for displaced workers. One thus moves in the direction of the corporate state, which implies greater emphasis on public control and enhances pressure for *local* control.

3.   In type C (international) firms, interest and relevant skill are in an international division, but with functional expertise remaining in the domestic divisions and domestically oriented staff departments. Decisions are less biased in terms of the type of foreign market entry strategy that will be considered, but are still heavily biased nationally. Initially, the capacity to exercise centralized control over foreign operations is weak and the pressure to grow rapidly, high. Hence, a joint venturing and contracting strategy may be adopted. But in time, pressure toward increased control and centralization emerge, and key positions overseas are filled with home-country nationals.

4.   In type D (multinational) firms, international interest and expertise are located throughout the firm, but most top corporate managers are still home-country nationals and initially lack international experience and skill. There is, nonetheless, an effort to make decisions less nationally biased, but an inability to effect a true centralization of control persists in headquarters, particularly if local equity participation continues to be permitted. As the firm grows overseas, political pressures develop to compel greater local control and, hence, subsidiary autonomy. In the meantime, as the firm gathers more environmental expertise in headquarters and perceives more clearly the advantages of greater integration, it will attempt to reestablish central control over its foreign operations, including the buying-up of local equity. Conflict with host governments tends to increase.

5.   In type E (transnational) firms, which are owned and managed multinationally, decision making is centralized, but free of national bias except as legally imposed. The firm loses loyalty to a single nation, thereby putting it on a collision course with its parent government.

6.   In type F (supranational) firms, management is free structurally, psychologically, and legally to allocate resources on a global basis in conformance with corporate goals insofar as they do not conflict with the international political regime controlling the corporation.

The point is made that if a firm's foreign market is perceived as growing relative to the domestic, all six corporate types are unstable except the last. Pressures in the system either propel a firm to the next level or push it back. An alternative to the supranational corporation, if the legal basis fails to materialize, might be the multinational or transnational association. If the center is owned and managed multinationally, it is thereby differentiated from a multinational association and becomes transnational.

Howard V. Perlmutter's three-type classification system, with some modification, identifies the characteristic behavior of the international, multinational, and *transitional* multinational firm (see Table 9.2). A shortcoming is that it does not describe a dynamic system—in that it does not specify the pressures pushing a firm from one orientation to another—nor does it go far enough. It fails to specify the distinctive orientation of the truly transnational and supranational firms. Neither does it refer to the interrelationship between orientation and structure, nor to the interrelationship between these two aspects and the priority of control centers.

9.3   Internal Structure

As already noted, whatever the type of corporation, a division, a "group," or a "headquarters" may be identified with a product line, a function (sales, production, finance), a region, a process (for example, exploration, refining, concentrating, smelting, shipping), or a class of customer (government or an industry). Coordination within a large organization may be necessary along more than one of these dimensions. For a firm expanding internationally a very real question is, which one of these linkages should be given priority and represent the primary chain of command? Which are the staff lines? Different line authority may be delegated along different dimensions, which brings one to the subject of the matrix (or grid) organization. Forgetting the customer and process-based organizational structures (which are unusual), the possible combinations are shown in Figure 9.9. Figure 9.10 shows a two-dimensional matrix management.

In U.S.-based firms, one is more likely to find the product divisions preeminent and portrayed in the vertical position; the functional, in the horizontal. Functional divisions are most frequently called "coordinating committees" or "groups." European firms are more likely to give priority to the functional division or possibly to make both the product and functional divisions vertical. The foreign trade organizations of Soviet bloc countries are almost invariably organized on a product-line basis.

The three-dimensional matrix management can be diagrammed most easily as in Figure 9.11. We assume the APF variety, which is possibly the most common for the big U.S.-based multinationals.

The obvious next question is, under what circumstances should a firm with international operations opt for one form or another, say for a PAF, an APF, or an FAP? Which are apparently the most common? Key questions

Table 9.2
Three Types of Headquarters Orientation toward Subsidiaries in an International Enterprise— the Perlmutter Model Adapted

Organization Design	Ethnocentric (international)	Polycentric (multinational)	Geocentric (transnational multinational)
Complexity of organization	Complex in home country, simple in subsidiaries	Varied and independent	Increasingly complex and interdependent
Authority: decision making	High in headquarters	Relatively low in headquarters	Aim for a collaborative approach between headquarters and subsidiaries
Evaluation and control	Home standards applied for persons and performance	Determined locally	Find standards that are universal and local
Rewards and punishments; incentives	High in headquarters, low in subsidiaries	Wide variation; can be high or low rewards for subsidiary performance	International and local executives rewarded for reaching local and worldwide objectives
Communication; information flow	High volume to subsidiaries of orders, commands, advice	Little to and from headquarters. Little between subsidiaries	Both ways and between subsidiaries. Heads of subsidiaries part of management team
Identification	Nationality of owner	Nationality of host country	Truly international company but identifying with national interests[a]
Perpetuation (recruiting, staffing, development)	Recruit and develop people of home country for key positions everywhere in the world	Develop people of local nationality for key positions in their own country	Develop best people everywhere in the world for key positions everywhere in the world

[a]If this term were to read "truly international company not identifying with the interest of any single nation except as legally imposed," then this column would describe the orientation of the true transnational firm.

Source: Adapted from Howard V. Perlmutter, "The Tortuous Evolution of the Multinational Corporation," *Columbia Journal of World Business* (January–February 1969), p. 12.

Figure 9.9
Possible Types of Matrix Management

First Level	Product P		Area A		Function F	
Second Level	Function PF	Area PA	Function AF	Product AP	Product FP	Area FA
Third Level	Area PFA	Function PAF	Product AFP	Function APF	Area FPA	Product FAP

Figure 9.10
A Two-Dimensional Matrix Management of the PF Type

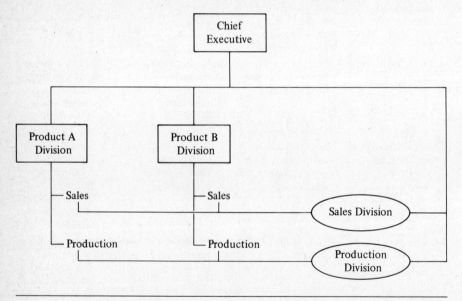

here have to do with specifying the most important similarities and dissimilarities.

Is each differentiated region essentially homogeneous in respect to functions and products, and is it significantly different from other regions along one or more important dimensions? If so, a regional structure is suggested.

Probable[10] firm characteristics: Those with products or manufacturing processes significantly influenced by environmental factors (such as taste,

---

[10]The term "probable" is used here for, so far as I can ascertain, this subject has not been researched in any systematic way.

Figure 9.11
A Three-Dimensional Matrix Management of the APF Type

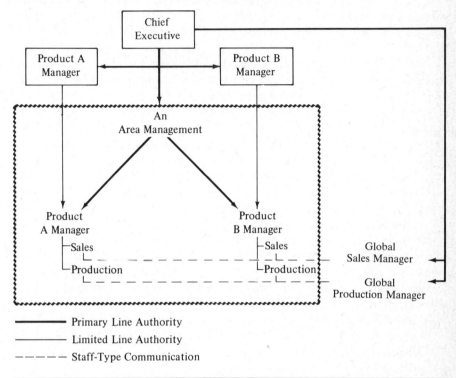

- ———————— Primary Line Authority
- —————— Limited Line Authority
- ————— Staff-Type Communication

law, factor mix, access, internal movement, politics, income, population size) that differ markedly from one definable region to another (definable in such terms as access and internal market integration, trade and investment impediments, homogeneity in taste and factor mix, relevant law, political pressures). This tends to be true generally for low-technology, mature, consumer-oriented products not closely related to one another and in respect to which political pressure for local control is likely to develop. Another probable characteristic is substantial economy of scale in production (meaning that plants will be large and that intraregional sales of component parts and final products are significant). Large-scale interregional sales or resource transfers are unlikely because of the environmental influence. **Does each differentiated product line possess essentially the same characteristics insofar as function and region are concerned, but remain significantly different from other product lines? If so, the product division approach is suggested.**

Probable firm characteristics: Those with products or manufacturing processes relatively little influenced by socioeconomic environmental factors (a standard product using a single technology with little factor substitutability possible, as in parts of the chemical industry) or influenced by factors not differing *consistently* from one definable region to another. This tends to be true for firms with several relatively high technologies, with new, capital intensive products that are not closely related. (Hence, interdivisional transactions will be few, but movement of a given product among regions will be great. Also, servicing on a regional or global basis—rather than on a national one—is probably most economic.)

Is each differentiated function essentially similar for different products and geographical areas? If so, a functional structure is suggested.

Probable firm characteristics: Those with a single or a few closely related products manufactured in the same plants, sold through similar channels to similar customers regardless of geographical area. Thus, environmental factors are minimal in respect to both product and manufacturing process, but may impact significantly on function.

Understandably, firms move slowly in relinquishing the time-honored notion of unity of command in favor of shared responsibility. But there are many pressures that may push a management in this direction. Different product lines may share common facilities in smaller national markets, but not in others. In different regions, similar problems appear; what happens in Country A may serve as a guide to the firm in Country B (three obvious examples: investment entry contracts, labor negotiations, a firm's political involvement). Also, functions may vary widely from product to product in some countries, not at all in others.

As a firm develops a full matrix management, the demands on the individual manager increase. He or she must now respond to different reporting requirements and act more as an integrator. Even greater training, maturity, and experience may be required.

Host-government pressures tend to push a corporation with multiple entities within a country to establish a national management for purposes of interfacing with the government. If such a headquarters is not in place, the government may face a number of relatively small enterprises; it has no ready way of communicating effectively with corporate headquarters. Research in Canada indicates that U.S. conglomerates with multiple and unrelated operations in Canada have tended to be less sensitive to Canadian national interests.[11] Figure 9.12 portrays a viable solution. In fact, it is now clear that at least some governments will hold all of the local subsidiaries of a single foreign parent collectively responsible for liabilities of any one of them (e.g., Brazil).

A similar situation arises whenever two or more countries enter into a continuing economic or political relationship such as a free trade area or common market. For a variety of reasons it may be highly desirable to have a regional headquarters to interface with the new regional institutions as lobbyist, negotiator, and as transmitter of information to corporate headquarters. It may also become virtually mandatory that the firm rationalize

---

[11]A. J. Litvak, C. J. Maule, and R. D. Robinson, *Dual Loyalty-Canadian/U.S. Business Arrangements* (Toronto: McGraw-Hill Co. of Canada, Ltd., 1971.

Figure 9.12
The National Headquarters Concept

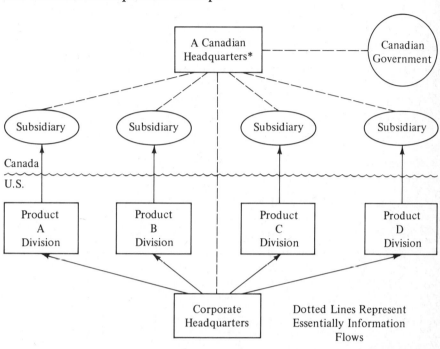

*Is not necessarily an incorporated operating entity.

production and other functions on a regional basis to take advantage of special regional arrangements, such as specialization agreements, complimentarity agreements, special financial institutions whose resources are available only to regionally oriented projects, and intraregional tariffs and other concessions.

9.4 Corporate Planning

Appropriate decision making in the control area is unlikely unless corporate goals have been spelled out and communicated, and a continuing planning process institutionalized to make the goals operational.

On the international level, this process is peculiarly difficult and time-consuming. Reasonable plans of affiliated foreign units depend upon special environmental factors facing each, plus the special interests of foreign partners (if any), local managers, local labor, and host governments. In addition, all the problems inherent in international and intercultural communication are present. It would appear that few companies with far-flung international operations do a really good job of planning. For many, it seems almost impossible. Some of the most frequently mentioned international planning problems are:

1. Inability to gain top-level support in the parent corporation for articulating and communicating corporate goals.
2. Lack of strategic integration of plans and operations between the domestic and international and among various international subunits.
3. Difficulty in gaining a personal commitment to planning at all management levels, at home and abroad.
4. Inability to provide an adequate and cost-effective information flow— including that relating to contingencies, such as inaccurate projection of sales or costs.[12]

In regard to the last point, a colleague of mine has classified defects of information into six categories:

1. *Persuasiveness*, that is, the degree to which information is perceived as "hard" as opposed to "soft," or tangible versus intangible. (Greater weight tends to be given to a hard fact, even though it may represent— or misrepresent—soft underlying data, or the soft information may be more important.)
2. *Delay*, which in some cases may be necessary—as in the perception of quality. (Delay may cause distortion because of inadequate recall of an event.)
3. *Distortion*, an example of which is the result of averaging or smoothing. (Important data may be hidden.)
4. *Bias*, which is reading information with a steady offset.
5. *Error*, which is reading information with a random offset. (It may well be the least important information defect.)
6. *Cross-talk*, which occurs when two information sources avoid the real problem. (An example would be responding to poor design by saying that the price was too high.)[13]

All of these defects probably tend to be exaggerated when one is interpreting information moving across national and cultural frontiers. The sophisticated international communicator is well aware of those defects and explicitly guards against them to the extent possible.

It seems obvious that commitment to long-run planning requires an incentive scheme built on something more than short-term performance. It also demands a personal identification with the fulfillment of overall corporate goals, rather than the purely local. In the absence of incentives consistent with the participation in, and support of, the planning process by affiliate and subsidiary managers—particularly those abroad—the latter may feed in wholly inadequate or misleading information. They may do so quite deliberately. In this manner they can shield themselves to a degree from overly centralized control and loss of subsidiary autonomy. For this

---

[12]Summarized from John S. Schwendiman, *Strategic and Long-Range Planning for the Multinational Corporation* (New York: Praeger, 1973).

[13]Jay W. Forrester, comments in a conference on corporate strategy, Sloan School of Management, MIT, September 2, 1982.

reason, really effective international long-range planning may be limited to the transnational corporations, and may be beyond the capacity of those at the international or multinational stages, *unless there is a very strong corporate culture* to which most managers, domestic and foreign, belong.

If a normative rule can be laid down at all, it is that control should be decentralized to the extent possible within the constraints of perceived managerial ability and the achievement of corporate goals. At the same time, it should be noted that national or even regional managers over time are likely to become emotionally attached to their respective areas. If so, reporting and decision making may become heavily biased, so much so that the firm will find it difficult, for example, to cut its losses and retire from hopeless situations when they develop. At the same time, it is quite clear that centralized control cannot be effective in the absence of both the necessary functional competence and adequate understanding of the environment involved. The final word may be that of Gianluigi Gabetti, former president of Olivetti Underwood: "If a multinational firm is not centralized, at least for control and coordination, all the advantages of its worldwide association are lost.[14]

9.5 Location of Tactical Decision-Making Authority

Operational or tactical decision-making authority may or may not be separated from that authority making strategy choices. The larger the firm, the more compelling separation becomes, particularly in the international case. In the firm driving toward in-depth penetration of foreign markets, the pressure for localizing tactical decision-making authority becomes most compelling due to the myriad of cultural variables relevant to such decisions. It is one thing for an international division or regional or corporate headquarters to specify, for example, that the strategy in regard to choice of channels shall be overseas agencies. It is quite another to ascertain the identity of agents to be used. A management remuneration policy is one thing: how much to pay Mr. X in Brazil is another. So it goes.

Experienced firms operating internationally tend to push all tactical decision-making authority down to the local (national) level unless there is compelling reason for retaining it at divisional, regional, or even corporate level. Some compelling reasons are tax and antitrust considerations, a high degree of integration between different national enterprises (in respect to sales, supply, finance, management), feedback effects (as in labor negotiations and relations with domestic customers), and political implications to which the parent government is sensitive (for example, U.S. trade restrictions with Eastern Europe or Cuba). A word of caution should be entered here. It is not at all clear that the formulation of corporate goals should occur at one corporate level, long-range planning on another, strategy selection on another, and tactical decision making on still another. Corporate headquar-

[14]As reported in *Business Abroad* (September 1969), p. 16.

ters is often in a position, by reason of greater breadth of information and a higher level of technical competence, to assist in tactical decision making, just as local subsidiary managers may be helpful in strategy determination because of their greater environmental knowledge.

9.6   Methods of Communicating Decisions

Possible choices in this area are informal indoctrination (or socialization), formal training, a company journal, conferences, personal visits by deci-sion-making personnel or their representatives, written plans, standard operating procedures, and budgets. Obviously, these choices are not mutually exclusive. To be considered in determining strategy in this regard are such factors as cost, managerial tenure, the number of entities and people involved, and the extent to which decision-making authority is retained by higher headquarters. Some observers here have categorized all of these approaches into *socialization* (the internalization of values and rules of behavior, which may or may not be written down), *bureaucratic administration* (formal rule making), and **centralization** (retention of authority at the center).

Experienced managers offer a few guidelines in the international area.

1. All decisions made by a level higher than that implementing the decision, by whatever means the decision may be communicated initially, should be committed to writing. (Exceptions: those felt to be politically and/or legally vulnerable.) Given the pitfalls of intercultural communication, this rule is more important than in comparable domestic situations.

2. Visits by decision-making authorities or their representatives should be on a regular periodic basis, not occasioned exclusively by crises.

3. Periodic conferences of key personnel of similar function from both domestic and foreign operations are of great utility in developing univer-sally valid strategies and in the delegation of tactical decisions to lower levels.

4. Management training and development assumes greater importance for foreign operations because of the differences in cultural backgrounds, in the meaning of management, in the status of managers, and in the sources from which managers are recruited as one moves from one national society to another. Such training facilitates both the decentralization of decision-making authority and improvement in the quality and effectiveness of those decisions made at higher organizational levels.

5. Periodic rotation of overseas managers to regional or corporate head-quarters may be one of the most effective ways of communicating overall

corporate goals and the rationale for corporate strategy, including the degree of control retained at each level.

9.7   Means of Reporting Performance

Reports of performance should flow in a reverse pattern to decisions. The
more decentralized the latter, the less the volume of the former. To require
unnecessary reports is costly, particularly for those moving across language
barriers, cultural frontiers, and great distances. Every report requirement
should be carefully justified.

The range of possible reports is similar to that of a purely domestic
operation, but certain difficulties arise peculiar to the foreign situation. One
of these is time lag, which may seriously reduce the value of a given report.
For that reason alone the means of reporting may have to be changed.
Essentially, there are seven ways to communicate internationally other than
by travel, all varying considerably in cost; namely, mail, telephone, cable,
telex, leased channel, computer conferencing, and international video conferencing. Which one is best in a specific situation depends on message
frequency, average length, destination, urgency, need for direct interaction,
and ease of personal communication. The various firms engaged in international communications supply analysts to assist individual firms in making
the most cost-effective choices.

Problems peculiar to foreign operations in establishing report strategy
lie in securing reports that contain information that may be properly evaluated, that is, compared with domestic and other national data. Some of the
complicating factors are differential inflation rates, shifting exchange rates,
imprecise statistical services, and different legal and accounting requirements.

9.8   Evaluation of Performance

Possible measures of overseas management performance, as in the domestic
case, include (1) conformance to decisions by higher authority, (2) local
profit, (3) contribution to consolidated profit, (4) rate of return on investment, (5) dollar volume, (6) cash flows, (7) physical volumes, (8) efficiency
(input-output ratios, such as annual added value per employee, or per
man-hour), (9) dollar flows, and (10) market share.

Assume that you are trying to evaluate the performance of operations
located in countries in which price levels are changing at rates different from
those in the parent country, and which are not adequately reflected in shifts
of local currency/foreign exchange rates. In such case, reports of two, three,
four, five, and six above will be exceedingly hard to evaluate; international
comparisons are unlikely to be valid. The point is that, in each case, relevant
factors *not* under the control of local management may be involved. Some of

these factors are government-enforced price controls, control over the re-valuation of assets, limits on depreciation allowances, and exchange rates prevailing at the time at which profits are remitted. You must also consider costs allocated by associated firms (such as the parent company) against the foreign operation (for example, price of materials, foreign wages and other benefits paid on behalf of nonnational personnel, and general overhead charges), the availability of local debt financing, and local currency valuation of foreign source assets. The problem is essentially that of sorting out current profit and loss from liquidation of assets and investment, plus that of isolating the consequences of *local* decisions.

Also subject to national differences, and hence not easily judged on the basis of standard measures, are input-output ratios (where product and process design differ due to market requirements, different relative factor costs, and varying plant sizes), physical volume (for similar reasons), and conformance to decisions by higher authority (because of communications problems, legal obstacles, and behavioral differences).

In evaluating the performance of associated foreign enterprises, many managements look only at *growth* (in terms of physical volume of sales in respect to the total market, such as market share in physical terms) and at *net convertible currency* flow. The latter includes all convertible currency investments, all expenditures made on behalf of the overseas firm (those that would not occur in the absence of the foreign operation) whether by the parent firm or a third-country enterprise, all cash remitted to the parent (dividends, royalties, fees, interest) or otherwise made available, and all income earned by the *parent* firm by reason of the foreign enterprise (such as profits on sales to the latter, remittances by third-country firms by reason of supply from or sales to the firm in question, taxes saved for reinvestment purposes, and profits on purchases from the foreign enterprise).

Any sort of financial control and evaluation system rests on a flow of accounting information, on which basis comparisons are made (either with other operating units, historical results, a budget, or competitors). Obviously, the accounting rules applied can significantly change a corporation's financial reports, which is important to managers, stockholders, and creditors. It should be noted that there are two general methods of translating financial statements from one currency to another, *monetary* and *temporal*. The first refers to a system under which financial items (cash, receivables, payables, loans, and debts) are translated at the year-end foreign exchange rates; all other items, at historic rates (those prevailing at the time of the underlying transaction). The temporal method refers to the translation of all current assets and current liabilities at the year-end foreign exchange rate; the translation of all long-term items at historic rates.

The extensive currency adjustments that took place after 1971 led the U.S. accounting industry, through its Financial Accounting Standards Board (FASB),[15] to set forth rules in respect to the disclosure of the effect of

---

[15]Replaced the Accounting Principles Board in 1972.

foreign currency translation on consolidated or foreign financial statements. These regulations specify the information that listed U.S. companies (i.e., those whose shares are publicly traded) must divulge on their balance sheets and profit and loss statements. These regulations have been changed or augmented several times since, but none have been completely satisfactory.

There are at least two basic problems. The first is to differentiate between net *operating* gains or losses arising from an operation and *capital* gains or losses; that is, to separate operating profit from liquidation of capital, or operating loss from accumulation of capital. The second problem is to translate foreign earnings into the currency used by the parent corporation at an exchange rate that is realistic, even though no international transactions take place—for example, the recording of capital assets, depreciation allowances, or reinvested earnings.

Standard U.S. accounting practice has been for U.S.-based parent firms (1) to state foreign fixed assets at their value when purchased, with perhaps a note specifying estimated current value, (2) to use LIFO (last-in-first-out) inventory accounting (which means that the flow of goods out of inventory should approximate current prices, but total inventory value becomes less realistic), (3) to state *current* assets and liabilities at the current exchange rate, and (4) to show long-term liabilities at the exchange rate on the date incurred (historic rate).

These rules do not solve the problem of multiple exchange rates or the classification of assets and liabilities. For example, is depreciation of fixed assets to be reported on a historic or current basis? In either case, a special replacement allowance or investment fund may be required. Another relevant query: How are costs calculated for a *dollar* profit and loss report? Some firms used a monthly average of exchange rates.

Such accounting difficulties as these render consolidated accounts exceedingly difficult to set up. At best, extensive notes are required. The introduction of the FASB regulations may have standardized the translation problems, and hence consolidation, but the extent to which the resulting reports reflect reality is another matter.

Conceptually, a firm has the choice of either consolidating the financial statements of all of its overseas holdings, only those firms in which it has more than 50 percent ownership, only 100 percent owned subsidiaries, only 100 percent owned subsidiaries in financially stable countries, or none. In the United States, it has been most common to consolidate the statements of all subsidiary holdings (i.e., those owned over 50 percent), with limited exception, but it has not been required (as it is in the United Kingdom, Canada, or Denmark). In fact, a U.S. firm is not permitted to consolidate its interest in a company in which it owns 50 percent or less, even though it exercises effective control. However, the stockholders of the parent company must receive the statements of such unconsolidated subsidiaries, in which case the translation problem remains, even though not that of consolidation.

Responding to pressures for international harmonization, the International Accounting Standards Commission was founded in 1973, its constit-

uency being 18 associations of accountants in 10 countries, including the
American Institute of Certified Public Accountants in the United States, plus
23 associate members in 18 additional countries. Its purpose was to formulate and publish accounting standards and to promote their worldwide
acceptance. In addition, the Commission of the European Community has
been active in trying to effect greater harmony among accounting practices
and laws within the nine member nations. It should be noted that one of the
impacts of the harmonization of financial reporting would be to ease the task
of controlling corporations with global spread. One of the difficulties is that
U.S. accounting practice is irreconcilably different from all others, most of
which use current foreign exchange rates for consolidation purposes and
defer some items in respect to reporting current income. In contrast, the
United States, as noted, accounts for certain items at historical rates, some at
the current rate, but all must be taken into current income.

What we have really been talking about is comparability of financial
statements of companies located in different countries. To the extent that
they are not comparable, these statements cannot be used as the basis for
allocating corporate resources or for evaluating the profit or loss of a particular enterprise against the profit and loss of those located elsewhere. The
many different legal requirements causing variations in accounting principles and practices from country to country often compel a firm to maintain
multiple financial reporting systems.

A firm may thus feel obliged to set up accounting procedures to satisfy
(1) host-country tax authorities; (2) parent-country tax authorities (who may
have different notions as to appropriate transfer prices, overhead allocation,
and depreciation allowances); (3) a banking institution (which may want to
ascertain a corporation's global debt/equity position or return on investment); and (4) internal control requirements. The need for this last arises
because a company's own allocation of cost and profits, rates of depreciation
and obsolescence, changes in reserve funds set up to cover a variety of
contingencies, and the exchange rates used for conversion purposes may
differ from those imposed by host- or parent-country governments. That is,
within the context of the firm, they can produce unrealistic and misleading
results.

9.9   Enforcement of Decisions (Maintenance
of Control)

A control system is purely informational unless sufficient pressure can be
built up to make the operational feedback conform, within a given range, to
that anticipated by the initiators of the inputs—the decision makers. How
does one bring this about when the system operates across international
frontiers? Important restraints on effectiveness in this case include those
provided by the legal structure of the countries involved, national interest as
perceived by political leaders, and the quality of communications. The

problems of good communications were dealt with in Section 5.1 and more briefly in the introduction to this chapter.

Basic methods of enforcement include legal pressure, business pressure, persuasion, and mutual benefit.

Legal pressure can operate only if one has a legal claim through guarantee, contract, financial obligation, or ownership. Even then pressure may not be effective if important political considerations or national sensitivities are involved. (See also Section 7.8). *Business pressure* can be generated provided an affiliated enterprise stands in an important sales, supply, management, or financial position in relation to the parent firm. Importance must be rated in terms of both the criticalness and uniqueness of that input.

If the foreign firm is substantially independent financially (i.e., it generates its own operating funds), is not tied by contract to the parent firm, and is not selling to or buying from the parent, control by the parent management may be exceedingly difficult even though technically it "owns" the foreign firm. The parent firm may be understandably reluctant to compound the problem by installing a management dominated by local nationals. The crucial element here is personal loyalty to the firm, the ability of the parent firm to *persuade* local management to abide by its decisions. Threat will be ineffective.

In the final analysis, persuasion is only effective if the person being persuaded feels it to be in his or her interest to be persuaded. If the parent mangement finds it impossible to frame a decision flowing to a foreign enterprise so as to embody *mutual benefit* in a positive sense, implicit or explicit, then the control structure is threatened with collapse. Something is wrong. *Reported* response may still appear to comply but not actual behavior. To the extent that the foreign enterprise involves the public interest, the mutuality of benefit must likewise encompass the national interests of the host country, as perceived by its authorities, if effective control is to be maintained. In all cases, a relevant query is: How important is the particular type of control the parent firm is trying to retain (important in terms of profit for the parent firm)? International business relations are much more sensitive to unneeded controls than are comparable domestic relations, and they are likely to be more costly.

In the ability to resolve the control problem and strike a mutually acceptable balance may lie the essential quality of good international management. To achieve such balance requires extraordinary flexibility, for each situation is unique, demanding a unique solution. The balance must be a constantly shifting one, as the capability of management and the size and nature of one's business changes—that is, if the cold war between headquarters and the field is to be kept within tolerable limits. Extraordinary sensitivity to the full range of the relevant variables, and the ability to weigh each with some degree of accuracy, is demanded. This capacity is the mark of the effective international manager.

CHAPTER 10

PUBLIC AFFAIRS STRATEGY

advocacy advertising space in publications or airtime bought to argue a point of view on a public issue.

discount rate the rate at which future earnings are discounted so as to provide an equivalent present value, which is normally equal to the interest rate.

high profile active strategy for representing the corporation's views to politicians, other business executives, labor leaders, and consumer groups.

international codes agreements formulated by two or more nations to regulate international corporate behavior.

leverage in the politico-economic context, the extent of a firm's advantage or power in a particular national market and the degree to which it can influence the local environment.

low profile passive strategy for representing the corporation's views.

philanthropy the act of making corporate resources available to activities or groups that do not enter into the production or sales function within the business planning horizon and that are not legally required.

political neutrality for a foreign corporation, nonintervention in local partisan politics except for public statements issued as attempts to influence policies, or other expressions or activities commonly tolerated for a local corporation. Any *covert* activity of a political nature on behalf of another government would be deemed a per se violation of neutrality.

political risk the probability of a political event that will impact on a firm to its disadvantage.

Corporate public affairs has to do with explaining corporate strategy to the corporation's many constituencies—employees, stockholders, creditors, consumers, suppliers, government, the general public. It also attempts to create a more favorable political-social-economic climate and reports the response, present and anticipated, to management. Finally, it presses for appropriate adjustment in corporate strategy so as to render the corporation more harmonious with its many-faceted environment at home and abroad.

Only in the last ten years have corporations generally realized that they are major actors in the formulation of both national and international public policy. As major forces in the allocation of the world's resources, corporations have a responsibility to indicate to the political sector how political decisions are likely to impact upon the national and global allocation system in interaction with ongoing economic and sociopsychological processes. Corporate representation is only now being accepted as a legitimate corporate function, as much so as for labor and other common-interest organizations. Possibly this development has been slower in the United States than in Europe and Japan. A tangible form of this corporate realization is the appearance of new staff departments in the larger corporations, variously known as public affairs, external affairs, government relations, or public policy.

One example is Union Carbide. In 1976, it became one of the first of the large U.S.-based multinationals to establish a corporate office to anticipate and address important social and political issues. In 1980, the company appointed what are called "issue managers" to focus attention on four areas of concern: energy; health, safety, and environment; international trade and investment; and capital formation and tax reform. The issue

managers work with top corporate decision makers and monitor various aspects of the external environment.[1]

Let it be noted that public affairs is quite distinct from the traditional public relations function, which is really part of corporate marketing in that it focuses on improving the corporate image in the eyes of the public (i.e., consumer) in order to enhance the acceptance of the firm's products in the market. Public affairs, in contrast, looks beyond the corporation itself. On one hand, it represents the corporate attempt to influence the social-political-legal (and indirectly, the economic) environment in which the firm operates and works to render the environment more congenial to the realization of corporate objectives, however these may be defined. On the other hand, public affairs is concerned with analyzing the implications of environmental changes for corporate strategy. In short, public affairs has to do with effecting a convergence between corporate strategy, political decision, and social change. At some point, a compromise tolerable to all major actors must be struck that is responsive to on-going social processes.

Public relations and public affairs functions may conflict when the corporation undertakes a public effort to alter some aspect of its environment if that effort is unpopular with a significant number of consumers. A case in point was the intense effort launched by a few U.S. corporations in 1977 to convince Congress not to enact legislation in respect to the Arab boycott,[2] which, it was alleged, would so damage the competitive position of U.S. firms in Arab markets as to virtually deliver those markets to Japanese and European competitors. At the same time, possibly many millions of American consumers were deeply offended by the Arab boycott. Whether they should have been was beside the point; they obviously were. One can argue for the phrase "public affairs" rather than "external affairs" in that among the actors in the nonmarket environment with which the corporation must relate positively are some who are *internal* to the corporation, namely, its stockholders and employees (including managers), not in their immediate economic roles but in their broader, societal roles. Since one can hardly call them external to the corporation, whatever their roles, this text uses the term public affairs, as do many corporations.

In setting public affairs strategy, the corporation faces several basic options.

1.   It can seek a **low profile** (passive strategy) or a **high profile** (active strategy).
2.   It can pursue its strategy alone, in concert with other corporations, or through nonbusiness intermediary institutions.
3.   It can select among a number of vehicles through which to implement public affairs strategy.

---

[1]See "Union Carbide Corporation and the Management of Public Affairs," a case prepared by John F. Mahon, Boston University, Graduate School of Management, 1980.

[2]The boycott imposed by many of the Arab nations against Israeli goods and the products of non-Israeli firms which continued to deal with Israel (the "blacklisted" firms). The boycott also attempted to block entry into Arab markets of firms trading with the blacklisted companies. Subsequent U.S. law prohibited U.S. interests from refusing to do business with blacklisted firms or providing information sought for boycott enforcement purposes.

10.1   Choice of Profile

Many corporations, although possibly a declining number, opt to pursue a neutral, or at least a hidden (covert), strategy in respect to efforts to change their social, political, economic, or legal environments. For example, in the debates preceding the controversial Tax Reform Act of 1976 and the anti-boycott legislation of 1977, few U.S. corporations were willing to take a public position. Apparently, many were so sensitive to the intense criticism in the U.S. of "multinational corporations" generally that they either assumed their overt opposition to the proposed legislation would be counterproductive, or they were intimidated by highly organized public pressure groups. One of the reasons for the antimultinational climate in the United States was undoubtedly the revelations of past covert attempts by certain corporations to alter their political environments overseas, most notably the ITT-CIA scandal in Chile allegedly involving an attempt to overthrow the national government, the United Brands effort to alter a tax law in Honduras by large payments to influential individuals, and the Lockheed effort to influence Japanese government military purchasing through multimillion-dollar "commissions."

One of the characteristics of the U.S. scene is the intense four-way adversary relationship between business, labor, government, and consumer, which some observers believe is building costs into the U.S. economy and thereby rendering U.S. business less competitive in world markets. These costs take many forms, but of overriding importance is the element of uncertainty introduced into business strategy. European and Japanese executives may be concerned about the relatively high fixed costs their more cooperative social and corporate structures imply, plus the alleged reduction in incentive. But GNP growth rates, employment levels, and relative rates of innovation, insofar as they can be measured, seem to indicate a relative loss of U.S. competitiveness. The cost of the cops and robbers game being played out by U.S. politicians, business executives, labor leaders, and consumer groups, all cheered on by the academic community, may prove to be exceedingly costly. It is a demonstrable fact that many corporations are so intimidated that they are unwilling, or unable, to communicate effectively with the political sector or with the public other than through the market. Suffice it to say that a high-profile public affairs strategy is very likely to be counterproductive unless the corporation has credibility with the target audience.

10.2   Choice of Mode

A corporation may choose to pursue a public affairs strategy identified directly with itself, to identify with the collective efforts of other firms, or to operate through nonbusiness intermediaries. Primarily, the choice depends upon the relative credibility of the corporation and the skills it can bring to bear. Lacking credibility, it may gain by joining other firms in whatever the enterprise might be. If business generally lacks credibility, as tends to be the case in the United States and many LDCs, a better strategy may be to support nonbusiness intermediaries that seem to be working toward constructive ends from the corporate point of view. Examples are universities, research institutes, and public media.

Firms operating internationally have only recently begun to fashion collective and representative organizations to research important international trade and investment issues and speak out with some authority and credibility. Among U.S. examples are the Emergency Committee for American Trade (ECAT), a lobby for freer international trade and investment composed of the leaders of 66 of the largest American firms and banks with international interests, and the Trade Action Coordinating Committee (TACC), a forum of about 100 representatives of national associations, law firms, and corporations committed to working for international trade expansion. Of regional concern is the American Association of Chambers of Commerce of Latin America (AACCLA), whose membership represents many billions of dollars of U.S. direct investment in Latin America. Other U.S. organizations active in presenting corporate views on international issues are the U.S. Committee of the International Chamber of Commerce (CICC) and the National Council for United States-China Trade. Another important international business forum in the United States is the National Foreign Trade Council (NFTC). Possibly the most highly organized of any national business community is that of Japan. Quasi-official industry associations linked to the Ministry of International Trade and Investment apparently are consulted before the Japanese government makes any moves in international trade and investment, so much so that a non-Japanese business executive negotiating with Japanese executives is never quite sure whether the negotiation is with a private firm or the government.

At the international level is the Trilateral Commission, which consists of prominent persons (chiefly business executives) from Western Europe, Japan, and the United States. Its purpose is to promote "the habit of working together" on political, economic, and security issues in the three regions and to seek to devise and disseminate proposals of general benefit to both the public and governments. Also operating at the international level is the Comité Internationale de l'Organisation Scientifique (CIOS), which is a confederation of national management and business organizations providing an international forum for discussion of issues and a vehicle for the establishment of common positions. At the secondary level are three associated regional federations, the Pan-American Committee of CIOS (PACCIOS), the Asian Association of Management Organizations of CIOS (AAMOCIOS), and the Counseil l'Européen de CIOS (CECIOS).

In the category of nonbusiness intermediaries in the United States stands the Conference Board, an independent, nonprofit business research organization headquartered in New York, whose purpose is to promote prosperity and security by assisting in the effective operation and sound development of voluntary productive enterprise. The Board has more than 4,000 associates and serves some 40,000 individuals throughout the world by means of its continuing research in matters of interest to business firms. Somewhat similar organizations exist elsewhere, such as the Nomura Research Institute of Japan. Because of the apparently objective, professional quality of much of their work, their reports enjoy a relatively high level of credibility.

10.3   Choice of Vehicle

Some of the vehicles for effecting corporate public affairs strategy include:

1. *Subsidized research*, participating in or supporting surveys and other research designed to prove the costs or benefits of a particular public policy or legislative proposal.
2. *Lobbying*, presenting views to various public bodies and influential individuals.
3. *Advocacy advertising*, space in publications or airtime bought to argue a point of view on a public issue, either in its own words or those of some scholar or well-known public figure.
4. *Corporate philanthropy* or charitable contributions, donations of funds to nonprofit organizations known to be sympathetic to one or more corporate policy positions, that are working to improve some environmental factor considered important to the corporation or that the corporation believes will improve the intellectual inputs to corporate policy formulation.
5. *Negotiating* with public and private bodies to improve the conditions under which the corporation acts.
6. *Restructuring the corporation* to be more reflective of major environmental changes (such as placing public-interest members on corporate boards).
7. *Volunteering corporate skills* to help resolve public problems.
8. *Bribes*, funds (or other material benefits) given to public officials or others to achieve a change of policy advantageous to the corporation.

We deal with a few of these in the following sections.

Advocacy Advertising

A device used frequently by the public affairs department is what has come to be known as **advocacy advertising.** Research by S. Prakash Sethi challenges the effectiveness of most such advertising in the United States. He concludes,

No amount of advocacy advertising will help unless there is a recognition that some of the criticism directed against business institutions is indeed valid. There must be a demonstrated willingness to change where current methods of operation and standards of performance fall short of societal expectations. Business must take steps to put its own house in order. Generalized statements of self-righteousness are ineffective in pre-

senting one's case. Nor does it help to explain away wrongdoing; e.g., illegal political payoffs and bribes at home and abroad, in terms of the "rotten apple theory" when such behavior is persistent and widespread, and equally well reported in the news media.

The cause of business is poorly served when corporate spokesmen concentrate their fire on critics; e.g., labor, radical groups, government bureaucrats, and environmentalists, and refuse to speak out against business practices that are illegal or considered socially irresponsible.[3]

If this be a valid assessment of advocacy advertising within the United States, consider the case of a large alien enterprise in a foreign country, particularly in an LDC with a prejudice against foreign business. The classic case of the misuse of advocacy advertising was the newspaper campaign of International Petroleum Corporation (a subsidiary of Exxon, then Esso) in Peru that labeled certain statements of high-level Peruvian government officials as untrue. Whether their statements were true or not was irrelevant. The point is that those designing the advertisements displayed a curious inability to imagine themselves in the shoes of the ordinary Peruvian and predict his reaction. The response, of course, was increased pressure for the expropriation of the IPC properties in Peru. It brings to mind those Americans who fully expected that a gringo-sponsored invasion of Cuba would spark a popular Cuban uprising against the Castro regime! A positive public response rests on a long record of behavior generally perceived to be beneficial in some sense by the majority of the relevant public, or—at the very least—not perceived to be harmful or deceitful.

Advocacy advertising, whatever its cultural setting, should not be seen as a public relations effort, but as a public *affairs* function, which means that it represents an honest effort to spell out the ramifications of certain political or social acts on employment, incomes, productivity, prices, sales, or investment. And it should only be used if the public credibility of the corporation is relatively high.

Philanthropy

Philanthropy or charitable contributions in the corporate context can be an important tool of the public affairs manager. *Philanthropy has to do with making corporate resources available to activities that do not enter into the production or sales function within the business planning horizon and that are not legally required*. Philanthropic expenditures are discretionary in the sense that corporate managers do not expect them to impact on costs, sales, or profits within the planning period. This definition, however, does not provide an easy categorization of many corporate expenditures. For example, on-site feeding of employees may well be a *business* expense, not philanthropy, if it is expected to affect productivity and absenteeism directly. Support of

[3]S. Prakash Sethi, "Advocacy Advertising as a Strategy of Corporate Response to Social Pressures: The American Experiences," paper presented on marketing and public policy (Cergy, France, September 30–October 1, 1976), mimeo., pp. 27–28.

research in respect to increasing yields on local farms, on the other hand, is probably philanthropy unless the firm itself is in agrobusiness and stands to benefit in some direct, short-term way. Does support for a technical institute engaged in research in a specific sector qualify as philanthropy? No easy answer is possible.

It would seem that corporate philanthropy is nonetheless generally perceived by the donors, and indeed, it must be internally justified on this basis, as supporting corporate goals. So what we are talking about is the expenditure of corporate resources for activities the donors believe will impact on corporate goals *in the longer run*. To say that the corporate goal is maximum profit is not adequate, for it begs several questions, specifically: (1) Maximum profit over what time horizon? (which quickly gets into consideration of perceived risks and discount rates); and (2) Maximum profit for whom? Management, labor, owners, customers, government? It can be argued that valid nonbusiness giving would satisfy corporate goals if:

1.   It is seen as *cost-reducing* over time (e.g., improves the relevant infra-structure, improves employee productivity or stability). In a very real sense such expenditures may be viewed as a corporate payment for society's expenditures from which the corporation derives benefit, such as the use of manpower trained with public and private resources external to the firm.
2.   It is seen as *risk-reducing* over time (e.g., improves the corporate image; supports the development of a climate compatible with long-term corporate survival, thereby reducing the probability of disruptive changes in market or production).

Corporate philanthropy may not be valid if it merely satisfies the personal desires of owners, managers, and/or employees. Many believe that the corporation is not the appropriate vehicle for generalizing the social priorities of such groups, which is exactly what it does if it uses its resources in support of activities unrelated to corporate objectives. If corporate re-sources are devoted to nonmarket-related purposes, one is on very slippery ground unless their allocation is supported by some general consensus, which is best reached through *political* processes, not corporate. Some cor-porations have moved in this direction by requiring votes of approval by employees, stockholders, or both, for major charitable commitments.

One of the problems is that there is no clear agreement about how to resolve some of the basic issues society faces. Even if we try to justify corporate philanthropy on the basis that it supports either national interest or world welfare, the problem of identifying those interests remains. The satisfaction of *national* interest in a world in which there is obvious need for global management of food, energy, exhaustible resources, and exploitation of space and the deep sea, begs a number of questions. In fact, it is not even clear that U.S. foreign policy, for example, is really responsive to the United States' own long-term national interests. Where does world welfare lie when one is called upon to support the notion of self-dependency in a world increasingly interdependent in reality? Some have emphasized the need for diverting resources in support of the poorest of the poor. Yet we know that we live in a world of finite resources. It seems unsupportable for corporations to make decisions on these issues in the absence of some sort of political consensus. In fact, it is not at all clear, given the apparent successes of certain socialist countries, that world welfare is best served by supporting traditional capitalist values in all parts of the world. How does one define world welfare? It would be presumptuous for a corporation to do so.

Corporate survival should not be viewed necessarily in terms of continued ownership of fixed assets, but rather as the maintenance of a reasonable stream of earnings—whether derived from direct investment, the sale of production inputs through contract (i.e., management skills, technology and associated skills, finance, capital goods, or other materials), or from providing access to international marketing and information networks. If otherwise valid corporate philanthropy is open and truly conceived as an effort to protect a profitable relationship with a given market—not merely in defense of a single ownership and control strategy—then it has claim to legitimacy. Otherwise, the validity of the act is brought into question, for it cannot be said to be truly risk-reducing in the long run. Obviously, any philanthropic act that runs counter to the basic interest of the host society compounds political risk, even though those interests may not yet be explicitly articulated. Therefore, corporate donations to support research designed to provide better understanding of the underlying dynamics of societies in which the corporation does business is of signal importance, although the research is of little value to the corporation unless it has access to that research and uses it in its decision making.

There are reasonable limits to even the most valid corporate philanthropy. Two tests might be suggested: the willingness of the corporate donor to make public both the fact of its philanthropy, and its true motivation.

Negotiation

Another device available to those responsible for the public affairs function is negotiation with public bodies to produce satisfactory politico-economic conditions. Corporate executives in the United States and elsewhere have been remarkably weak in this area. The hallmark of the effective negotiator is the ability to understand what moves and concerns the people on the other side of the bargaining table, the pressures to which they are responding. A common pitfall is insensitivity to the other side's need to save face, a need that is not unique to the Oriental, nor to the politician. Although they manifest it in different ways, virtually everyone endeavors to save face. Any negotiating ploy that forces another person into a losing position, or into a position that will subject him or her to ridicule or public condemnation, is bound to set up a countervailing force. The battle may be won, but not the war. A corollary is that face-destroying rudeness or anger in a negotiation is inexcusable and probably self-defeating unless carefully calculated in advance. It should be realized that there are always several possible explanations for the behavior one witnesses.

For example, a negotiation became bogged down in Turkey some years ago. The Turkish government had summarily reneged on an agreement with a U.S. firm that had been the basis for the company's investment of substantial resources. The U.S. management immediately jumped to the conclusion that this act, plus the obstinance exhibited by the principal Turkish negotiator, was generated either by ignorance or the desire for personal gain through some sort of illegal payment. It failed to appreciate several key facts: the Turkish negotiator was very nationalistic and was strongly committed to getting the best deal for his country; he had a very limited staff for evaluating the technical and economic soundness of the proposed project; Turkish law made him *personally* responsible for the feasibility of the project under negotiation; he had quite sincere doubts about the price; and he had no prior experience with the U.S. company. The company president rushed into the situation and requested an audience with the Turkish prime minister. In so doing, he was assuming that (1) his company's position was thoroughly defensible, (2) the Turkish negotiator was acting without the knowledge and support of the prime minister, and (3) the Turkish negotiator was not acting in good faith. Fortunately, the president became conscious of these assumptions prior to the appointment with the prime minister and gained a postponement on the grounds of illness. It later developed that there were some technical errors in the company's proposal, that the price could be scaled down, that the Turkish negotiator had acted with the support of the prime minister, and that the negotiator was scrupulously honest. Had the company president gone to the prime minister and impugned either the integrity or competence of the Turkish negotiator, the company would have been in serious trouble. The matter was resolved amiably with the submission of a somewhat different proposal, with full credit given to the astuteness of the Turkish negotiator. In fact, the changes made were not really material, but the Turks were convinced by this act that the proposal was sound and properly priced. Face had been saved.

Before responding, an experienced negotiator speculates very carefully on all of the possible explanations for the behavior exhibited by the other party and then devises ways to probe the system to ascertain the most likely explanation. Such an analysis presupposes adequate insight into the socio-political system in which the other negotiating party is operating. For example, if a negotiator is unsure of his or her technical ability to evaluate a particular proposal, negotiations may be delayed until the negotiator can build up a personal relationship with the other party, thereby creating an element of personal trust and confidence. In some societies, this personal relationship is a necessary prelude to striking any bargain.

In complex international business negotiations, experienced negotiators say it is wise to negotiate informally before or during the formal sessions. For example, the informal negotiation might take place between lawyers, between engineers, or between accountants from each side for the purpose of reaching a one-to-one agreement before bringing up specific technical subjects for formal negotiation. Others caution about the possibility of a negotiation being spoiled by "bad actors"; that is, people who insist on passing judgment on matters outside the areas of their own competence. The worst sin is for a negotiating team to enter negotiations without a consistent position among team members on all important issues, and without fall-back positions having been defined. But falling back to a lesser position in one area should always be contingent upon successful negotiation in another. Otherwise, one is the victim of the "ratchet effect," as point after point is bargained away.

A very useful device in preparing for an important negotiation is a simulated negotiation, in which members of one's own company are assigned to represent the other side as vigorously as possible. It is revealing to note how unprepared many corporate representatives are to state the conditions they seek in terms of the interests of the other party. Take the typical LDC case, in which a foreign company is trying to negotiate satisfactory conditions for entry. Whatever the negotiating team proposes should be justified in terms of the political and economic priorities of the host country, whether they be foreign exchange conservation, export promotion, employment and income generation, income distribution, or technology or control transfer, to mention a few. This means that the corporate negotiators should be fully familiar with micro- and macroeconomic theory, the various theories of economic development, international trade and investment theory, local development plans, and the political realities of the local scene, as well as the technical aspects of the proposal. Very few corporate negotiating teams bring these skills to the negotiating table. As the level of sophistication of host LDC government negotiators increases, corporate negotiators are frequently outgunned.[4]

One further observation is made by experienced and successful negotiators. Once a negotiation has deteriorated into acrimony and personal hostility, change the negotiators. Bring in a new team. This is particularly true on the interface between a large alien corporation and an LDC government.[5] And, one might add, to strike an agreement that will remain viable, the corporate negotiators must be able to anticipate the impacts of that agreement and assess the probability of unfavorable political reactions that might force a subsequent change in the bargain. At this stage, scenario writing is a useful technique.

---

[4]It should be noted that the Georgetown Law Center (Washington, D.C.) and the UN Centre on Transnational Corporations have been running training seminars for government negotiators.

[5]Some of these same points are made by John Fayerweather and Ashok Kapoor, *Strategy Negotiation for the International Corporation* (Cambridge, Mass.: Ballinger Pub. Co., 1976).

Illegal Payments

Bribe or illegal payment is a device to be used only under the most extreme, desperate circumstances, for it must be assumed that the details will become known publicly sooner or later, probably sooner. Disclosure only takes one disgruntled knowledgeable employee, one honest official, or one astute and courageous journalist. Anticipation of the impact of ultimate disclosure must be a factor in the decision.

In the United States, the 1976 Tax Reform Act denies tax deferral and the crediting of foreign wealth and income tax against U.S. tax liability in respect to foreign revenues from a country in which the corporation has made an illegal payment. Also, U.S. corporations are required to maintain controls to give reasonable assurance that such payments will not be made without headquarters' knowledge. The result is that not only have many large corporations begun to monitor very closely any questionable payments made overseas by their personnel, but some have issued explicit guidelines on the issue. The relevant IBM statement reads:

IBM will not make contributions or payments to political parties or candidates. Nor will IBM bribe or make payoffs to government officials, civil servants or anyone. This is a single worldwide policy. If you ever are approached for what you believe is a questionable payment, report the circumstances to your manager as soon as possible.

In many countries political contributions by corporations are illegal. In other countries they are legal, but IBM will not make them in either case. Nor will IBM provide things other than direct cash payments which may be considered contributions. For example, if you want to campaign for a political candidate, the company will give you reasonable amounts of time off from work without pay, commensurate with your duties. IBM encourages people to be involved in politics, but on their own time and at their own expense. If IBM were to pay you while you were campaigning, your salary could be considered a contribution to the candidate or party you were supporting.[6]

Issued in several languages, the booklet containing this statement is distributed to all IBM employees in decision-making positions, and they are annually requested to sign a statement to the effect that they have read and understand the guidelines. It should be emphasized that such a rule may place the individual manager in a difficult dilemma if he or she is being judged purely on annual sales or profit achievement. The more competitive the situation, the greater is the dilemma, and possibly the less effective the corporate guidelines.

What should be realized is that "large-scale payments by multinational corporations do not represent an aberration to be analyzed in terms of a decline in morality (business or general) or comparative ethical or legal systems." Stephen J. Kobrin, the author of this observation, goes on to point

---

[6]"IBM Business Conduct Guidelines" (undated), p. 10.

out that such payments "are a manifestation of three interrelated and more general issues that in turn are a function of developments in technology as applied to production and communication." These are:

1. The concentration of economic and thus political power in the modern corporation; the fact that business has "gained a power and is not sensitively subject to control by the market."
2. The emergence of significant nongovernmental transnational political actors.
3. The presence of powerful actors within a given nation-state that are responsive to external forces and not entirely under the control of the host government. (This last point, perhaps, should be subsumed under the first two.)[7]

He concludes: "The basic issue is that of changes that are necessary in both socioeconomic and political institutions to cope with the major changes that have taken place in the nature of productive enterprise,"[8] to wit, its size, internationalization, and politicization.

The problem of illegal payments (or more broadly, nonbusiness payments) is more complicated than U.S. law suggests. They may best be analyzed in terms of initiating pressures, forms of payment, objective of the payment, mode of payment, and impact within the parent country (see Figure 10.1). The corporation may be under pressure to make such a payment because of either competitive pressure or pressure from its parent government to gain some political or military advantage (e.g., the CIA pressure on ITT in Chile to serve as a conduit). The payment may be made directly or through an intermediary. It may end as a personal gain for a public official in government, politics, labor, or some other influential sector, or it may go for some social purpose, such as a project that benefits the society at large. It may be in the form of money or some desired service rendered gratis or below market price, such as an "inspection trip" to corporate headquarters. The specific object of the payment may be to expedite the achievement of a legal objective (such as moving goods through customs), to create a competitive bias in favor of the donor (as in government purchasing or in prohibiting import of competing goods or services), to achieve an objective illegal under local law, to influence national economic policy or political outcomes, to achieve an objective illegal under parent-country law (such as evasion of U.S. export controls, antitrust law, taxes, etc.), or to further parent-country policy objectives. Obviously, these are not all mutually exclusive categories.

The mode of an illegal payment may be overt or covert. The payment may have no impact on the parent country, or it may have a negative or positive effect. For example, the payment may cause the loss of business by

[7]Stephen J. Kobrin, "Morality, Political Power and Illegal Payments by Multinational Corporations," *Columbia Journal of World Business* (Winter 1976), p. 109. Reference in item 1. is to V. P. Key, Jr., *Politics, Parties and Pressure Groups*, 5th ed. (New York: Crowell Co., 1964), p. 25.

[8]Kobrin, "Morality," p. 110.

Figure 10.1
A Classification System for "Unusual" or "Illegal" Payments Overseas

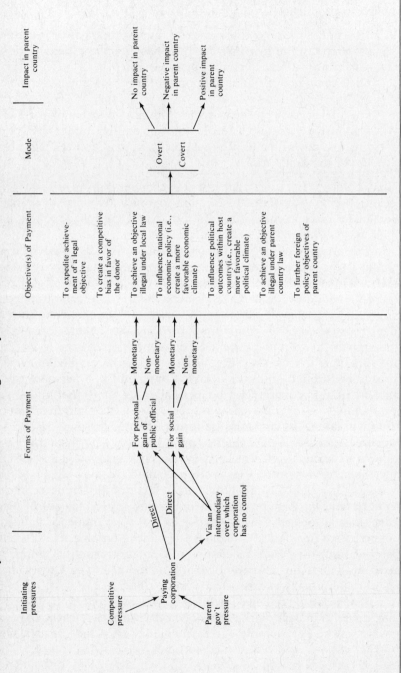

other parent-country firms or undermine parent-country foreign policy. Examples of the latter could be contributions to a political party known to be hostile to parent-country interests, stimulating demands for military equipment contrary to parent-country interests, or committing an act illegal under parent-country law. On the other hand, the payment may have a positive impact on the parent country; it could produce employment and profits for business generally through subcontractors and others, improve the balance of payments, or support governmental policy. Examples of the last could include gaining access to critically needed raw materials, undermining an unfriendly government, or inducing the acceptance of parent-country products.

As can be perceived from these comments, and from Figure 10.1, what is generally considered to be reprehensible, at least in the United States, is a direct payment generated by competitive pressures for the personal gain of a government official for any purpose other than to further U.S. policy objectives, particularly if it is covert and produces a negative impact in the United States. An overt act might still be reprehensible if illegal under U.S. law, such as corporate support of foreign political groups (which may be perfectly legal under foreign law, as in Canada), or if it produces a negative impact in the United States. But there are many gray areas. What of corporate sponsorship of a visit by host-government officials to the parent country in an effort to improve the host country's political image and, hence, influence national policy of the parent country? This is apparently what Mobil did in 1969 when it sponsored the visit of a Nigerian government official to the United States in order to try to offset pro-Biafran sentiment in the United States. What of making corporate facilities available to a parent-government effort to overthrow the host-country government? What of payments to labor leaders? What of the distribution in Ecuador by Texas-Gulf of pamphlets prepared by the U.S. Information Agency extolling the benefits of private oil distribution? We have now probably crossed the line of what is doubtful to what is fully acceptable. Even more clearly acceptable was the financing of school buildings' construction in Mexico by Ford dealers. We have now moved into the area of charitable donations or philanthropy, the motive of which may well be to influence national economic policy and/or political outcomes to be more favorable to the donor company.

The skills required for an effective public affairs function become apparent when one lists the tasks involved. The list includes: (1) constantly scanning the corporate environment to be able to order the priorities of public issues pressing upon it; (2) deriving some measure of the cost effectiveness of a public affairs effort on a given issue (will the gain in a changed environment be worth the alienation of individuals and interests, not to mention the expenditure of corporate resources?); (3) effective communication; and (4) negotiation with public authorities in order to match corporate strategy with the perceived public interest.

10.4   Environmental Analysis

Obviously, the common denominator for all vehicles of public affairs strategy is environmental analysis, which in turn rests upon a carefully designed and accurate information system. Public affairs strategists must also be alert to sociopolitical processes that impact on the market well after the usual time horizon for normal business decisions and that can only be quantified approximately. The more dynamic the environment, the greater the uncertainty, and the higher the rate by which future earnings are discounted. The result is a very short time horizon for many business decisions. In the contemporary world, long-term business planning can usually be no longer than five years if it is to have any impact on current decisions. Corporate executives are normally evaluated upon *annual* performance, but public affairs executives must think in much longer terms. To have an impact on corporate activity they must be very senior and influential people with direct access to the corporate president and board of directors and must have assured tenure. They must be assisted by political and social analysts. For the first time, corporations are now beginning to employ political scientists, cultural anthropologists, and sociologists, not only economists, to add more balance to analysis. Even so, most corporations were apparently caught completely by surprise by the upheavals in Iran (1979) and Lebanon (1982). Business had considered both countries relatively stable!

It follows that an important part of the public affairs function is the monitoring of corporate impact on various measures of public welfare, measures depending upon the political priorities of the countries involved, both parent and host.

Monitoring Issues

In the case of the United States, coming high on the list should be the ratio of imports (from foreign subsidiaries, associated firms, licensees, and technology contractors) to exports (from the corporation's domestic operations), given the fact that the larger U.S. corporations are under constant attack from labor on the grounds that by investing and contracting overseas they are "exporting jobs."[9] Another sensitive issue in the United States is the matter of illegal payments overseas. Revelations by corporations at the behest of the Securities and Exchange Commission have excited considerable public attention.

Many U.S. corporations have also felt obliged to respond to various pressures from stockholders, employees, consumers, and others by examining with care their policies in the Republic of South Africa.[10] The relevant

[9]An example is *Union Carbide's International Investment Benefits the U.S. Economy*, a 35-page study by the Union Carbide Corporation, first issued in October 1972, and updated November 1975.

[10]The U.K. government in 1976 began requiring U.K.-based corporations operating in South Africa to report their policies regarding black employees.

political question is whether the continued presence of the corporation supports or subverts apartheid. Of direct concern to a corporation's decision makers is the probability of a majority black government, when that might occur, and which corporate policies to pursue in order to preserve corporate interests through such a transition. It could be argued that, even if the withdrawal of U.S. corporations from South Africa might greatly enhance the probability of revolutionary change, the use of foreign corporations to trigger a revolution is not a valid use of corporations, whether one favors that revolution or not. However, as representatives of U.S. society—and hence, to a certain extent, of U.S. values—U.S. corporate executives undoubtedly feel obliged to push the advancement of their black employees in South Africa to the limit of the law, possibly beyond. To do so requires careful monitoring of the changing legal and political climate of South Africa and of the performance of affiliated firms there. Indeed, given the increased concern in the United States with human rights everywhere, any U.S.-based corporation fails to monitor this dimension of its operations at its own peril in countries under attack from the point of view of alleged violations of human rights, whether it be South Africa, Chile, the Soviet Union, El Salvador, the Philippines, Argentina, or Korea.

Other areas of particular concern to the public affairs officer of a U.S.-based corporation monitoring response within the United States are foreign affiliates' participation in any international boycotts and any major environmental pollution they may cause (particularly atmospheric and oceanic). The first is now illegal and the second can destroy a corporation's credibility at home.

Consumer safety is another issue that has become relevant, the most celebrated international case being that of the Swiss-based Nestlé Corporation and its infant formula. Widely publicized allegations accused Nestlé advertising in Third World countries of extolling the virtues of bottle feeding without effectively warning users of the disadvantages, particularly in the Third World environment. World opinion was aroused and an international consumer boycott stimulated. Finally, the United Nations itself, via the World Health Organization, acted to pass a guideline on the subject (over U.S. objections). Part of the fallout was that a U.S. company subsequently desisted from marketing a new, highly nutritious "weaning food" developed specifically for Third World countries. Management was afraid to put it on the market.

When one considers the matters to be monitored abroad in response to anticipated political pressures in *host* countries, the list lengthens considerably. For each country in which the corporation operates, its public affairs department should be measuring on a *continuing* basis the impact of corporate activities on balance of trade, balance of payments, net domestic product, employment, and income distribution (overall, by region, by sector, private vs. public, and by important groups—tribe, ethnic group, political division, and the like). In addition, the corporation is wise if it periodically employs expert independent analysts to examine the overall political vulnerability of the corporation in each country where important corporate assets are located. A key measure of the failure of the public affairs function is the number of times the corporation is faced with an unanticipated political event. The other key measure is the ability of the public affairs department to suggest financially feasible strategies that permit the corporation to survive what would otherwise prove to be a costly change in the political environment.

Political Risk Assessment

Indeed, one of the most difficult public affairs tasks is the assessment of **political risk,**[11] by which I mean determining the probability of a political event that will affect the firm to its disadvantage. Typical impacts: the imposition of an unexpected cost (such as a tax), loss of some degree of management control (such as inability to lay off employees), blockage of earnings (such as the imposition of foreign exchange controls), loss of assets (expropriation), physical loss (such as destruction of assets due to violence or the kidnapping of personnel). In fact, all could be subsumed under unanticipated increase in cost resulting from nonmarket forces. The point is that abrupt political change does not translate into political risk for the corporation unless that change impacts on cost.

As the probability of one or more of these events increases, the public affairs analyst should be responsible for alerting management and suggesting ways of influencing the anticipated political event so as to render it less onerous (less costly), to shift the burden of the anticipated politically induced cost to an external agency, and/or to adjust corporate strategy to minimize that cost.

The sophisticated corporate analyst does not assume a linkage between sudden political change and corporate well-being. Hence, aggregate measures suggesting an apparent political discontinuity, say a coup, are inadequate guides to corporate behavior. One needs to interpret that coup in terms of impacts on the corporation of the sort listed above. I suggest that political risk is a function of: (1) pressures within the surrounding political system, (2) the capacity of that system to adjust so that these pressures are kept within tolerable limits, (3) the degree of **leverage** possessed by the firm (market advantage), and (4) responsiveness of corporate strategy. What may constitute very high political risk for one firm may mean zero risk for another.

A "manager of international business environments," the principle analyst for a very large U.S.-based multinational, explained to me that political risk, as viewed by his management, was not an absolute; it was as much a function of corporate activity and policy as of independent political events. If the economics of a project were attractive, corporate strategy

[11]A basic work in this area is Stephen J. Kobrin, *Managing Political Risk Assessment, Strategic Response to Environmental Change* (Berkley; University of California Press, 1982).

would be adjusted so that the political risk would be reduced to a tolerable level. Of course, this assumes flexibility of corporate strategy.

The art of political risk assessment lies in sensing the level of pressure a given political system will tolerate. At what point will structural changes be forced? Obviously, the more rigid the system, the more likely such changes will occur in the face of a given level of pressure. The relevant questions are: What is the nature of the critical pressures? What are the measures of a system's rigidity?

One can only list some specific critical pressures, for each national society is highly idiosyncratic in this respect; all of the pressures interrelate and interact, both among themselves and with other dimensions of the socioeconomic-political environment. The list of important indicators of pressures includes:

1. Increasing wealth and income disparity, particularly if identified with ethnic, religious, and/or regional groupings, and if consumption differences are visible.

2. Deprivation of economic or social status of a formerly important group (e.g., military officers) or a large number of individuals, particularly if concentrated geographically.

3. Large-scale and accelerating rural-urban movement, particularly if led by a large, unattached, young male population.

4. Loss of land rights by a significant segment of the rural population to large town-dwelling landlords, particularly if they are of different ethnic, religious, or tribal identity.

5. Mounting external debt, dwindling domestic reserves, deteriorating credit position, and increasing scarcity of essential imports, particularly if involving imports to which a significant part of the population has become accustomed.

6. Accelerating affluence without serious effort to equalize its impact among various groups and economic classes.

7. Inability of the government to maintain law and order in important areas.

8. Mounting corruption at high levels of government, which may be indicative of leaders' shortening time horizon.

9. Declining real incomes after a long period of growth.

10. The presence of persistent, organized, violent (actual or potential) opposition under charismatic leadership—labor, religious, or political.

The capability of a political system to tolerate such pressures, even at high levels, lies in its capacity to respond by introducing an appropriate adjustment mechanism. A competitive political system with multiple power centers and a long record of more or less peaceful adjustment may be best able to respond effectively to pressures. But one should not be misled by labels. A single-party system, in which multiple factions are held together by a strong charismatic leader, may be highly representative and responsive. Competition and representation simply take place at a different level under different labels. On the other hand, a competitive, multiparty system may not represent important segments in a population.

Until very recently, there has been extraordinary contrast between economic and political inputs to corporate decisions. The latter have been treated either as constants or random variables, almost never subject to rigorous analysis by expert analysts, as economic inputs have been. In contrast with their regard for economic analysis, virtually everyone claims the skills and insights needed for political analysis. All one need do is read the *New York Times* or a comparable paper. If political turbulence is reported, the political risk discount figure becomes infinitely high. Of course, the political crisis may be wholly irrelevant to the business climate. We thus derive our first trap for the unwary, the "crisis syndrome." Of particular danger is the second trap, the "old hands syndrome"—those who know because they were there. A classic case was the old China hands, principally missionaries and businessmen, who scoffed at the notion that the Communists could ever take over in China. This suggests a very serious problem in establishing an effective political intelligence system, for long-established local managers may well insist on having the last word. Yet they are very unlikely to be sensitive to new political currents that do not intrude into the social gatherings of the more affluent part of the society. This introduces the third trap, the "well-groomed syndrome." Apparently no manager of a subsidiary of a U.S. firm in pre-Castro Cuba had any notion that the "bearded unwashed in the hills" were about to take over the country. The revolutionaries were not well-groomed, respectable members of society, and so were not worthy of attention. The result was that not a *single* U.S. firm bothered to take out a U.S. government guarantee against expropriation of its Cuban assets. It is almost certain that a skilled political scientist specializing in Caribbean affairs would have specified a probability of something more than zero for a Castro-led takeover. It is also clear that the corporate interest in political intelligence tends to be relatively high at the point of entry (i.e., the time of its investment decision) into a country, but thereafter is somewhat reduced. This leads to the fourth trap, the "entry syndrome." Some firms now maintain an *ongoing* profile for each country in which they have significant operations. These profiles are produced by trained political analysts, whether within or outside the firm, using input from local management but drawing upon independent evaluations as well. One alarm signal may be triggered by a significant difference between the assessment by local management and the independent political analyst.

Let us assume that a high probability of political discontinuity is specified for a country. This fact may not translate into political risk for the firm if its leverage is great—that is, if it is perceived as the sole purveyor of essential goods and services at a given price, or if the internal corporate balance of transfers (incoming capital, technology, and skills set off against outgoing fees, royalties, and dividends) is still very much in favor of the host country. What corporate executives often overlook is that a firm's leverage is very likely to be reduced over time. Once again, the International Petroleum Company in Peru is a case in point. Initially, it was investing foreign savings, technology, and skills, for which there was no other source at comparable price. And it was producing essentially for external markets to which it had low-cost access. Over time the flow of new capital dwindled to a trickle. The essential technology had been transferred and local skills developed. What was not available locally could be purchased from a variety of independent service organizations. Finally, the local market was absorbing virtually the entire production. Obviously, the firm had lost most of its initial leverage, and its political vulnerability was greatly enhanced as a result. Still, IPC might have survived if it had anticipated political events in Peru and, sensitive to its loss of leverge, had adjusted its strategy from one of ownership and control to that of a seller of services—technology, technical skills, marketing, management, and international financing—and a buyer of product.

Hence, political risk analysis must cover all four levels; political pressures, the capacity of the political system to adjust, corporate leverage, and the responsiveness of corporate strategy. This point is lost by those professing to reduce political risk to a pure numbers game. In fact, there is considerable evidence that many corporations have dropped the idea of expressing political risk in a single number that can be used for discounting purposes. Not only is there a tendency for financial analysts and others to overinterpret such numbers, but it is conceptually invalid to use a single number because political risk varies depending upon corporate response. There is no single political risk factor, hence, no single **discount rate.**

Forecasting Function

We have been speaking here of relatively short-term environmental changes. Public affairs should also concern itself with plotting the probable course of much longer term social, political, and economic processes likely to impact on the corporation, such as:

1.   The appearance of socially responsible governments in the LDCs (i.e., more honestly responsive to the interests of their own societies).
2.   Broadening dispersion of high-level technical and managerial skills.
3.   Widening disparity in per capita well-being between the poorest and richest nations.
4.   Growing inequality of incomes within certain countries.
5.   Rising demand for environmental and consumer protection in the more developed countries.
6.   Increased importance of countertrade of various forms.
7.   Worldwide shortages of certain commodities, given present price structures (e.g., energy, food, and the like).
8.   The appeal of the OPEC model of cartelization among commodity producing nations.
9.   Shift in liquid assets to commodity producing countries, initially the oil producers.
10.   Growth of employee participation in decision making.

11. Increasing entry of women into the labor force and resulting change in family structure.
12. Aging population in industrialized countries.
13. Declining relative importance of the U.S. economy vis-à-vis the world economy (in terms of total production, international trade, innovation).
14. The increasing internationalization of production (i.e., increasing integration of national economies).
15. Internationalization of organized labor.
16. Regionalization of markets.
17. Possible worldwide slowdown in technological innovation.
18. Increased international mobility of labor, legal and illegal.
19. Increased scale of illegal and unreported economic activity.

Some likely derivatives of these underlying forces are:

1. Persistent worldwide inflation.
2. A floating exchange rate system.
3. Loss of faith in the market allocation process and increased pressure for government intervention.
4. Slowdown in the application of new commercial technology.
5. Accelerating shift of manufacturing from the more-developed countries to the less-developed countries.
6. Increasing nationalistic identification.
7. Shift of economic power toward the LDCs.
8. Reduced implicit politico-economic clout of the United States.
9. Increasing economic interdependency.
10. Multinationalization of ownership and management of many large corporations.
11. Increasing unreliability of official statistics.
12. International agreements relating to the control of large corporations operating internationally.

10.5 International Codes

The last point needs expansion, for corporate public affairs analysts are becoming increasingly concerned with the possibility of **international codes,** for such codes could greatly restrict corporate strategic options. Given the many efforts to put together a set of guidelines for international corporate behavior, it is apparent that at least some bodies have concluded that the nation-state is an inadequate vehicle for controlling the larger corporations operating internationally. The upshot is that at least five codes

---

[12]*International Investment and Multinational Enterprises* (Paris: Organization for Economic Cooperation and Development, 1976).

[13]*Guidelines for International Investment* (Paris: International Chamber of Commerce, 1972).

have been proposed: by the Organization for Economic Cooperation and Development,[12] by the International Chamber of Commerce,[13] by the Council of Europe,[14] by the Nonaligned Countries,[15] and by ten Latin American and Caribbean nations.[16] In addition, the five-nation Andean Common Market has articulated a *regional* code ("Decisions 24"), and both the European Economic Community and the Association of South-East Asian Nations have been discussing codes, as have various international labor bodies. One should also note the codes Japan and Sweden have urged upon their corporations operating overseas. Finally, the United Nations, as a result of a report issued by the UN Commission on Transnational Corporations in 1974,[17] gave birth to the UN Centre for Transnational Corporations in 1975. United States policy on the subject, enunciated in 1975 by Secretary of State Henry Kissinger, apparently remains unchanged:

The United States believes that the time has come for the international community to articulate standards of conduct for both enterprises and governments. The U.N. Commission on Transnational Corporations, and other governmental bodies, have begun such an effort. We must reach agreement on balanced principles.[18]

For a code to be really effective, several conditions might be suggested:

1.   It must apply to the behavior of both corporations and states.
2.   It must not penalize those corporations attempting to abide by the code.
3.   It must not penalize the small corporation or reward the large.
4.   It must not introduce added costs so as to reduce aggregate flows of private capital, technology, and skills from the more-developed to the less-developed countries.
5.   The code must be stated in sufficient detail to be operational.

All of the codes thus far proposed fail to satisfy more than one of these conditions. Although several satisfy the first condition, those corporations trying to conform would be penalized. Their strategy selection would be more restricted than for those corporations choosing to ignore the guidelines. And there is no explicit reward for their "good behavior" other than enhanced public image, which, in the LDCs, may not be widely perceived as a particularly valuable attribute. Until it becomes quite clear that host governments are more protective of the rights of alien corporations demonstrating sensitivity to local interests—which the guidelines purport to encour-

---

[14]Resolution 639 (Strasbourg: Parliamentary Assembly, Council of Europe, 1976).

[15]"Draft Statute for the Treatment of Foreign Investment, Transnational Corporations and the Transfer of Technology" (Lima: Conference of Ministers for Foreign Affairs of Non-Aligned Countries, August 25–29, 1975).

[16]*Commission on Transnational Corporations, Report on the Second Session*, Supplement No. 5 (United Nations: Economic and Social Council, 1976), pp. 17–34.

[17]Bear in mind that, in UN usage, the term "transnational" applies to any corporation operating internationally (international, multinational, transnational, multinational and transnational associations, and international service companies). See Chapter 9.

[18]September 1, 1975.

age—then good behavior derives no benefit. Do host governments in fact differentiate in terms of ownership policies, availability of local resources, and profit remittance permits? There seems to be precious little evidence that they do. To my knowledge, only one government has been collecting information on how corporations with which it is negotiating have behaved elsewhere.

Each new governmental intervention in the market, whether on a national or international level, tends to reward the large corporation; it can afford the specialized staff or counsel to plot its course through—or around—the regulations. A small firm cannot. Also, the addition of further restrictions, assuming that the code becomes effective, translates into more entry barriers, reduced competition, and increased costs of desired transfers of capital, skills, and technology. The exact reverse is needed, that is, an improvement of markets. None of the proposed codes includes measures that will really do that.

Finally, none of the codes is sufficiently detailed to be operational; and indeed, if they were, they would undoubtedly conflict with one or more national codes. Even a stricture that a corporation not tolerate any discrimination on the basis of race, ethnic origin, or political activity introduces a problem. What does a corporation do about the laws and regulations in Malaysia, Indonesia, and the Phillipines regarding the Chinese? What of similar rules in respect to the whites in Zambia or the blacks in South Africa? What of enforced political discrimination in Communist countries? Business is required by law to discriminate. Should it be forced to withdraw wherever it is required to do so? Consider the area of restrictive business practices and competitive policy. Is an agreement between a corporation and a host government to keep out all competition a restrictive business practice?

In order for a code to be effective, *enforcement at the national level* is required. Given the very different intensity of national needs for infusions of foreign capital, skills, and technology, it is difficult to see how such a code could be effective. If not, the bad behavior—this time a country—would be rewarded. Countries would have to avoid the prohibited practices as well as corporations.

Because of these and other difficulties inherent in the idea of an international code as presently conceived, I am driven to the conclusion that eventually a very different approach will evolve. This approach would rest on several premises, specifically:

1. Corporations behaving in what has been politically determined as a socially acceptable manner should be rewarded.
2. A principal area of conflict among nations generated by international business should be addressed; namely, the distribution of taxable income.
3. There should be some measure of effective *international* control over unilateral breach of agreement between host government and alien corporation.

4.   Each country should specify upon the entry of an alien corporation the behavior it expects.[19]

It should be noted that among the principal problems perceived by host governments in dealing with alien business are the lack of public information regarding corporate activities, the alleged use of corporations to further *parent* government policy objectives (including the extraterritorial application of parent government law), conflict over the allocation of taxable income, and the inability (or unwillingness) of many governments to enforce their own laws.

Some observers have suggested that corporations satisfying certain conditions should be registered with an international agency. The conditions: international activity at some specified level, a corporate commitment to disclose specified information about its activities, and a corporate commitment to adhere to a set of operating principles. The international agency suggested in this context is the International Bank for Reconstruction and Development, perhaps in the form of a functionally enlarged International Centre for the Settlement of Investment Disputes (ICSID). Both corporation and nation-state might feel restrained from treating an agency under such auspices in a cavalier fashion.

As a reward for its cooperation, a "registered corporation" would be given special status by countries signatory to the convention establishing the international agency. This might take the form of:

1.   Taxing only local-source income, such income to be determined objectively by calculating the average of local assets/global assets, local sales/global sales, local employment/global employment ratios. (The international agency would establish the accounting rules and receive global operating statements.)[20]
2.   Permitting the registration of a corporation's shares on local stock exchanges (i.e., acceptance of an internationally accepted disclosure statement).
3.   A host government and corporate commitment to submit differences to international arbitration before the ICSID.
4.   Exemption by a corporation's parent government of the corporation from withholding taxes on dividends, interest, and royalties paid to individuals or corporations domiciled in other signatory countries.
5.   A World Bank-backed guarantee against loss due to uncompensated expropriation and unilateral breach of contract by signatory nations.

---

[19]Many are now doing so. See Richard D. Robinson, *National Control of the Entry of Foreign Business* (New York: Praeger, 1976); also *Foreign Investment in the Third World: A Comparative Study of Selected Developing Country Investment Promotion Programs* (Washington, D.C., International Division, Chamber of Commerce of the United States, 1980); and *Performance Requirements for Internal Business, U.S. Management Response* (New York: Praeger, 1983).

[20]At the very least, signatory countries should recognize the tax sparing principle for registered corporations domiciled within their jurisdictions. (See p. 245.)

6.   Exemption by signatory governments of requirements for performance bonds or guaranties.

7.   A commitment by host governments to treat corporations as national corporations.

Further rules that might render such a convention more attractive:

1. Registered corporations could only merge with one another or acquire one another on the basis of prior clearance by the international agency. (Signatory nations would have to agree to give such clearance legal status under national law.)

2. Any member state could bring charges against a registered corporation before the ICSID on the grounds that it was not living up to its commitments made upon entry or subsequently. A finding of guilty could result in revocation of registered status.

3. Likewise, a corporation could bring charges against a member state before the ICSID on the grounds that the state was not living up to its commitments made upon entry or subsequently. A finding of guilt could lead to an order to pay damages.

4. Failure to maintain strict political neutrality on the part of foreign controlled and/or owned enterprises, foreign personnel, and contractors in host countries could void all governmental guarantees that may be offered. **Political neutrality** might be defined as nonintervention in partisan politics except as a corporation might attempt to influence policies by means of *public* statements or by other means of a nature commonly tolerated for a local corporation. Any *covert* activity of a political nature on behalf of another government could be deemed a per se violation of neutrality.

5. Failure to adhere to all local laws on the part of foreign-owned and/or controlled enterprises and contractors would be a bar to recovery in event of expropriation or unilateral breach of contract by the host government, even in the absence of effective, prompt, and adequate compensation (unless the law is discriminatory or of an ex post facto nature, that is, if it constitutes a host-nation violation of agreed-upon entry conditions).

6. A host government commitment to recognize foreign ownership of tangible and intangible rights, and/or management control of same, for 20 years (unless a shorter period is agreed upon at the time of entry). These rights should be inalienable during such period if (1) the rights are established locally in accord with local law and upon the consent of a signatory government, and (2) the foreign investor and/or contractor adheres to the entry conditions *unless* adherence is made impossible either by the host government or by a change of circumstances beyond the control of the foreign interest involved.

In speculating upon the reality and utility of such an international control system, you might bear in mind that in all probability, the preeminent form of international business in the future will be international federations of locally owned firms, to which the central organization will sell research findings, technical assistance venture capital, debt capital, and access to international marketing and information systems. The central organization itself is very likely to be owned by nationals of many different states. As ownership and operation broaden geographically, the rationale that would require the central body to register as a legal entity under the laws of any *one* national state appreciably weakens, and the argument for the recognition of private, internationally chartered corporations becomes compelling.

One can predict with some confidence that in the last decades of the 20th century international business will constitute a powerful pressure in the direction of *internationalizing* the process of political socialization, through the institutional relationships it creates and the flow of communication inherent in them. Even Communist societies may be included, for the private ownership of the actual machines of production is not a necessary prerequisite for this relationship. In many countries, joint public-private ownership of large sectors of production has already occurred, and in some of these situations private foreign enterprise is participating.

A number of forseeable technical developments will likewise push in the direction of international, rather than national, development of innovations such as deep-sea mining, weather control, supersonic transport flight, worldwide television networks, use of outer space, and arctic exploitation, not to mention the pressing need for the global management of the environment, of exhaustible resources, and of food and water. A prophetic study on this subject some years ago concluded: "Current concepts of national sovereignty are not well suited to the orderly regulation of these advances nor to their development for maximum utility with minimum conflict. Policy planners will find it increasingly necessary to explore new types of supranational organizations.[21]

International business leaders are now transcending national frontiers in their willingness to undertake anything, anywhere, in association with anybody, so long as it promises a reasonable long-run return. By legally elevating the transmission of the business services suggested here to the international level, the business organizations involved would be, at least in part, insulated from abuse by nationalist political authorities to further the ambitions of any state against another. One can sense that there already exists an international business community, the members of which have ceased being emotionally committed to the perpetuation of particular cultures and value systems. This community has members in both the more

[21]*Possible Nonmilitary Scientific Developments and Their Potential Impact on Foreign Policy Problems of the United States* (prepared by the Stanford Research Institute, for the Committee on Foreign Relations, Senate, 86th Congress, 1st Session, September 1959), p. 1.

developed and less-developed worlds, and in both capitalist and communist nations.

The significance of this development may be enormous. Political scientist Hans J. Morganthau once wrote to me, "When the national state will have been replaced by another mode of organization, foreign policy must then protect the interest in survival of that new organization." He then suggested that such organization would come into existence only by conquest or by "consent based upon the mutual recognition of the national interests of the nations concerned." I contend that there is perhaps another route that has been largely overlooked—specifically, the expansion of internationally constituted private groups (i.e., business) whose mutual interests are contrary to the continued existence of national sovereignty as presently constituted. Already these groups have significant impact on national foreign policy. It is conceivable that they will of themselves create a supranational organization possessed of not insignificant power. As Morganthau observed, foreign policy must then protect the interest in survival of that new organization.[22]

The distinguishing characteristic of the international business approach to international relations is that it envisages institutional, functional, nonpolitical, multinational relationships that are conducive to the weaving of an ever-larger fabric of common interest and loyalty, thereby eroding the concept of national sovereignty and conflicting national interests. In the end it is possible even to imagine the appearance of privately owned supranational corporations, registered, controlled, and taxed by an international organization,[23] perhaps—as suggested earlier—by some agency of the International Bank for Reconstruction and Development. But there is a very long road to travel. International business needs a theory, a unifying purpose, and internationally skilled managements to give it reality. It is hoped that this volume contributes to bringing that reality closer.

---

[22]Morganthau's comment on these ideas: "What you say about the problem of national sovereignty is entirely correct." (Personal letter to the author, *June 1958*.)

[23]So far as I know, this idea was first suggested by Eugene Staley in his *War and the Private Investor* (New York: Doubleday & Co., 1935).

GLOSSARY

absolute prohibitions   Unconditionally prohibited import or export of certain goods or services to or from a nation.

absolute quotas   Limits that require excess imports to be returned or held in bonded warehouses until quota period ends.

acquisition   The take-over of one firm by another. In a sense, one firm buys another.

advocacy advertising   Space in publications or airtime bought to argue a point of view on a public issue.

agent   One who buys nothing from a firm, its principal, but who acts on the firm's behalf as defined by agreement, for which agent receives a fee and/or commission.

affiliate   The status of a company that is less than 50 percent but more than 10 percent owned by the parent corporation.

American depository receipt (ADR)   A receipt issued to a non-U.S. citizen who owns shares in a U.S. corporation by a bank or other entity who holds the shares in trust.

antitrust laws   Laws that prohibit business from engaging in anticompetitive practices, such as price fixing.

area expertise   The capacity to grasp the cultural, social, political realities of a society.

arm's length transaction   A transaction between two or more unrelated parties.

attachment   A legal process by which property is officially seized as security for payment of a claimed debt.

balance of payments   Essentially the record of a nation's annual cash flow (movement of liquid assets and liabilities) in relation to the rest of the world, balanced by any increase or decrease of the nation's international monetary reserves.

bilateral trade agreement   An agreement between two countries that commits the two to exchange specified amounts of listed goods and services over a given amount of time.

black market   The illegal purchase or sale of currencies or goods.

blocked account   Financial assets that cannot be transferred into another currency or out of the country without the government's permission.

branch   An unincorporated entity, legally and financially indistinguishable from the parent firm.

capital intensive   Processes and/or products using a high percentage of capital per unit of output relative to labor.

cartel   An organization of suppliers that controls the supply and price of a commodity.

cash-against-documents   Cash payments made once shipping documents have been delivered to the buyer through a commercial bank.

central banks   Government institutions with authority over size and growth of the national monetary stock. They frequently regulate commercial banks and usually act as the government's fiscal agent.

centralization   The retention of authority at the center, usually with the top-level management of the parent corporation.

centrally planned economy   National economy with almost no free market activity, with government ownership of all major factors of production, government control of labor, and government-determined economic policy.

C.I.F. (cost, insurance, and freight)   A term used in the delivery of goods from one party to another, accounting for the costs of the goods, maritime or other transportation, insurance premium, and freight charges to a designated destination.

clearing dollars   The value of the imbalance of exchange between two countries committed to a bilateral trade agreement.

codetermination   50-50 owner-employee representation on the board of directors.

commercial purpose   The effort to fulfill some human need or desire through the transfer of goods and services from one condition or place to another, or from one person or group to another, for a mutual profit stated in explicit terms on a quid pro quo basis.

common market   A regional group with no internal tariffs, a common external tariff, and harmonized domestic law to facilitate unrestricted factor movement.

company resources   Available finances, personnel, technical knowledge, skills, goodwill, intangibles (patents, copyrights, trademarks, trade secrets), distribution system, political leverage, and so forth.

comparative advantage   The concept that nations undertake international trade to sell goods and services they can produce at relatively low cost (relative to other goods and services each might produce) and to buy those that other nations produce at relatively low cost.

competitive position   The degree to which a firm can meet the prices, quality, delivery, and credit terms offered by other firms.

confiscation   Seizure by a government of foreign-owned assets that is not followed by prompt, effective, and adequate compensation.

consignment   A transaction in which a seller ships goods to a second party but retains title. The second party sells the goods on behalf of the original seller on mutually agreed upon terms.

contract manufacturing   Manufacturing of a product or input by one company for another company under contract. The two companies may or may not be related by stock ownership, common parent, or otherwise.

contractual joint venture   The agreement by contract of two or more legal entities to supply certain assets to a joint undertaking, assume certain operational responsibilities, and receive earnings as defined by contract.

control   The relationships and devices designed to assure that strategy decisions are made by designated authority in conformance with corporate goals, that tactical (or operating) decisions conform to the selected strategies, and that actual operations are in accord with decisions.

controlled foreign corporation (CFC)   A U.S. corporation that is majority owned by U.S. shareholders, each of whom holds at least 10 percent.

convertible exchange   A currency that may be sold for other currencies and over which there are relatively few exchange controls imposed by the issuing government. Also called *hard currency*.

corporate culture   The rules perceived by corporate employees that describe behavior within that corporation.

cultural cluster   A grouping of nations perceived as culturally similar.

cultural distance   The distance separating people from one another in terms of language, history, and values.

culture shock   The disorientation and distress caused by the removal of familiar clues that give meaning to behavior, values, perceptions, and institutions.

cumulative stock   A preferred stock whose specified dividend, if missed, must be paid in arrears before any dividend may be paid on common shares.

currency area   A group of countries whose currencies are relatively freely convertible, which enforce similar foreign exchange control systems, if any, and hold reserves of scarce or "hard" foreign currencies in a common pool.

debt   Borrowed funds normally constituting a fixed obligation.

deemed paid   In U.S. tax law, the notion that a subsidiary corporation has paid the corporate income tax of its subsidiaries.

degree of integration   The percentage of a product manufactured by one plant; or, more broadly, the extent to which a company produces its own goods or purchases inputs from external suppliers.

devaluation   The loss of value of one currency in terms of another currency. Also called *depreciation*.

development banks   Worldwide, regional, or local banks that aid LDCs (or depressed areas in more-developed countries) in economic development by lending or investing money, often at terms more favorable than the market.

direct investment   An investment of capital made with the intent of exercising some control and assuming some degree of participation in management.

discount rate   A percentage by which a figure may be reduced to provide a more realistic value.

distributor   One who contracts to buy a firm's goods or services for sale to third parties.

domestic international sales corporation (DISC)   Subsidiary corporations of a U.S. company that are incorporated in a state of the United States for the purpose of exporting from the United States. They are given certain tax advantages.

domicile   The country in which an individual or corporation is legally present.

draft   An unconditional order written by the seller directing the buyer or its agent to pay a specified amount of money at a specified time. Sometimes called a *bill of exchange*.

dual taxation   The taxing of both corporate profits and stockholder dividends.

dumping   The sale of goods at less than fair market value.

earned income   Income derived from labor, production, sales, or other active participation in business (salary, wages, bonuses, commissions, etc.). *Unearned income* (or passive income) is a return on investment of money or time (interest, dividends, royalties).

Edge Act corporations   Domestic subsidiaries of U.S. banks incorporated under the Federal Reserve Act to engage in international banking and to finance foreign projects through long-term debt and equity.

efficiency   The relative cost of a product or process. The greater the efficiency, the lower the relative cost.

entry agreement   An explicit agreement between host government and alien corporation made upon the latter's entry through direct investment.

Entry agreements commonly impose time limits on the alien's rights of ownership, schedules for phasing out alien employees from certain categories and for increasing local value added, and include host government guarantees to honor the alien's rights for the duration of the agreement.

equity joint venture   An enterprise in which ownership is shared among two or more corporations (or owners) of different nationalities, each of whom contributes certain assets, shares risk to some extent, assumes some degree of operational responsibility, and receives a share of earnings via dividends.

Eurodollar   Dollar accounts banked outside of the United States.

evaluation   The increase of value of one currency in terms of another currency. Also called appreciation.

exchange rate   The price one pays in one currency for another currency, expressed as a ratio (at five pesos for one dollar, the dollar/peso exchange rate is 5; the peso/dollar exchange rate is .20).

Export-Import Bank   U.S. government agency that lends to foreign customers to facilitate export of U.S. goods. It can also give loan or investment guarantees to U.S. exporters.

export-oriented   A firm where international interest and expertise are limited to a staff department and are restricted to searching for and developing export markets only, but where real authority lies in the domestic divisions.

expropriation   Seizure by a government of foreign-owned assets. It is not contrary to international law if it is followed by prompt, adequate, and effective compensation. If not, it becomes *confiscation*.

factoring   Generally, the sale of a receivable to a bank or other financial intermediary. More specifically, the outright sale to a bank of accounts receivable without recourse to the seller, the bank thus assuming the entire risk so long as the seller avoids disputes relating to the delivery and quality of its merchandise.

flexitime   Flexible scheduling that permits employees to choose their own work hours within a given time frame.

floating rates   Exchange rates that vary according to market pressures.

foreign base company income   Income received by a foreign base corporation from outside the country in which it is incorporated.

foreign base corporation (FBC)   A subsidiary located in a country other than that in which its parent is domiciled for the purpose of receiving and holding funds.

foreign exchange   Claims that one nation has on the goods and services of another. Very frequently, these claims are in the form of foreign bank accounts.

Foreign Insurance Credit Association (FICA)   An association of private American insurance companies that, in cooperation with the Export-Import Bank, provides credit-risk insurance in connection with export sales.

foreign international sales corporation (FISC)   A foreign subsidiary of a domestic international sales corporation.

foreign reserve   A government's holdings of foreign exchange, gold, IMF drawing rights, all of which the government may use to pay its international obligations.

foreign tax credit   The credit taken by an American taxpayer against American income tax for taxes on income paid to a foreign government.

foreign trade organization (FTO)   Organizations in the USSR and other Communist countries, chiefly engaged in procuring goods and services from foreign suppliers, or selling same to foreign customers.

forward contract   An agreement to buy or sell something at a given time in the future for a specified price.

free trade area (FTA)   A regional group with no internal tariffs.

friendship, commerce, and navigation (FCN) treaties.   Basic agreements between nations about such matters as treatment of each other's citizens and corporations, often including a most favored nation provision.

general trading companies   A company engaged principally in the distribution of a wide range of goods and services worldwide.

gray market   Illegal transactions tolerated by a government even though aware of their existence.

gross national product (GNP)   The market value of all final goods and services produced by the national economy over a given period of time, usually one year.

guestworkers   Foreign workers who are brought into a country by legal means to perform needed labor.

hard goods   Merchandise (also known as *hardware*, as opposed to *software*).

hedging   Selling forward currency exchange, borrowing, or using other means to protect against losses from possible currency exchange rate changes that would affect value of assets and liabilities.

high profile   Active strategy for representing the corporation's views to politicians, other business executives, labor leaders, and consumer groups.

host country   The country in which foreign investment is made.

human resources   The labor, skills, and knowledge embodied in people available to an organization.

IMF drawing rights   The capacity of a government to borrow the equivalent of foreign exchange from the International Monetary Fund.

income elasticity of demand   The relationship between change in demand for a good or service and change in the level of income.

indexing   Accounting for the effects of inflation on assets and liabilities by adjusting the amounts in order to preserve original tradeoffs. Also refers to the similar process used to keep employee compensation at a steady real value over time.

inferior good   A good for which consumption decreases as income rises.

interest arbitrage   The movement of short-term funds between countries as borrowers and lenders try to taken advantage of differences in interest rates.

intermediates   Manufactured or processed goods which are inputs into a good produced for delivery to the final consumer.

internalization   The process by which a corporation brings a skill or function within its own organization.

international base salary   In corporate remuneration, a common scale of pay for all personnel regardless of nationality, with a variety of extras to compensate for specific costs incurred by employment overseas.

international business management   The generation, maintenance, and control of international flows of people, information, funds, goods, and services for a commercial purpose.

international codes   Agreements formulated by two or more nations to regulate international corporate behavior.

international corporation   A firm where international interest and relevant skill are in an international division, but with functional expertise remaining largely in the domestic divisions.

international depository receipt (IDR)   A receipt issued to a foreigner who owns shares in a corporation domiciled in another country by a bank or other entity which holds the shares in trust.

international law   A body of principles and practices which have been generally accepted by nations in their relations with other nations and with citizens of other nations.

investment center   The locale of a corporation's investment decisions.

joint venture   The participation of two companies jointly in a third enterprise. Both contribute assets, both own the joint venture to some extent, and they share risk.

know-how contract   A contractual agreement to transfer technology that is not covered by patent, copyright, trademark, or secrecy. The subject matter is considered to be in the public domain. Payment is designated as a *fee*. Also called *technical assistance contract*.

labor intensive   Processes and/or products requiring a high usage of labor per unit of output relative to the capital used.

labor management   Authority of labor is theoretically preeminent to that of management. Also called *self-management*.

lag   Postponement of import payments or a delay in the receipt of export proceeds.

lead   Prepayment for imports or the early receipt of export proceeds.

learning curve   The graphic representation of a company's increasing efficiency (lower per unit cost) as it becomes more skilled. Also called the *experience curve*.

less-developed countries (LDCs)   Countries with low per capita income, low levels of industrialization, relatively high illiteracy, and often political instability.

letter of credit (L/C)   A document issued by a bank upon request of a buyer stating that it will honor drafts drawn against it by a specified seller if the terms and conditions set forth in the letter of credit are satisfied.

leverage   The debt/equity ratio. Also, in the politico-economic context, the extent of a firm's advantage over other firms in a particular national market and the degree to which it can influence the local environment.

license   A contractual agreement to permit another to use a functional or design invention protected by patent, a unique literary or artistic expression protected by copyright, a unique identification protected by trademark, or technology and/or skills of a secret nature. Payment is designated as a *royalty*.

long position   The net position of an individual or institution whose assets (future inflows) exceed its liabilities (future outflows).

long-term arrangements (LTAs)   Bilateral or multilateral agreements calling for the restriction of exports of a specific commodity by one or more producing countries to one or more importing countries whose markets are being disrupted. Also called orderly marketing arrangements (OMAs).

low profile   Passive strategy for representing the corporation's views to politicians, other business executives, labor leaders, and consumer groups.

management prerogative   A contract under which a firm has the right to exercise managerial control over another firm in the event of certain specified eventualities, such as dropping below a minimum sales volume or profit level.

manufacturing interchange   A setup where each of several plants manufactures a specified set of parts, all exchange with one another, and all assemble the same products.

merger The joining of two or more firms in the formation of a new legal entity. The original firms disappear as separate legal entities. The owners of the merging companies then own the new entity.

minority board participation Minority representation for employees on the board of directors.

minority-owned joint venture Less than 50 percent but more than 10 percent ownership of a joint venture. Also called an *affiliate*.

Mitbestimmung German for *codetermination*.

mixed venture One in which the host government is part owner, or in which equity is owned jointly by public and private interests.

most favored nation (MFN) The policy of nondiscrimination in international commerce by extending to all MFN-status nations the same treatment granted to any one.

multinational association A general trading or service company, linked internationally by a web of contractual relations with largely locally owned and managed associated firms.

multinational corporation (MNC) Generally, an internationally integrated production system over which equity-based control is exercised by a parent corporation that is owned and managed essentially by the nationals of the country in which it is domiciled. As distinguished from other kinds of large corporations that operate internationally, a *multinational* is a firm where international interest and expertise are located throughout the firm, but most top corporate managers are still parent-country nationals.

multiple pay scales Salary structures that remunerate parent-country personnel at a rate comparable to their home pay and all other personnel at relevant local rates.

national A person of a given nationality. Where a firm is establishing a business overseas, employees from the nation where the firm is domiciled are *parent-country nationals* or expatriots; employees from the nation where the new business is located are *local nationals*; employees drawn from elsewhere are *third-country nationals*. Either of the last two may also be called *nonnationals* in respect to the firm's home nation.

nenko seido The Japanese seniority-based pay system.

net exposure The difference between a firm's exposed assets and exposed liabilities, with exposure being measured in terms of the effect of a devaluation on the value of the assets or liabilities.

netting The offset of payables and receivables between related companies so that only the net balance is actually transferred.

neutral tax A tax that neither stimulates nor depresses particular types of income, forms of business organization, location of production, or seat of control.

newly industrializing countries (NICs) A group of less-developed countries that have been industrializing rapidly.

obsolescing bargain The situation where a foreign firm's contribution to a foreign society is perceived to be steadily diminishing relative to what the firm is receiving.

off-shore income Income that for tax purposes is not reported in the country where it was earned. Also called *split* income.

100 percent ownership The equity position of owning 100 percent of the voting stock of an enterprise. An enterprise is normally considered *wholly owned* if the principal owner holds 90 percent or more of the voting stock.

open-account Sales on the basis of unsecured credit, in which the seller ships goods and subsequently bills the buyer.

open-door policy A policy of granting employees access to higher management in order to register complaints about the behavior of their immediate supervisors.

Overseas Private Investment Corporation (OPIC) A U.S. government agency that insures private U.S. investors against risks of expropriation, war, or currency nonconvertibility.

parallel financing An arrangement by foreign borrowers (governments and businesses) with a consortium of banks in different countries to float largely identical bond issues in each country at the same time, each in the currency of the issuing country.

parallel trading Two or more firms acting in concert either to take a country's goods or services as partial or full payment for products or services sold there, or to supply goods or services in exchange for those received, or both.

parent company A company that owns subsidiary companies.

Paris Union The popular name for the International Convention for the Protection of Industrial Property, which provides that if a patent application is filed in one member country, the applicant may file in other member countries within one year, with priority running from the date of first application. Also called the *Paris Convention*.

participating debt A negotiable security that bestows on the holder rights in the form of profit participation up to a given percentage of annual net profits distributed. It is always callable by the holder and is not considered part of a corporation's capital.

participative stock Preferred shares that participate, beyond the fixed rate, with common shares in the distribution of earnings.

passive income   (see *earned income*)

paternalism   A system where the patron (an individual, group, or corporate entity) provides for employees' personal as well as employment needs, with minimal participation in decision making by the employee.

pegged exchange rate   The fixing of the rate at which a foreign currency may be bought and sold by government decree.

per se violations   Business practices deemed to be illegal under antitrust laws without proof of any adverse effect on competition.

philanthropy   The act of making corporate resources available to activities that do not enter into the production or sales function within the business planning horizon and that are not legally required.

piece rate   A rate of pay based on the number of pieces (units of product) a worker produces per unit of time.

political neutrality   For a foreign corporation, nonintervention in partisan politics except for public statements issued as attempts to influence policies, or other expressions or activities commonly tolerated for a local corporation. Any *covert* activity of a political nature on behalf of another government would be deemed a per se violation of neutrality.

political risk   The probability of a political event that will impact on a firm to its disadvantage.

portfolio investment   Investment with an equity position of less than 10 percent and with no managerial responsibility.

preemption   The right of first refusal in relation to the issue of additional stock by a company.

preferred stock   Shares with a claim on profit before distribution to shareholders of common stock.

private arbitration   Resolution of disputes by use of private intermediaries according to rules and procedures provided ahead of time in the parties' underlying commercial contract.

product   The embodiment of a package of services, or value-added chain.

profit center   The place in an organization where profits are legally recorded. Full financial *consolidation* means the parent firm is the profit center; full financial *integration* means that profit centers are located wherever there is an advantage to be realized, although under central financial control of the parent firm.

profit sharing   Compensation in addition to workers' basic pay package that is keyed to the company's profitability and intended to create a greater area of common interest between owners and employees.

public affairs   The efforts by a corporation to explain corporate strategy to its constituents and gain their support, to create a favorable political-social-economic climate for the corporation's business activities, to keep corporate management informed of response, present and anticipated, and to advocate changes in corporate strategy that will put the corporation in closer harmony with its environment.

purchasing power parity   The theory that, in an efficient foreign exchange market, changes in relative prices of two countries' goods correspond to changes in the exchange rate between their currencies.

qualifying shares   The shares required by law for an individual to be a corporate founder or to sit on a board of directors.

quality circles   Groups of workers who meet periodically during work hours to discuss ways of improving product quality, efficiency, and employee morale.

quotas by source   Limitations or bans on imports from "enemy" countries or those against which trade sanctions have been decreed.

rationalize production   To split apart existing plants and bring together new bundles of processes or products to make production more efficient.

registered user   Someone other than the owner of a trademark who is recorded as such and who has use of the trademark, sometimes rests on assurance that adequate quality control will be exercised by the owner over the manufacture of the goods by the licensee.

repatriation   The transfer home of assets held abroad, or of earnings.

ringi-seido   A characteristic of Japanese system of management; literally, "the system of submitting a proposal to one's superior for approval."

risk   Outcomes whose probability can be inferred from previous experience.

Scanlon plan   A plan to increase employees' interest and effectiveness by involving them in a committee system that evaluates plant efficiency and management, and offering them financial incentives to find ways to achieve savings as measured against the historical ratio of labor cost to value of production. Named after its creator, Joseph Scanlon.

short position   The net position of an individual or institution whose liabilities (future outflows) exceed its assets (future inflows).

shushin koyo seido   The Japanese system of lifetime employment.

silent language   The signals communicated by means other than words, such as spatial relationships, timing, gestures, and sequences.

social costs   Costs a firm incurs in damage suits, legal expenses, work stoppages, insurance premiums, building and maintaining security systems, taxes, compliance with government regulation, and general training of employees not covered by public education.

socialization   The internalization of values and rules of behavior by employees of a corporation.

software   Human skills and technology, as opposed to *hardware*.

sogo shosha   Japanese general trading companies.

sovereignty   The rights and powers a national government holds over the territory within its borders and the people and organizations within those borders.

speak-up policy   A policy of encouraging employees of all types to register complaints with their supervisors.

special drawing right (SDR)   An international reserve asset, a paper money, created by the IMF and allocated to members in accord with agreements among them. SDRs may be used only for intergovernmental transactions and between the IMF and governments.

special tariffs   Duties imposed in specific instances, often to equalize import prices relative to fair market prices.

spot rate   The rate of exchange between two currencies on a specific date.

strategy   An element in a consciously devised overall plan of corporate development that, once made and implemented, is difficult (i.e., costly) to change in the short run.

structure   Organizational rigidities, or relationships, difficult to alter significantly in the short run.

subnational market   A market smaller than a national market, defined geographically, by income level, by ethnic identity or some other distinguishing characteristic.

subpart F income   In U.S. tax law, the total of a company's U.S. insurance income, illegal bribes paid to foreign officials, and foreign base company income.

subsidiary   An incorporated legal entity, in which the parent owns a controlling interest, that possesses legal liability distinct from the parent and, hence, a separate financial structure.

superior good   A good for which consumption increases as income rises.

supranational   A firm where management is free structurally, psychologically, and legally to allocate resources on a global basis in conformance with corporate goals insofar as they do not conflict with the international political regime controlling the corporation. It is not legally under the law of any nation-state.

switch trading   a complex system of barter trade involving a number of firms and intermediaries.

tactical decision   A decision that sets up little or no institutionalized resistance to making a different decision in the near future.

tariffs   Amounts charged when goods are imported into a country. Also called *duties*.

tariff rate quotas   Tariff rate increases with quantity imported.

tax haven   A country with no tax or a very low tax rate on foreign source income and accumulated earnings; popular domicile for subsidiaries which act as holding companies (or foreign base companies) for corporations domiciled in high-tax countries.

tax holiday   An exemption from tax granted by a government for specified income for a given amount of time.

tax treaties   Two-nation agreements defining source of income for tax purposes and providing for consultation in the event of double taxation, among other things.

Theory X   One of two theories in a dichotomous management classification system developed by Douglas McGregor, positing, among other ideas, that efficiency is measured solely in terms of production, that people prefer the security of a definite task delegated by a hierarchical authority to freedom of choice, and that workers are motivated solely by economic needs. Equated with the classical theory of management.

Theory Y   An alternative theory of management based on the participative model and drawing upon a normative management theory derived from Maslow's need hierarchy. The theory posits that individuals will exercise self-direction and self-control in the service of an objective to which they are committed, that people seek responsibility, and that the conditions of modern industrial life realize only a part of the average person's potential.

time horizon   The time over which the inputs and outputs (cost and benefits) relevant to a decision or plan are considered.

trademarks   There are four varieties of trademarks: *true trademarks* identify a product with a specific manufacturer or source; *service marks* identify the services of an individual or a corporation; *certification marks* indicate that a product is of a certain quality, is manufactured in a specific location, or bears some other factual characteristic; *collective marks* indicate membership in an association or organization of some sort.

transfer prices   The prices at which goods, services, and funds move among related companies.

transnational   In addition to multinational ownership and management, a firm whose decision makers develop loyalty of a sort that transcends national identity, thus eliminating covert or psychologically based national bias in decision making.

turnkey operation   A project undertaken by a firm under contract to design and construct a plant. If the training of operators is involved as well, it is called **turnkey-plus**.

uncertainty The probability of an unpredictable outcome, which may be approximated by use of a normal distribution curve based on minimum and maximum estimates.

uninational Involving or operating within the boundaries of one nation. A uninational enterprise is a business established, owned, and operated by the nationals of the country where it is located.

unitary taxation The taxing of only corporate profits, as opposed to *dual taxation*; also used to describe a system of sourcing corporate income for tax purposes by applying the ratio of local assets, sales, and/or employees to the global totals.

unit-of-account financing Financing in securities denominated in several different currencies held in fixed relationship.

universalists Those who believe that all managers share certain kinds of behavior regardless of their cultural milieu.

valuable rights Rights which may be leased or sold, such as the right to use patents, copyrights, trade secrets, and trademarks, or any right bestowed by a commercial contract (e.g., the right to buy something at a stipulated price).

value added The value added to a product or material by reason of the processing undertaken by a company, or within a country.

vertical consistency The degree to which managers at all levels within an organization use similar styles of decision making.

voluntary import quotas Quotas in the form of reduced imports by private foreign business on a voluntary basis.

voluntary marketing arrangements (VMAs) Unilateral commitments by a country to limit its exports of a particular product to another country; sometimes used interchangeably with **long-term arrangements** (LTAs).

workers council A body of workers' representatives, or of both workers and management, institutionalizing management-labor relations at the enterprise level.

Webb-Pomerene association An association (U.S.) whose members are authorized to use joint facilities, fix prices, and allocate orders. The association must engage solely in export trade, and is subject to numerous other restrictions.

zaibatsu Japanese industrial-banking cartels formally associated with general trading companies.

Appendix: List of Acronyms

Alphabetical list of the acronyms or initials of some of the more important international organizations and terms used in this text.

AACCLA American Association of Chambers of Commerce of Latin America

AAMOCIOS Asian Association of Management Organizations of CIOS

ADB Asian Development Bank

ADR American depository receipt

AFL-CIO American Federation of Labor and Congress of Industrial Organizations

AID Agency for International Development

AIEC Association of Iron Ore Exporting Countries

ANCOM Andean Common Market

ANRPC Association of National Rubber Producing Countries

BTN Brussels Tariff Nomenclature

CACM Central American Common Market

CCCF [French] Central Fund for Economic Cooperation

CDC Commonwealth Development Corporation

CECIOS European Council of CIOS

CFC controlled foreign corporation

CICC [U.S.] Committee of the International Chamber of Commerce

CIOS International Committee of Scientific Organizations

CIPEC Council of Copper Exporting Countries

COCOM Coordinating Committee

CPC Community Patent Convention

DGB German Trade Union Federation

DISC domestic international sales corporation

EC   European Community

ECAT   Emergency Committee for American Trade

ECLA   Special Coordinating Committee for Latin America

EEC   European Economic Community

EPC   European Patent Convention

EPO   European Patent Office

FASB   Financial Accounting Standards Board

FBC   foreign base corporation

FCN   friendship, commerce, and navigation [treaties]

FDI   foreign district investment

FICA   Foreign Insurance Credit Association

FISC   foreign international sales corporation

FMO   [Dutch] Financial Corporation for Development

FTA   free trade area

FTO   foreign trade organization

GATT   General Agreement on Trade and Tariffs

IADB   Inter-American Development Bank

IBA   International Bauxite Association

IBRD   International Bank for Reconstruction and Development
(also called World Bank)

ICFTU   International Confederation of Free Trade Unions

ICI   Imperial Chemical Industry

ICSID   International Center for the Settlement of Investment Disputes

IDA   International Development Association

IDR   international depository receipt

IFC   International Finance Corporation

IFU   [Danish] Industrialization Fund for Developing Countries

ILO   International Labor Organization

IMF   International Monetary Fund

IPI   International Patent Institute

ISIC   International Standard Industrial Classification

ISO International Organization for Standardization

ITS International Trade Secretariat

LAIA Latin American Integration Area

L/C letter of credit

LDC less-developed country

LTA long-term arrangements

MFN most favored nation

MNC multinational corporation

NATO North Atlantic Treaty Organization

NCUSCT National Council for United States-China Trade

NIC newly industrializing countries

OEF [Japanese] Overseas Economic Fund

ODC Overseas Development Corporation

OECD Organization for Economic Cooperation and Development

OMA orderly marketing arrangements

OPEC Organization for Petroleum Exporting Countries

OPIC Overseas Private Investment Corporation

PACCIOS Pan-American Committee of CIOS

PCT Patent Cooperation Treaty

PEFCO Private Export Funding Corporation

SDR special drawing right

SEC Securities Exchange Commission

SIC Standard Industrial Classification

SITC Standard International Trade Classification

TACC Trade Action Coordinating Committee

TAT thematic apperception test

TUG [British] Trade Union Congress

UAW United Auto Workers Union

UBEC Union of Banana Exporting Countries

UCC   Universal Copyright Convention

UNESCO   UN Educational, Scientific, and Cultural Organization

VMA   voluntary marketing arrangements

WIPO   World Intellectual Property Organization

INDEX

Accounting,
  and international firms, 281
  procedures, 304
Accounting Principles Board, 302n
Acquisitions, 67
  definition, 57
  and U.S. antitrust law, 67
  legality of,
    and U.S. Justice Department,
      230–231
    vulnerable to U.S. antitrust, 228,
      229, 230
Adams, J. C., 133n
Advertising advocacy, 312–313
  definition, 307
  as public affairs function, 313
  as public affairs vehicle, 312
Advertising agencies, 46
Affiliates,
  and decision making, 268
  definition, 153, 155
  management of,
    and decision making, 269
  success of,
    and decision making, 269
Age,
  in selection of overseas manage-
    ment, 127, 128
Agents,
  definition, 25, 41
Agricultural cooperatives,
  exempt from antitrust law, 227
Alexander, William Jr., 130n
Alien firms
  restraints on, 160–163
Aliens, nonresident,
  U.S. taxes, 253
Alpander, Guvenc G., 145n
American Arbitration Association,
  234
American Association of Chambers
  of Commerce of Latin Amer-
  ica, 311
American depository receipts, 189
American Federation of Labor and
  Congress of Industrial Orga-
  nizations, 99, 100
American Graduate School of Inter-
  national Management, 131
American Institute of Certified Pub-
  lic Accountants, 304
Andean common market, 63, 329
  and international arbitration, 235
Antitrust.
  See Law, antitrust
Arbitration,
  enforcing foreign awards, 234,
    235
  private, 234
    definition, 219
  and U.S., 235

Area expertise,
  definition, 115
  and selection of overseas man-
    agement, 126–127
Argentina,
  patent licensing, 236
Asian Association of Management
  Organizations of CIOS, 311
Asian Development Bank, 194
Assets,
  exposed,
    definition, 210
  physical,
    as cost in joint enterprises, 170
  revaluating,
    as risk-modifying device, 201
Associates,
  acceptable to international firms,
    165
Association of Iron Ore Exporting
  Countries, 61
Association of Natural Rubber Producing Countries, 61
Association of South-East Asian Na-
  tions, 329
Attachment, 198
  definition, 181
Australia,
  antitrust agreement with U.S.,
    230
  and credit insurance systems,
    215n
Austria,
  and credit insurance systems,
    215n
  and patents, 237

Bahamas,
  and financing subsidiaries, 195
  as tax haven, 185
Balance of payments
  pressure, 206
  and source financing, 191
  surpluses,
    and demise of direct invest-
      ments, 13
Balzer, Richard, 86n
Bank accounts,
  confidential, 198
Banker's acceptance, 213, 214
Bargaining, 127n
Barrett, Gerald V., 144, 145n, 149,
  149n
Barter, 48
A Basic Guide to Exporting, 31n
Bass, Bernard M., 144, 145n, 149,
  149n
Battle Act, 31
Belgium,
  and credit insurance systems,
    215n

Benefit/cost analysis, 170–171
  and fixed ownership policies, 172
  ratios, 171–172
  and local societies, 161
Benefits. *See* Pay scales and other
  benefits
Berne Convention of 1886, 241
Biases, 72
  cultural,
    awareness of, in selection of
      overseas management, 126.
  distance, 22
  engineering, 21, 72
  nonmarket, 21–22
  of past success, 22
  power, 21
Bilateral trade agreements, 72
  definition, 25, 48
Blocked funds, 193
Bonuses, 110
Borrowing,
  as conflict area, 169
Boycotts, 257
  and host governments, 183
  and profit centers, 183
  and tax credits, 254–255
  vulnerable to U.S. antitrust law,
    230
Branches,
  definition, 25, 41
  foreign,
    and capital allocation, 259
    and mining enterprises, 259
  and local law, 222
  as type of corporate organization,
    221
Bribes,
  definition, 253n
  as public affairs vehicle, 312
  and taxes, 257
  See also Payments, illegal
British Commonwealth,
  and trademark laws, 241
British Trade Marks Act of 1938, 241
Brussels,
  as headquarters for multination-
    als, 293
Brussels Tariff Nomenclature, 30n
Bureaucratic administration,
  definition, 300
Business,
  volume of,
    and management policies, 226
Business America, 31n
Business International, 31n, 86, 209
Business pressure,
  and enforcing decisions, 305
Business trust,
  as type of corporate organization,
    221–222
Buy American Act, 47n